THE STORY OF
SADLER'S WELLS
1683–1977

'EVENING', AFTER THE PAINTING BY HOGARTH, 1738
WITH SADLER'S WELLS IN THE BACKGROUND AND THE
SIR HUGH MYDDELTON INN

THE STORY OF
SADLER'S WELLS

1683–1977

DENNIS ARUNDELL

Old Sadler, land surveyor to the king,
Laying foundations, chanced upon a spring . . .
'Ods Life!' he cried. 'Here flows a natural wine
With healing salts imbued!' and built a shrine.

CHRISTOPHER HASSALL
(Prologue for the Gala Performance,
Twelfth Night, 1956)

DAVID & CHARLES
Newton Abbot   London   North Pomfret (Vt)   Vancouver

Arundell, Dennis
  The story of Sadler's Wells, 1683–1977
  – 2nd ed
  1. Sadler's Wells Theatre—History
  I. Title
  792'.09421'43   PN2596.L7S3
  ISBN 0–7153–7620–9

First published in Great Britain in 1965 by
Hamish Hamilton Ltd
Second extended edition published
by David & Charles (Publishers) Limited in 1978

© Dennis Arundell 1965, 1978

Set in Monotype Bell
and printed in Great Britain
by Redwood Burn Ltd, Trowbridge
for David & Charles (Publishers) Limited
Brunel House Newton Abbot Devon

Published in the United States of America
by David & Charles Inc
North Pomfret Vermont 05053 USA

Published in Canada
by Douglas David & Charles Limited
1875 Welch Street North Vancouver BC

CONTENTS

LIST OF ILLUSTRATIONS

'Evening', after the painting by Hogarth, 1738, with
Sadler's Wells in the background (left) and the 'Sir
Hugh Myddelton' inn (right)
(*Finsbury Public Library*) *Frontispiece*

vi

PLAN

INTRODUCTION TO 1978 EDITION

SKILFULLY written by Dennis Arundell, with most thorough research, this story of the Sadler's Wells Theatre will be read with great pleasure by actors and true theatre-goers alike.

I first met the author at Cambridge, where he got his classical and music degrees, when in the late twenties I joined Anmer Hall's Repertory Company at the Festival Theatre for which he wrote some music while becoming noticed as an actor. A few years later we met again as actors at the Old Vic, when Miss Lilian Baylis had pulled off a double by restoring the Sadler's Wells Theatre.

This helped us all, as it meant some weeks at the Old Vic and some at the Wells with more time to rehearse the next play. We alternated with the opera and ballet, and occasionally to our delight we met the other companies in the restaurant or coffee bar. Dennis was then an accomplished actor and also wrote the music for our songs: they were perfect 'period' pieces in Elizabethan style or for Restoration ballads. Later on he became a producer of plays and especially operas both here and on the continent.

This exchange of theatres only lasted a short time: then plays stayed at the Vic and ballet and opera at Sadler's Wells. The great trouble at the Wells was acoustics. I brought in the expert, Bertie Scott, and asked *why* I could not be heard? The answer was that there are no *boxes* on each side of the proscenium but only flat hard concrete walls: the speaking voice bounces off these walls and the audience on the opposite side from each wall cannot hear. On the other hand the wall makes a *splendid* sounding board for a singer: so Sadler's Wells became the nursery for opera and the Royal Ballet.

I come last to the great history of the theatre. Built as a music-house in 1683 to entertain visitors to the famous wells, it was then in the country outside London, with trees and lanes of great beauty. It failed as a spa, but became famous as a theatre in *all* its glorious forms—Shakespeare, music hall (with Grimaldi and Marie Lloyd), ballet, opera and splendid spectacular productions.

Now, in 1977, the ballet is returning there. Long may it run! As there have been performances near various wells of old London since at least 1390, may Sadler's Wells flourish and please the public for a thousand years to come!

FLORA ROBSON
1977

APOLOGIES AND ACKNOWLEDGEMENTS

1978 Edition

IN A STORY covering events of nearly three hundred years there are bound to be omissions, some justified and some disappointing.

Justifiably Roger Machell of Hamish Hamilton and my friend from Cambridge days jibbed at including the full details from the contemporary account of the 'Hibernian Cannibal' in the first edition, just as I decided not to include the story of the artist who refused to wear another's costume for moral reasons nor to mention the deeds nor misdeeds of this or that performer or manager. In those pre-permissive days we also agreed to leave the details of Lady Squab's 'modest ditty' to be read by those who wished in *Pills to Purge Melancholy* (1682–1720).

Disappointingly the sheer number of operas and ballets and, more recently, visiting companies has meant the omission of an artist, an event, or a performance that should have been mentioned, such as Sir Geraint Evans' Leporello in his early days.

I apologize for any mistakes, especially for my careless misnomer in the first edition of John Fryatt (given as John Frear on pages 265 and 282) who proved from the start to be another indispensable artist first at the Wells and later ta Glyndebourne and elsewhere. The Smith who joined the Wells in 1838 (page 122) was not C. J. Smith who during the previous five years had been actor, Harlequin, head of the Melo-Dramatic Department and eventually stage-manager. The invaluably accurate staff producer John Donaldson corrected my misstatement on page 220 that Marjorie Shires, Marion Lowe and he were with Carey instead of with James Robertson and pointed out that Robert Thomas's height on page 234 was 5ft 6in.

Misprints in the index should be corrected on page 279 to Crouch, Frederick, 133; on page 285 Jacopi should be Iacopi; page 296 *Baiser de la Fée, Le*, 209, 211; page 297 *Origin of Design, The*, 197; page 299 *Immortal Hour, The*, 233; and on

xii

page 303 the dramatized *Oliver Twist* 123 is missing. I also regret the worrying inadequacy of applying single adjectives to many performers of successfully varied achievements, and the omission of the names of many on whose co-operation the success of all productions depended.

All criticisms are from printed or authoritative sources without comment from myself, as are the financial or political details, except where definitely stated.

I have personally examined the many press-cuttings on Sadler's Wells Opera when at the Wells, which are now tumbled in huge cardboard boxes in the Coliseum basement together, I am told, with some of the pre-Wells Old Vic. I suggest—although it would cost money—that for the sake of theatrical and operatic history they should be put in order and housed in their respective theatres.

I also wonder, in view of the valuable work done by the Sadler's Wells Foundation under the Charity Commissioners since 1968, what 'the Lady', Lilian Baylis, would say about V.A.T., seeing that in 1934 after lobbying for years she gained remission of the Entertainment Tax for her contributions to British artistic culture.

For help in collating the unexpectedly complicated material for the new Postscript section I am most indebted to Douglas Craig, the Director of the Wells, who in spite of temporary incapacity vetted and improved my script, and to all his staff, especially Derek Westlake, the General Manager, Joseph Karaviotis, the Financial Controller of the theatre, and Claire Thornton, the Press Representative.

Thanks are also due to staff members of the Coliseum, Frederic Lloyd of D'Oyly Carte (also a Governor of Sadler's Wells Foundation), and to others mentioned in the text, especially to David Humphreys, who has spent days researching, consulting, correcting and helping to put my rough draft into shape.

D.A.
November 1977

FOREWORD

ENTERTAINMENT is built on human relationships ranging between author and composer, performer and director, audience and management including staff. What first intrigued me to find out more about the second oldest existing theatre in London were the anecdotes about Sadler's Wells in various stage reminiscences—Tom Dibdin's Memoirs, Boz's *Memoirs of Joseph Grimaldi*, John Coleman's *Players and Playwrights I have known*, *The London Pleasure Gardens of the XVIIIth Century* by Warwick Wroth and *The Drama of Yesterday and Today* by Clement Scott.

When I joined the Old Vic Company in 1933 I knew that a Mr. Sadler had started entertainments in the eighteenth century to encourage people to drink his health-giving waters, that Charles Dibdin Junior gave water-shows, that Grimaldi was the first 'Joey' clown, that Phelps ran Shakespeare seasons at the place, and opera and ballet were new there.

Surprised that little had been written about the Wells apart from Edwin Fagg's sixpenny pamphlet, occasional articles and a few pages in books such as Edward Dent's *A Theatre for Everybody* and the 1938 tribute to Lilian Baylis under the title *Vic-Wells*, I was still more astonished when delving showed that Sadler gave entertainments before he knew he had a well, that the water-shows were short-lived, that Grimaldi was a straight actor, that Phelps by no means presented only Shakespeare, and that opera and ballet had been given there over a hundred years before.

Pinks's *History of Clerkenwell* (1881) was of course of value (while reading this I found my Cornish forebears had had their near-London house in Clerkenwell till the eighteenth century), but chiefly important were fourteen huge volumes of Wells press-cuttings, pictures, song-sheets, etc., of the Percival Collection in the British Museum (Crach 1 tab. 4 b 4) made about 1866 and the excellently filed similar collection, but coming up to date, started for the Finsbury Public Library by the late Harry G. T. Cannons, former Librarian.

A lucky chance remark led to my land-lady (why is there no real feminine of 'landlord'?) Miss Olive Lloyd-Baker, whose family had owned most of the land round and including Sadler's Wells, kindly inviting me to examine the archives in Hardwicke Court, Gloucester—hence hitherto unpublished documents connected with Rosoman, King, Wroughton, Dibdin, Grimaldi and Mr. Siddons (pp. 14–15, 25–26, 30–32, 37, 63–64, 92–94, 104, 109–110, 114–116).

I am also most grateful to Raymond Mander and Joe Mitchenson not only for two pictures but for the loan of the embryo notes for a Wells history by our late mutual friend, Arthur Beales; to my old friend, Sir Michael Redgrave, for the photograph of his father; to George Nash of the Enthoven Collection, Victoria and Albert Museum, and his staff; to my friend George Wood, O.B.E. ('Wee Georgie Wood') for vaudeville information; to the Society of Theatre Research for permission to quote from the invaluable *Memoirs* of Charles Dibdin the Younger, edited by George Speaight; and to reproduce the plan on p. 60; to Macmillan and Co. for quotations from Sir John Gielgud's *Early Stages*; to Macgibbon and Kee for the same from Richard Findlater's *Grimaldi*; to W. H. Allen and Co. for quotations from Anton Dolin's *Markova*; to the Barnes Museum of Cinematography at St. Ives, Cornwall; to British Actors Equity; naturally to Norman Tucker, C.B.E. and the Sadler's Wells management, especially Douglas Bailey; to Miss Rankin and the Vic-Wells Association; to Reginald Rouse, the Finsbury Librarian, and above all to Miss Margaret McDerby who tirelessly gave me enthusiastic help in the Finsbury Library.

In reducing my notes on two hundred and eighty years of theatre history I have naturally had to skim over innumerable shows and the achievement of innumerable Wells people ranging from Tony Easterbrook, the present Production Manager, who worked so hard on my *Flying Dutchman* production, and friends of mine on the other side of the curtain such as Bunty Chase, Syd Kingham, Neville Currier, Ronnie Brooks and others to orchestral players and the always co-operative chorus singers who have all contributed enormously to the Wells story—no doubt even Mr. Douse, a singer, who was found dead on a Holborn dunghill in 1783.

It is only ironic that the part of the story I know best has had to be in some ways less human than the earlier part, as I have had to leave out anecdotes which, however amusing, might seem to qualify my great affection for the Wells.

D.A.

1965

CHAPTER ONE

MR. SADLER'S MUSICK-HOUSE

1683–1746

IN THE high ridge to the North of the City of London, from where one can look down on St. Paul's, there are many springs—one reason perhaps why the Romans encamped there before routing Boadicea's forces in the valley below at Battle Bridge near the present King's Cross Station, and certainly why Sir Hugh Myddelton, when digging his artificial stream in James I's time to bring country water to London, chose as his New River's Head the ground where the headquarters of the Metropolitan Water Board still are. Even in the basement of the nearby house I have lived in for over twenty years there are signs of underground water, and in the London blitz of the Second World War some were drowned in their basements when bombs blew open the hillside.

In the twelfth century many of these springs were known, among them the Clerks' Well (Clerkenwell), the Skinners' Well, St. Clement's Well, Fag's, Tode, Loder's, Rede or Rad Wells, and the Holy Well, which last had been famous for many cures; and long before Henry VIII's time there had been a building near the Holy Well to afford diversion to the water-drinkers. All the Wells had been festival-centres at least—the parish clerks had acted at the Skinners' Well with three-day performances of *The Creation of the World* before Richard II from July 18th, 1390, and again before Henry IV in 1409, when the play was followed by jousting against four Frenchmen by four Englishmen including Sir Richard Arundell. On St. Bartholomew's Day wrestling matches took place both there and at the Clerks' Well.

At the Reformation, the wells were stopped up: they were said to promote superstition because the priests of Clerkenwell Priory persuaded people that the virtue of the waters came from the efficacy of their prayers, and gradually the wells were

1

forgotten. But this did not put an end to the enthusiasm of the
district for entertainment. In Shakespeare's day his Globe and
Fortune Theatres were rivalled by the blood-and-thunder Red
Bull, just off St. John Street, where the great Edward Alleyn
acted; and not far away for over thirty years towards the end
of the seventeenth century Thomas Britton, the small-coal man,
gave his famous concerts with the best musicians.

By 1683, on the country footpath from Clerkenwell to Islington crossing the New River by a wooden footbridge, Dick
Sadler had already opened his Musick-House in which singers
and entertainers amused the public. He was a Surveyor of the
Highways for which gravel was needed and, as he had good
gravel in the garden of the Musick-House, he employed two
men to dig there. One day that summer, when they had dug
pretty deep, one of them found his pickaxe strike something
very hard but could not break it. So, thinking it might be hidden
treasure, he carefully uncovered it and found that his discovery
was a broad, flat stone. This he loosened and lifted and saw it
was supported by four oak posts, while under it was a large
stone well arched over and curiously carved.

He called his fellow labourer and asked whether they should
show it to Mr. Sadler; but the other, having no kindness for
Sadler, disagreed and proposed that, as they had found it, they
should simply stop it up again and take no notice of it. The
man who had found it consented at first, but soon, out of curiosity perhaps, found himself strongly inclined to tell his master,
and one Sunday evening he did so.

Sadler at once went to see the well and, fancying from the
curious stonework that its water might be medicinal—formerly
had in esteem but somehow lost—he took a bottle of it to an
eminent physician, explaining how it had been found and asking
his opinion. After tasting and testing it, the doctor told him it
had a strong mineral quality and advised him to brew some beer
with it which he should take to persons the doctor would recommend to him. This Sadler did, and some of them found it did
them so much good they asked for roundlets (that is, small
casks) of it instead of bottles so that, after it had had so good
an effect during most of the winter of 1683–4, the well-known
Dr. Morton, Fellow of the College of Physicians and later
Physician in Ordinary to William III, advised several of his

patients the following summer to take it. Visitors to the Musick-House began to drink it, and most London physicians recommended it to their patients, so that by the end of the summer of 1685 five or six hundred people frequented the Musick-House constantly every morning for the water.

Soon after this, Sadler discovered two more wells, one in a cellar, the other in the garden of the house opposite; and these three wells he named Sadler's New Tunbridge Wells, after Tunbridge Wells in Kent which, in the previous fifty years, had become more fashionable than even Epsom or Bath.

The waters of the first well discovered were carefully described by Dr. T. Guidott—no mean authority in view of his writings on Bath and other British springs, though he was so conceited that he sometimes seemed quite mad, especially when his blood was overheated by too much bibbing. He said they had a steel taste, not as strong as those at Tunbridge Wells, and were so inoffensive that more could be drunk of them than of any other liquor. The great Robert Boyle found that the water weighed 3 oz. 4 dr. 36–9 gr. as against the 3 oz. 4 dr. 43 gr. of common water.

It is uncertain what mineral properties the waters had other than nitrous sulphur which moved the drinker to stool at the first taking or, if he had a very foul stomach, to vomit. A prospectus describing the uses of the waters announced that they were good for dropsy, jaundice, scurvy, green sickness and other distempers to which females were liable ('not convenient here to be mentioned'), as well as for ulcers, fits of the mother, virgin's fever, and hypochrondriacal distemper, making the patient brisk and cheerful. The water should be drunk early in the morning after a leisurely walk to Sadler's Wells, and should be warm—a quarter of a pint of scalding milk to three pints of the water. From four to ten glasses a day should be taken, with a twenty-minute stroll round the gardens after each second glass, for two to six weeks running.

Nothing should be eaten while taking the waters except a few caraway seeds, some preserved angelica or elecampane (a medicinal root of the aster family), though a pipe or two of tobacco might not be harmful nor, after the drinking, a glass of Rhenish or white wine—Sadler was said to be a confectioner, a tobacconist, and a wine-merchant!

About midday, some light food such as sage-tea, milk-porridge, mutton-broth or even roast mutton or lamb was allowable, but no bohea or green tea which tended to be 'cholicky'. There should be no violent exercise but only sedentary occupations such as reading, writing, or needlework: nor should fruit or malt liquor be taken till dinner, and no immoderate drinking, while 'that bane of Englishmen', brandy, would be pernicious. People were recommended to seek a doctor's advice.

A season's subscription was one guinea; but the water was available even to those of limited means, as non-subscribers were charged only 6d. a glass with some capillaire—that pleasant old drink made with sugar, white of egg and orange-flower-water.

To make the walks between medicinal glasses attractive, Dick Sadler laid out ornamental gardens and arbours with a marble basin for the water: he also built a long room with a stage at one end on the lawn outside the Musick-Room and engaged posturers, tumblers, and rope-dancers to perform in the open at no extra cost to the water-drinkers. He took as partner the fiddler Francis Forcer, who was both dancing-master and composer (some of his songs had been printed in 1679 by John Playford in *Choice Ayres and Dialogues*); visitors could dance to the strains of a musician with pipe and tabor who sat on a rock of shell-work; while every evening in the season (that is, during the summer) one Pearson played the dulcimer from five to eight.

Sadler's success led to immediate printed comment—praise at the expense of Epsom and Tunbridge in 'A Morning Ramble, or, Islington Wells Burlesqt':

> Those are good but for one disease;
> To all disorders this gives ease,

and an attack in 'An Exclamation from Tunbridge and Epsom against the new found Wells at Islington', disparaging the local suburban bawds, loitering apprentices, strong ale and milk made from rotten turnips and hogwash.

That first year, 1684, two songs praised the new Wells—the first for its 'Sweet gardens and arbours of pleasure', the second more satirically for the preparations made there for young wives that have unkind husbands, announcing:

London lasses make ready,
  Repair for Islington;
Young widows, young wives or lady,
  While all your husbands are gone,

recommending the power of the water, the bowls, gardens and arbours, and telling husbands how to get that time-honoured sign of cuckoldom, 'Gilt antlers well grafted and tall'.

Scarcity of contemporary records makes accuracy difficult, but it seems that the medical popularity of Sadler's Wells soon declined. Certainly already in 1685 one John Halhed, owner of the Fountain Inn, finding the old chalybeate well there, named it 'London Spaw'; he boasted that it was better than other waters in the locality and cunningly let the poor drink it free. He did not achieve a great success. (The site is now a pub at the corner of Exmouth Market and Rosoman Street, some two hundred yards west of Sadler's Wells. There an old well, maybe the Skinners' Well, was found only in 1963.) Three months later Sadler sold the Islington Wells south of the river and the large gardens to a shady London merchant, John Langley, who renamed them Islington Spa or New Tunbridge Wells, and they soon strongly rivalled Sadler's only remaining well, which the dramatist Nahum Tate scathingly called 'Sadler's Pump'.

John Evelyn, the diarist, went the next year to see the New Spa Wells; but a year later Islington was emptied by the rival attractions of Tunbridge and Bath, and by 1691 a poem ridiculed 'Islington Wells, or, the Threepenny Academy', and was dedicated to all pretty young girls who visited them 'To render their bodies more apt to conceive'. The author of these verses rose at 6 a.m., and when he reached his arbour the place was already packed by scented—and odorous—people: fashionable beaux, scarlet-coated commanders off to Flanders, a linendraper and other tradesmen pretending to be city fops, strumpets, tricksters and country people, all drinking the waters, which two old women gave away free, joining in a raffle or gambling in the game of Royal Oak, while

The *Musick* Plays, and 'tis such *Musick*,
As quickly will make me or you sick.

Three violins and a bass murdered tunes from the Opera—

presumably from Purcell's *King Arthur* and *Dioclesian*, Cambert's *Ariane*, Lully's *Cadmus and Hermione*, or Locke's *Psyche*, the recent popular opera successes.

Sadler tried to compete by giving his waters free on a medical certificate, but his spring somehow stopped flowing until 1697, so his entertainments had to become the chief attraction. Every Monday in August at least during 1697 there was a vocal and instrumental concert with double the usual number of performers from 11 a.m. till 1 p.m., admission 6d., while in 1698 the concert began an hour earlier with a full orchestra of strings, oboes, trumpets, and kettledrums. This development of the music may well have been due to Francis Forcer, who about this time took as partner a glover named James Miles, after whom the wooden theatre was renamed Miles's Musick-House: which suggests that Sadler had either died or retired.

Not that music was the only entertainment offered to Sadler's water-drinkers. In May 1699 the house was as full 'as if an *Elephant* had been [going] to Dance a Jigg' or a sermon was to be preached by the 'Salamanca Doctor' Titus Oates (released, after the Revolution of 1688, from life imprisonment for perjury over the Popish Plot, 1678). The reason was to see a 'Hibernian Cannibal' do something that would turn a foul stomach as well as a gallon of emetic. (Non-squeamish scholars can read the more nauseous details in the British Museum: the beginning of the description is indication enough.)

A table in the middle of the room was spread with a dirty cloth and on it bread, pepper, oil and vinegar, but no knife, plate, fork or napkin. When the room was filled with a crowd craning to see 'his Beastlyness's Banquet', the lord of the feast came in with a smutty face and wearing a buffoon's cap. He sat down and a live cock was put into the ravenous paws of the ingurgitating monster who first pulled out a few tail and wing feathers. Next he clapped a few oats in his mouth, which he extended to the width of a lady's chamber-pot; then he held up his living morsel, which pecked out several of the oats and played at bob-cherry with him for a considerable time, to the great diversion of the company. At last he—in short, he ate the living bird, feathers, guts and all, leaving the spectators to change colour and be sadly troubled with the hiccups, while he washed it down with a pint of brandy and wagered for another five-guinea fee he would do the same again in two hours' time. (Later he is said to have eaten a live cat.)

A fuller description of Sadler's entertainments in about 1699 was given in Edward Ward's contemporary verses entitled, 'A Walk to Islington: with a description of New Tunbridge-Wells, and Sadler's Musick-House'. In this the author with his lady of pleasure, after visiting New Tunbridge Wells, decided to trudge on to Sadler's for the sake of the organ, as women always like music and dancing. Inside the House they went upstairs where pairs of lovers were eating cheesecakes while organs hummed and fiddles were scraped and the guests kept drumming on the tables for more ale. Poor Tom, the waiter, could only cry out, 'Coming, sir, coming'.

Cakes, wine, pastries, custards, and tobacco were also available, and when Ward and his companion had refreshed themselves after their walk they looked at the paintings round the outside of the gallery: these were all of classical gods in suggestive love-scenes—Neptune and a Nymph, Apollo and Daphne, Jupiter and Europa. Then they looked down into the pit below where butchers and bailiffs and 'vermin trained up to the gallows', informers, thief-takers, deer-stealers, bullies, old straw-hatted whores and their dupes were dancing, skipping, ranting, raging, drinking, smoking, lying, swearing and, when they were caught stealing away without paying, fighting with those serving the drinks.

To quieten the hubbub, a dumpy singer ('Lady Squab with her moonified face') stood in her usual place by the organ, her hands on her belly, and sang her 'modest ditty', 'Rub, rub, rub; rub, rub, rub; in and out ho!' Then came a fiddler in scarlet, who showed off his finger-work in the upper register, though he looked like a fierce soldier. Then a plain and sluttishly unattractive eleven-year-old girl in tinsel, so impudent one could be sure 'she knew how to sin by the time she was seven', danced with a number of rapiers which she pointed at her throat and then spun round on her heel so fast that the wind under her petticoats fanned her and cooled her before and behind. Next came a young boy with quicksilver in his heels but 'a gallows in's face' who danced a jig and made strange 'Music-House Monkey-like Faces'. Last of all came honest, fat, old Tom, who seemed to be in charge, dressed as a clown:

He cocks up his Hat, draws his Heels to his Arse,
And makes his own Person as good as a Farce.

This brought the show to an end.

After 1700 the waters were no longer advertised, and though the few remaining records seem to indicate that the entertainments continued, conditions at the Wells were deteriorating. City wives and apprentices were drawn to Miles's Musick-House in 1701 to see 'a strange sort of monster that does everything like a monkey; mimics man like a jackanapes, but is not a jackanapes; jumps upon tables and into windows, on all fours, like a cat, but is not a cat; does all things like a beast, but is not a beast; does nothing like a man, but is a man!' While they were watching this acrobatic clown, a family of rats gnawed through the ropes by which a stuffed alligator was suspended from the ceiling, and rats and alligator fell together on the crowd below —sufficient evidence of the state of disrepair of the wooden theatre.

Four years later Francis Forcer was dead; he left all his property to his son Francis by his will, dated 1704, which, however, contained no mention of Sadler's Wells. It seems probable, therefore, that James Miles was now running it. In 1711 Sadler's Wells was called a nursery of debauchery in the trouble-making publication *The Inquisitor*; and a year later a quarrel over women between Mr. French, a lawyer of the Temple, and Mr. Waite, a Lieutenant of a Man-of-War, ended with the murder of Waite near the organ-loft. But a contemporary tract suggests that any disorder was not the fault of the proprietors; it says that Sadler's Wells, otherwise Miles's Musick-House, was so well known to most people in town that the writer need not describe it (a pity, from our point of view!) beyond saying that many go there daily to divert themselves in all innocence, while the proprietors are only getting an honest living, but nevertheless it is frequented by many unaccountable and disorderly people.

By 1714 its music and dancers, to say nothing of the toothsome ale, was making this 'fam'd House' more reputably popular than the London Spa with its old huts and drunken nine-pin players or New Tunbridge Wells

> where dejected Scrapers us'd to tune
> Their catcall-Instruments from Six to One,

and where the ancient drooping trees were unpruned and no ladies were to be seen. Four years later, it was the music that drew strolling damsels, half-pay officers, peripatetic tradesmen, tars, butchers, and others to the Wells when it opened in March, as it did up to 1825.

The only musical performer at this time of whom we know anything was Bat, or Bartholomew, Platt, who about 1723 sang in a Sadler's Wells pantomime[1] called *Harlequin Director*, a 'cantata' by George Hayden, 'A cypress grove, whose melancholy shade'—'a composition which would have done honour to some of the ablest masters of the time', wrote Sir John Hawkins in his *History of Music*. This implies that good music was liked at the Wells, but the snobbish Sir John says that the same Bat Platt, 'a favourite singer with the vulgar', used to sing there, dressed as a madman, another song by Hayden called 'New Mad Tom', 'to the great delight of all who mistook roaring for singing'. However, this dramatic showpiece, in imitation of Purcell's 'Mad Tom', was so popular that a print was made of Platt as that character and several of his Wells songs were published as ballad sheets, among them one by Henry Carey (of 'Sally in our Alley' fame), who lived in Clerkenwell, and another that was printed in D'Urfey's *Pills to Purge Melancholy*.

Charles Macklin (*c.* 1697–1797), who made his name in 1741 by his naturalistic Shylock, is said to have appeared at Sadler's Wells under one of the Forcers—perhaps as tumbler, wrestler or cudgeller, all of which he had been. Towards the end of the eighteenth century, the veteran actor gave an account of the theatre that seems to fit the earlier Forcer régime better than the later, especially as in the earlier period Macklin was taking odd jobs in London. His account, in answer to an enquirer, begins, 'Sir, I remember the time when the price of admission *here* was but *threepence*, except for a few places scuttled off at the sides of the stage at *sixpence*, and which were usually reserved for people of fashion, who occasionally came to see the fun. Here we smoked and drank porter and rum and water as much as we could pay

---

[1] Until influenced by early nineteenth-century burlesques, a 'pantomime' kept its original Greek meaning of 'all mime' and told a story without words—an art that developed into ballet.

for, and every man had his doxy that liked it, and so forth; and though we had a mixture of very odd company (for I believe it was a good deal the baiting-place of thieves and highwaymen), there was little or no rioting. There was a *public* then, Sir, that kept one another in awe'.

Asked whether the entertainments were anything like those given at the time of the interview, he answered, 'No, no; nothing in the shape of them; some hornpipes and ballad-singing, with a kind of pantomimic ballet, and some lofty tumbling—and all this was done by daylight, and there were 4 or 5 exhibitions every day'. He then went on to relate how the proprietor always had a man stationed outside who, when he thought the waiting crowd was enough to fill the house, ran to the back of the upper seats and called out 'Is Hiram Fisteman here?'—whereupon the performers brought that programme to an end.

In 1724, Miles, who had run Sadler's Wells for about twenty-five years and through his entertainments was the favourite of beaux, butchers, and bawds, died leaving most of his possessions to his daughter Frances (who had married Francis Forcer the younger), but his will did not mention Sadler's Wells. The younger Forcer had attended Merchant Taylors' School, matriculated at Lincoln College, Oxford, and been called to the bar in 1703. Whether or not he had been helping his father-in-law after his father's death, he was in 1730 granted a lease of the place by the ground landlord, Thomas Lloyd, son of the Chancellor of Worcester. In spite of unsavoury competition at Stokes's Amphitheatre at Hockley-in-the-Hole by Clerkenwell Green—bull- and bear-baiting as well as women fighting, even with swords—he boldly presented in his opening year Edward Ward's *Prisoner's Opera* (two years after the *Beggar's Opera*), in which Platt sang the part of the Prisoner. Besides competition, two other factors were against him: the danger of the sparsely populated neighbourhood (Mr. Jones, the City Marshal, was robbed by three footpads on entering Spa-field in 1733), and the growing popularity of the larger New Tunbridge Wells, which had as many as seven hundred people at 7 a.m. (some sober sots arrived as early as 5 a.m. to recover) and one morning was visited by George II's daughters, the Princess Royal,

Princess Amelia, and Princess Caroline,[1] and nearly two thousand people to whom Pinchbeck, the toy-man, sold fans showing a view of the place.

Forcer then in 1735 applied for a licence to charge admission for organized entertainments as well as for liquor, claiming there had been music, rope-dancing, ground-dancing, a short pantomime, and the sale of liquors at Sadler's Wells forty years before. His application was refused but, being told he would not be interfered with, he advertised the usual diversions for 5 p.m. daily with an occasional performance between 1 and 2 p.m., naming only the new pantomimes, most of which had 'Harlequin' in the title. Even the Licensing Act of 1737 that stopped all theatres except the Royal Patent Theatres of Drury Lane and Covent Garden (and in the summer the Haymarket) from giving drama without musical accompaniment did not deter him: he at once announced that the house was 'entirely new modelled and made every way more commodious than heretofore for the better reception of company'.

The signboard of the new-modelled house appeared in Hogarth's picture 'Evening', painted in 1738 (the year Bat Platt died); it showed a dyer with his family and his cuckold's antlers outside the Sir Hugh Myddelton's Head, which was almost opposite the present Wells main entrance. Inside was a group seen in the smoke of what some think was the Sadler's Wells Club, though I can find no reference to a club till Rosoman formed one some eight years later.

Local competition was strong that year with pantomimes at the New Wells near London Spa, at another New Wells in Goodman's Fields, and concerts at one of Nell Gwynn's old houses, Bagnigge Wells, in what is now King's Cross Road, where an old commemorative plaque can be seen today nearly opposite the steps into Granville Square (Arnold Bennett's *Riceyman Steps*). So from 1739 Forcer stressed in his advertisements of rope-dancing, tumbling, singing, and grand dances, both serious and comic, that Sadler's Wells adjoined the New River Head. The shows for many years began at 5 p.m. so that they could end before nightfall.

Here in full is the advertisement for Saturday, 13th September

---

[1] Sir John Arundell allowed a path to be made for them over his Coldbath fields by Mount Pleasant.

1740: it is not only typical but gives the earliest list of Sadler's Wells performers and the earliest admission costs I have found. It is headed:

SADLER'S WELLS FOR THE BENEFIT OF MR. AND MRS. RAYNER.[1]

At Sadler's Wells, adjoining to the New-River Head, Islington, this Day, will be perform'd, The Usual Diversions of that Place. Likewise a New Dance by Mons. Baudouin, Mons. Froment, Mr. Davenport, Mrs. Woodward, Mrs. Rayner, Mrs. Davenport, The Parting Lovers.

Also a Dance call'd The Pigmalion, by Mons. Froment, Mrs. Rayner and others. With a new Balance by Mr. Rayner.

The whole concluding with a new Pantomime Entertainment call'd The Birth of Venus, or, Harlequin Paris, Concluding with the Loves of Zephyrus and Flora.

N.B.—There will be a variety of Rope-Dancing by Mademoiselle Frederick Kerman, lately arriv'd.

Box 2s. 6d. Pit or Gallery 1s. 6d.

Box, of course, means a seat in a box and shows that what we call the circle was in those days a series of boxes—as it is in many eighteenth-century opera-houses abroad today—where the élite sat protected from the rabble below who occupied the ground floor up to the orchestra, as they did till the mid-nineteenth century.

The Pigmalion was so successful that it was revived in 1741 when the company was joined by one of the first stars of Sadler's Wells, Mr. Hendrick, the famous Ladder-Dancer, lately arrived from Russia: that he was later called Mr. Hendrick Kerman suggests that the 'Mademoiselle Frederick Kerman' of the advertisement may have been carelessly printed, or that he was a female impersonator. The Ladder-Dancer's arrival in 1741 helps to date William Garbott's poem 'New River' which gives many interesting facts about Sadler's Wells and people connected with it at that time. It insists that though Forcer improved the place, it was Miles who first secured fame for it so that the garden was still known as Miles's Garden, where you could smoke under the trees, watch the fish or catch them, admire the two swans

[1] Till nearly 1900, leading performers were entitled at the end of a season, and if outstanding more frequently, to a benefit performance, at which guest artist friends often appeared and from which the beneficiary took all receipts after usually being charged the theatre's expenses.

> Which to the *Garden* no small Beauty are;
> Were they but *black*, they would be much more rare;

feed the ducks, and drink ale: indeed

> So good it is, it's prais'd by all Men's Tongues,
> Healing as *Balm of Gilead* to the *Lungs*.

As for the management, the poem said Miles was obliging in his way, but Forcer was more polite and polished and was not to be blamed for giving up the Bar he was called to at Gray's Inn for another which was more profitable, though the individual payments might be less, because there are far more clients —after all,

> Monarchs have Money rais'd from Subjects' Smoak,
> And thought they did not less majestic look;
> Then who can blame if, by his Care and Pains,
> Forcer doth Money raise from Barley-grains?

Charles II had taxed tobacco first, and William III coal, and perhaps Forcer made a nice profit by still brewing ale from Sadler's Wells water, but the water was no longer alluded to medicinally except by implication.

The entertainments in the 'Show-Room' included the bold Dutchman with his back-leaps on the rope (surely Kerman) with as his assistant an excellent clown, who made even the best people laugh (including the Duc d'Aumont, 1709–82, the great art-collector); the famous tumbler, Dominique, who came over from Paris in 1742, doing a head-first fall from the upper gallery with a somersault in the air which made the women shriek before he landed gently on his feet; a Black Scaramouch, a Harlequin, and many others.

All these one could see cheaper there than 'at The House' (which may mean the New Wells, Spafield, but more likely means indoors); at the Show-Room (which I take to mean a place where the entertainers showed the crowd in the garden a taste of the programme to be given in the new-modelled wooden theatre), 'You only pay for *Liquors*, not the *Show*'—and this included neat brandy, Southam cider, and wine. Even indoors, for some years the price of admission was only the purchase of a pint of wine at 2s.; for that in 1742 so many came to see Dominique throw a somersault through a hogshead of fire, hear Mr. Heemskirke sing a Mad Dialogue by the late Mr. H.

Purcell as well as the Cries of London by special request, watch Kerman's Ladder-Dance and finally enjoy a new entertainment called *The Americans Triumph over the Savages*, that the footway from Clerkenwell was widened for carriages. In addition, the piazza was built at the eastern end of Forcer's house (as shown in the 1745 print), opening almost where the iron gates are today after turning from Rosebery Avenue into St. John Street.

In 1743, after being four days 'very ill of the new distemper', the tall, athletic, handsome old gentleman Francis Forcer died, stipulating in his will that 'my Lease of the House wherein I now live called or known by the Name of Sadler's Wells . . . and all the Scenes and implements Store furniture & Household stuff and things thereunto belonging shall be sold', the proceeds, after paying his debts, to go to his wife Catherine[1] and his daughter Frances, wife of George Savage.

Much to the wrath of the regular Patent Theatre actors at Covent Garden and Drury Lane, Fleetwood at the Lane imported 'mummers' from Sadler's Wells, which was then taken over by John Warren. He so lowered the standard that in May 1745 Sadler's Wells was included in a list of places condemned by the authorities who were determined to clean up any spots in London seducing people into luxury, extravagance, idleness and other illegal wickednesses which were destroying family life 'especially at a Time when we are engag'd in expensive Wars, and so much overburdened with Taxes of all sorts'. So many loose, disorderly, idle people resorted to Sadler's Wells that the Grand Jury of Middlesex seems to have closed the place. The Wells therefore had no audiences to lose, as the Patent Theatres did, when London panicked in December 1745 on hearing that Bonnie Prince Charlie and his anti-Hanoverian army had come as far south as Derby, only to turn back unexpectedly.

But things changed in 1746, when on 7th February (1745 Old Style) the ground landlord, the Rev. John Lloyd, leased to Thomas Rosoman, late manager of the New Wells, Spafields (where now the street bears his name), and Peter Hough, who had been a tumbler there and at Goodman's Fields, 'all that Messuage or Tenement commonly called by the Name of

[1] His second wife? See p. 10: or some think this was a third generation Francis Forcer.

Sadler's Wells' for twenty-one years at a yearly rental of £100 plus all rates and taxes. This lease—according to the rough, very fragile draft in the possession of the Lloyd-Baker family at Hardwicke Court, Gloucester, included 'the Brewhouse Storehouse Stables Granary Sheds Yards Walls Gardens Walks Trees Outhouses & other Buildings together with the Stage Benches & Galleries thereunto belonging and also all Ways Passages, Lights Pavem^ts. Water Springs Wells Watercourses Cellars Vaults Fixtures p^r of its Commoditys & App^ts whatsoever to the s^d Messuage or Tene^mt & pre^mis belonging or in any wise ap^ptaining.'

So Rosoman and Hough reopened Sadler's Wells in April 1746 and thereby started twenty years' prosperity for the old wooden theatre with a resultant success that continued virtually unbroken for nearly one hundred and fifty years and made the name of Sadler's Wells famous up to the present day.

CHAPTER TWO

THE REIGN OF ROSOMAN

1746–1771

THE SADLER'S WELLS that Rosoman took over in 1746 can be seen in the same year's *Universal Harmony, or, The Gentleman and Ladies' Social Companion* of 1745, a collection of songs, where it illustrates 'A New Song on Sadler's Wells; set by Mr. Brett'. This is the earliest print of the place, and a later description of it points out that, as three of the seven first-floor windows had what were then modern sashes, that part had probably been added to the Musick-House when Forcer made it habitable. The small detached building may have been the Well-house itself (it is in the correct relative position), and on the New River are the two swans referred to in Garbott's poem.

The song idealizes the pastoral 'Joys of Sadler's Wells', with its 'vary'd sweets all round display'd', 'Musick's charms in lulling sounds' and 'Zephyrs with their gentlest Gales' (the local breezes of the high neighbourhood are constantly mentioned in verses of the time, and are still preferable to the comparative airlessness of the City below): its lyrical praise is so like good taste advertisements of today that it may well have been commissioned by Rosoman himself.

He certainly considered his audience, opening at holiday-time at 2 p.m. and 6 p.m. instead of the usual 5 p.m., and he tried from the start to set a standard of good quality—not that he undervalued rope-dancers and tumblers (more than eight in his opening programme as well as Hendrick's Ladder-dance and 'The Young Giant', fifteen years old and seven foot four); but he also announced an entertainment of sung music 'never perform'd before'.

This was *Tithonus and Aurora*, 'interspers'd with a New Piece in Grotesque Characters', *The Aukward 'Squire, or, Harlequin Philosopher* (in which he himself played Harlequin, the character

16

1730

1746

1792

BATT PLATT   RICHARD WROUGHTON

SADLER'S WELLS, 1813

for which he was well known). This would seem to have been a conventionally classical opera with an act of a comic show interpolated in each interval in true *intermezzo* style—a breaking of continuity as much in the fashion of the day as advertisements now are in commercial television—and ending in true Purcellian style with a Grand Dance in the Palace of Aurora, all done with entirely new costumes, scenery and music.

Rosoman kept up this ambitious opera-intermezzo programme for some five years, the classical stories set to music being *Minerva and Ulysses, or, The Fate of Polyphemus* (1746), *Meleager and Atlanta, or, The Calydonian Chase* (1747), *The Fate of Narcissus* (1748), and *Jupiter and Alcmena* (1750)—if only the scores still existed!

He also presented a musical *Scipio Africanus* (Beckingham's Lincoln's Inn Fields play of 1718 with music, or Buranello's Haymarket opera of 1742?); and in 1749 he produced a version of Theophilus Cibber's Drury Lane pantomime of 1733, *The Harlot's Progress*, based on Hogarth's famous prints, to which he added a representation of Ranelagh Gardens as decorated for the recent Jubilee Ball. Equally topically he celebrated the defeat of the Young Pretender at Culloden with a new song in honour of the Duke of Cumberland, 'The Royal Hero's Return'. 1750 saw the personal appearance of Hannah Snell, who had made her name by enlisting in the Marines as James Gray and was only found out when wounded at the siege of Pondicherry. The following year (1751) a benefit was given for twenty-two sailors who, after being shipwrecked in 1745, had since been slaves to Muley Abdullah, Emperor of Fez and Morocco—their appearance in the irons they had worn in slavery profitably following the publication of the book on their experiences, *Barbarian Cruelty*, by one of them, Thomas Troughton.

Rosoman realized the value of good variety and good music equally. In 1746 he engaged the famous Rayner family of ropedancers (Miss Rayner jumped on the rope with a pair of candlesticks fixed to her feet), but he also welcomed Mrs. Smith's singing of 'To Song and Dance' from Handel's oratorio *Samson*, announcing it as having been 'sung by Signora Frasi at the King's Theatre in the Haymarket'. Then, in 1750, not only did the great bass singer, Thomas Reinhold, who had followed Handel to London, come to sing Purcell's 'Mad Tom', but the attractive Michael Maddox began his seven-year popularity at Sadler's Wells: while standing on a wire he played the violin, trumpet and drum, balanced a coach-wheel, stood on his head while the wire was in full swing without using his hands, even discharging a brace of pistols at the same time. For perhaps his most famous and difficult trick it was announced that he

> puts a Straw on his Foot, tosses it from thence to his Face, from his Face to his Shoulders, from his Shoulder to his Face again,

keeping balance the whole time.

To avoid any risk to respectable people on their way home through the lonely fields after sitting in the theatre from 5 p.m., Rosoman announced that

> . . . as we hope all will be right,
> All shall be over by Ten at Night.

Long shows indeed! No doubt to avoid the management's being prosecuted for charging for theatrical entertainment, patrons were admitted on purchasing a pint of wine or punch, and there was always British ale brewed on the premises, duly advertised in the same metrical form as the pastoral lyrics under the print of Sadler's Wells:

> Haste hither, then, and take your fill.
> Let Parsons say whate'er they will,
> The ale that every ale excells
> Is only found at Sadler's Wells.

To help the sale of drink Rosoman also sold shrimps.

It has been said that about 1750 John Wesley turned the Wells into a Methodist tabernacle, but that was the New Wells, not Sadler's, which was, however, closed with the other Minor Theatres in 1751. But as Rosoman immediately complied, he easily got his first theatre licence in 1753 under the Minor Theatre Act, which permitted, rather than licensed, certain smaller London theatres; and he started the custom of opening a new season on Easter Monday, the shows now beginning at 6 p.m.

The following year Rosoman had himself and his cronies— the Sadler's Wells Club—painted by Frank Hayman—a picture that used to hang in the Sir Hugh Myddelton's Head, but has unfortunately long been lost. According to a list compiled some forty years later by Mark Lonsdale, then the manager of the theatre, these Sadler's Wells friends included various tradesmen, and the following men of the theatre: Rosoman in the centre with his hand on his pug-dog; a dancer who went by the nickname of Bug Nose because of his warts; the scene-painter Holtham; the Wells tailor Rawson—known as Tailor Dick; Davenport the Ballet Master (teacher of the great comic Charles Mathews who first danced at Sadler's Wells in 1753); the painter Greenwood; Hough (Rosoman's partner); Maddox the wire-dancer, in a blue and gold theatrical dress; Peter Garman, rope-dancer and tumbler; and the tumbler Billy Williams, popular at the Wells for at least twelve years, till he collapsed dancing on its stage and died on Sunday, 7th June 1754.

From that season on, when the New River was enclosed by high wooden 'pallisadoes' to prevent angling, netting, bathing 'and the putting in of dogs', Rosoman devoted himself to management, giving up his part of Harlequin to Maddox who, however, retired from his hazardous occupation, having saved £6,000. In his place Rosoman engaged a performer who drew the whole town, another equilibrist on the wire, Isabella Wilkinson, whose playing in her precarious position of the cymbal, violin, pipe and tabor, and drum, pleased even those who before this could not look on feats of this kind with any patience:

> Such feats, so strange, yet pleasing to the view,
> They seem at once both art and nature too.

So sure had Rosoman been that she would pack the house that, before she appeared, he engaged her for three seasons running at a salary rising from £100 to £300 a season—roughly from £5 to £15 a week (not bad money in those days). At the same time, he gave up brewing ale, and converted the brew-house into a dwelling-house, Miss Wilkinson being the first tenant. The Queen of Hungary, formerly the Turk's Head, opposite the Wells Coach Gates, served coffee, tea and hot loaves from 4 o'clock for early comers.

For the world, the great event of 1756 was the war with France; but for the Wells it was the continuation of the City Road by building the New Road from Islington to Paddington. It was started in May, and by September there were so many

coaches, carriages and horsemen using it as far as it had gone
that dust was spoiling gardens near it, such as those of Bedford
House, as well as the fields. As a result any building nearer to
the New Road than 120 feet was forbidden. This made it dangerous from the risk of footpads, and Mr. Justice John Fielding
(half-brother of Henry, the author of *Tom Jones*) as magistrate
at Bow Street often arranged for a horse patrol to protect
nobility and gentry travelling between the fashionable squares
(for example, Grosvenor Square) and the City.

To nerve his audiences for the lonely way home, now that the
shows began later, Rosoman had already started advertising
when there would be moonlight or 'Cynthia' (a practice kept
up for many years), and he added attraction after attraction to
draw them to the Wells—Mr. Franklyn, an ingenious artist
who, with two bells on each foot, two on each hand and four on
his head, played tunes, triple peals and bob-majors by jerking
his arms and legs and nodding his head backwards and forwards;
a version of Henry Carey's popular *Contrivances* which had been
farce, comi-farcical opera and ballad opera; and the return of
Maddox from retirement, jealous, possibly, of Miss Wilkinson's
success: certainly they tried to outdo each other on the wire—
she by not only giving a variety of curious new balances (one
wonders what) but also dancing a hornpipe and playing a concerto on the violin; and he adding to his famous act with the straw:

> He takes a wine glass and holds it in his mouth, then kicks the
> straw, which he catches in the glass in a balance, after which he
> tosses it out of the glass and catches it on the edge.

Rosoman was a good public relations man: a seat in a box
cost 2s. 6d., in pit or gallery 1s. 6d.; those who bought a pint
of wine or punch at 2s. a bottle were admitted; and anyone who
had a ticket was entitled to a pint of wine or punch for 3d.—he
even had threepenny tickets printed stating that the pint was
gratis: no wonder the place was filled, as a poem called 'Sadler's
Wells' said, with footmen pretending to be beaux, maidservants
who had used their mistresses' make-up so badly they rivalled
any painted whore, apprentices with their oaken cudgels, slat-
tern females, city rakes, all outdoing each other—

> Here hat with hat, with ribbon ribbon vies;
> Wig threatens wig, and eyes contend with eyes.

Most of the men smoked clay pipes, and in the noisome fumes men and women drank each others' healths till the 'flashy sing-song feast' was over and all rushed for the door and so back to their lodgings, servant and master, maid and mistress, where

> Each easy cuckold then to bedward creeps
> Miss hugs the 'prentice, Tom with Mary sleeps.

Yet it was not all flashy. At the desire of several persons of quality Rosoman's programme in 1757 included a new music and dancing show called *As You Like It* (musical Shakespeare or a sort of revue?); and he realized the publicity value of giving to charity: from a performance at increased prices of 5s. and 2s. 6d. with no wine or tobacco allowed, but with a special horse patrol for the New Road, he handed over £65 12s. to the Marine Society to clothe men and boys going on board His Majesty's ships. The following year he similarly helped the Duke of Newcastle's police force scheme for giving 'asylum or refuge to orphan and deserted girls of the poor'.

In the winter of 1758 there was a rumour that Miss Wilkinson had been drowned with all the other passengers on board the *Dublin* on the way to Ireland: this was not true (though it was true of that unpleasant character the actor-dramatist Theophilus Cibber; of Franklyn the twelve-bell man; and of 'the pride and wonder of the world', Maddox, 'our Balance-Master'). A year later, Miss Wilkinson's wire failed and she broke her leg in two places, while Rosoman's partner, that 'facetious mortal' Peter Hough, died—apparently on the stage, his epitaph being:

> Here lie the bones of Peter Hough
> Of Sadler's Wells, and that's enough!

In 1760, tactfully falling in with the proclamation of the new twenty-two-year-old (but not entirely moral) King George III against immorality, a woman's magazine attacked the performances at the Wells:

> Do you think that a woman's exposing her limbs, and writhing her wretched body, into the most indecent postures, is an edifying instruction to the youth of either sex? . . . Most of the unhappy wretches who pay their lives as forfeit to the law, are such as frequent these ill-conducted places of recreation, where their

imaginations are enflamed to a degree of madness, that makes them run on any crime and danger for the gratification.

This may have been as sincere as attacks against sex and violence in films and television today, but it may also have been started by fear inside the Patent Theatres that places like the Wells were becoming serious rivals. Certainly in the following year Samuel Foote's sarcastic pleading in his prologue to *All in the Wrong* at Drury Lane seems rather too genuine:

> If at Sadler's sweet Wells, the wine should be thick,
> The Cheesecakes be sour, or Miss Wilkinson sick,
> If the fume of the pipe should prove pow'rful in June,
> Or the Tumblers be lame, or the bells out of Tune,
> We hope that you'll call at our warehouse at Drury—
> We've a curious assortment of goods, I assure ye.

The Wells must have been popular indeed because in 1762 it was found worth while to arrange for the sale of tickets through a London agent at Old Slaughter's Coffee-House in St. Martin's Lane.

Miss Wilkinson might no longer be able to do her wire act, but she could still play the musical glasses, while another Miss Wilkinson—Caroline—appeared as Columbine (it is difficult to disentangle the two, but a doubly broken leg is not an aid to dancing).

The programmes were still varied: rope-dancing was always popular, with Mrs. Preston having two baskets tied to her feet and also performing on a deal board laid loose on the rope, while Garman first had two boys and then even two men tied to his feet. Waters balanced half a pound weight on top of a straw(!); Mathews still tumbled and danced; and popular singers appeared, including Miss Brown, who later created a part in the West End in Linley's *Duenna*, and the versatile Andrews: his songs varied from patriotic attacks on the Grandees of Spain, who had just joined the war against England, and the vain projects of France over Canada, to comic impersonations such as a Somerset farmer's son up on a visit to London, who declared that Wells was 'better by half nor the play' at Drury Lane.

In the autumn of 1762 Rosoman allowed the young gentlemen of Mr. Rule's Academy to act Addison's *Cato* and the first part of *The Miller of Mansfield* before a numerous and polite audience on a Sunday to great applause—and as the actors were amateurs Rosoman could put on the first spoken play at the Wells without contravening the law.

The following year Rosoman engaged a Drury Lane dancer as Ballet Master and chief dancer, and with him came the Drury Lane dancers: this was not a direct clash with the Patent Theatres as the Wells opened only in the summer, and artists at the Patent Theatres, which had only winter seasons, were allowed to take outside engagements in the off-period. But this engagement added to the immediate prestige of the Wells and ultimately benefited the place enormously, for the new Ballet Master was Giuseppe Grimaldi who had been at Drury Lane for five years.

Either Giuseppe or his father Nicolini (authorities vary) had been known as 'Iron-Legs', but he himself, strangely enough, had first come to London from the Netherlands to be Queen Charlotte's dentist. He was not the first or the last stage performer to have another profession as a sideline, but as a dentist he made odd claims—that he could draw teeth or stumps without giving the least uneasiness in the operation (before the days of anaesthetics), fill hollow teeth with lead, and even fix another person's tooth of equal beauty and service in place of a broken one, 'although this operation is so curiously difficult as to be questioned by many, and particularly some of the profession'.

Drury Lane had not been doing well; the old custom of admitting the public for half-price after the third act had had to be restored after riots. Garrick himself, joint-partner at the Lane, took advantage of the end of the war with France to go on a year's grand tour of the Continent—only to catch typhoid and become so thin that he wrote saying that, better than returning to the Lane, he could apply to Sadler's Wells because he now could thread through the smallest tumbler's hoop.

Another link with Drury Lane in 1764 was the Wells production of *The Tempest*, presumably Garrick's version of the Dryden-Shakespeare-Purcell work castrated into an opera, as Theophilus Cibber had said (forgetting his father's Shakespearean distortions). At the Wells the music was stressed to avoid trouble, and Andrews added a patriotic song alluding to the British heroes of the late war—Granby, Wolfe, and Clive among them. Three days later the show was given for Grimaldi's

benefit at Drury Lane. The same year *Don Quixote* was produced (perhaps also an arrangement from Purcell?).

The entertainments had become so popular and, presumably,
profitable that in the summer Rosoman announced that Sadler's
Wells would be pulled down at the end of the season and rebuilt
in a most elegant manner.

In October 1764, then, the old wooden theatre was destroyed,
and the new theatre was up and tiled in seven weeks at a cost
of £4,225.

A builder by trade, Rosoman had already built over the
ground of the old New Wells (today part of Rosoman Street),
and probably made the English Grotto Garden there with its
rainbow water-mill and magic fountain, which about 1840 became the home of the *Clerkenwell News*, its first-floor windows
still to be seen at the corner of Garnault Place and Myddelton
Street.

The new, enlarged, brick Sadler's Wells with its elegant iron
gate and pallisadoes opened at 6 p.m. on Easter Monday, 8th
April 1765, and, though altered and further enlarged at various
times, it remained virtually the same to within a year or two of
1883. Its walls were still standing in 1927, and its last remains
were taken down only in 1938.

Rosoman added a handsome house for himself at the New
River end of the theatre and put up an iron chain and lamps by
the river to prevent people from falling in—a few years earlier
a woman servant, fetching coal in the dark, had been drowned,
and more recently a woman leaving the theatre had been pushed
in, 'undesignedly by her brother-in-law, with whom she had
some words'. For the convenience of the audience, he had the
backs of the seats fitted with shelves for wine-bottles and glasses.

The programmes that first year exemplified Rosoman's flair
for varying them: besides tumbling, dancing, singing, equili-
brists, and music, he found such novelties as a Scaramouch
Dance by a boy of six; the strong Venetian Colpi turning a fast
Catherine Wheel on the slack-wire with fireworks on his feet;
Miss Wilkinson on the wire for the first time since her accident
(by command of H.R.H. the Duke of Gloucester) doing Maddox's trick with the straw. Rosoman also brought back famous
old singers such as Mrs. Lampe (Isabella Young, Dr. Arne's

sister-in-law and widow of the composer Johann Frederick Lampe) who had sung in Arne's *Eliza* in London twelve years before.

The most far-reaching event of 1766 was a new twenty-one-year lease between Rosoman and Thomas Lloyd, acting for his nieces, now the real owners. This bound Rosoman to apply each Michaelmas to the Middlesex Justices for a public entertainment licence, and to do nothing to prejudice such a licence while undertaking to see that 'the utmost Decorum and Decency' were maintained. The most important condition in the draft lease, still in the archives at Hardwicke Court, was that Rosoman should undertake to keep Sadler's Wells open every summer by giving performances regularly

> so that the said place may not be any ways prejudiced or discontinued as a place of publick Entertainment.

Important people began to visit the shows. *Harlequin Restor'd, or, The Country Revels* was revived for His Excellency Hamed Aga, Ambassador from Tripoly, in 1767 at the benefit of young Master Herryman, who appeared at the Wells for the next sixteen years and on this occasion sang a new song by Dr. Arne, 'In Love should there meet a fond Pair'. But Rosoman's programmes were not always approved; a writer in 1768 implied that although the place was always packed, 'they must be easily pleased, who go to Sadler's Wells for entertainment'.

But Rosoman picked his entertainments and artists well: young Parsons, who sang at the Wells from 1767, later became well known in West End comic operas by Shield, Jackson, and Linley, as well as in Arnold's *Spanish Barber*, the first *Barber of Seville*. A popular act was Signor Spinacuti's wonderful monkey, Le Chevalier des Singes (a man dressed up?), who walked and danced on the tight-rope with the pole, balanced on the wire both with and without the pole, and on the slack-rope vaulted and turned the Catherine Wheel to admiration. Following Garrick's *Falstaff's Wedding* at Drury Lane in 1766, Rosoman presented *Shakespeare's Choice Spirits, or, Falstaff in Pantomime* two years later, thus anticipating Garrick's Shakespeare Jubilee performances of 1769.

The Gagnuer family introduced 'a new-invented Tumble called the Tranplain' (the trampoline); and Rosoman engaged two new tight-rope dancers, Lawrence Farci and his wife—the name reappears as Ferci and even Ferzi—who stayed for years and soon introduced into their act their three-year-old daughter and their son aged two (performers started young in those days —a practice even then condemned by some as a dreadful exhibition 'to gratify the avarice of unnatural parents').

Rosoman's business sense can be seen from his tough contract with the two Farcis in 1769: they had to appear for two seasons as often as required, not only in their own act but also in the various pantomimes, masques, dances, and other entertainments performed every night (for years every artist at the Wells had to take part in any production), and they had to get written consent to appear at any other theatre (except the Theatres Royal). For all this their joint salary was seven guineas a week together with one benefit night a season 'upon their paying the Usual Charge & Expence thereof'.

Rosoman was certainly careful in financial matters. According to Macklin he at first put his money in the Bank of England, but when he learned how to invest angrily demanded it back, accusing the Bank of cheating him out of his interest. He then put all his money into the three per cents and with his first dividend gave a public dinner to those friends who had advised him.

From 1771 it became the custom at the Wells to present two big musical entertainments or pantomimes a year. That year, Rosoman introduced a new musical instrument:

> The Trombe Marine e Timpano, which has all the Effect of a first and second Trumpet, and a Pair of Kettle Drums, and will be performed on every Evening by the inventor,

as well as a solo on the Welsh Harp, a trumpet Concerto by Mr. Jenkins, and—for one night only—a duet for two violins by Kotzwara (the Bohemian composer who later wrote the famous 'Battle of Prague').

Still following his policy of reintroducing past famous singers, Rosoman brought to the Wells Thomas Lowe, the very popular creator in 1740 of Arne's 'Under the Greenwood Tree' and 'Blow, blow, thou winter's wind': he was over fifty when he joined the Wells in 1771, but sang there every summer for the next eleven years. He was not a good musician, but had a fine voice and had sung in the first performances of five of Handel's oratorios.

In Smollett's novel, *Humphrey Clinker*, published in 1771, the character Winifred Jenkins describes going to the Wells:

> I was afterwards of a party at Sadler's Wells, where I saw such tumbling and dancing on ropes and wires that I was frightened and ready to go into a Fit. I tho't it was all enchantment, and believing myself bewitched, began for to cry. You know as how the witches in Wales fly on broom-sticks; but here was flying without any broom-sticks or thing in the varsal world, and firing of pistols in the air and blowing of trumpets and singing, and rolling of wheel-barrows on a wire (God bliss us!) no thicker than a sewing thread; that to be sure they must deal with the Devil. . . .
> A fine gentleman with a pig's tail and a golden sord by his side, came to comfit me and offered for to treat me with a pint of wine; but I would not stay; and so in going through the dark passage he began to show his cloven futt, and went for to be rude; my fellow sarvant Umphry Klinker bid him be civil, and he gave the young man a dous in the chops; but i' facking Mr. Klinker warn't long in his debt; with a good oaken sapling he dusted his doublet, for all his golden cheese-toaster; and fipping me under his arm carried me huom, I nose not how, being I was in such flustration.

Rosoman's partner Decastro, the comedian (his real name was Rutherford), had bequeathed his Wells shares to his widow with reversal to Rosoman if she married again: this she did, so that now Rosoman owned them all. Having previously sold a quarter of the shares to a goldsmith named Arnold for £2,500, in 1771 Rosoman sold the remainder to Thomas King, Garrick's friend and rival·at Drury Lane, for £7,000 (£9,000 some versions say) and retired.

King, now aged forty-one, educated at Westminster, had given up the law for the stage, acting for Garrick when eighteen. After appearing for Sheridan at the Smock Alley Theatre, Dublin, and managing the Bath Theatre for a year, he rejoined Garrick at Drury Lane in 1759, and the year before he took over the Wells was actor and manager of the King Street Theatre. He announced that he was not quitting his profession as actor at Drury Lane (at about £8 per week), but would take over from Rosoman on 1st December 1771.

CHAPTER THREE

PAGEANTRY, PATRIOTIC AND OTHERWISE

1772–1785

BEFORE KING could open, rumours started that the style of entertainment at the Wells would be changed and that there would be no more wine for spectators. King scotched both stories, stressing that the wines would be the best and the general entertainment much as before, though conducted 'on a Plan more brilliant, more extensive, and consequently (to the Proprietors) much more expensive than has hitherto been pursued'. But King as a straight actor (his Lord Ogleby in *The Clandestine Marriage* was famous), naturally preferred something more obviously dramatic than the customary 'Harlequin' pantomimes which he still revived, and his opening programme for 20th April 1772 showed new ideas. Advertisements had hitherto given no special prominence to performers' names; from King's advent they read more like present-day theatre bills: the names stand out and performers are thus built into attractions. The opening bill started:

PERFORMERS AS FOLLOW

SINGERS	Mr. Lowe, Mr. Kear, a young Gentleman, Miss Dowson, and Miss Froment.
PRINCIPAL DANCERS	Sieur Daigueville and his Pupils, Mr. Atkins, Miss Froment, and Signor Radicati.
TUMBLERS	Mr. Thompson, Mr. Rayner, Mr. Porter, and Mr. Garman.
ROPE DANCING.	Mr. Ferci, his Pupil, and Mr. Garman.

Then came the name of the new musical piece: *The Monster of the Woods*, and after that:

Ballet Master   Sieur Daigueville.
Composers of the different Musical Pieces: Mr. Fisher, Mr. Hook and Mr. Dibdin.

King obviously believed not only in the value of names but in encouraging young artists: all three composers were under thirty—John Abraham Fisher whose concertos for piano and oboe, as well as his music for *Monster of the Woods*, now called an opera, were published by Clementi; James Hook, later well known for his musical theatre works; and Charles Dibdin who at Drury Lane in 1768 had made a great hit both as composer and as actor in his own *Padlock*.

Everything was done to attract the public; the theatre was newly decorated, and the orchestra enlarged. A seat in a box plus a pint of Port, Lisbon, Mountain or Punch, was 3s.; one in the pit 1s. 6d. and in the gallery 1s., a pint of the same drinks costing an extra 6d. A second pint, which in the past had always cost 1s. 3d., would now cost only 1s., 'the Price paid at every other public Place'.

To satisfy the regular audience, King revived the 1766 pantomime *Trick upon Trick* and ladder-dancing of Maddox's days, now performed by the brilliant Mons. Richer, who was a regular attraction for eight years. But Dibdin specially wrote two interludes—*The Ladle, or Belphegor, or The Three Wishes* and *The Mischance* (from the *Barber of Bagdat*) as well as the popular 'Brickdust Duet'. Dibdin, indeed, proved that music could be the chief attraction. For 1773 he wrote *Vineyard Revels, or, Harlequin Bacchanal* with specially designed scenery and *The Whim-Wham, or, Harlequin Captive* which 'was received by a crouded audience with universal applause' and established the Wells as a rival to the Haymarket for pantomime. His *Cave of Enchantment*, 1774, preceded by *The Bower of Flora* (all airs and choruses without recitatives and so 'more sprightly and engaging than such poetical trifles usually are'), was said to be merely a vehicle for his lively music, though the machines and painting were admirable, while 'sprightly' was the word again used for his additions to yet another revival of *Harlequin Restor'd* (1748); which showed that, for all his dramatic preferences, King was practical enough not to despise the popular Harlequin pieces, nor novelties such as the two Sigels from Paris, a strong-man act.

For the 1775 season King had the Wells, as it was now called for the first time, redecorated in 'peculiar state', but the result was pleasingly cool and delicate—milk white, pale green, and a beautiful pink.

Even more musical pieces than usual were given: Dibdin's *Raree-Show Man*, *The Pilgrim*, *The Grenadier*, and his larger *Harlequin Neptune* (at the Easter Monday opening the audience was annoyed because the scene-shifters—'having kept Easter-Monday as well as the scene spectators'—changed a scene too soon, and Harlequin went against tradition by striking the scene to be changed with his hand instead of his magic sword). Revivals included *Tit for Tat*, by the late Henry Carey and Barthelemon, and *The Farewell, or, India Hoa!* by Samuel Arnold, Covent Garden composer and owner of Marylebone Gardens, in which the choruses with drum and fife were singularly pleasing.

King also introduced a Signor Rossignol who mimicked sounds, not only playing with the orchestra 'on a Fiddle without Strings' but especially imitating the songs of birds; his varied shows that year pleased several of the nobility, including the Prince of Hesse Cassel. Some society folk, of course, as always, thought such popular entertainments beneath them, but King was generally praised for what he was doing at the Wells: as a local poetaster wrote:

> . . . the nice coxcomb, and the beau
> Say, all its *phizgigs* are *so so*,
> The entertainments *horrid low*.
>
> May all such false refiners swing,
> And every British spirit sing,
> 'Of Sadler's Wells *God save* the KING!'

So confident did King feel about the Wells that on 4th August 1775 he wrote to Thomas Lloyd, asking for a fourteen- or twenty-one-year extension of the lease no less than twelve years before the current one was due to expire. He offered £50 more a year in rent (making it £150), and an extra £50 'by way of fine', explaining that, though he claimed the theatre now was 'better & the Scheme more reputable than heretofore, yet I must assure you, on my word of honour, the profits (which I believe I hinted to you before) are not equal to what they were when the place was frequented by the meaner sort of people only, and the exhibitions were in a narrower compass'. He then promised that 'if my offer is accepted I can cheerfully continue to expend money on various pieces, dresses, paintings, and other improvements within and without the building & may look on them as stock in trade, which will in their turns become profitable by their use at distant periods'. Without a guarantee that the lease would be renewed to him, the Wells might be let to 'some Person who (ignorant of the situation of matters) may dream of acquiring mountains of wealth, and offer more than I, who am acquainted with the concern, cou'd think of giving; in which case, my property, the acquirement of risque, fatigue and many an anxious hour, must be sold for a tenth part of it's cost, or taken away as nothing better than second hand Rags, old canvas and fire wood'.

A guaranteed extension of the lease might well safeguard the money he and his friends had put into the Wells even if he died, so he proposed to watch 'the two Theatres' (Drury Lane and Covent Garden) for a likely young man of good principles and understanding, with a tolerable turn for business, whom he could train. He would give him a small share of the concern, but he couldn't expect such a young man to 'sink any money, nay to give up any part of his present pursuits for a situation which has not got a *certainty* of longer continuance'.

In short, King was another of those who were determined to do all in their power to keep the Wells as a theatre for many years to come, realizing not only its present popularity but its promise for the future.

It was a year before Mr. Lloyd replied, but King meanwhile had got permission from the New River Company to put up a low wall and ornamental iron railing along the Wells walk by the river which would prevent the rabble from 'throwing in their dogs, etc.' He also introduced several more Dibdin pieces, *Sister Witches, or, Mirth and Magick, The Impostors*, and *The Savoyard's Holiday*, and Hook's *Easter Monday*, as well as reviving the old Elizabethan Egg Dance, brilliantly performed, over twelve eggs laid out on the stage, by Master Williamson (like a sword-dance) but blindfold. By this dance Williamson did great credit to his teacher, Mr. Grimaldi, 'the best Clown we ever saw', one critic said, adding: 'In scenes, when the business was not very engaging, he last night afforded great entertainment, without doing that violence to nature and probability, which mimers in general imagine they may commit in defiance of censure.'

When Mr. Lloyd eventually replied, the following August, he accepted King's proposal on condition that the £150 yearly rent suggested for the remaining twelve years of the current lease was raised to £200 for a further fourteen. King sent Lloyd two silver tickets of admission to the Wells, and in January 1777 agreed to the increase. His search for the young man of good principles had been successful: in March he wrote begging for a settlement about the lease as he was scheduled to open according to custom on Easter Monday (31st March) 'and as I have a conditional agreement with Mr. Wroughton of Covent Garden Theatre, shou'd the writings between you and me remain unexecuted till that time it will intail a very great inconvenience on, S^r, y^r very hble Servt & sincere well wisher Tho. King'.

At last the conditions were agreed to by Miss Katherine Lloyd, the real owner, according to the only remaining page— the last and undated—of the lease that is still in the Hardwicke Court records.

Twenty-eight-year-old Richard Wroughton had for the last eight years been making a name for himself in elderly character parts at Covent Garden and was immediately given the chance to justify King's confidence in him by being left in charge of the opening of the 1777 season which was to include Hook's *Wizard of the Silver Rock* and *The Norwood Gipsies* and Dibdin's *Razor-Grinder* and *Yo Yea! or, The Friendly Tar*, as well as Signora Rossi's tight-rope act playing the fiddle 'in various attitudes' and making 'a curious display of Two Flags'. King himself went to create the part of Sir Peter Teazle in *The School for Scandal* at Drury Lane on 8th May.

A year later King made further alterations to the auditorium, raising the ceiling and increasing the rake of the floor of the boxes and pit floor, thereby improving both the ventilation and the sight-line. Gradually the Wells became fashionable. The Duke and Duchess of Gloucester visited it, and in Fanny Burney's novel, *Evelina*, published that year, when the London family, the Branghtons, are discussing where to take their country cousins, Mr. Branghton asks the heroine,

'Pray, Cousin, have you been at Sadler's Wells yet?'
'No, Sir.'
'No! Why then you've seen nothing.'

There was considerable fear that summer of an invasion by
France which was supporting the American Colonies in their
revolt; so many of the items presented at the Wells took on a
patriotic tone which continued for years. England now resembled a huge camp, so not only was there an entertainment of
music and dancing called *A Trip to Coxheath* (where many
troops were stationed near Maidstone) 'with a distant View
of the Camp & a Roast-Beef Chorus', but Signor Ferzi on the
tight-rope went correctly through military exercises 'to the
satisfaction of all the Gentlemen of the Army who were present'.

Interest in events in India—where the re-establishment of
Warren Hastings as Governor-General of Bengal and the new
solvency of the East India Company—gave topicality to Hook's
Oriental Magic, or, Harlequin Nabob that year, with scenery by
Greenwood (the son of Rosoman's painter and the Wells designer for fifteen years). In this same year Dibdin's *Old Woman
of Eighty* and *She's Mad for a Husband* were produced, while
Dibdin himself became composer to Covent Garden. In September 1778, thirteen years of the Wells lease were put up for sale,
perhaps to raise extra capital.

In 1779 the British fleet was sent to the West Indies in the
struggle with France and Spain over the American Colonies and
was crippled off Grenada. So the Wells gave *All Alive at Jersey,
or, A Fig for the French* with airs from Arne, his son Michael,
Dr. Samuel Howard and others, as well as various emblematical
decorations and a Grand Naval Prospect: then, after seventy
French and Spanish ships had been off Plymouth in the summer,
9th August saw the complicated production of *The Prophecy, or,
Queen Elizabeth at Tilbury*. In this there was an emblematical
frontispiece with a small transparency at the top in which was
seen both the destruction of the famous Spanish Armada and a
moving perspective of the present Grand Fleet.

For the increasing carriage-trade the footbridge was widened
and built of brick. In June 1780 Lord George Gordon started
the would-be patriotic 'No Popery' riots, and the story goes
that after the rioters outside the old clown Grimaldi's house
opposite the Wells gateway told him he must write 'No

Popery!' on it, they laughingly left him and his premises un-molested when he immediately wrote 'No Religion at all here!'

To protect the London Streets during the riots, soldiers were encamped in St. James's Park; so the Wells gave *All for Scarlet, or, Ding Dong to the Park* with 'A Striking View of the Camp near the Canal, and an exact Representation of its Environs', and this was soon followed by revivals of *Harlequin Neptune* and *The Prophecy*, altered to end with a Military Exhibition, a song and chorus in honour of the Loyal London Military Association, and, above allegorical figures of France and Spain suing for peace, as every Briton hoped they would, 'Fame in the Act of crowning Britain's hope and boast'—the fifteen-year-old mid-shipman son of George III, Prince William Henry, afterwards William IV.

For King, however, good theatre outweighed patriotism, and on Easter Monday, 1781, he daringly presented two French artists who were so fine they remained Wells favourites for several years—Alexandre Placide Bussart, the 'French volti-geur', tactfully renamed Signor Placido, who appeared both on the rope and as a tumbler (before Louis XVI and Marie An-toinette he had jumped over twelve pairs of soldiers with per-pendicular bayoneted muskets), and Paulo Redigé called 'The Little Devil' (in contrast to Nevit who performed at Astley's four-year-old Amphitheatre Riding School as 'The Great Devil'). Redigé's performances on the tight-rope were 'such as cannot be described' and had never before been seen in Britain.

For these two and for Saunders, who stood on his head on a drinking-glass balanced on a slack-wire in full swing, H.R.H. the Duke of Cumberland, the Earl of Chesterfield, Lord Jersey, Sir William Watkyns Wynne and others, gave particularly loud plaudits on the following Saturday—possibly hardly noticing the appearance of one who in time was to become the best-loved performer in all the history of Sadler's Wells: Joe Grimaldi.

The Easter Monday announcements said there would be 'Dancing by le Mercier, Langrish, Master & Miss Grimaldi, & Mrs. Sutton.' At that time Master Grimaldi was just over two years old—he had been born, according to the registers of St. Clement Danes, on 18th December 1778—and he stayed at the Wells for fifty years, working at Drury Lane or Covent

Garden each winter. His mother, Rebecca, Mrs. Brooker, 'a short, stout, very dark woman', had danced at Drury Lane and Sadler's Wells from infancy and later played old women and utility parts, and his eccentric father was sixty-five when Joe was born. Tom King was fond of the child and often gave him a guinea to buy a rocking-horse or a toy cart.

In July 1781 topicality, till now usually patriotic or providing a pantomime scene, was represented by a satirical song: one Dr. James Graham, aged 34, had established in the Adelphi a Temple of Health with a Celestial Bed on which infertile couples were guaranteed fertility for a large fee (one duke paid £500), and a lecture was given on a naked female (later said by some to have been Emma, Lady Hamilton, in her youth): from the song, sung at the Wells by the popular Mr. Doyle as one of the Doctor's porters, we gather that admission simply to view the Bed cost 5s., while its mystery is explained in the following lines:

> Come see
> Where electricity
> Tickles ye all from the top to the toe—

something novel indeed, for the earliest Electrical Researches, by Henry Cavendish, are dated 1771–81.

Easter Monday 1782 fell on 1st April, so the curtain went up at 6 p.m. (with the front doors facing New River Head opening at 5 and the back door under the portico at 5.30) on *April Day, or, Who's the Fool?*. Eleven days later Admiral Sir George Rodney, K.B. (as he had been since his St. Vincent victory), captured the French Admiral, the Comte de Grasse, off Martinique as the French were sailing to join Spain in attacking Jamaica. This the Wells, ever up to date, celebrated only eight weeks later in *Huzza for Old England*, showing the late action in the West Indies with transparencies dropping in to show 'the gallant de Grasse surrendering his sword to Victorious Rodney', whose wife and two daughters saw the second night's performance. The piece included lines typical of the popular patriotic songs of the day:

> From morn to eve the bold affray,
> Was heard in thunder loud;
> But Gallic tops, by close of day,
> To British Rodney bow'd;

> When loth to leave so brave a foe,
> He took De Grasse himself in tow,
> Tol, lol, etc.

In the autumn a benefit was given for those bereaved by the sinking of the *Royal George*, while under repair at Portsmouth for rotten timbers, with the loss of 800 lives; a few days later the chain on which old Grimaldi swung young Joe round like a monkey broke, depositing him in the lap of an old gentleman to their mutual alarm; and shortly after that Saunders, while on the wire, balancing a French Horn on his lips, played a minuet without using his hands.

During 1782 fine old Thomas Rosoman, who had retired to Hampton, died worth, they said, £40,000, of which £6,000 went to his widow and the remainder (apart from a handsome legacy to Hough, his late partner, who had been dead for years) to his three children, 'neither of whom, however, is to receive a shilling till the day of their marriage'; and at the end of the season Thomas King became manager of Drury Lane in place of Sheridan, leaving the Wells, of which he was still the official lessee, to be managed by Richard Wroughton together with a goldsmith, Thomas Arnold (son of King's partner of the same name), and Serjeant, the trumpeter of Drury Lane Theatre.

The new working syndicate at once redecorated the theatre, making a complete semicircle of the front of the boxes, ornamented with festoons, intersected by a light stripe, and lit with glass lustres instead of patent lamps.

In the 1783 season, for the safety of the audience outside the theatre, the management had a patrol of horse and foot stationed from 8 to 11 p.m. along the New Road as far as the Tottenham Court Turnpike and along the City Road to Moorfields as well as to St. John's Street and across Spa Fields to Rosoman Row. This thoughtfulness encouraged society to take the risk: among the visitors were the late King of Sardinia's brother and the French Ambassador with a large party ('it seems quite the fashion, and is visited by people of the first distinction'). The Duke and Duchess of Richmond went to see *The Enchanted Wood, or, Harlequin's Vagaries*, with Placido and the Little Devil as Harlequin and Pierrot; in this, a transparent scene was introduced of the Diving Bell by the *Royal George* under the water at Portsmouth showing how a man went to fix the tackle. The *Public Advertiser*, which also sneered at the failing Opera with its castrati, scoffed at the Wells, which

> as usual in the summer months, exhibits a mockery of dramatic entertainment to crowded mariners and their red-ribboned Mollies, where the convivial pint of Portugal wine, vintaged in Southampton, wets the lips of the tar and his temporary wife, Jack eyeing with delight the dexterity of the rope-dancer, whilst Madam is thinking of somewhat for supper at the Ship and Anchor at Wapping. Hilloa here—avast there—hip in a third place—a song in a fourth—damn my eye in a fifth—pint of wine, waiter, in a sixth—orange, boy, in a seventh—and then hats off, hats off, all over the house, give a true picture of this favourite and long established place of public resort, where more genuine good humour and real happiness in the audience are to be found, than in any the most fashionable theatres of the metropolis.

The success of the Wells led the new owners, Mary Lloyd and her husband the Rev. William Lloyd Baker (they were first cousins, her aunt Mary having married his father the Rev. Thomas Baker) to have the property valued with a view to selling; the valuer thought it worth £3,700 and that the present leaseholders should give £4,000, but they considered the time too precarious for spending money, so the idea was dropped.

The programmes in 1784 were much as usual, with the topicality of the Little Devil passing through 'an Air Balloon all on Fire' only two days after the famous Lunardi made an ascent in a balloon for the first time in London. But an attraction that Wroughton said brought him a clear profit of over £7,000 was Scaglioni's troupe of performing dogs acting *The Deserter* under their leader Moustache, to which all London flocked. When the royal Duke of Gloucester went to see them (mistaking the thirty-five-year-old Wroughton—whom he had seen only in old men's parts at Covent Garden—for the manager's son), the theatre was like the Opera House on a Saturday night during the height of the season with princes, peers, puppies and pickpockets all crowding to see the illustrious 'dog-stars'. In his *Life and Times*, the dramatist Frederick Reynolds wrote:

> Moustache, as the Deserter! I see him now, in his little uniform, military boots, with smart musket and helmet, cheering and inspiring his fellow soldiers, to follow him up scaling ladders, and storm the fort. The roars, barking and confusion, which

resulted from this attack, may be better imagined than described.

At the moment, when the gallant assailants seemed secure of victory, a retreat was sounded, and Moustache and his adherents were seen receding from the repulse, rushing down the ladders, and then staggering towards the lamps [the footlights] in a state of panic and dismay.

How was this grand military manœuvre so well managed? . . . these great performers having had no food since breakfast, and knowing that a fine *hot supper*, unseen by the audience, was placed for them at the top of the fort, they naturally speeded towards it, all hope and exultation, when just as they were about to commence operating . . . the smacking of whips, and other threats, drove the terrified combatants back in disgrace.

1785 was almost as successful with dancing dogs; a wonderful hare beating a drum; bulldogs with English grit drawn up twenty feet by a balloon surrounded by fireworks rather than loose their hold; two horses dancing a minuet; the laughable singing duck; and the learned pig which, by means of 'Typographical Cards', set out names, reckoned the number of people present, told the time 'by looking on any Gentleman's watch', revealed any lady's thoughts, and distinguished colours.

It was this animal whose joy of life Dr. Johnson defined so speciously to an objector who failed to see any happiness for the pig in such a performance:

Not see what his happiness consists in, you astonish me; is not a consciousness of superior achievement happiness; is not being the first of his class happiness? But above all this, consider, Sir, the pig's learning has protracted his existence. Had he been illiterate, he had long since been smoked into hams, rolled into collars of brawn, and consigned to the table of some luxurious citizen, as the companion to a fillet of veal, or a Norwich turkey. Now he is visited by the philosopher, and the politician, by the brave and the beauteous, by the scientifick and the idle. He is gazed at with the eye of wonder, contemplated with the smile of approbation, and gratified with the murmur of applause.

CHAPTER FOUR

ROPE DANCERS AND THE BASTILLE

1786–1793

IN 1785, Wroughton and his partners, having bought Tom King's shares for some £12,000, took sole charge of the Wells. Dispensing with animals, the new management applied to Parliament for a licence to give Sadler's Wells, as the oldest of the non-Patent Theatres, a monopoly of pantomime. This was passed by the Commons, but the Chancellor, Lord Thurlow, had it thrown out by the Lords—to the joy of the. prime monopolists, Drury Lane and Covent Garden.

Wroughton still aimed at getting the best performers of whatever country, so that in 1786 artists from all parts of the Continent were said to be eager to appear at the Wells, where the nightly audiences were numerous and contained 'the first people in the kingdom', many of whom sent their servants to keep their booked seats till 8.30 when empty seats were sold at half-price—the usual London theatre custom.

The Little Devil and La Belle Espagnole (Signora Spagniola, a rope-dancer from Paris who had been very successful on her first appearance the year before) continued to appear and made Mrs. Wroughton jealous. The beautiful Spaniard actually danced with two swords on her feet, and her husband, Mr. Macquire, won a case against Wroughton for engaging her, without the consent of her lord and master, at four guineas a week instead of the twenty he asked. Other foreign attractions were Louis Porte, known as L'Hercule du Roi, who supported twenty-five people on a twelve-foot-long table and balanced on his teeth a ladder with a boy on top; the slack-wire clown Pietro Bologna with his wife, his sons Jack and Louis, and his daughter Barbara, 'well-behaved, honest people', said the well-known actor Tate Wilkinson, their act being 'on the whole, the best conceived and the most worthy of attention of anything of the kind I ever beheld'. One of Pietro's tricks was to play two flutes through his nose at the same time. The seventeen-year-old London-Italian Jewess, Miss Romanzini, sang Cupid in the pantomime.

Many thought Maria Romanzini was destined to be 'the Billington of the Wells' and, though in fact she sang there only that one season, she soon became the great Mrs. Billington's rival by her singing in musical plays by Arnold, Storace, and Kelly. Under her married name, Mrs. Bland, she remained a famous ballad-singer for nearly forty years; she was a sister-in-law of Mrs. Jordan, the well-known actress who composed 'The Blue Bells of Scotland'.

Among popular British artists were the dancer Lassells Williamson, who had married Mary, the daughter of his old teacher Grimaldi; and the singers Herryman and Robert Dighton, 'the best singer at Sadler's Wells', who was also an artist and caricaturist of his colleagues. When not singing, Dighton ran a print-shop at Charing Cross, some of the proceeds from which, to the extent of thirty-seven guineas, were stolen from him with his watch by a man with a pistol in Spa-fields 'not much after six o'clock, and hardly dark': which shows how dangerously solitary the Wells neighbourhood was in those days.

The audiences appreciated such musical scenes as *The Gates of Calais, or, The Roast Beef of Old England*, based on Hogarth, and especially applauded the topicality of *The Earth Bath, or, Modern Quackery*. This was a satire on Dr. Graham's latest catch-penny Temple of Health device—a promise of a hundred years' health, vigour, and beauty by the same lady who had adorned the Temple five years before, but now called Vestina, Goddess of Health. She appeared either stark naked or up to her neck in mud with a head-dress of flowers, feathers and pearls, to the accompaniment of lectures given by Anne Kemble, which much embarrassed her now famous elder sister Mrs. Siddons, since she insisted on calling herself Anne Siddons. Vestina's assistant junior priest, incidentally, was young Dr. Mitford, whose daughter, the future author of *Our Village*, was born the following year.

In 1787 the theatre, now fitted with side-boxes for separate parties after complaints that society visitors were jostled by rougher people, opened with a troupe of eight acrobatic Spaniards headed by Joseph Dortor or Doctor who appeared at the Wells as clown for many years. Dibdin's *England against Italy* was given and also *Hooly and Fairly, or, The Highland Laddie* with lyrics from the celebrated Allan Ramsay. One of the greatest attractions was a three-year-old child, known as the Fairy of the Wells, who in the character of Jack Ratlin sang the favourite 'Fal de ral Tit' with great exactness and trod the stage like an old performer.

But 1787 and 1788 were in one respect a trying time for the Wells. Wroughton and Arnold again petitioned Parliament—this time for a regular licence to present dancing, singing and musical pieces not seen at the Royal Theatres (provided no piece lasted more than half an hour and no more than two such pieces were given nightly) from 25th March to 10th October. They claimed that the Wells not only had been the first but, until about fifty years previously, the only theatre apart from the two Patent Theatres, and a licence had been granted to the Wells annually since 1753.

The authorities insisted that other theatres would want licences, and it was beneath the dignity of the Crown to grant a Patent for selling drink and exhibiting rope-dancing. Tom King, of course, spoke in favour of the petition, but Sheridan was jealously against it. A decision was so often adjourned that in 1788 the Wells had to break its long-established custom of opening at Easter and wait till Whit Monday.

Finally Parliament decided against the petition, claiming that the Wells had already been breaking the law for too long—which suggests that the Wells had been illegally slipping spoken dialogue into its 'all-musical' scenes; at the same time permission seems to have been granted for musical pieces, provided all dialogue was set to music, but for a shorter period than requested—from Easter Monday to 19th September.

In 1788 old Grimaldi died in his seventies (72, the papers said, 75 the burial register of the Northampton Chapel in Exmouth Market); and young Joe—now rising ten—had his Wells salary of 15s. a week as a baby performer cut to 3s. as help to the property-master, the carpenter and the painter (though Sheridan raised his equal salary at Drury Lane to £1 a week unasked, the sum his mother was getting at the Wells).

Child-entertainers still being an attraction that year, the ten-year-old Infant Hercules turned a somersault on the rope, and in the musical piece *Saint Monday, or, A Cure for a Scold* there appeared Master Abrahams, just fourteen, who, when two years older and under the name John Braham, started his amazing career as the first tenor of his generation in Italy, Paris and London, where he eventually built the famous St. James's Theatre (pulled down in 1958).

Another species of amusement, 'being quite nouvelle', was the exhibition of fights with broadsword, small sword and battleaxes between M. Durenci and M. Bois-Maison (was his real name Woodhouse?): these were made dramatically plausible, though too numerous, some thought, by being fitted into a Charlemagne story called *Les Quatre Fils Hemond* (or *Aimon*, or *d'Aimond*), or, in simpler and more popular English, *The Four Valiant Brothers*.

Specialists were still expected to take part in dramatic pieces, just as most actors of the day were expected to be versatile, as the casting of this romantic drama shows:

Charlemagne	. .	Signor Bologna (*Clown to the rope*)
Roland, his son	. .	M. Bois-Maison (*Swordsman*)
Officers of the King's Party		Dubois (*Rope-dancing clown*)
		Dighton (*Singer*)
		Meadows (*Singer*)
		Herryman (*Singer*)
		Dortor (*Ladder-clown*)
		Boyce (*Harlequin specialist*)
Four Brothers, Renaux	.	M. Durenci (*Swordsman*)
Danvis	.	M. Redigé (*the Little Devil*)
Dousdique		Holland (*Dancer*)
Cademuse		Louis (*Dancer*)
Officers of Renaux's Party		Lawrence (*Tumbler*)
		Lowe (*Singer*)
		Brouguier (*Dancer*)
		Huntley (*Tumbler*)
Princess St. Clair, Renaux's Wife	. .	Miss Bithmere (*Dancer*)

Yet Durenci's acting was so finished that one critic recommended 'our English Tragedians to take a lesson', Miss Bithmere in her last scenes of distress with him was 'positively Siddonian'—both without a spoken word—and Dubois's miming was brilliant.

The same cast was also excellent in the *Commemoration of The Glorious Revolution* 'on the Landing of King William in 1688 being exactly One Hundred Years since', with emblematic scenes and broadsword and dagger fighting—'an Entertainment that would do credit to the first Theatre in Europe', the *World* said, and especially at the end of the season in the new pantomime *The Witch of the Lakes* with its jokes, its atmospheric music, and its magnificently realistic scenery (by the Wells designer, Greenwood) of Fingal's Cave, the New Town of Edinburgh, the moonlit Glen, the Cumberland Lakes, the Cataract—'a chef d'œuvre of stage effect . . . taken from a part of the Highlands, near Glen Ammon, a few miles beyond Perth', and the Newcastle Moors with coal-pits, mixing up Ossian and Harlequin and ending with the reel of Tulloch-Gorum.

Such variety drew a more and more distinguished audience— the Portuguese and Danish Ambassadors, the Duke of Hamilton, the Duke of Gloucester's young son, and even George, Prince of Wales, were all attracted by one of the best pantomimes for years in any theatre: as an 'impromptu' verse had it, the Circus, Astley's, the Haymarket and the Royalty might all be popular,

> But that which most of all the publick takes,
> Is Wroughton's treat, the Witches of the Lakes.

No wonder the Patent Theatres were worried to read that 'for richness of subject, warmth of stage colouring, and adroitness of general execution, no place equals the old place—Sadler's Wells', and out of that excellent care in every department of the theatre, arising from Wroughton's thorough apprenticeship in stagecraft, grew the standard of dramatic sincerity that is always invaluable.

In the winter of 1788–9, the Thames froze over and George III for the first time went really mad. He recovered with the thaw, and Wroughton not only opened the Wells season with 'God Save the King', but presented in commemoration of the King's happy recovery *Britannia's Relief, or, the Gift of Hygeia* with horses and carriages in an exact reproduction of the Royal Procession to St. Paul's on 23rd April between Temple Bar and Ludgate Hill. The naturalistic scene-painting made the pageant so true to life that, though the rainy summer affected other theatres, the Wells was thronged by persons of the first distinction.

In the same programme there was another historical romance,

The Rival Cavaliers, or, Bertrand and Matilda, with even more varied combats with mace d'arme, poignard, small sword, sabre and javelin according to the custom of ancient chivalry; Dibdin's *Fortune Hunters, or, You May Say That*; and, starting a custom, last season's final spectacle to open the new season—*The Witch of the Lakes.*

Acrobats and dancers still appeared, but contemporary interest was more and more the chief attraction: *The Mandarin, or, Harlequin Widower,* with its Feast of Lanterns and 'the very laughable Trio of "Ching Chit Quaw"', reflected the growing taste for things Chinese shown by the Prince of Wales's new decorations in his Royal Pavilion at Brighton; and the characters of the two boy chimney-sweeps in *The Two Little Savoyards,* expressing the hope of better things to come, reflected the ideas which, springing from British ideals, burst into revolution with a thunder-clap on 14th July 1789 with the fall of the Bastille.

All London theatres immediately reflected Fox's enthusiasm for what he described as the greatest and best event in history by rushing to reproduce the human drama implicit in it. Covent Garden's *Bastille* was banned, no doubt because, at a Royal Patent Theatre, it might seem to have official approval, which the government could not risk, but the Royal Grove gave its version as early as 17th August, and a day later the Royal Circus gave another.

Sadler's Wells, with greater artistic integrity and business sense, did not join the grabbing rush to cash in; Wroughton's management, 'anxious for proper and well grounded information, upon a subject of such general attention, have preferred waiting for authentic drawings and descriptions, which having been recently communicated by Mr. Delcourt, who was on the spot, at the moment: the whole of the picturesque arrangements are now preparing for public inspection, by Mr. Greenwood and others'.

At last then on 31st August the Wells presented *Gallic Freedom: or, Vive La Liberté* with full realism and factual accuracy, showing:

> The first assembling of the Bourgeoisie in the Faubourg St. Martin . . . The Manner of their proceeding to the Assault of the BASTILE, and their previous Conference with the Governor . . .

The Massacre of the Citizens who passed the Drawbridge . . .
The Cannonade and general Attack . . . The Skirmish with the
Garde Criminelle . . . The forcible Entry into the Governor's
House, with the Transactions which there took Place, previous
to the Beheading of M. de Launay by the Mob . . . The actual
Descent of the Soldiers and Citizens by Torch Light, into the
SUBTERRANEAN DUNGEONS . . . the Discovery of the un-
fortunate Objects confined in the horrid Recesses of the Place . . .
The affecting and happy Restoration of several Prisoners to their
Friends and Connections. And the Plundering and final Demoli-
tion of the BASTILE by an exasperated Populace . . . With an
ADDRESS from LIBERTY, who is represented as rising out of
the Ruins of that once dreadful Prison.

The *Public Advertiser* for 28th September, from which this
description is taken, stresses that the music, scenery, dresses and
decorations were entirely new, while the scenes as drawn on the
actual spot were brilliantly painted, especially that of the subterranean dungeons, 'where the greatest horror, both from
Scene and Actors, is created. The Figure in the Iron Cage is,
we hear, the work of Mr. Johnson the machinist, and wonder-
fully well executed. . . . Finer scenes of greater effect have not
been produced at any Theatre for many years.'

This realism is all the more remarkable when it is remembered that all dialogue had to be accompanied by music. At the
same time Wroughton, remembering how in the starkest
tragedy Shakespeare introduced comedy for relief and contrast,
added comic humour which was 'highly relished by the spectators, particularly the laughable ballad that was sung by the
mob'. Critics and audience alike were enthusiastic: 'our tribute
of praise and thanks is due to the painter, the actor, and poet,
for the whimsical lines of:

> The grand monarch's a noodle
> To fight for Yankee Doodle,
> *Et contre les Angloise* (sic)

'which is a neat and excellent hit at this moment'. Those lines,
sung to the tune of *Marlbrouk*, certainly roused the audience
against the French Monarchy for helping America in her War
of Independence.

For these three shows—the Procession to St. Paul's, *The
Mandarin* and *Gallic Freedom*—people were 'turned away for
want of room every night', while for the rest of this season

servants were allowed to keep their master's places only until
7.30, instead of the usual 8.30, and the 1789 profits were considerable.

This new custom of reproducing a recent event on the stage
continued at the Wells in some form for about twenty-five years,
and Wroughton was scrupulous for accuracy of presentation.
Three near-contemporary reproductions were put on in 1790.
The first was *The Austrian Peasant, or, the Battle of Fockschau.*
Though called a burletta to conform with the licence, it showed
the field of battle on 1st August 1789 when the Hungarians
defeated the Turks—'the Manœuvres of the Infantry, Cavalry,
and Artillery of the allied Armies of Austrians and Russians,
commanded by the Prince of Saxe Cobourg and General
Suwarow, and the Defeat of the Ottoman Forces, under the
command of the Saraskier Hassan Pacha, previous to the taking
of Belgrade by Marshal Loudohn'. The second (not three weeks
later), *Historical English Heroism*, depicted the *Guardian*, a
frigate commanded by Lt. Riou 'in her very Perilous Situation
in the South Seas, embayed amongst the stupendous Floating
Islands of Ice': and was so convincing that at one performance
'the tear of sensibility was observed stealing down the cheek of
the Duke of York' who was there with the Duke of Orleans,
the Duke of Bedford, Col. St. Leger, and a large party. The
well-acted parts of the Abbé and the Boatswain were both taken
by the Little Devil (who of course also gave his usual rope-act
during the evening).

The Duke of York was George III's second son, and Orleans,
a great friend of the Prince of Wales and later notorious as
Philippe Égalité, was then on a mission to London concerning
the political relations between the Paris revolutionaries and
King Louis, whose attempted compromise at the grand National
Fête on 14th July provided the third realistic news-show of
1790.

To be sure that the Wells would this time be the first to stage
this world-event, Wroughton himself had gone to France—
'lately the mournful scene of tumult and bloodshed, but now the
happy spot of freedom and harmony'—so as to be present at the
meeting of the King with his people. The result was *The Champ
de Mars, or, Loyal Foederation*, presented on 2nd August. So

effectively did the productions show the King joining in the labours of the loyal citizens, with popular *chansons*, French marches, and a troop of boys in uniforms who 'heightened one of the best fancied Dances, with the National Cockades, yet introduced on the English stage', that it not only 'made you exist for a moment on the actual spot' but also enabled the whole audience to 'catch the enthusiasm of the moment, as if by electricity, and *Vive le Roi! Vive le Roi!* seems to be echoed from the very heart of every spectator'.

It seemed that while the Revolution had brought mutual understanding, things in India were more serious. Tippoo Sahib had invaded the protected state of Travancore, but as Lord Cornwallis and Colonel Stuart, aided by the Mahrattas and the Nizam, were victorious, this was celebrated by the Wells in July 1791 (without omitting the *Champ de Mars* or, of course, the varied acts) with *Tippoo Sahib, or, East-India Campaigning*, the music by the Covent Garden composer William Reeve. This show was hailed as 'the best ever', the spectacle including:

> the Assistance of the Friendly Brahmins; With the Attack and Destruction of their Pagoda, By Tippoo's Soldiery. The cruel treatment of the English Officers, under General Mathews, when confined in the Subterraneous Prisons at Seringapatam, with their intrepid refusal to serve under the Enemy's Standard, and their resolute conduct when receiving the Sentence of Death, by Poison. Also the Bravery of a Detachment of Sepoys, who defeated a part of Tippoo's Army, released several Prisoners, and particularly signalized themselves by Capture of an Elephant,

as well as an 'Eastern Divertisement, with Parasols', the Duke of York's black musicians, and a broadsword fight between the still popular Bois-Maison and Durenci.

Wroughton must have felt the responsibility of such shows too much for him for, while retaining an eighth share himself and letting young Arnold keep a fourth (Serjeant had retired), he formed a new syndicate to save the Wells (there was a rumour it was to become a Methodist Chapel); shares had dropped so low that one eighth was bought for only £60.

The new partners, apart from Wroughton and Arnold, were John Coates, a Bermondsey tanner who had an eighth; Richard Hughes, experienced as a manager of theatres at

Plymouth, Exeter, Weymouth, Truro, Guernsey, Penzance, and Dartmouth after having been in Roger Kemble's touring company; and Kemble's unbusiness-like son-in-law, whose wife Mrs. Siddons was now the Drury Lane attraction—Hughes and William Siddons owning one quarter each and together holding the receipts. For them Mark Lonsdale, who had started working in the wardrobe but was 'a man of great theatrical genius', and had been at the Wells since the 'eighties, continued as 'author and conductor' (that is to say, resident dramatist and producer) till 1800.

For the 1792 season the Hughes-Siddons management not only redecorated the theatre and made the detachment of those sitting in the boxes from the rest of the audience even more secure, but also sold books descriptive of the performances for 6d., at the same time raising the price of a box-seat by 6d. to 4s.

The improvements resulted in more carriages than usual, bringing the Duke of Clarence, the Duke and Duchess of York, the Duke of Bedford, the Duchess of Gordon, Lady Ann Fitzroy 'and a long et cetera of rank and fashion'.

Apart from revivals of the previous year's successes, there was the topical *Mars's Holiday, or, A Trip to the Camp* (at Bagshot Heath) with Reeve music; a 'Domestic Tale' straight from the Paris theatre L'Ambigu Comique, *La Forêt Noire, or, The Natural Son* (the story founded on fact: how an illegitimate child, abandoned in the forest, was adopted by robbers who attacked his mother when warned by the whistle they had given the child to summon aid; rescued eventually by his father, an army man, he was reunited with his family); and *The Fourth of June, or, Birthday Loyalty*, 'A Local Allegorical Effusion'. There was the usual variety—the brilliant rope-dancing, singing actor-clown Baptiste Dubois revived the Egg-Dance after seven years; the singer Dighton appeared in such character parts as an Old Hag; the dancer Signora Marchesini (her real name was Rossi, though she had been known in Bath as Miss Mitchel) played a 'clarionet concerto' at her benefit; while young Grimaldi, honoured for the first time by a share in a benefit performance (a sign he had some status in the company at last), acted Jacky Suds in *Mars's Holiday* and the Dwarf in the pantomime, and earned his first press-notice: 'The comic abilities of this youth are very great—we wish him his deserved success.'

HIS FIRST APPEARANCE,
AS A MONKEY

HIS LAST APPEARANCE

GRIMALDI
AT THE WELLS

AS THE WILD MAN

'THE ACCIDENT'

A WATER PAGEANT

Financially the 1792 season was a success: apart from interest on capital, the profits came to £2,633 4s. But 1793 (when Macklin, then well over ninety, often went to the Wells) was an exceptional year for the world, a situation reflected at the Wells. On 21st January King Louis XVI of France was executed, war with France was declared on 1st February, and in March the Austrian Netherlands, occupied by the French, was invaded by British troops under the Duke of York. At the Wells, now the oldest theatre building in London, the Easter opening on 1st April started with the singing of 'God Save the King', 'Rule, Britannia', 'Britons, strike Home', and 'The Wooden Walls'. An allegorical sketch, *The Hall of Augusta*, depicting the four continents, Scotia, Hibernia, and Londina (played by Joe Grimaldi's mother) was much appreciated 'at this interesting period, when the distracted state of the Continent certainly leaves a large balance of national happiness in favour of *The Land we Live in*' (the title of a 1791 production of which this new piece was an elaboration).

The outstanding feature in the opening programme was the introduction of the 'inimitable Mr. Richer from Petersburgh': this was Jack Richer, son of the famous ladder-dancer and tumbler of twenty years before, 'one of the handsomest and best-made men in England'. His dancing, with his 'exquisite ease and unaffected natural grace', on a three-inch-wide rope was said to be infinitely more pleasing than that of nine-tenths of the professional dancers on the stage; while his leaps, nearly as high as himself, terrified those who saw him for the first time. (He somehow did even the Egg-Dance on the rope.) So popular did he become that his fame was later declared comparable to that of the great dancer Gaetano Vestris, the original 'Dieu de Danse', who had so captivated London that Parliament had been prorogued for his benefit:

> Not long ago, we all do know it true,
> The *Vestris Mania* rag'd the town quite through;
> The Ladies of St. James's nought could say
> But '*Vestris! Vestris!* have you seen him, pray?'
> The City Dames would not be out of fashion;
> There '*Westris!* charming *Westris!*' was the passion.

(So Sam Weller's cockney pronunciation was as early as that.)

Who could have thought the *Mania* would have flown
From the Haymarket up to *Islington*;
Or e'er a sigh be given by our Belles,
From the grand *Opera* to Sadler's Wells?
Yet there, at present, Fashion keeps her Court;
Both Belles and Beaux do to the haunt resort;
And crowded Boxes nightly there do ring
With 'RICHER! charming RICHER is the thing.'

A fortnight later, on 15th April, *The Sans Culottes & the Grand Culottes, or, the Invasion of Holland*, with music by Reeve, was given: it depicted the attack by the Sans Culottes (one of whom was played by young Grimaldi) from Antwerp under Dumourier (Dumouriez is the more usual spelling); the defence of Williamstadt helped by English sailors; the burning of Maesdyck (Maastricht); and the arrest of Dumourier, ending with his declaring for the King with *Vive le Roy*.

In May the Wells was praised for introducing a fresh novelty every week, outstanding among them being *The Prize of Industry, or, the Village Rejoicing Day*, showing rustic ceremonies and a spinning competition in an Oxfordshire fête; and Harlequin's allegorical war with the powers of discord in *Pandora's Box, or, the Plagues of Mankind*, in which Dubois guyed the latest fashion in clothes and 'the perverted taste of those who are weak enough to adopt it', while young Grimaldi came out of the box as Hatred with Mary Bates (granddaughter of Mrs. Holmes, the Wells Wardrobe Keeper and Mantua Maker) as Pride—two children who would in the future affect the Wells respectively for better and for worse. In July the French were defeated at Valenciennes by Coburg and the Austrians, not very capably assisted by the Duke of York and his troops; and this event was reproduced in *The Honours of War, or, the Siege of Valenciennes*—which, naturally, gave special credit to His Royal Highness.

On 2nd August Marie Antoinette was removed from the Temple to her new prison in the Conciergerie, and the stage presentation of the 'persecution of an unfortunate Female, who was once the envy and the admiration of Europe', *Les Innocens Enfermées, or, the Royal Prisoners*, at the moment being acted in the Flemish theatres, was introduced at the Wells by Mrs. Parker, a dancer, at her benefit on 23rd September. She herself as the Queen separated from her children admirably performed, and drew tears from the whole audience. Her prison scene . . . where she throws herself on a bed of straw, with the effect of dropping of the curtain to Storace's Tune of Lullaby—had a wonderful effect.

So quiet an ending with that charming melody from *The Pirates* proves Reeve a more sensitive theatre-musician than is usually supposed.

No wonder that such poignant realism, with or without words but with suitable music, should have reduced the audience to tears, especially as many were refugees from France who had for some time so compared 'this elegant little Theatre, and their own dirty Ambigu Comique on the Boulevards at Paris, that you hear nothing but exclamations of Bravo! bravo! charmant! superbe! magnifique!' But to follow *The Royal Prisoners* with 'A Favourite Comic Song, by Mr. Dighton' seems strange to us. Still, the audience expected variety, and it was reported that 'a train of coronets is altogether as familiar to the eye in the Wells Yard as at St. James's Square'. Financially, this season was nearly as good as that of the previous year—a profit of £2,614 8s. 4d., and after the season spoken drama was again presented at the Wells, but by inadequate amateurs—John Home's *Douglas* and *Ways and Means, or, A Trip to Dover* by George Colman the younger, while further changes at the Wells were soon foreshadowed by the arrival of the second generation of the Dibdins.

CHAPTER FIVE

DIBDIN STEPS IN

1794–1802

WHEN THE first theatrical Dibdin, the singing-acting-author-composer Charles, began writing for the Wells in 1772, he was the father of two illegitimate sons by Mrs. Harriet Davenet, a chorus singer at Covent Garden. Harriet, whom he deserted in 1773, was the daughter of Mrs. A. Pitt who for nearly fifty years had been well known at Covent Garden for parts such as the Nurse in *Romeo and Juliet*. The elder son, born in 1768 just after his twenty-three-year-old father's success both as composer and actor of the part of Mungo in Isaac Bickerstaff's *Padlock*, was christened Charles Isaac Mungo; when old enough, he was apprenticed to a pawn-broker, Mr. Cordy. The younger, born in 1771 and named Thomas John after his father's much-loved brother (to whose memory he had written the famous 'Tom Bowling') and John Richards, secretary to the Royal Academy, found when he was eighteen that the stage, hereditary on both sides, was his life, so by the time he was twenty-two he had acted, written and de-signed for nearly twenty provincial theatres.

From Haverford West, where he wrote and sang a new song every week, Tom early in 1794 sent to his mother at Islington a burletta he had written one rainy day—*Rival Loyalists, or, Shelah's Choice*—to place if she could.

At the Wells the 1794 season had begun with four British subjects, the Scottish *Haunted Castle* (at the Wells set in Spain), and *The Monk and the Miller's Wife*, altered from the 1787 production *Hooly and Fairly*; a pantomime dance *Irish Courtship, or, the Bull at Athlone*; and *Penmaenmawr, or, the Wonders of Wales*, with Harlequin Glendower showing many parts of Wales, the Welsh Charity School in Gray's Inn Lane, Temple Bar (which, as a 'continued scene of inconvenience and interruption' should be removed), Carlton House (residence of the Prince of

Wales), and a Grand Eisteddfod with Mr. T. Jones at the harp.
Then, far away in Carmarthen, Tom Dibdin (or Tom Pitt,
as he was then called) read with surprise in a London paper that
on 12th May, together with a new historical piece, *William Tell*
(in which Dubois in the title-rôle did an excellent shooting-
trick), there had been performed his *Rival Loyalists*, inaccur-
ately announced as a 'favourite burletta'. He at once came up to
London. Dighton, who sang in it, told Tom he would do well
as a minor dramatist and introduced him to Hughes, Arnold,
and the 'clever, eccentric, and good-hearted' Mark Lonsdale.
After discussion with his wife of just a year, Nancy Hilliar that
was, Tom Dibdin agreed to accept £25 (half what he indig-
nantly thought he should have got 'for the credit of "the
Islington stage" '), though he was in fact paid only £5.

But for another £5 he agreed to write a new burletta for the
Wells, *The Apparition*, with his wife in a principal part and
receiving a salary for the rest of the season; while 'should she
and my muse succeed', they would both be engaged for the following year and he should act as well. So Mrs Dibdin and their
baby daughter came to London; they stayed at the Wells for
three years.

On the Glorious First of June, as it came to be called, Admiral
Howe was victorious off Brittany. So three days later *Sons of
Britannia, or, George for Old England* contrasted modern France
with old England, showing 'the Triumph of British Loyalty over
Gallic Madness', and at the end of July this victory was celebrated with the spectacular *Naval Triumph, or, The Tars of Old
England*, with a historical display 'to that brave defender of his
country's fame, Earl Howe'. In August there was a reproduction
of the *Attack on Fort Bizzotton & Surrender of Port au Prince*,
dedicated to Sir John Jervis.

Mark Lonsdale's romantic *Valentine and Orson, or, the Wild
Man of Orleans* had been produced in June with such success that
it became a Wells classic for years. Dubois, a stage veteran of
nearly forty years, was remarkable as the Wild Man. In these
days when mime is seen only occasionally and then, however
brilliant, never in a long-sustained part, it is worth reading of
his convincing versatility. He could play on the same evening
with equal truth a complete fool and a dignified character, but
was particularly happy in a malicious part, changing from smiles

to threats, from approbation to abhorrence in a masterly way. As a pursued murderer his terror, guilt, confusion and revenge made one 'almost suppose the fiction approached reality'. As Orson he 'displayed a thorough insight into human nature, debased', mixing a monkey's tricks and sagacity with gleams of matured reason. As a Moor, fighting to the last, he was no longer European but moved like a savage, trying to find a firm footing ready to dart like a tiger on his prey. And yet after *Valentine and Orson* he also gave a 'most wonderful and unexpected performance on the Cymbals'.

Tom Dibdin's *Apparition*, renamed *The Village Ghost* to avoid confusion with a Haymarket piece, was given in September, and at his own benefit in October he presented a new burletta called *The Whirligig*. A benefit was given for Mrs. Boyce, a former Wells dancer, and her children on the death of her husband (who had been a valuable tumbler and Harlequin for eight years) after a short illness 'brought on by one of those overheats to which those of his pantomimic industry are so liable'; and the famous Bologna family left the Wells to join the Royal Circus. 'Joe Grimaldi, now fifteen, had his salary raised to £4 per week, so with his friend Robert Gomery he took a six-roomed house in Penton Place, letting off part of it to Mr. and Mrs. Lewis, minor Wells performers.

The profits this year showed a considerable drop to only £856 12s., but at least it was a profit; and there were great hopes from young Dibdin as a writer. He first acted at the Wells in 1795 in his own burletta *Gaffer's Mistake* and then, remembering a visit to Holyrood, wrote *The Fall of David Rizzio* which lasted forty nights, thanks largely to the impassioned acting of Dubois—who played equally well the naïve but sly Ephram Yankey, attendant on the title-rôle in *Harlequin Munchausen*: in this piece a crocodile swallowed a living lion and a fire insurance office was produced out of a phoenix's nest, transformation-scenes becoming popular.

William Reeve wrote the music for Tom Dibdin's *Chevy Chace, or, Douglas and Percy*, and for the topical *England's Glory, or, Britain's best Bulwarks are her Wooden Walls*, which reproduced the most brilliant naval actions since 1793 including the picture of the Glorious First of June by the well-known Drury Lane designer, Loutherbourg. After the marriage of the

Prince of Wales to Caroline of Brunswick on 8th April, a picture of Neptune presenting her to Britannia had been added to a new ballet, *The Lord of the Manor, or, the Village Nuptials.*

For novelties that year, Master Baux, aged six, played a violin concerto and two Indian Chiefs from the Catauba Nation in North America, the first to appear in Europe, gave exhibitions (only four days after they landed) of their dexterity with the tomahawk and with the bow and arrow as well as specimens of their war-song and dances. Advertisements announced: 'N.B. Those who wish for a nearer communication with the Indian Chiefs than the Stage exhibition will admit of, may be gratified, by applying at the Middleton's Head Coffee-house, near Sadler's Wells.'

In spite of such originality, the Wells this year showed its first loss for many years— £183 14s., after allowing for interest on capital.

In 1796 Lonsdale joined Covent Garden, though he remained deputy manager at the Wells, where Tom Dibdin took his place as stage-manager—a post equivalent to that of the present-day producer or director. His first piece that season was the serio-comic entertainment *The Talisman of Orosmanes, or, Harlequin made Happy* with Joe Grimaldi as the Hag Morad who travelled nefariously round the world in a necromantic box.

Though Reeve still wrote most of the music, Tom brought in Alexander Moorhead as leader of the orchestra and his brother John as viola player and composer, having known them three years before at the new Manchester Circus. For novelty there was a Sicilian family of strong men (Saccardi lifting with his teeth a table with people on it, a weight of half a ton), and there was a brilliant ventriloquist, the one-legged Mr. Askins from Staffordshire with his invisible familiar 'little Tommy'.

Lonsdale's *Venus's Girdle, or, the World Bewitch'd*, in July was indirectly to change the Wells, for in it (apart from young Grimaldi as an Old Woman and his mother as Lady Simpleton) was fifteen-year-old Mary Bates (who had popped out of *Pandora's Box* in 1793) as Cupid—and young Charles Dibdin met her behind the scenes. At the end of the season, Mary Bates asked that her 15s. a week salary should be raised to a guinea and a half as she had been acting at the Wells for seven years.

This was refused, and she went back to her hotel-keeper parents in Holyhead—but Charles could not forget her.

War with France and Spain had begun again and the French had been defeated by Jervis and Nelson off Cape St. Vincent in February 1797, so the opening programme that year included *Britain's Defenders, or, a Fig for Invasion*, a serious piece but, to satisfy the licence, announced as a 'Serio-comic Sketch': it was founded on a story about 'French Criminals' on the Welsh coast, and in it Joe Grimaldi played a French Prisoner—and danced in a comic ballet.

Whether or not Wales was really nervous of invasion, Mary Bates came back to London and was married at St. George's, Hanover Square, to Charles Isaac Pitt, as Charles Dibdin called himself, on 13th June—not 14th June, as he wrote in his autobiography. Having left the pawnbroker's, he had already failed as 'Mr. C. Dibdin Junr.' at the Royalty with his solo entertainment *Sans Six Sous*, in imitation of his father's successful one-man show of songs, poems and stories at the Sans Souci in the Strand at the same time. He now joined the great Philip Astley's Amphitheatre of Arts at Lambeth as a stage-writer and trick-scenery inventor—sheer bluff as his only experience of the stage (against which he had written vehemently when he was nineteen) was one burletta sold to the Royalty, and models (which he himself says were impracticable) for a twenty-four-scened pantomime that he took to show Philip Astley. His wife was engaged to sing at Astley's. Both were underpaid because 'a Horsewoman was their Prima Donna'. Tom Dibdin left the Wells at the end of the season, deciding that legitimate drama out of town was better than minor theatricals in town, and rejoined Mrs. Baker's Kent circuit of theatres, though he still kept in close touch with the Wells.

The last two seasons had resulted in losses—£339 16s. in 1796 and £250 17s. 4d. in 1797; but the first two years of the Hughes-Siddons syndicate, 1792 and 1793, had been so profitable that Mrs. Siddons probably put up the money to save her husband and the Wells, for in December 1797 Mme D'Arblay (Fanny Burney), learning from Princess Augusta that Mrs. Siddons 'had bought the proprietorship of Sadler's Wells', recorded 'I could not hear it without some amusement; it seemed, I said, so extraordinary a combination—so degrading a one, indeed,—that of the first tragic actress, the living Melpomene, and something so burlesque as Sadler's Wells.' Fanny Burney had recommended the Wells in *Evelina*, published twenty years before, but that was for country cousins in a novel; now she had royal friends, and the Princess thought the combination 'as ill fitted as the dish they call toad in the hole; which I never saw, but always think of with anger,—putting a noble sirloin of beef into a poor, paltry batter-pudding!'

Thomas Campbell in his *Life of Mrs Siddons* (1834) thought she alluded to Sheridan's defaulting in her pay in her letter of 7th January 1798: 'I can get no money from the theatre. My precious two thousand pounds are swallowed up in that drowning gulph, from whom no plea of right or justice can save its victims'—but the round figure and the phraseology reads more like an investment such as in Sadler's Wells. There is an unverifiable story that she acted there, retorting to Miss Burney who protested, 'I will play anywhere so long as I am paid'.

For 1798 the Wells economized: they paid the dancing-master Anthony Bruguier, in his twelfth year at the Wells, together with his two daughters only four guineas a week—4s. more than twenty-year-old Grimaldi got as a useful swordsman and (surprisingly) villain: but Grimaldi was now called 'Mr.', and his 'utility' friend Bob Gomery was allowed to play leading parts. They had lost La Belle Espagnole and Richer, who had replaced the Little Devil; but in place of the invaluable Dighton, who left in 1797, were lucky enough to get 'Jew' Davis, as he was called, from the Royal Circus—brilliant in everything but dancing, but difficult, as came out later; and they kept the versatile Dubois.

The outstanding items this season were the opening pantomime, *The Monster of the Cave, or, Harlequin and the Fay*, and two patriotic pieces. The first of these, *The Prisoners, or, an Escape from France*, staged the Scarlet Pimpernel-like rescue of Sir Sidney Smith, hero of Acre, from imprisonment in the Temple in Paris by counterfeit soldiers and fake orders (the French version), or his escape when the coach transferring him to the General Depository nearly ran over a child and struck a post (the British version): either was a truly romantic story because, the British government having offered 4,000 French prisoners in exchange for him, Smith had to hide in the woods near Le

Havre before reaching Folkestone in a fishing-boat. The Wells version was produced only twenty days after the event.

The other patriotic production was Lonsdale's 'Historical Ballet of Action', *Alfred the Great, or, the Patriot King* (with Grimaldi as the villain Oscitel)—memorable now only because in it Davis sang Tom Dibdin's 'Snug little Island' or 'Tight little Island' (which began 'Daddy Neptune one day To Freedom did say—'). Tom records that he got only five guineas from the Wells for this song, while Longman's the publishers (who, according to him, made £900 out of it) gave him only £15. This year Tom joined Covent Garden.

By June it was obvious that the Wells was not doing well, for in that month Mrs. Siddons wrote to a friend that she was alarmed about finances—Sheridan had not settled with her and Mr. Siddons was engaged in speculations which threatened 'equally formidable pecuniary losses'. Events did not prove her wrong—the 1798 loss was £555 0s. 4d. plus interest on the capital.

Hughes and Siddons redecorated the theatre for 1799, re-engaged Richer, introduced two fine dancers M. St. Pierre and Mlle St. Amand, and produced a 'new serious Ballet of Action with Songs' called *Arden of Feversham*, and a 'Heroic Pantomime', *Don Juan, or, the Libertine Destroyed* (based on Purcell or Mozart?). That year Joe Grimaldi married the manager's eldest daughter, Maria Hughes, at St. George's, Hanover Square, on Saturday 11th May, after which there was a wedding supper at the Wells and a dinner for the Wells carpenters on Sunday.

But the event of 1799 that led to a transformation of the Wells was the wardrobe mistress's letter to her grandson-in-law, Charles Dibdin the younger, saying that Lonsdale was resigning. After checking with Tom, Charles at once showed Hughes samples of his writing and applied for his wife to be engaged as singing-actress at two guineas a week, while for three he would manage the theatre (starting four weeks before the opening), writing all the pieces and inventing all the transformation-scenes, hitherto largely devised by young Grimaldi. These terms were impertinent, as his stage-experience at thirty-two had been as author for less than two years, occasional singer, and unsuccessful actor for one night; while his business ability, picked up when a pawnbroker's shopman and an insolvent editor, had been tested in show-business for little more than a year.

Not that he was incompetent: but, less experienced than Tom and certainly not as clever as their father, he had inherited the self-assurance that had been justified in the first Charles Dibdin, and was expert at sales-talk.

Hughes, not seeing the difference between reproducing London successes in the provinces and the original creation necessary for a London theatre, was so financially uneasy (this year the loss at the Wells was £630 and no interest paid) that he swallowed the bait, eager to get anyone prepared to do three men's work and provide a singing wife for roughly what was paid to Joe Grimaldi alone—for he beat Charles Dibdin down to two guineas for himself.

From the first, Charles Dibdin the younger swamped the Wells with his work, strictly according to contract. Apart from a Pastoral Ballet and Richer on the tight-rope with Dubois as Clown, the opening programme of the 1800 season was entirely from his pen—a Musical Bagatelle *Old Fools, or, Love's Stratagem*; a Historical Ballet of Action *Boadicea, or, the British Amazon*; comic songs; and the pantomime *Peter Wilkins, or, Harlequin in the Flying World* in which Grimaldi played Clown for the first time—Guzzle the drinking Clown with Dubois as Gobble the eating Clown.

Dibdin (as he shall now be called to distinguish him from his brother Tom) claimed—perhaps justly—that it was he who encouraged the comic side of Grimaldi ('there was so much *mind* in every thing that he did') after Hughes had told him what a clever lad he was: Dibdin watched him at rehearsals 'exhibiting his "Monkey Tricks" to the Performers' and jotted down any whimsicality he could make use of; he also claimed that it was he who designed for Grimaldi in *Peter Wilkins* the multi-coloured clown costume that became traditional in place of the former usual outré livery worn by a red-faced, red-haired rustic booby (though Dibdin had just attributed the change to Grimaldi himself, who certainly introduced the red half-moons on the Clown's cheeks).

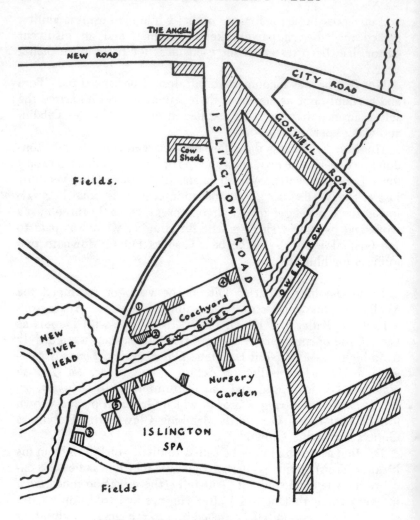

THE ENVIRONS OF SADLER'S WELLS

Based on Horwood's Atlas, 1799

Key: 1. Sadler's Wells Theatre. 2. Mr. Hughes's private residence. 3. House in which Charles Dibdin lived, 1798–1803. 4. House in which Charles Dibdin lived, 1803–1819. 5. The Myddelton's Head, a theatrical tavern, later the site of Deacon's Music Hall.

The present theatre is on the same site, and faces the same way as the old, with the stage at the east end. The entrance foyer is on the site of Mr. Hughes's residence. Rosebery Avenue now runs over the last hundred and fifty yards of the course of the New River. Islington Road is now St. John's Street, and New Road is Pentonville Road.

Admittedly Dibdin's transformation-scenes were brilliant—a pill turned into a duck, Ward's Medicine Shop to Jarvis's Coffin Shop, and a drum into a temple ('one of the prettiest scene changes we ever saw', *The Times* said). His detailed descriptions with drawings of the changes from Columbine's Tomb to willows and shrubs, and from a Post Chaise to a Wheel Barrow (from his autumn pantomime of this year, *Chaos, or, Harlequin Phaeton*) are in the Percival Collection in the British Museum, and should be studied by all stage-designers today to see how in those days complete changes of both shape and colour could be almost instantaneous.

Incidentally, at the opening performance of *Chaos* Dibdin, 'running in a passion, across the stage' (as only an amateur would) to put something right, fell through an unfastened trapdoor and would have had a bad accident if he had not supported himself on his elbows.

One artistic change seems to have been happening gradually. The general public more and more accepted, if it did not appreciate, opera. Several new dancers, including one with the name of a famous stage family—Miss Lupino (afterwards Madame Noblet), had come from Paris to the Wells via the Opera House (today's Her Majesty's Theatre); Richer took the title-rôle in *The Deserter* by Monsigny. 'The Music the same as at the Opera House', but in the King's Theatre version as altered by the elder Dibdin in 1773; Dubois burlesqued an Italian air in *Chaos* (accompanied by Grimaldi on a salt-box); and there was a new serious Ballet Pantomime which obviously had an operatic basis.

This was *The Daughter of the Air*, said to be a Persian romance from the German 'as it is performed in Vienna, having been commanded four times by the Emperor', with music by Mozart: presumably a version of *The Magic Flute*, which had already been given in Vienna at the Theater auf der Wieden about three hundred times since its first performance ten years before. The Wells probably was the first theatre in England to perform a version of this opera, eleven years before the usually recorded date of the first British performance.

The Wells achieved social recognition in 1800 by being able to announce that it was 'under the patronage of His Royal Highness the Duke of Clarence', and so it remained for thirty years till the Duke became the Sailor King William IV, when he still remained the theatre's patron. His interest in the Wells may have been encouraged by his mistress Mrs. Jordan and her sister-in-law Mrs. Bland, who had sung there, and fostered by the influential friends of Mrs. Siddons to bolster up her husband's speculation. The Wells programmes took on a naval tinge and sailors came to regard it as their own theatre. Once during *Boadicea* when the Queen, exhorting her people against their enemies, cried:

> If your breasts conceal one coward care,
> Alone I go!

an honest tar in the gallery tried to climb down to the stage, shouting to her and to his mate, 'I'll be damned if you do! Here, Jack! Let's go, and we'll show 'em as tight work as we did under his Honour, Admiral Nelson!'

Despite such encouragement, both royal and naval, the 1800 season again resulted in a loss—£180 (the smallest for six years).

For the following season Dibdin's salary was raised to three guineas a week (his wife still drawing two), while during the winter, when salaries normally lapsed, he was to get two. He revived his brother's *Alonzo* in 1801 and his father's *Henry and Louisa, or, the Deserter in Naples*, but almost all pieces were from his own pen, including three topical news-shows. The first, seen by the Duke of Clarence and the Duke of Norfolk only nineteen days after the actual event (2nd April), was the 'late glorious victory at Copenhagen' showing the battle of the two fleets and transparent paintings of the three North Fleet heroes, Parker, Nelson and Greaves. In June *Egyptian Laurels*, representing the Battle of Alexandria, was given; and a month later the new Grand Junction Canal in London was celebrated with *A Trip to Paddington*.

In *Egyptian Laurels* 'the real invincible Flag of Bonaparte, copied from the original by permission' was shown; and all the flags that had been taken and destroyed were displayed by Davis as an officer of the 'gallant Scotch Forty-second'. The piece included Dibdin's musical 'Death and Apotheosis of Sir Ralph Abercromby'. Grimaldi (whose wife had died in childbirth the previous October) appeared in it in the character of O'Doody and gave 'an Irish comparison between English and Egyptian Wonders, Including Mamelukes and St. Luke's, Pyramids and Obstacles, Crocodiles and Monopolists, Mummies and Men Milliners, the Fortunes of War and Peace, etc. etc.' The same programme contained one special novelty: it was announced that 'Master Carey, the Pupil of Nature, will recite Rolla's celebrated Address from the Tragedy of Pizarro.' In after-years Dibdin was specially proud of having introduced this child, great-grandson of the composer Henry Carey (a natural son of George Savile Carey, Marquis of Halifax), for the boy, as the great actor Edmund Kean, turned out to be more famous than any of his forebears.

Towards the end of the 1801 season, during which Dubois left (through jealousy of Grimaldi, Dibdin said, but more probably because his request for a rise in salary was refused), Dibdin presented his topical thriller about thirty desperadoes who were then terrifying Genoa. In this, *The Great Devil, or, the Robber of Genoa*, Grimaldi played both the robber lieutenant Nicola, and another part, and had nineteen changes of costume; Davis played Bridget. That Davis was there at all worried Dibdin, who had refused what he thought an unreasonable request so as to get Davis to leave, as Dubois and Richer (last rope-dancer to appear at the Wells) had already done. Davis was always ready to annoy other people: earlier that season, while playing the Moorish King in a piece called *The Ethiop, or, the Siege of Grenada*, he had pretended his shoulder was dislocated, and so had forced Dibdin to act for the first time since his failure on the stage in Liverpool. Dibdin was so nervous that, although he had written the show, once he got on the stage he could not recollect one incident in the part.

One evening in *The Great Devil*, when Grimaldi drew his pistol from his boot, it exploded and damaged his foot, but he was nursed by young Mary Bristow, a small part actress who had joined the Wells from Drury Lane; he married her on 24th December and they were happy together for thirty years.

When the season and the current lease ended together, Hughes asked the Rev. W. Lloyd Baker in November for a twenty-one year lease from 1801 at £200 a year instead of the normal £250, not only because the Wells had lost so much in the last five years but also because they wanted to reshape the theatre at a cost of between £1,200 and £1,700. Siddons wrote in December giving details of the recent losses, and claiming that much would have to be spent to make the theatre even safe: had their attractions proved remunerative, there could have been no objection even to an increase of rent. He went on to say,

> By the proposed Erection of an Entire new inside the Building will be a stable one for fifty years to come, which of course will be a great security to the ground Landlord, but shoud (*sic*) the Rent increase and the Customers decrease what chance can we have for a reimbursement of the money about to be expended? In truth, Sir, to convince you of our disastrous Situation, we are ready & Willing to sell the concern for one-half the Sum we paid for it on our coming in.

The Proprietors were also appealing against the Land-Tax and so, pending a decision by the Commissioners, Wroughton wrote to Lloyd Baker in January 1802 asking that a new lease might be drawn up in Siddons's name alone, without any mention of the proposed rebuilding which might make the Commissioners think there were funds to spare, 'as all Persons in Parish Offices think a public Place of this sort little short of a Mine of Wealth and are ever very ill-natured respecting the necessary claims on them'. He promised, however, that Lloyd Baker's representative, Mr. Lewis, could check the architect's contract and see how the building was getting on—'the Place is completely gutted and a very pretty, handsome Theatre will soon be ready'.

On 1st March 1802 Lloyd Baker, always considerate, granted the Siddons syndicate a twenty-one year lease at £210 a year, and the new theatre was ready for opening on Easter Monday, 19th April. The auditorium had been altered according to a model by Hughes from square to semicircular by the architect Cabanel (builder of the Surrey Theatre, the Coburg—the Old Vic—and the interior of the Amphitheatre, Westminster Bridge) whose sister was the Wells' principal dancer, later well known as Mrs. Helme. As Dibdin said, 'the alteration certainly was not made before it was necessary; for it was, I think the dirtiest and most antique Theatre in London'. The proscenium ends of the gallery now had three boxes a side, boxes filled the circle, there were four stage boxes, an extensive pit and a large gallery: the boxes, built like those of Drury Lane, could be booked by the night, week, month, or season, though the prices were the same as before (box-seats 4s., pit 2s., gallery 1s.): but half-price was no longer allowed at 8.30, and the shows, which started at 6.30 p.m., were over by 10 p.m. The stage was about 33 ft. wide and about 90 ft. deep in all, the usual acting depth about 74 ft.

A print of what was then called the 'New Theatre, Sadler's Wells' was made by Robert Andrews, the scene-painter at the Wells from 1796 to 1818, 'whose professional eminence has never been surpassed' in spite of his rapidity of working, thought Dibdin; while his rival at Covent Garden, John Richards, admitted that 'Little Bob, Sir, is a Giant in the Art'. The print shows the theatre's beautiful situation by the New River, the house of Mrs. Hughes, the entrance to the boxes, pit, and gallery, and in the distance 'the residence of Mr. C. Dibdin, manager', which can still be seen today through iron gates on the left just as Rosebery Avenue turns into St. John's Street, and north of this is Goose Yard, part of the farm where his mother and sister lived. Under the print is a vignette of the previous theatre.

In the 1802 programmes, Siddons wrote a burletta prelude praising the new theatre with the historically inaccurate title of *Old Sadler's Ghost, or, The Wells in the Days of Queen Bess*; Grimaldi and his friend young Jack Bologna had broadsword and battle-axe fights in *St. George, the Champion of England*, while in *Ko and Zoa, or, the Belle Sauvage*, in which Grimaldi had the passionate part of Ravin, there was a six-handed combat (violence is nothing new in entertainment!).

For novelty Grimaldi sang in the 'fine, deep-toned voice' Tom Dibdin said he had, about the 'fashionable Transparent Dresses', and the back of the stage was opened to show all the carriage ground which, with the stage, formed a racecourse for ponies, three times round making a one-mile heat and finishing on the stage: but the magistrates stopped the races because of damage done to neighbours' palings 'by the boys clambering up them to get a peep'.

For one benefit at the end of the season, there was a sparring-match between Belcher, then Champion of England, and the famous Mendoza, which inspired Dibdin, after the season was

over, to exhibit Belcher and other first-rate pugilists; but again
the magistrates interfered so, rather than risk losing the licence,
he closed the theatre. On 21st November Joe Grimaldi's son,
Joseph Samuel William, was born. But shortly before that something happened that changed the history of the Wells.

At the end of the season Dibdin, as was customary, called on
the management to see if his yearly contract would be taken up
for the following season and, as Hughes was out of town, he
saw Siddons who 'hummed and ha'd so about it, I plainly saw
that there was "something rotten in the State of Denmark",
and felt rather fidgetty lest I should be out of an Engagement for
some time'. But Dibdin's luck was in: while Siddons was called
from the room, 'as I sat close to the Table, I unconscious of any
improper design, cast my Eyes upon a short, open note, which
lay close before me, and in which a treaty for the purchase of the
Wells was mentioned'. When Siddons came back, Dibdin
learned that all the proprietors except Hughes were determined
to get out, while John Fawcett, a popular actor at Covent
Garden and stage-manager there, was ready to step in with the
two dramatists Frederick Reynolds and Thomas Morton.

Dibdin at once asked if the deal had gone too far for him to
make an offer and if he would be acceptable as a purchaser, to
which Siddons replied 'he would as soon sell his share to me as
to anybody; he only wanted to sell it, and did not care who was
the purchaser; that it cost him £4,000, and if he sold it to the
parties proposing to treat for it, he should only receive £1,200
for it; but there were reasons which determined him to give it
away rather than keep it'. Did Mrs. Siddons insist?

When Hughes came back, he advised Dibdin to join with his
brother and Andrews the scene painter, and some clever composer, to take over the Wells, because 'being all young, all professional, and more gifted with the spirit of enterprise than
older men, the Concern . . . might flourish as it had formerly
done'. Hughes offered to be security for Dibdin who, with his
brother, approached William Reeve, the composer, who was
enthusiastic; so were their acquaintances Thomas Barfoot (a
bankrupt grocer in 1794 but later married to the rich daughter
of Penton, the North London builder) and William Yarnold Esq.
of Finchley.

So Hughes retained his quarter interest of ten shares; Andrews and Reeve bought Wroughton's five and Coates's five; Yarnold and Barfoot Arnold's quarter for £620; and the two Dibdins Siddons's quarter between them for £1,400—£200 more than he had quoted because they paid down only £100 each (Charles's £100 being advanced by his ex-master, the pawnbroker), the rest to be paid in yearly instalments of £100 with interest, the shares being mortgaged to Siddons.

To celebrate, the new management had a grand dinner—at which, Dibdin says, he drank too much.

CHAPTER SIX

WATER AND CLOWNING

1803–1806

FROM 1803 the Wells changed, and the change was typified by a new type of advertisement announcing the management's decision to revive the old custom of providing the audience with wine—

NEW SADLER'S WELLS

New Proprietors
New Management
New Performers
New Pieces
New Music
New Scenery
New Dresses
New Decorations
and
Old Wine
at 1s. 3d. per pint!!!

This strikes a cheap note and shows that commercialism had come in: yet to announce new décor was good, as usually old stuff had been used over and over again in different shows.

Dibdin said they were 'determined to do everything upon a liberal and magnificent scale; and to give such Salaries as would tempt performers of Merit to engage with us'; but the first thing he records of his first year as proprietor is that his own salary was raised to four guineas a week for the summer and three for the winter. From outside the Wells the only worthwhile artists employed were the singing actors King and G. Smith, while Townshend from Covent Garden, engaged as leading man at £12 a week for three seasons, lasted only one, preferring the Horns Tavern in Kennington, which he had just taken.

The best artists were already Wells favourites—Grimaldi, Jack Bologna, Jew Davis, and Hartland (a pupil of Dubois, and an excellent harlequin, serious pantomimist, clown and 'Pero'— as Dibdin spelt 'Pierrot'). Mme St. Pierre and Mrs. Davis were re-engaged, and Mrs. C. Dibdin of course headed the list of women: Dibdin's half-brother Cecil Pitt played in the orchestra and his half-sister Harriet joined the dancers (they were the illegitimate children of the actor George Mattocks): or rather she came on last of the figurantes and in crowd scenes, which was not surprising as she was short and squat. Dibdin ignored the dangers of nepotism.

When the season opened, the interior of the theatre was lit entirely by wax candles, while the approaches to it were lit by lamps and guarded by patrols. In the first night's programme Grimaldi played Sir John Bull with song and quintet in *New Brooms, or, the Firm Changed*, Thrumbo, the Giant's Dwarf, with comic song, in *Jack and the Beanstalk* (young Master Menage played Jack, and the Giant was the 6 foot 6 'Patagonian Sampson', Belzoni, once barber, monk, hydraulic expert, and later well known as an explorer), and the Clown in *Fire and Spirit, or, a Holiday Harlequin*. In the same programme Belzoni lifted eleven men on an iron apparatus with the top man as high as the flies of the theatre (one evening the weight broke the stage and all were precipitated into the water below).

But the most remarkable part in the opening programme was a rhymed operatic piece founded on the recent seduction by fraudulent marriage of the daughter of the keeper of the Char Inn near Buttermere and called *Edward and Susan, or, the Beauty of Buttermere*. Susan's real name was Mary Robinson, and her seducer John Hadfield (sometimes misspelt Hatfield) was hanged for the crime five months after the Dibdin version was produced: shortly after the opening the Wells gave a benefit performance for the real beauty of Buttermere.

On 11th July Mary Lamb wrote to Dorothy Wordsworth, telling her that she and her brother Charles (whose pretty house in Duncan Terrace, near the Angel, still stands) 'went last week with Southey and Richman and his sister to Sadler's Wells, the lowest and most London-like of all our London amusements— the entertainments were Goody Two Shoes, Jack the Giant Killer and *Mary of Buttermere*! Poor Mary was very happily

married at the end of the piece, to a sailor her former sweetheart. We had a prodigious fine view of her father's house in the
vale of Buttermere—mountains very like large haycocks, and a
lake like nothing at all'—(which hardly supports Dibdin's enthusiasm for the artist, Andrews, and seems unfair, to judge from
his picture of the Wells). 'If you had been with us, would you
have laughed the whole time like Charles and Miss Richman
or gone to sleep as Southey and Richman did?'

Whatever Dorothy Wordsworth might have thought of it,
her brother William left his imaginatively innocent opinion in
Book VI of his *Prelude*—Residence in London. This was begun
in 1799 and not published till 1850; in it he not only records his
memories of *The Beauty of Buttermere*, but recalls his visits to
the Wells—five between 1788, when he was eighteen, and 1802.

> Need I fear
> To mention by its name, as in degree,
> Lowest of these and humblest in attempt,
> Yet richly graced with honour of her own,
> Half-rural Sadler's Wells? . . . here more than once
> Taking my seat, I saw (nor blush to add,
> With ample recompense) giants and dwarfs,
> Clowns, conjurors, posture-makers, harlequins,
> Amid the uproar of the rabblement,
> Perform their feats.

He then tells how Jack the Giant-Killer could no longer be seen
by putting on a coat with the word 'invisible' flaming from his
chest. He also saw at the Wells

> dramas of living men,
> And recent things yet warm with life; a sea-fight,
> Shipwreck, or some domestic incident
> Divulged by Truth and magnified by Fame;
> Such as the daring brotherhood of late
> Set forth, too serious theme for that light place—
> I mean, O distant Friend! a story drawn
> From our own ground—the Maid of Buttermere—
> And how, unfaithful to a virtuous wife
> Deserted and deceived, the Spoiler came
> And wooed the artless daughter of the hills,
> And wedded her, in cruel mockery
> Of love and marriage bonds.

As the heroine he remembered the tall, dark, over-made-up
Mrs. Dibdin contrasting with her lovely stage-infant,

in cheek a summer rose
Just three parts blown—a cottage-child,

but he feared the boy might later have proved real life more
dramatic than the stage by growing more like the drunken,
indecent audience than the real

nameless babe that sleeps
Beside the mountain chapel, undisturbed.

This first season under the new proprietors was not without
its troubles: when Dibdin produced his *Philip Quarll*, with
Grimaldi as the hero living among monkeys, some ladies in the
audience thought their tails indecorous and disgusting. Still the
shows, if unimportant, were varied. In June *Goody Two Shoes,
or, Harlequin Alabaster* (in which Grimaldi as the Clown got an
'and' before his name) showed Balloons à la Française, or Aerial
Invasion, frustrated by Harlequin, and included a song comparing the mammoth's skeleton on view in London with Boney-
party; in July Grimaldi, as Gorthmund, Prince of the Assassins,
in *The Old Man of the Mountains*, was joined by three of his
followers in an eight-handed fight against Richard Cœur de
Lion, Philip of France, Sultan Saladin, and the Grand Master
of Jerusalem, and finished in a cauldron of fire (though like most
of the pieces even this ended patriotically with 'May the Arms of
the King of England procure Peace'); in August, when the
Volunteer system began, Dibdin was as skilfully satirical as any
revue-writer in *The British Amazons, or, Army without Reserve*,
by versifying the inattentive chatter of an all-women committee
meeting. The show ended with the female volunteers in scarlet
doing military exercises accompanied by patriotic songs praising
the loyalty of all British counties, and a vision of Bonaparte in
the Temple of British Victories.

The performers counted more than the pieces in which they
appeared: Grimaldi was so versatile—comic dwarf, singing
clown, hero or villain (as well as Negro Duettist with Davis)—
that he was re-engaged for three years at a high and rising
salary; while Mrs. Dibdin had her small salary raised a guinea,
Dibdin pledging himself never to increase it further, though less
popular and less industrious performers, he said, sometimes got
double as much.

Hearing from Hughes that if the Fawcett syndicate had taken

the theatre they might have introduced on the stage a stream from the New River, Dibdin decided on a fresh novelty—the presentation of shows on real water.

So, all through the winter of 1803, workmen worked day and night behind locked gates. They ripped up the stage, traps and cellar work (thereby entailing preparation for a different method of scene-changing) and built on dwarf walls 2 ft. 4 in. high and the same distance apart an irregularly shaped tank, like a brewer's, 90 ft. long, 24 ft. wide at its widest and 10 ft. at its narrowest, and 3 ft. deep, with two branches extending to the side walls of the theatre. The stage was made to be raised out of sight, while another tank, 15 ft. square and 5 ft. deep, was later put in the theatre-roof for real waterfalls.

It took twelve men, four at a time, twelve hours to fill the tank from the New River, by an Archimedes wheel, through a series of troughs: the water was renewed every three weeks, or more often if the weather was hot. During the day the performers used to bathe in the tank when it was sweet water, 'which was not always'. Later, an agreement was made with the New River Company to lay water on from the main for £30 a year, and then the water was changed more frequently.

The 1804 season was planned to open the new water-theatre with *The Siege of Gibraltar*. Experts from the dockyard at Woolwich at once made 117 model ships 3 ft. long on a scale of one inch to a foot, exact in rigging, with workable sails and specially cast brass cannon, which fired and recharged in action. The ship's crews were manufactured on the same scale, and the ships were to be manœuvred by boys and young men specially engaged to swim with the ships to their positions. 'The Expense occasioned by this was enormous,' Dibdin said (a letter to the New River Company says the conversion cost nearly £1,000), 'but—it was not "throwing a sprat to catch a herring", it was baiting with a whale to catch a Leviathan'.

The Saturday before the first performance the 'water-boys', whose salary was 2s. 6d. extra to go into the water and a glass of brandy before and after, showed signs of striking, so Dibdin threatened to sack them: but he also dosed them with brandy as if they were staying, so they stayed. They were always provided with fires and towels when they came out; but some drank and smoked when only half dry ('for they were generally of the lower orders'), and two died, one of consumption, the other having taken medicine before going in. When in the water (only for some five to ten minutes) they wore 'thick, duffil trousers'.

On the opening night, 2nd April, after a Dance, a musical piece and a pantomime, a drop scene was lowered showing the English Grand Fleet in battle line against the fleets of France and Spain; it had been painted by Andrews to fill the whole proscenium which was mechanically enlarged some eight feet. Behind it the stage was raised in hearing of the audience while gusts of air agitated the act-drop—an operation that could take twenty minutes.

At last the act-drop, which had earned rounds of applause, was raised to disclose 'so unusual a sight in a Theatre, as a Sheet of Water', with the Rock and fortress of Gibraltar on one side and the ocean on the other:

> It acted like electricity; a pause of breathless wonder was suc-
> ceeded by stunning peals of continued acclamation; and when the
> Ships sailed down, in regular succession, 'rolling on their way',
> their sails shifting to the wind; their colours and pennants flying;
> and their ordnance, as they passed the front of the stage, firing
> a grand salute to the Audience, the latter seemed in an extacy.

Ships were dismasted and sunk, 'red hot balls' from the gallant *Heathfield* blew up the Spanish gun-boats (*L'Orient* was 'really blown-up in first-rate style'), so that the reflection of the fire in the water 'was truly magnificent', and when 'Sir Roger Curtis saving the Spanish sailors from a watery grave' was represented with real boats in the foreground (the 5 to 6 in. high mariners on the ships of the line masked by smoke) manned by 'children for sailors, picking up other children, who were instantly seen swimming and affecting to struggle with the waves, the enthusiasm of the Audience exceeded all bounds; and I think' (wrote Dibdin) 'that there was no person who witnessed in 1804, *The Siege of Gibraltar*, at Sadler's Wells, will assert other than that it was one of the most novel, imposing and nationally interesting Exhibitions they ever saw'.

For classical scholars, Dibdin at first called this entertainment ΩKEANEIA, but pleased the pit and gallery by announcing 'that the Entertainment of the Public may not consist of Water only; the Proprietors will provide the best Unadulterated Wine at 2s. 6d. per bottle'. In the gallery a fat man named Wren, who sold Spirits and Water, Porter, Spruce Beer, etc., announced stentorianly between the pieces, 'Come, Ladies, give your minds to drinking'. One night a sailor, doubting that it was genuine water on the stage, plunged in and testified to his mates in the 'elegant lingo peculiar to the unreflecting Sons of Neptune' that it was real, and this became a nightly practice till Dibdin threatened to have one of the swimmers arrested.

This season showed a profit six times more than the previous year had done, because of the Aqua-shows, as they were called. Dibdin said that 'Grimaldi and the Water were the Alpha and Omega'—or, as Thomas Greenwood put it in his *Rhyming Reminiscences,*

> Attraction was needed, the town to engage,
> So Dick emptied the river that year on the stage;
> The house overflowed, and became quite the ton,
> And the Wells for some seasons went swimmingly on.

Yet not so swimmingly.

Novelty soon dates: *The Siege of Gibraltar* when revived the following year no longer attracted. Water was effective only when used in a novel way, as in the Caledonian Melo-dramatic Romance *An Bratach, or, the Water-Spectre* (Dibdin loved erudite titles) when the Spectre rose through real water in Fingal's Cave and the heroine was thrown into the water (Mme St. Amand—now Mme Louis—doubled by a slim boy when swimming) or in *The Talking Bird, or, Harlequin and Perizade* which, though Asiatic, ended with a boys' boat-race before a panorama of the new London Bridge. But Calder's defeat of France and Spain off Finisterre was celebrated only in musical dialogue; and when a musical piece called *The Rival Patriots* ended with the Battle of Trafalgar, the audience resented the same ships being used as had been seen in the *Siege of Gibraltar*.

Another disappointment was Michaeleto Sanchez walking upside-down by unbolting iron shoes in a board ten feet above the stage: on his first night he fell at the first step, saying, 'Laids and Gemps, tonight I very Moash fright; you coime again tomorrow night, I do de whole Board'—but Dibdin sacked him.

The 1806 season, it would seem, was up to standard only—
or chiefly—in Grimaldi's famous dance of vegetables in *Harlequin and the Water-Kelpie* and his Grand Combat in *The Invisible
Ring, or, the Water Monster and Fire Spectre*. Incidentally, he
had been engaged at Tom Dibdin's suggestion by Covent
Garden for three seasons, but with permission still to appear at
Sadler's Wells, so that Dibdin complained that as soon as a
performer was good he went to Drury Lane or Covent
Garden (a habit that, quite understandably, has not yet died
out!).

An intimate picture of back-stage at the Wells at the turn of
the century was written by the theatre watchman of the time,
one R. Wheeler, from the Clerkenwell Workhouse, about 1828.
The early copy in the Percival Collection of Sadler's Wells
records at the British Museum was quoted in part by George
Speaight in his edition of the memoirs of Charles Dibdin the
younger: Speaight says it is malicious but entertaining, while
'each reader will decide for himself just what weight should be
given to these jaundiced memories of a disgruntled old work-
man': he adds that there are few alternative witnesses to set
against Wheeler—Grimaldi avoided personal comment on Dibdin; Lamb admired his whimsical literary style; Holcroft respected him; and Dibdin's own moralizing memoirs indicate that
he was a man of principles (there is a family tradition that he
used to conduct prayers for his company, on the stage, before
the curtain went up).

Jaundiced or not, Wheeler's views seem borne out by letters
to Lloyd Baker; by the opinions of Thomas Hood and of the
actor Cape Everard; by Dibdin's own actions and writings;
even by Grimaldi's silence.

It is also a fact that so-called theatre underlings instinctively
know the truth about their managers and all events affecting
their theatre, sensing correctly how a show is doing, what
changes are planned and why (something every theatre manager
would do well to remember). They may get hold of the wrong
end of the stick, but it is usually the right stick. Wheeler is
quoted here only in so far as he says something new or pointed,
and always with his own spelling but repunctuated, as he wrote
with hardly a break.

He begins:

> My old friend,
> I have at length in compliance with your desire sat down to give you some account of the Sadler's Wells management as it was called. Tho fresh in my memory it is an old Story, for I have often quoted some parts of it, as a kind of moral lesson to many— tho I do not think it would be any to those who speculate in the management of Theatres.

The theatre had not done well under various managers for some time, though they had 'the best ability engaged' as performers, at the head of whom stood Mr. Grimaldi (the only artist to whom Wheeler gives that prefix, so presumably the elder), unparalleled in his line as Pantaloon; Dubois, and the 'unprincipled and in manners, language, brutal' Jew Davis, whose 'Practice and dirty Jokes' finally led to his expulsion from the theatre 'tho such a favourite with the Gallery, that it was said they never would be able to get on without him—but they did in Young Grimaldi', with whom Dibdin was always at war. Then there was Dighton who was 'brought one night to the theatre in a Hamper' to avoid some legal trouble, and St. Pierre from the King's Theatre 'who got up very attractive ballets' with Mme Louis, possessor of 'a host of talent': as Mme St Amand, she had come from the Paris Opera house, after her husband had been guillotined, to dance at Covent Garden, and then became Mme Louis (her second husband was a scamp and robbed her of everything). Mme Louis played Columbine to the Harlequin of Jack Bologna or Hartland, and the heroine to Hartland's hero in the serious spectacles that ended the programmes for many years. 'By such artists the theatre was supported and not by the trash that was written for it.'

Poor singers were engaged, till after the death of Mrs. Dibdin in 1816, and female performers, unless under contract, never stayed,

> for the manager's wife, Mrs. C. Dibdin, could bear no rivalry, and a song encored wd dismiss the lady singing it from ever singing it again, and at the end of the season from the Theatre.

For instance, in 1806 Dibdin announced as a reason for refusing an encore demanded by the audience from a Miss Bloomgren that the show would end too late: a voice from the boxes called out 'Was there no Petticoat reason?' No answer.

There was never any jealousy among the men, but only the voice of Garland, 'a humorist, and tho in his line a good theatrical machinist and carpenter, withall a social good companion and friend to every one in distres', was heard behind the scenes in the evening, for Dibdin forebade talking off stage. He never allowed his performers in the green room between their appearances, 'wh. made them in 1820, when Howard Payne had the Theatre and gave them one, wonder what it was for'.

Wheeler's opinion of the managers is even more enlightening. Hughes was too ready to listen to gossip about inefficiency, too liable to lose his temper, and delighted in 'the most abject servility'. Dibdin was mean: when Wheeler was night-watchman, he did odd jobs at his previous trade of shoemaker and at re-servicing knives and forks to make a little extra money, but this was always docked by Dibdin from his theatre salary, which he considered covered everything done in theatre time—and Wheeler never got a farthing of some £16 due to him.

The managers were surprised when the *Siege of Gibraltar* was such a success, 'full houses was the reward of having a leaden tank full of putrid water—for it was not renewed once in two months'. (Was Dibdin or Wheeler more accurate on this point?) The success of the *Siege* turned the managers' heads—'Mr. Hughes was able to save more money, Mr. Barfoot to be able to carry on his attentions to the Ladys' (Mrs. Barfoot every night watched from a box his latest fancy, a small-part dancer named Bates, whom he later had to marry when a widower), 'and Mr. Dibdin to give dinners and Partys from one end of the year to the other . . . it was the ruin of nearly all of them.'

As for Dibdin's engaging his wife as an artist, Wheeler was of opinion that, however it might help support their ten children,

it was, in addition to his own Idleness and Conceit, eventually the ruin of the theatre, if the Possession of a handsome salary raised to 400 p annum, two clear benefits for himself and wife, her salary (such as a manager wd give his wife), a house rent free delightfully situated, to say nothing of the Patronage of the situations (not a trifle) would have made a man of literary habits happy. This was the situation.

Wheeler adds that, though Dibdin should have been grateful to the Wells as the only theatre where his 'very mediocre ability' would have been endured, Dibdin bothered only about the pantomime and the grand spectacle, few of which were needed—at most two of each a season of six months, and often they were revivals:

> Was it any Wonder that a Theatre managed in this way should have come to ruin, which with the ability of Reeve and his wishes he often Expressed might have been made an English Opera house.
>
> Idleness and mediocre ability united with conceit destroyed it at last. Such was the fate of Sadler's Wells.

CHAPTER SEVEN

GRIMALDI TO THE FORE

1807–1818

A T THE end of his memoirs Dibdin certainly stresses that a theatre manager must 'study and accommodate the interest, reputation, feelings, and prejudice of his Performers', cultivate talent where he finds it, discard favouritism, win loyalty by 'an occasional half-holiday' rather than by the rod, and never regard the performers as 'merely passive mediums of his interest and convenience'. But he wrote these words some fourteen years after he left the Wells and some four years after leaving the theatre for good, having failed at both Astley's Amphitheatre and the Surrey—to judge from his benefits. Perhaps he had learned his lesson by then, or perhaps these admirable views were inserted, with the rest of his moralizing, into *My Professional Life*, as he called his memoirs, with a view to publication, though they were not printed until 1956. His description of his 'mode of management' begins with the words, 'I have found strictness of discipline, discreetly and good-naturedly kept up, indispensable to the welfare of a Theatre. . . . The Manager who is not firm, will always be imposed upon.' This sentiment, taken with the prayers before performance, might suggest that his management of the Wells, softened as it was by memory, may have been as unfriendly as Wheeler described.

But one thing Dibdin undoubtedly could do: though his vaudevilles were, as Wheeler said, trash, they were effectively written for a popular audience, mainly because they cleverly exploited the performers.

The 1807 season opened with the pantomime *Jan Ben Jan, or, Harlequin and the Forty Virgins*, an Oriental tale suggested by the Rev. Mr. Maurice of the British Museum and so advertised in Oriental lettering, in which Grimaldi, specially starred in the advertisements, made his comic song 'Me and my Neddy' so popular that watches were made with faces like his when singing it. In his honour the old Turk's Head opposite the eastern Wells entrance, later the Queen of Hungary and then the King of Prussia, was known as the Clown at the Wells.

During a new water-spectacle, *The Ocean Fiend, or, the Infant's Peril*, in which there was a wonderful reflection on the water of a palace in flames (produced by the new 'Redfire'— strontia, shellac, chlorate of potash and charcoal), a bulky country lady in the centre box was so startled by the throwing into the tank of what appeared to be a four-year-old child ('a precociously talented Girl'—'I was rather partial to the race', said Dibdin) that she burst out with, 'O, damn it, they've thrown the child into the water!' The 'child' was, in fact, a life-size doll, soon rescued by a Newfoundland dog.

The audiences provided the greatest news of 1807. Not only did the *Forty Virgins* and Grimaldi attract high society, but on one occasion in July a deaf-and-dumb man, sitting with a crowd of sailors in the gallery watching Grimaldi, suddenly—during a violent peal of laughter—cried out, 'What a damned funny fellow!', regaining the speech he was said to have lost through intense heat abroad: after the show he celebrated at the Sir Hugh Myddelton, and next day met Grimaldi and Dibdin.

But on Thursday 15th October, during a benefit performance of *The Ocean Fiend*, the Wells was the scene of a tragedy as dreadful as it was unnecessary. Hearing shouts from the pit of 'A fire! A fire!', the audience of 2,000 panicked and, though assured by Dibdin through a speaking-trumpet that there was no cause for alarm, they stampeded. (Only a few years before, Astley's had been burned down, and the Wells had given a benefit.) People from the back of the gallery threw themselves desperately into the pit below, those in the boxes on to the stage: the last scene with its real water had not started, or some would have been drowned.

Those fortunate enough to get out of the auditorium failed to clear the exits, so that those behind thought the doors were shut, and 'screams, oaths and exclamations reigned throughout'. Some jumped down by way of the chandeliers and escaped unhurt, but—apart from the damage to the theatre, musical instruments, girandoles, etc.—eighteen people lost their lives, and

TIPPO SAHIB

MRS. EGERTON AS JOAN OF ARC   THE SIAMESE TWINS

many more were badly injured. All the victims (except one aged thirty) were between nine and twenty-five years old: one, a boy of twelve, had been trampled to death. The bodies were laid out in the various rooms:

> In the first room were five men and five women; they were placed upon temporary tables round the room, with their clothes on, as they met their death; the faces of some of them were much disfigured, being quite black from the effect of suffocation. In the next room there were two women, two boys and three men, laid out in the same manner; and in the third room lay a beautiful young girl, whose body appeared as if it had been much trampled upon. It is a remarkable fact, that of all these persons, not a single limb was broken, though many had received violent contusions.

Others, after being bled, recovered:

> A husband and wife were both carried for dead into this place. On opening the vein of the wife, there was no emission, but on a like incision being made in the arm of the husband, the blood burst forth, and after a few minutes of suspended animation, his senses returned, and the first object which attracted his eye was his own wife, a corpse by his side. A paroxysm of frenzy was the immediate consequence, and he was borne off from the scene of death in this dreadful situation.

On the morning after the catastrophe, Dibdin wrote to his brother: 'Dear Tom, We have sat up all night in the treasury: eighteen dead bodies are lying in the music parlour: come directly.'

Grimaldi, not being in *The Ocean Fiend*, had gone to bed early, only to be wakened at midnight by repeated knocking at his door, which he at first thought was 'an intellectual amusement not at that time exclusively confined to a few gentlemen of high degree'; then, finding it was friends assuring themselves he was safe, he rushed to the theatre. The rest is better told, like the above quotations, from Boz's *Life of Grimaldi*, written partly by the thirty-three-year-old Charles Dickens, who thought it twaddle, but chiefly by his father:

> On arriving there, he found the crowd of people collected around it so dense, as to render approach by the usual path impossible. Filled with anxiety, and determined to ascertain the real state of the case, he ran round to the opposite bank of the New River, plunged in, swam across, and finding the parlour window open, and a light at the other end of the room, threw up the sash and jumped in *à la Harlequin*.

What was his horror, on looking round, to discover that there lay stretched in the apartment no fewer than nine dead bodies! yes! there lay the remains of nine human beings, lifeless, and scarcely yet cold, whom a few hours back he had been himself exciting to shouts of laughter. Paralysed by the sad sight, he stood awhile without the power of motion; then, hurrying to the door, hastily sought to rid himself of the dreadful scene.

It was locked without, and he vainly strove to open it, so knocked violently for assistance. At first the family of Mr Hughes were greatly terrified at hearing these sounds issuing from a room tenanted, as they imagined, only by the dead; but at length recognising the voice, they unlocked the door, and he gladly emerged from the apartment.

Only twenty shillings were found on the bodies, which had almost certainly been robbed: robbery in fact was the cause of the whole tragedy.

Two couples, Vincent Pearce, who worked for Whitbread's, John Pearce, up from Wiltshire to look for a butcher's job, an old woman, Sarah Luker or Locher, and Mary Vine, when spoken to by the constables on duty in the theatre to keep order, had, though not drunk, defiantly started a fight at the bar, claiming that a man had insulted them. Others said these four had begun fighting among themselves so that in the confusion they could rob the crowd, and started shouting 'A fight! A fight!' which was misheard as 'A fire! A fire!' The two couples were charged with causing a commotion, but said they did not care, as they could not be hanged for it: one man got six months, the other four; the old woman got fourteen days; Mary Vine had absconded.

The coroner sat the morning after the tragedy at the Sir Hugh Myddelton's Head and brought in a verdict of 'killed, casually, accidentally and by misfortune', adding that no blame attached to the management. 'The Accident', as it was always called in accounts of this period of the theatre's history, happened only four nights before the end of the season; so the Wells closed at once.

But it reopened a fortnight later for two benefit performances in aid of the sufferers and of relatives of the deceased; all the artists gave their services. Dibdin himself sang his burlesque song 'B.C.Y.' and a Mr. Morris presented an 'Exhibition of Gas Lights' (in the same year, this novel method of lighting

was used for the first time in London in Pall Mall). The proceeds were £257 16s., increased by the Wells to £290 7s.
instead of £300, which would not have looked like genuine
takings.

As a result of this tragedy the sale of wine in the theatre was
discontinued at the magistrate's suggestion, but shows went on.
The 1808 season, instead of opening as usual with the aqua-
drama from the end of the previous season, began with another
idea from Hughes: the use of a dry stage in front with a waterfall at the back. But the only piece with this device, *The White
Witch, or, the Cataract of Amazonia*, failed because the waterfall,
effective by day, was deficient in lamplight; moreover, on the
first night Miss Jellet, who had just lost her mother, had real
hysterics on the stage when, as the heroine, she saw a cloud
descend with the words, 'Behold the spirit of your departed
Mother': Dibdin had forgotten to have it changed.

Grimaldi's songs were now important enough to be specially
mentioned in the advertisements. In *Harlequin Highflyer, or,
Off she goes*, he sang 'Oh! my deary!' and 'A Bull in a China
Shop'. Others of his songs that year were 'Odd Fish', 'Whip
Club', 'Looney's Lamentation for Miss Margery Muggins'.
In *Thirty Thousand, or, Harlequin's Lottery* he sang, 'Smithfield
Bargain, or, Will Putty' (very topical because of the proposed
removal of Smithfield Market to a spot between the Angel and
the Wells): this might increase the value of the Wells site, as
Thomas John Lloyd Baker wrote to his father, but would damage
it as a theatre.

Dibdin certainly cashed in by showing in his pantomimes
actual shops whose proprietors, allowing him discount, shared
mutual advertisement, packing the theatre free—170 of them,
Wheeler said.

But it was Grimaldi, in *The Wild Man, or, Water Pageant*,
who gave the most outstanding performance of 1808. In this
story from Cervantes he was wonderful in the title-role, largely
modelled on Dubois's famous Orson, especially in the scene that
showed 'The Power of Music over the Savage Mind'. This
scene Dibdin wrote, he says, to give Grimaldi's talents full
scope, and it drew from him such an impressive exhibition of
the various passions of the natural mind that the scene was

'perpetually introduced as an attractive feature on Benefit nights, at almost every Theatre in Town, and many in the country, under the title of "The Power of Music"'. The editor of Cumberland's collection of plays said that the scene as played by Grimaldi (who also composed the incidental ballet) 'was tragic expression and dumb show of the rarest excellence', while Ackerman's Repository commented that as the Wild Man 'he is beyond any thing we could have conceived possible, when only delineated by dumb show'. Many of the audience were reduced to tears.

William Robson vividly described in *The Old Playgoer* how Grimaldi showed 'the very height of pantomime action' in this scene, in which the only music was played on a small silver flute, first pensively, then changed through *moderato, furioso*, and *affettuoso* into a happy jig:

> As a wild man, of the Orson kind, he is about to tear a child to pieces, whose father, destitute of other means of conquering him, tried the power of music. The first fierce glance and start, as the sound struck upon his ear, were natural and fine—the hands hung as if arrested, the purpose was at pause.
>
> As the plaintive air of the flageolet continued, it was really wonderful to watch that which you felt was the natural effect of the music upon such a being—and when, at length, the savage heart became so softened that his whole frame shook convulsively, and he clasped his hands to his face in an agony of tears, he never failed to elicit the proudest triumph of the actor's art—the sympathetic drops from the eye of every spectator. And, when the measure was changed to a livelier strain, the picture became almost frightful, for his mirth was in as great an extreme as his grief—he danced like a fury!
>
> I have seen him play this a dozen times at least, and was as much affected by the last exhibition as the first.

The 1810 water-piece illustrated two new trends—the growing popularity of Scottish shows (which Dibdin couldn't explain) and the dramatization of recent literary works: it was *The Spectre Knight*, founded partly on one of Raphael Holinshed's legends, partly on Scott's poem *Marmion*, published in 1808. This was a great success; and the pantomime *Bang Up, or, Harlequin Prime* (so called from catch-phrases of the day chiefly connected with the four-in-hand mania) ran it close. But the latter's success was largely due to a song by Dibdin that

Grimaldi made one of his most famous. As Dibdin says, his Grimaldi songs lost half their effect when sung by anyone else because they were written to exploit Grimaldi's peculiarities of expression:

> Many songs *sing* well (technically speaking) that would read *ill*. Even Nonsense, in its place, can have a meaning . . . those who never heard him cannot be made to understand how words so utterly destitute of humour, and music so entirely guiltless of merit, could have been rendered effective.

No doubt Reeve, who would have preferred to be writing opera, knew equally well how best to set such words to music for a great artist to make popular for very many years to come. (If these words seem dully simple, one should remember what a comedian did with 'I stopped and I looked and I listened' or can do with 'I thank you', 'I'm in charge' and 'very dodgy'.)

Tippety-witchet, or Pantomimical Paroxysms.

This very morning handy
My malady was such,
I in my tea took brandy
And took a drop too much. (*Hiccups*)
Tol de rol, etc.

Now I'm quite drowsy growing,
For this very morn,
I rose while cock was crowing,
Excuse me if I yawn. (*Yawns*)

But stop, I mustn't mag[1] hard,
My head aches—if you please,
One pinch of Irish blackguard
I'll take to give me ease. (*Sneezes*)

I'm not in cue for frolic,
Can't up my spirits keep,
Love's a windy colic,
'Tis that makes me weep. (*Cries*)

I'm not in mood for crying,
Care's a silly calf,
If to get fat you're trying,
The only way's to laugh. (*Laughs*)

At the end of 1810, George III became mad for the third and final time, and in 1811, when the Prince of Wales was made

[1] Chatter.

Regent, the Wells, freshly painted and with new lustres which 'had a very brilliant effect', opened with Dibdin's *Dulce Domum, or, England the Land of Freedom*, the first scene being his brother's cottage at Betchworth. In this Grimaldi's brother-in-law, George Bristow, appeared as Napoleon so as to get hissed, while Grimaldi sang his topical songs 'A Peep at Turkey' and 'Massena's Retreat' (from Torres Vedras only a month before), and brought the house down with his patter: 'O give me little England, where a man's head is his own freehold property, and his house is his castle; and whoever touches a hair of the one, or the latch of the other without leave, is sure to get the door in his face and his head in his hand.'

In his burlesque of Michael Kelly's well-known musical play *Blue Beard* (Drury Lane, 1798), Grimaldi's caricature of the chief singer, Miss de Camp (now married to the actor Charles Kemble) even made her laugh heartily herself when she saw it. Now that the Wells pantomime slightly overlapped that of Covent Garden, to which he was also under contract, he had to go by coach to appear at both on the same evening: on one famous occasion the coach failed to arrive and he ran through the streets in costume followed by a cheering mob till he found a coach in Holborn.

In 1812 he earned £8 a week at Covent Garden and £12 at the Wells, where his second benefit made £225 for him, though the theatre was supposed to hold only £200. Still he got into difficulties, and on one occasion had to be smuggled out of the Wells in a sack when bailiffs were after him.

In the aqua-drama *Johnnie Armstrong, or, the Caledonian Outlaw* (after Sir Walter Scott), in which there was a most inapposite song about the recent battle of Salamanaca and the fall of Madrid, he burlesqued the famous song 'Robin Adair' with his 'Moggy Adair'. In a Chinese pantomime that ridiculed the latest fashionable manias of the boxing ring (christened 'the Fancy' in 1811) and the Metallic Tractors, a much advertised cure of diseases by magnet, he sang his famous 'Thinks I to myself'. His comedy scenes were greatly helped by the engagement of Barnes as Pantaloon—Grimaldi had got him also into Covent Garden.

As the profit for 1812 was only £134, Yarnold and Andrews (who stayed on as scene-designer) sold out their shares to

Hughes, Reeve, Barfoot and Dibdin, for nearly three times as much as they had originally paid in 1802. Dibdin later regretted his purchase and recorded, 'It had been more prudent, if I had not augmented my share; for the *tide* of our *Water* had a *turn*, about three Seasons after, which brought on me some very embarrassing perplexities.'

From 1813 on, though there were still Intermezzos, Dances, Ballets, and so on, Dibdin confined his activities to the Harlequinades and Aqua- or Melo-dramas—literally music-plays. In that year the Wells and all the buildings on the ground, including Arnold's old house, were insured for £2,000. The season began with the first Wells dramatization of a recent novel—*Rokeby Castle, or, the Spectre of the Glen* (Scott's novel had been published in 1811); for this Dibdin said he had two ships made as large as the tank would hold which 'produced thunders of unqualified applause'; another version being that a crowded house was very satisfied, though the ships often ran aground,

> but this, indeed, was not surprising when a man was enabled to walk round one of them, with the water not higher than his knee; by which means it manifestly appeared, to the great relief of the audience, that even if a shipwreck had been the consequence, there was no imminent danger of drowning.

For topical pieces there were *Vittoria, or, Wellington's Laurels* and *The Battle of Salamanca* with real soldiers engaged nightly to reproduce the famous moment when English and French marched coolly up to each other, locked bayonets, and paused—till 'the determined aspects of the British Soldiers produced such an appalling effect upon the élite of the Emperor, that they suddenly and simultaneously, turned tail, and ran off, at speed'.

For Mrs. Dibdin's Benefit that September, tickets were printed from a copperplate by Cipriani of 'eight little Cupids, or Zephyrs, or some species of the fairy family, clustering and climbing, like Bees or Butterflies, upon stems of flowers, etc.', to which Dibdin had two more added to represent their ten children.

Grimaldi, more down to earth, was this year elected Chief Judge and Treasurer of the Wells self-governing Court of Rectitude. There were two judges, prosecuting and defending

counsel, clerk and treasurer who posted lists of fines each
Saturday, and these were saved till the company thought it fit
to have a dinner. Among the rules were the following:

> Any person making use of profane language shall be fined for
> each offence 1d.
> Any person calling another a b-g-r, shall be brought to trial.
> If any person takes the liberty of taking another's property from
> his pocket (which has been the case) though in a joke, he shall be
> brought to trial.
> Any person coming drunk, and disturbing the company, shall be
> brought to trial.
> If any person brakes wind in the room he shall be fined 1d. for
> the first offence, and 2d. for the second.

Grimaldi was now so well known that James Smith (of
Rejected Addresses fame) praised him in *Tributary Stanzas to
Grimaldi the Clown* for 'brushing the cobwebs from the brows
of care', for his song, for his 'Newgate thefts', for setting 'the
mind from critic bondage loose', and for making young and old
of both sexes cackle:

> Even pious souls, from *Bunyan's* durance free,
>   At Sadler's Wells applaud thy agile wit,
> Forget old Care, while they remember thee,
>   'Laugh the heart's laugh', and haunt the jovial pit.

The profit of 1813 was only £105; but the 1814 season more
than doubled that, partly no doubt because of the new sensational Harlequin, Ellar, whose tricks were brilliantly described
by Leigh Hunt, including the famous head-spinning act that he
had learned from Bologna and that sounds incredible:

> In comes Harlequin, demi-masked, parti-coloured, nimble-toed,
> lithe, agile; bending himself now this way, now that way,
> bridling up like a pigeon; tipping out his toe like a dancer; then
> taking a fantastic skip; then standing ready at all points, and at
> right angles with his omnipotent lath-sword, the emblem of the
> converting power of fancy and lightheartedness.
>   Giddy as we think him, he is resolved to show us that his head
> can bear more giddiness than we fancy; and lo! beginning with it
> by degree, he whirls it round in a very spin, with no more remorse
> than if it were a button. Then he draws his sword, slaps his
> enemy, who has just come upon him, into a settee; and springing
> upon him, dashes through the window like a swallow.

Ellar first appeared at the Wells in the opening pantomime,

Rival Genii, or, Harlequin Wild Man, in which Grimaldi celebrated the February Frost Fair on the Thames with his song
'Frost Fair, or, the Disasters of Mr. Higgins and Mrs. Wig-
gins'.

There were three aqua-dramas this season. The first was
notable for the appearance of the new dramatic actor Campbell,
who stayed a Wells favourite for years. The second, *Vive le
Roi, or, the White Cockade*, celebrated the restoration of Louis
XVIII to the throne of France after Napoleon's abdication in
April, showing his grand entry into London from his retirement
at Hartwell in Buckinghamshire, and 'an aquatic Fantoccini on
the river Seine', the figures, boats, and sea-horses in the water
worked by intricate machinery, but too far from the audience to
be effective. In the third, *The Corsair*, from Byron's poem of the
same year, Grimaldi played the title-role: he was rumoured to
be going to play Othello.

In *The Corsair* Dibdin wrote a comic song about the glorious
uncertainty of the law, considering 'the inability of a Man's
claiming his paternal Estate, when he came of age, from the
circumstance of his having been born on the 29th February; his
proper birthday, therefore, coming but once in four years'—a
dilemma exploited sixty-five years later by Gilbert in *The
Pirates of Penzance*.

On 20th June peace was proclaimed and the Wells 'presented
one blaze of refulgence, from thousands of illuminated lamps'
and extensive transparencies; and that season Grimaldi cleared
nearly £480 by his two benefits.

By 1815 theatre taste was changing. It was fashionable to
dramatize recent exciting novels, and audiences accordingly began to prefer drama—spectacular or farcical—to variety acts.

Dibdin accordingly took a chance with the licensing authorities. As he himself explained, 'At the Wells, whether I was
right or wrong, prudent or imprudent, after some time, using
an intermezzo of recitative singing, in rhyme, and speaking in
Prose, I "*did a bit of march of Intellect*", dismissed the Piano
from the Orchestra, and introduced dialogue, spoken in prose
only; I say *I* did, for with me, at Sadler's Wells, originated this
Custom, which was soon after adopted, and has since been continued at all the Minor Theatres.'

Occasional speaking in a song, like Grimaldi's eulogy of England in 1810, could hardly have been interpreted by the law as being spoken drama, so it was easy to extend it into a speech or even dialogue: then it was a short step from a musical performance with dialogue to a spoken drama with music.

The Wells, as Dibdin says, had already performed three-act operas by calling them burlettas or entertainments (for example, *The Deserter* and *The Daughter of the Air* in 1800), while other Minor Theatres had produced even Shakespeare 'interspersed with Sing-song'. So the introduction of dialogue into the Wells programmes, though not unprecedented, went far towards freeing the Minor Theatres 'from the narrow, and ambiguous limits, which the Act, whence they are authorised, *is said* to confine them to. It has been said that this will probably be the case soon, by virtue of a new Act made expressly for them.' He wrote this, of course, in 1830 shortly before the new Act he anticipated became a reality, but his own anticipation of the event began as early as 1815.

1815 was a year of trouble for the Wells. Mrs. Dibdin was ill; and Grimaldi, though not yet thirty-seven, began to have difficulty with his breathing, and occasionally could not appear. At his first benefit that year his son, J. S. Grimaldi, made his first Wells appearance as Scaramouch, having previously played Friday to his father's Robinson Crusoe, probably at Covent Garden.

Both Richard Hughes and William Reeve died this year, leaving their Wells shares to their widow and daughter respectively, and these two, relying on their major shareholdings, now apparently began—like all amateurs in power—to interfere with the running of the theatre. As Dibdin says, he had hitherto been uncontrolled manager, backed by Hughes, Reeve, and his own brother, but now 'it began to be a Committee Theatre: I had more to please than the public; and . . . by trying to please everybody, I could scarcely please anybody'. While he had been unshackled, 'the Concern was always prosperous . . . Indeed, no Theatre has a fair chance of success . . . unless the direction is restricted to one Person—a Theatre should be like an absolute Monarchy—as a limited Monarchy it will dwindle—as a Republic (of Proprietors and Committees) the administration will get into confusion, and confusion is the forerunner of defeat.'

In this Dibdin was proved right for, though previous years had shown only small profits, 1816—the first committee-run season—showed a loss of £570 (a drop of some £800). This cannot be accounted for solely by the programmes, though they were not up to date—*Iwanowna, or, the Maid of Moscow* celebrated the 'awful destruction of Moscow' four years too late, and Waterloo, in the summer of 1815, seems to have been ignored. Individual performers alone, however good, could not draw an audience—a ten-year-old boy from Paris, Master Hyacinthe Longuemare, walked up a tight-rope from stage to gallery and back with fireworks far more effectively than a recent similar performance at Covent Garden:

> The feat is performed here by a very graceful boy, instead of an indecent lusty woman; and instead of gazing in terror lest a clumsy mortal fall, we are pleased with the apparent realization of a fairy's flight.

Dibdin also engaged, apart from two nieces of his own, the clever Clown and Pierrot, Paulo, son of the famous Wells artists La Belle Espagnole and the Little Devil (who had died after striking his head on an iron screw when stage-hands did not hold the carpet for him to make his harlequin leap through a window); the dog Bruin which momentarily saved the Wells in the aqua-drama *Philip and his Dog*; and one Crawley, a Carcase Butcher, who sang louder than any other singer except the famous Incledon and filled the theatre with everyone from Smithfield Market who gave him thunders of applause—but as he could not sing new music, he was got rid of at the end of his first season.

About now two people came to the Wells almost every night —J. P. Malcolm, author of *Londinium Redivivum*, to see the shows, and an old gentleman, John Stewart (late private secretary to the Nabob of Arcot, and known as 'Walking' Stewart, since he had walked through most of Europe) to sleep in a box.

On 16th August 1816 Mrs. Dibdin, who had suffered from epilepsy since she was eight, died, and of her Dibdin wrote: 'As an actress and singer she was much admired, as a mother exemplary, and as a wife inestimable—the effects of her being a christian . . . She acquiesced in everything I proposed to her, and during the nineteen years we were united she never contravened my wishes.' Dibdin obviously dominated his home as well as his theatre.

Because Grimaldi, owing to a difference of opinion with the management, had not been engaged, *Forget me not, or, the Flowers of Waterloo* played in 1817 to an audience of only forty in the boxes, one hundred in the pit, and a gallery only half full. Grimaldi had been 'shabbied from his old familiar boards' by Dibdin. Grimaldi's version is that, as he asked for twelve guineas a week instead of £12, his right to a second benefit in the season was cancelled; Dibin's version is that Grimaldi had not only demanded an unspecified increase in salary, but had insisted on taking lucrative provincial engagements at the height of the season. Certainly his appearance in the provinces (when he played not only the wild man in *Valentine and Orson* but Bob Acres in *The Rivals*) paid him well— £32 for each of some fifty performances while at the Wells he got about £2 for each of some 180 performances plus two benefits of about £150 each after paying £60 for the expenses.

When Paulo appeared in Grimaldi's place there was a near-riot. Placards appeared outside Grimaldi's house, 'No Paulo!' or 'Joe for ever!' though there were a few with 'No Grimaldi'. The Wells lost £2,534.

How bad things were is clear from a most informative letter written on 22nd December by Dibdin to the Rev. Lloyd Baker in Gloucestershire (the paragraphing has been added to ease reading):

> My dear Sir,
> We have very seriously considered your Proposal of a Lease for 21 Years from Christmas 1815 at a Net Rent of £350 per annum and repairs £375. Allow me, before I reply to your proposition, to give you a true Statement of our hopes for the last *Six* Years.

He then gives the figures for 1812 to 1817 already quoted, and points out that the net loss for the six years amounted to £2,401, an average loss per annum of £400 5s. He goes on with a complaint often heard since:

> Sadler's Wells is not nor ever will be what it was; We are considered by the Public as out of Town, and the very great notice the Circus and Astley's have risen into (tho' formerly nothing in comparison with the Wells) has decreased the value of our Concern considerably.

In consequence we are obliged to adopt, at an *enormous* Expence, some peculiar features which *they* cannot procure—(as, for instance, the *Water Exhibitions*) and when that feature fails we are sure to lose money till we find another: and the Search for such an one sometimes 2 or 3 Seasons. The *Aquatic Exhibition* HAS lost its *prime* attraction; added to which *Astley* has made a Reservoir and is going to adopt it next Season: so that now we do not stand [*illegible*—alone?] in that feature.

The Times too are so bad for Theatres, that added to the great increase of the [*illegible: torn*] it will, probably, be 2 or 3 Years before they turn in our favour; and in a Theatre the worse the Season the more Money we are obliged to expend (and the common interest of that Money is considerable) and we must lay out a very considerable Sum for such Season to (in the *technical* Phrase) *pull up*—yet there is no rational prospect of a return at present—it is most probable we shall lose more.

Now, my dear Sir, as we wish nothing but what is reasonable we trust you will consider all this. I should remark that raising us for the year already past & paid seems unreasonable & cuts a Year off the proposed Lease—and as we *must* expend a great deal of Money on the Theatre independently of the Repairs your Terms are certainly too high, especially as Rents when augmented generally arise from the Landlord's laying out Money on the Estate himself for which a reasonable addition may be made to the Old Rent of *so much* per Cent for the Money laid out.

We conceive that no rise ought to take place till the End of the present Term, and we trust you will have no Objection to add 21 years to the present Lease at *such* Terms (commencing at the period when the present ceases) that We can with confidence meet: so, upon my Word, I must fear it will take us the whole of the present to *recover* what we lost in the last 5 years; supposing our Business improves, of which there is actually no prospect at present.

All Theatres are bad now. Drury Lane is a very ruinous Concern—the others struggling with every Difficulty. From the high Character for Candour the *late* Mr. Hughes always gave me of you, I am sure, you will see this letter in a fair and reasonable Light, and awaiting your answer for our further Guide,

I am, My Dear Sir,
For myself and Partners
Your respectful Servant
CHARLES DIBDIN

A lease of twenty-one years was granted at £330 per annum (though Lloyd Baker's surveyor, Bunning, thought £280 enough, considering the state of the roof), subject to an outlay of £370 in substantial repairs (slightly less than the original offer that Dibdin queried, but not as low as the Hughes family suggested—rent £260, repairs £370, or rent £250, repairs £500, or rent £300 if Lloyd Baker paid for the repairs).

Dibdin points out in his memoirs that after the Peace of Amiens, receipts fell seriously till the war started again, and that takings had dropped again now there was general peace, though he is wrong when he says this was the first year since he was proprietor and manager that the Wells had lost money.

In 1818 Grimaldi and Barnes, who had left together, returned, Grimaldi having now become a proprietor by buying five shares (an eighth part) from Mrs. Hughes who, he said, begged him to come back on his own terms, which certainly now included permission to make a provincial tour late in each July.

As Dibdin could not help recording, 'The return of Mr. Grimaldi was hailed with shouts of applause; and all, before and behind the curtain, appeared happy at seeing him "at home".' But the only shows of interest that year were two necessitating the revival of the water exhibition—*The Gheber, or, the Fire Worshippers* from the 1817 poem 'Lallah Rookh' by Thomas Moore, who also suggested the Hibernian *O'Donoughue, or, the White Horse*.

The critics found 'the more pleasing aquatic performances at Sadler's Wells probably better than the grand theatres of Naples, Turin, or opera-houses at Dresden, Stutgardt and Manheim with squadrons of horses or whole fleets', and even when Grimaldi was away in July his pupil, Hartland, caused bursts of applause by his performance in *The Wild Man*. In place of the late William Reeve, John Whitaker, organist of St. Clement, Eastcheap, who had written the *Iwanowna* music, and G. Reeve 'were in their music brilliant and effective' and the sixteen-year-old Miss M. A. Tree, Mrs. Charles Kean's sister, was an excellent singing-dancer at £6 a week: yet 'we lost more money this season, than in the former'. Grimaldi says each shareholder lost £333 13s., and Dibdin records, 'We dropped the Curtain, on the last night chopfallen.'

So in 1819, though Dibdin was at the Wells at the start of the season on Easter Monday, 12th April, a dispute with the other partners (which he thought should no more be disclosed than disputes between husband and wife or sworn friends, as being incomprehensible to outsiders, 'especially as they are not always thoroughly understood by the Persons disagreeing, themselves, while both sides are generally, somewhat in the wrong') led him to resign in favour of Grimaldi, 'and from that time to the present, I have never done anything for Sadler's Wells'.

CHAPTER EIGHT

HOT CODLINS

1819–1828

DIBDIN says that he opened the 1819 season, but resigned before Whitsun: Grimaldi's version—that he had resigned before Easter and was with difficulty persuaded to stay on till Whitsun—is more plausible. Certainly when in the rush to the gallery at the opening fourteen-year-old John Meeking was trampled to death, it was Grimaldi who came before the curtain to appeal for order.

Before leaving, Dibdin had superintended the addition of upper stage-boxes, the remodelling of the orchestra, separation of the pit pay-office and the box office, elevation of the pit and the enclosing of both pit and gallery for better ventilation and acoustics. He also—to please his partners, he says—had melodramatized *Macbeth* into *The Weird Sisters, or, the Thane and the Throne*, 'the only time I ever took such a step . . . It is probable that Macbeth was murdered as well as Duncan'. About the same time he was imprisoned for debt (refusing a surprising offer of help from a tearful Jew Davis) and with him Barfoot, whose second wife, now drunk and dissipated, was a spectacle in the Clerkenwell workhouse, as Wheeler recorded. The designer, Robert Andrews joined Drury Lane at £4 12s. 6d. a week.

But Dibdin's alteration of the 1805 *Talking Bird* pantomime brought the season a profit—as Grimaldi said, no doubt through the most famous of all his songs (one that only the day before I wrote these words I heard sung slightly differently by Ron Moody from his musical play on Grimaldi which was given during the winter of 1962–3 at Bristol):

HOT CODLINS

A little old woman her living she got
By selling codlins, hot, hot, hot;
And this little old woman, who codlins sold,
Tho' her codlins were not, she felt herself cold;

So, to keep herself warm, she thought it no sin
To fetch for herself a quartern of - - -

And when, at the end of each verse, the obvious rhyme was
shouted by the audience it was greeted by Grimaldi with 'Oh
for shame!'—the same shocked mock-amazement that great
comedian of recent times, Sir George Robey, used to show at
any suggestively understanding laugh.

> Ri tol iddy, iddy, iddy, iddy,
> Ri tol, iddy, iddy, ri tol lay.

> This little old woman set off in a trot,
> To fetch her a quartern of hot! hot! hot!
> She swallow'd one glass, and it was so nice,
> She tipp'd off another in a trice;
> The glass she fill'd till the bottle shrunk,
> And this little old woman, they say, got - - -
> Ri tol, *etc.*

> This little old woman, while muzzy she got,
> Some boys stole her codlins, hot! hot! hot!
> Powder under her pan put, and in it round stones;
> Says the little old woman, 'These apples have bones!'
> The powder the pan in her face did send,
> Which sent the old woman on her latter - - -
> Ri tol, etc.

> The little old woman then up she got,
> All in a fury, hot! hot! hot!
> Says she, 'Such boys, sure, never were known;
> They never will let an old woman alone'.
> Now here is a moral, round let it buz—
> If you mean to sell codlins, never get - - -
> Ri tol, *etc.*

—the last rhyme being probably a word we no longer use—
'fuz', i.e. drunk.

Other items of interest that year were a revival of *The Great
Devil*, with Grimaldi and Miss Tree; an African Ballet of
Action *Mungo Park, or, The Treacherous Guide* (Park, the ex-
plorer, had been killed in 1806 when his canoe upset in the
River Niger, but his death was not confirmed till 1812); *The
Padlock* (called a burletta), Miss Turner singing the popular
'Hope told a flatt'ring tale'; a musical interlude *The Caliph
and the Cadi, or, Rambles in Bagdad* by a promising young
writer, J. R. Planché; a melodrama *The Czar, or, a Day in the*

Dockyards (the same story as that of Lortzing's later opera *Czar und Zimmermann*); and a *Don Juan* with Grimaldi as Scaramouch and Donna Anna played by Miss Tree, of whom Thomas Hood wrote,

> Then next Miss M. A. Tree
> I adored, so sweetly she
> Could warble like a nightingale and quaver it.

She later this year sang Rosina in *The Barber of Seville* at Covent Garden, first produced in London the year before.

A press-notice said the Wells was sure to regain its former prosperity, thanks to Grimaldi's thoroughness; but constant cramp and rheumatic pains after performances forced him to give up management, though he remained a proprietor and performed as often as he could. His place as manager was taken in 1820 by a twenty-eight-year-old American actor-dramatist, Howard Payne, already known for his tragedy *Brutus*, who resented being called the American Roscius.

Most of Payne's presentations were revivals; but, George III having died on 29th January, there was a most unsuitable insertion in the Persian pantomime, *The Yellow Dwarf, or, Harlequin King of the Golden Mines* (from Madame Bunch's Fairy Tales), of a preview of George IV's Coronation Procession, including the Challenge of the Champion on horseback—but naturally not foreseeing his backing in, as he did at the actual Coronation of more than a year later.

Two horses were a sensation in the Equestrian Melodrama *Albert and Elmira, or, the Dumb Boy and his Horse*, in which there was a fight from their backs in the water; but the most interesting production was *The Robbers*, after Schiller, with Payne as Charles de Moor, presumably well musicalized, as was also Tom Dibdin's version of *Douglas* given for Payne's benefit with the famous *pas de deux* from Covent Garden's *Mother Goose* by Bologna and Grimaldi; the falling of a spark from a candle or a lamp on to the stage nearly started a panic.

As this was the last year Grimaldi was a regular player at the Wells, Thomas Hood wrote his

ODE TO JOSEPH GRIMALDI, SENIOR
' This fellow's wise enough to play the fool,
And to do that well craves a kind of wit.'
—TWELFTH NIGHT

Joseph! they say thou'st left the stage,
  To toddle down the hill of life,
And taste the flannelled ease of age,
  Apart from pantomimic strife—
    'Retired—(for Young would call it so)—
    The world shut out'—in Pleasant Row!

And hast thou really washed at last
  From each white cheek the red half moon?
And all thy public Clownship cast,
  To play the private Pantaloon?
    All youth—all ages—yet to be,
    Shall have a heavy miss of thee!

Thou didst not preach to make us wise—
  Thou hadst no finger in our schooling—
Thou didst not 'lure us to the skies'—
  Thy simple, simple trade was—Fooling!
    And yet, Heaven knows! we could—we can
    Much 'better spare a better man'.

Among those Hood could spare he lists 'Dibdin—all that bear
the name'. He goes on to miss that 'oven-mouth, that swallowed
pies', 'Thy pockets greedy as thy mouth', his ears that got
cuffed, his flapping, filching hands, his foot that was 'often made
to wipe an eye', his witty pair of legs with their striding 'some
dozen paces to the mile', his motley coach, his vegetable man—

Oh, who like thee could ever drink
  Or eat—swill—swallow—bolt—and choke!
Nod, weep, and hiccup—sneeze and wink?—
  Thy very yawn was quite a joke!
    Tho' Joseph Junior acts not ill,
    'There's no Fool like the old Fool' still!

Joseph, farewell! dear funny Joe!
  We met with mirth—we part in pain!
For many a long, long year must go,
  Ere Fun can see thy like again—
    For Nature does not keep great stores
    Of perfect Clowns—that are not *Boors*!

Many changes were coming quickly.
Though the season was said to have been a success, Payne
gave up (Wheeler said his finances should have been more
secure); Barfoot sold his shares to his son-in-law, Mr. Dixon
of the Horse-Repository; and Dibdin's were bought in by the
other shareholders, while nineteen-fortieths of shares or interests

in 'This valuable Property, With its Appurtenances' had been put up for auction in July, with three years' lease from the previous Christmas still to run and the privilege of taking a new lease for twenty-one years as from the previous Christmas.

The remainder of the lease for three years was taken in 1821 by Mr. Egerton, a Covent Garden actor, who brought with him his stately wife, a fine dramatic actress, and Mr. Keeley (later to become a well-known comedian). Egerton kept on Hartland and Campbell from the Wells company, but Grimaldi (because he had no reserve of strength) quarrelled over a clause in the contract which gave his old friend Egerton the right to hire him out and refused to appear at the Wells.

Egerton aimed at better acting and better drama—a thing deplored by the paper *John Bull*, which thought it abominable to have 'actors in earnest' at the Wells. So on 9th July Mrs. Egerton appeared as Madge Wildfire in a dramatization, or melodramatization, of Scott's four-year-old *Heart of Midlothian*; at last drama really started at the Wells and—an important sign of serious intent—free passes for tradesmen were abolished.

Because George IV was to be crowned on 19th July, poor Queen Caroline, who had come in for criticism by demanding a box for the coronation, caused further unfavourable comment when she tried to gain some recognition by visiting all the Minor Theatres. She came to the Wells on 12th July (as did many pickpockets) with only one carriage and in her usual style of dignified simplicity, accompanied only by Lord and Lady Hood and Alderman Wood. As soon as they entered the decorated box the audience cheered, and 'God Save the Queen' was 'called for from every part of the house, and performed by the *corps dramatique*'. On the day of the coronation, when all theatres were open at the King's order, 'God Save the King' was sung with equal acclamation.

In August one of Douglas Jerrold's first plays, *The Chieftain's Oath, or, the Rival Clans*, was performed: it was based on the old Ossian story of *Oscar and Malvina* (Covent Garden, 1791), and in its last scene the moon could be seen 'rising (as in nature) large and red, decreasing in size and becoming paler as she ascends, her beams being reflected on the lake of real water peculiar to this theatre'. The scenery—worth imitation by the major theatres, it was said—was by a Greenwood of the third

generation to paint at the Wells. But the season resulted in a
loss, of which Grimaldi's share was £90.

The theatre was redecorated for 1822 in a delicate pink with
blue for the drop curtain and the box hangings, the proscenium
doors in white with gold lattice-work on the front of the boxes,
and gold lyre and cornucopia on the proscenium instead of the
Royal arms.

Egerton, planning to discontinue the water-scenes, presented
the popular *Tom and Jerry, or, Life in London*. Adapted by the
author of the original, Pierce Egan, this version, said to be the
best, introduced, unlike those at Astley's, the Surrey and the
Adelphi, 'the celebrated Poney Races': this was made possible
by building platforms over the orchestra so that the ponies,
passing into and round the pit, gave the audience 'a perfect and
safe view of the whole Race'. The production, with thirty scenes
designed by George Cruikshank, had well over a hundred performances. The race-track was also used to comic effect by
Keeley who walked along it in *Hookey Walker, or, Eight Miles an
Hour*.

Tom and Jerry made *John Bull* change its tune and recommend
an early visit to the Wells, 'lest the powerful *fiat* of the Lord
Chamberlain should reduce the performance to the ordinary
jump and jingle of the olden days'. The Lord Chamberlain did
not interfere, and Egerton concentrated on dramas ranging from
Joan of Arc, or, the Maid of Orleans to *Rival Indians, or, the
Faithful Dog*. He also revived *Valentine and Orson* with a real
bear; and in *Jack and Jill*, to show George IV passing Tilbury
Fort on the way to Scotland, expensive machinery raised the
stage to the roof in sight of the audience, disclosing the real
water instantaneously without the former delay in filling the
tanks.

After that, Egerton reintroduced water-shows with enthusiasm. The 1823 season had two Esquimaux, Niakungetok and
his wife Coonahink, performing evolutions on real water; a
water-fight in *The Island, or, Christian and his Comrades*, based
on Byron's poem about Captain Bligh of the *Bounty*; and
Nerestan, Prince of Persia, or, the Demon of the Flood, in which
Mrs. Egerton played the Prince. She also played the romantic
lead in *The Indian Maid, or, Sailors and Savages* (based on
Arnold's *Inkle and Yarico* of 1789), but was criticized because

'she puts on an appearance of superiority which evinces a *silly vanity* of distinction above her compeers. Now, all this is very well in your satin-clad potentates, and hopeful princes; but it is most unseemly in parts like Yarico where every thing should be artless and natural.' With the production of serious drama serious dramatic criticism was obviously starting, and this year's literary extravaganza on *Dr. Syntax* seems to have been better appreciated than *The Russian Mountains* with sledges sliding down an iced plane of wood at breakneck speed from high at the back of the stage to the back of the pit: the same was done at the London Hippodrome early this century when a dramatic escape into water was shown—but at the Wells the audience also was allowed to travel down the slide.

After three Egerton seasons the Wells was let for 1824 to 'Little Williams, of ham and beef celebrity', Llewellin Watkin Williams, son of the owner of an Old Bailey boiled beef house. He was also lessee of the Surrey Theatre, and employed his company both there and at the Wells, running them from one to the other during the evening by special carriages. Grimaldi supervised the Wells shows for Williams, but the scheme did not work in spite of such performers as Charles Kemble's son, Henry, in *Ora, or, the African Slave* and an 'Actress of All Work'(as quick-change artists were called), Miss Vincent, aged eight, and in 1825 Williams, going bankrupt, gave up his theatres. At the invitation of the proprietors 'the veteran' Tom Dibdin (he was fifty-four) chose to return to run the Wells, while the Surrey, on Tom's suggestion, took his brother instead —'rather reluctantly', as Dibdin himself wrote.

Tom and the other shareholders—Richard Hughes, son of the late proprietor, Jones, Reeve's solicitor son-in-law, Dixon of the repository, and Grimaldi, who was given £4 a week and lodgings at the Wells to supervise—spent £3,000 on improvements: they made Rosoman's old private house at the New River Head end of the theatre into box-offices, wine-rooms and saloon, open from 11 a.m. to 11 p.m. They reintroduced the retailing of wine and entrance at half price at 8.30.

By now the nearby fields were built over (present-day Myddelton, Wilmington and Lloyd Squares), and new audiences were expected: there was even Taylor's Sadler's Wells Coach 'the

Grimaldi' which left Paddington at 6 p.m. for the Wells and
waited till the show was over.

Tom revived many of his own slight pieces, written for other
theatres, and at last had his amusing sketch from the French,
Garrick and his Double, acted—he had written it for Bannister,
but it had not been played before lest the story (of Garrick at a
country inn being taken for an impostor because another visitor
had already been accepted as Garrick) might cause offence.
(Some papers, remarking that the Wells played drama, asked
why it was not licensed.) Tom also encouraged good music—
The Devil's in Doctor Faustus, or, Mephistophilis in Town had a
Weber overture and sixty-four airs by

> Dr. Arne, Blow, Bishop, Busby, Carolan, Dibdin, Kelly, Locke,
> Linley, Macgregor, Nicholson, Dr. Pepusch, Purcell, Rizzio,
> Reeve, Rossini, Rauzzini, Stroace, Whitaker, etc.

and he opened one programme with the *Freischütz* overture and
another with that to *Zaira*.

While Tom Dibdin organized the shows, Grimaldi was the
resident manager, as can be seen from a song by the father of
Thomas Greenwood who later was Samuel Phelps's partner: it
was discovered by E. L. Blanchard and runs in part:

The History of Sadler's Wells; or a Chapter of Managers

────

(To the tune of Collins's 'Chapter of Kings')
The merry Charles Dibdin then ruled the roast,
Who the family genius and talent could boast;
Of frolick and fun Nature furnished a stock,
And truly a chip he was of the old block,
    And, barring all pother, not one or the other
    Has written much better in turn.

Charles in council adopted his ancestors' plan,
Allowing a pint of old port to each man;
But now like their ancestors, morals were shrunk;
Modern dandies each night in the boxes got drunk.
    And, barring all pother, each Manager, brother,
    With the audience got drunk in their turn.

Grimaldi, indignant, determined to reign,
But soon yielded the sceptre to young Howard Payne;
Yet somehow or other, his reign was cut short,
For management was not at all Yankee's forte.
    And, barring all pother, yet, somehow or other,
    Payne managed one season in turn.

Next Egerton rose, and dispelling the mist,
Determined fresh troops of the line to enlist;
Who appeared one and all, when he opened his plan,
And swore they would triumph or fall to a man.
  And, barring all pother, he, somehow or other,
  Had a lease for three seasons in turn.

Grimaldi a second time took his degrees,
To whom little Williams had yielded the keys;
With voice, heart, and hand, each man joined the cause,
And Joey enjoyed all his well-earned applause.
  And, barring all pother, Joe, Momus's brother,
  Now governed the tank in his turn.

Wheeler's story of Charles Dibdin's having parties every night
is borne out by the lines saying the managers at that time got
drunk with the audience.

The 1825 season resulted in a loss of nearly £1,400, and
Tom Dibdin changed the whole system at the Wells by a bold
novelty—a winter season (the 1787 licence for performances
only between Easter Monday and 19th September apparently
being tacitly disregarded).

That first winter season opened at Christmas with Tom's
George Barnwell melodrama, a *Humphrey Clinker* burletta and a
Don Giovanni burlesque and lasted ten weeks. Then, leasing
the theatre to W. H. Williams for his successful one-man impersonation show *Walnuts and Wine* till 6th March, the proprietors were uncertain whether to reopen at Easter or not.

Richard Hughes Junior wrote on 10th March to Lloyd Baker's
agent pointing out that the losses from 1815 to 1820—some
£8,000—had resulted in some of the shareholders selling their
shares to make the concern solvent, and in the preceding year
they had spent some £2,500 on repairs and decorations: at the
same time 'it is but natural to cling to an object while there is
hope of some fortunate hit turning up however distant'.

Belatedly it was agreed to go on with the season, leaving
Tom Dibdin a bare three weeks 'to write and prepare three new
pieces for representation, deducting three or four hours each
day during a fortnight's busy rehearsal'.

The opening productions, as might be expected, were not of
great interest but once more the Wells was temporarily saved
by stunts. A mad elephant at Exeter Change had recently died,

so Campbell wrote a topical play named after it, *Chuneelah*, which was successful for many nights; later, for the first of many times, the public paid 2s. (children 1s.) to see the Inflation and the Ascent from the grounds of a Balloon—carrying twenty-three-year-old Mrs. Graham, 'the only English Female who has handled such a stupendous machine entirely herself'. Then the heat of the early summer 'inspired my "governors"', said Tom Dibdin, to try another outdoor attraction—pony races: boards were erected to hide the races from passers-by, and for publicity riders with flags and bugles paraded the streets in racing costume daily, distributing bills descriptive of cups, plates, bits, etc. The 'Little Newmarket Races' for horses of under thirteen hands, starting on 19th July at 6 p.m., were a fair success when the heat was damaging all London theatres. There was one race for a silver cup; two for five horses once round; one for two horses twice round; and even a race for female jockeys. Thanks to the balloon ascents and the races, the Wells recovered.

Among the more interesting stage-shows was a version of the 1823 dialogue-opera *Clari, or, the Maid of Milan* by Henry Bishop, to Howard Payne's libretto. It included the apparently British 'Home, sweet home', the only thing for which Payne is remembered today (ironically enough, he never settled in a home of his own), and was called *Force of Conscience, or, the Play's the Thing*. Mrs. Fitzwilliam played the lead. In *Tom and Jerry* the characters took part in the races; George Hook Lupino appeared as a 'blue monkey'. But the winter season, though it started well with *George Barnwell*, suffered when George IV's brother, the Duke of York, died early in 1827.

There were two remarkable productions in June 1827—a version of Edward Fitzball's most popular melodrama *The Flying Dutchman*, with twenty-four-year-old J. S. Grimaldi as Vanderdecken, the Dutchman—a non-speaking part except at the beginning and the end; and two days later a version of the story of the Weber opera *Freischütz* called *Sixes!!!!!!!, or, the Fiend*, for which Joey Grimaldi left a sick-bed 'to prop the falling fortunes of the former scene of his early fame' by playing Hock, a drunken soldier.

The pony races, however, were stopped by the courts; the romantic *Paul Jones*, Payne's performance in *The Murdered Monk*, and the stuffed figure of an animal new to London in

The Giraffe, or, The Cameleopard did little good; and in September young J. S. Grimaldi was brought home dangerously ill with a brain fever induced by love and brandy.

The winter season started unremarkably, but on Thursday 27th February 1828 an interesting experiment was made: a concert with an orchestra of forty-two conducted by J. C. Nightingale, organist of the Foundling Hospital, which included selections from *Israel in Egypt* and *Judas Maccabeus* in which Mrs. Fitzwilliam sang.

Music was becoming popular at the Wells, for before the winter season ended *Clari*, 'The Favourite Romance', was revived four times, and for Tom Dibdin's benefit *Inkle and Yarico* and two scenes from *The Beggar's Opera* were given—Macheath being played by Miss Hague, 'the Young Lady who was so favourably received in *Clari*' (Harriet, daughter of Charles Hague, Professor of Music at Cambridge).

Then came this announcement—for the last performance by Grimaldi at the Wells, Monday, 17th March 1828:

> To greet his Friends, ere he retires
> To rural Scenes and Village Spires,
> *Grim* takes a Night to say Adieu,
> And thank his Patrons *tried* and *true*.
> To find relief from many woes,
> He seeks retirement and repose;
> But can he go—and cease to grieve,
> Such zealous hearts and friends to leave?
> Oh! no! for '*Forty Years*' they've back'd him,
> 'Till *Sickness* and *Old Time* attack'd him—
> Come, then, on Monday, as above,
> His heartfelt gratitude to prove,
> No more he'll press—'The Die is Cast',
> His next appearance—is—HIS LAST!!!

The show was to last five hours, from 6 p.m. with half-price about 8.30.

He had been persuaded to give this last benefit performance (which raised £315 for him), all the artists and technicians giving their services, by the composer Michael Kelly's charming niece, the Drury Lane singing actress Frances Maria Kelly (who later built the Royalty Theatre to show off her drama students and spent most of her long life of ninety-two years trying to elevate the stage in public estimation; she died in 1882). Covent

Garden refused Grimaldi the theatre for a benefit there, so Lord
Segrave arranged for one at Drury Lane which produced out of
the sale of tickets and gifts some £580.

For his farewell performance at the Wells, apart from other
items, the burletta *Humphrey Clinker* was given, Campbell sang
'Bound 'Prentice to a Waterman', Mrs. Searle (whose pupils
had been supplying the ballets for some time) did her skipping-
rope dance, Payne juggled, and the celebrated *pas de deux* that
Ellar used to do with Joey was done with Joey's son, while
Grimaldi himself appeared as Hock in *Sixes, or, the Fiend*—the
part Tom Dibdin had written specially for him.

At the close of the performance Grimaldi came on to the stage,
dressed in black with a white waistcoat and gloves and, ad-
vancing to the footlights while a crowd of performers arranged
themselves around, addressed the audience with much feeling.
These were his words:

> Ladies and Gentlemen,—I appear before you this evening for
> the last time in this theatre. Doubtless, there are many persons
> present who think I am a very aged man: I have now an oppor-
> tunity of convincing them to the contrary. I was born on the 18th
> of December 1779[1] and, consequently, on the 18th of last Decem-
> ber attained the age of forty-eight.
>
> At a very early age—before that of three years, I was intro-
> duced to the public by my father at this theatre; and ever since
> that period have I held a situation in this establishment. Yes,
> ladies and gentlemen, I have been engaged at this theatre for
> five-and-forty years.
>
> By strict attention, perseverance, and exertion, did I arrive at
> the height of my profession, and, proud I am to acknowledge,
> have ofttimes been honoured with your smiles, approbation, and
> support. It is now three years since I have taken a regular en-
> gagement, owing to extreme and dangerous indisposition: with
> patience have I waited in hope my health might once more be
> re-established, and I again meet your smiles as before;—but,
> I regret to say, there is little or, in fact, no improvement per-
> ceivable, and it would therefore now be folly in me ever to think
> of again returning to my professional duties. I could not, how-
> ever, leave this theatre without returning my grateful thanks to
> my friends and patrons, and the public; and now do I venture to
> offer them, secure in the conviction that they will not be slighted
> or deemed utterly unworthy of acceptance.
>
> To the proprietors of the theatre, the performers, the gentle-
> men of the band—in fact, to every individual connected with it, I

---

[1] He was wrong: it was 1778.

likewise owe and offer my sincere thanks for their assistance this evening. And now, ladies and gentlemen, it only remains for me to utter one dreadful word, ere I depart—Farewell!—God bless you all! may you and your families ever enjoy the blessings of health and happiness.—Farewell!

And so to a packed theatre the most classical clown that ever raised laughter in a care-crowded world said good-bye to the stage. At the end he called out 'God bless you', his thanks were displayed in fireworks, and he retired to the green-room, weeping with an intensity of suffering that it was painful to witness and impossible to alleviate. He did not recover for some days.

CHAPTER NINE

'ORF WITH HIS ED'

1828–1837

FROM NOW on and for the next twenty years summer and winter seasons at the Wells virtually merged so that, apart from short breaks before Easter and Christmas, there were performances all through the year.

Tom Dibdin, though still a shareholder, gave up being manager before the summer of 1828, when J. B. Blackstone, the Adelphi's rising comedian, took over the Wells to present the Adelphi-type of strong drama with atmospheric music: for example, *Jack Sheppard, the Housebreaker* (played by J. S. Grimaldi); *The Green-eyed Monster*; *The Fatal Ravine*; *The Old Oak Chest*; the very successful *Napoleon, or, the Emperor and the Soldier*; and *Guy Fawkes, or, the Gunpowder Treason* (another young Grimaldi lead).

At the start of the winter season the popular Wells actor, Campbell, began his four-years' management of the theatre with the usual sort of programmes. *The Plague of Marseilles*, with its reproduction of the 1720–1 'Depopulating Scourge' which killed off nearly half the 100,000 inhabitants, and of the final saving of the town, was wildly applauded; and his own *Gambler's Life in London*—so full of moralizing that the Press thought one of old Joey's petty larcenies would do more good to the rising generation than twenty morals: 'but so it is—the march of intellect has banished mirth from Sadler's Wells. What will it not effect next?'

'Improvement' was in the air. The New River Company had closed the passage (formerly known as Lovers' Walk) between Arlington Street and Myddelton Square, and when the Rev. William Lloyd Baker objected, Thomas Cromwell, the parish clerk, explained: 'It was become the common resort of abandoned women, reputed thieves, and the dissolute frequenters of the theatre and house of entertainment in the neighbourhood, to

109

the nightly annoyance of all the respectable inhabitants of the vicinity, who had made repeated representations to the Board upon the subject.' Lloyd Baker, however, said it was a necessary short-cut to Pentonville and so 'of more private consequence to me than the board are aware of'.

The Wells proprietors, too, supported moral uplift by stressing that their amusements offered 'lessons of the most virtuous and moral principles':

> The Leading Pieces are generally Melo-Dramas . . . which for purity of diction, classicality of language, and delicacy of sentiment, may vie with the productions of their competitors, those 'vast Leviathans', the Metropolitan Theatres.

Their ballets could be excelled only by the Opera-house; while their final 'Comic Operatic Burlettas' at least equalled those of other Minor Theatres. Besides, only people appropriately dressed were admitted to the Private Boxes ('the regulation respecting dress is most strictly observed').

In the summer of 1829 female attendants in the saloon served young visitors (for whom several boxes were reserved) with tea, coffee, fruit, etc., while the shows would begin 'precisely at a quarter past six, and positively close before 11'.

Discussions about the short-cut continued and in June Grimaldi was persuaded to write to Thomas Lloyd Baker (who represented his father) suggesting that if the New River Company wanted a new road, it should be at that company's expense:

> We are well as we now are—it might prove advantageous, or it might not—it is a speculation—but if Mr. Baker has an idea it will benefit his Estate, we should be most happy in contributing our mite, at the same time, we trust Mr. Baker would give it his serious consideration and have no objection to grant us an extension of Lease—I know not what length our lease has to run, but think about twelve or thirteen years. Now if he will make it a Twenty-One years from Christmas next we cannot have the least hesitation by conforming to the proposed application.

The controversy went on, and the passage is the same today— Myddelton Passage, still useful to those of us who live westwards of the Wells.

The 1829 programmes were most varied. There was another dog-show—the founded-on-fact *Dog of Montargis* (where its statue can still be seen) with the dog 'ringing the doorbell, seizing the lantern, lighting Gertrude to the spot, and after-wards discovering the murder'. The title-rôles in Reeve's *Paul and Virginia* were played by Miss Helme and Miss Adami respectively (Miss Helme, 'by the bye, seems particularly par-tial to the—hem!—what we must not mention'). A dramatized version of Mrs. Opie's 1801 novel *Father and Daughter* was given, under the more theatre-filling title of *The Victim of Seduction*, as well as Campbell's *Deamon of the Desert, or, the Murderer's Sacrifice*.

The most popular show that year was *Blackeyed Susan* with Campbell as the sailor William: this was played a hundred times between 24th August and January 1830, rivalling the hundred-odd performances of the original production at the Surrey in the same season with the more famous T. P. Cooke, who had actually been seven years in the Navy.

Miss Helme played Macheath in *The Beggar's Opera*—'although a part totally unsuitable to the fair pretensions of a lady, yet it was assumed with much spirit and effect'; the Young Disloqué's postures, contortions and evolutions, and Ducrow's statue-poses (Hercules and the Lion, the African afraid of the Thunder, the Dying Gladiator) attracted great attention; and—most daring at the time—Campbell at his benefit acted in Cibber's popular 'improvement' of *Richard III*.

There was a version of *The Lady of the Lake*, there were operas—Storace's *No Song, no Supper*, Shield's *Lock and Key*, and Reeve's *Cabinet*—and as a great novelty a coloured actor, F. W. Keene, appeared as 'The African Roscius' (to make the public think it was the famous Aldridge then playing Othello under the same description at Covent Garden) in the opera *The Slave* and the ballet of action *Obi, or, Three-fingered Jack*.

The Duke of Clarence, patron of the Wells, came to the throne in 1830 as William IV, remaining their 'august patron', so there were three special programmes of the usual mixture, including new words to 'God Save the King' and a ballad 'A British Sailor wears the Crown' and even a new loyal drama, *William and Adelaide*. Though other programmes remained as mixed as before—melodramas, ballets (now more exhibitions of technique than the dramatic mimes they had been), topical shows and such stunts as Xavier Chabert, who claimed to drink and wash in boiling oil, walk on red-hot irons, and stay in an oven till 600 degrees were registered, and the famous man-monkey, M. Gouffé, who ran round the edge of the gallery and jumped from the proscenium to the stage—more and more worthwhile works were given. Operas that year included Bishop's *Miller and his Men*, O'Hara's delightful *Midas* and *The Golden Pippin*, Arne's *Love in a Village*, Dibdin's *Waterman*, and Boieldieu's *John of Paris* (arranged by Bishop), with the surprising addition of Rosina's 'Una voce' from *The Barber of Seville*, but sung with such feeling by Miss Crawford that it was encored. Miss Helme, however, was now using her good voice too wildly and was too fond of interpolating cadenzas. In January 'a gentleman', who had been refused permission by Covent Garden to play it there, though willing to pay for the privilege (a common procedure at the time), appeared in Massinger's *A New Way to Pay Old Debts*, and this may have urged Campbell to play the famous Sir Giles Overreach himself in February. As no protest came from the licensing authorities, between the end of July and September the Wells actors, headed by Freer, 'the Kean of Sadler's Wells', daringly played *The Merchant of Venice*, *Richard III*, *The Iron Chest*, *Pizarro*, *Romeo and Juliet*, *Othello*, *The Castle Spectre*, and *Venice Preserved*, while *Father and Daughter* was given a new title, *The Lear of Private Life*, more in key with classical drama than *The Victim of Seduction*.

Each play was, of course, only part of an evening's programme and must, therefore, have been 'arranged' and even had songs introduced. What the performances were like can only be guessed from contemporary comments on the great topical piece of the year, *The Charter, or, Death or Liberty*, a brave attempt to emulate the topical plays of forty years earlier; but the stage was too small for 200 extras needed for the reproduction, only a month after the event, of the July revolution in Paris that put the *roi-citoyen* Louis-Philippe in power. One reporter, describing one scene, wrote:

> An urchin of the Polytechnic school—apparently four years of age—is beset by two soldiers. Nowise daunted, he pulls from his breast . . . two *diamond-edition* pistols, and presents one at each of his assailants. Having nothing except *guns* with which to defend themselves against their *formidable* antagonist, they are, of course, panic-struck, when he *throws away* the pistols, and stabs them both.

PHELPS AS WOLSEY

PHELPS AS MACBETH AND, WITH MISS GLYN, AS HAMLET

MISS HUDDART.   MR. KNIGHT.   MR. MORTON.   MISS L. ADDISON.   MR. WILLIAMS.   MR. PHELPS.   MR. BRANSON.   MR. H. MARSTON.   MR.
MISS COOPER.   MR. SCHARF.   MR. G. BENNETT.   MR. HOSKINS.

SADLER'S WELLS THEATRE.—FROM A SKETCH MADE IN THE GREEN ROOM.—CHARACTERS IN "THE MERCHANT OF VENICE."

THE PHELPS COMPANY IN THE MERCHANT OF VENICE

Later, this account goes on, Campbell threw away his sword and fought a soldier with bare fists and of course won, while Freer rolled about most pompously, and shouted most lustily . . . Williamson looked 'the soldier every inch' and sung very sweetly. Mrs. Searle acquitted herself most creditably, but she would look the Amazon better if her legs were a *little* thicker.

The outspoken critics of those days give a pretty clear picture of the standard at the Wells in 1830 by their comments on the various players: Campbell was good at Frenchmen and melodramatic parts but too much inclined to dash 'at "all in the ring"', while in his favourite sailor-parts 'he speaks as if for a wager, and he is consequently unintelligible'; J. F. Williamson was a good singer 'and knows it'; Villiers always seemed to have 'a paper of plums' in his mouth; Miss Pitt was 'a very harmless personage' who 'sings like a tea-kettle'; Mrs. Searle dances and gets up ballets well, but nods and leers to her friends impudently; Miss Adami should be used more. Lastly, Freer had talent, but stamped and strutted—to watch him was like 'looking at tragedy through a magnifying glass'—he had an excellent voice and always gave a good reading, but 'he trots about the stage at the rate of eight miles an hour!' The scenery was musty, but 'dancing *is* good at Sadler's Wells'. Young Grimaldi was not mentioned, probably because he was then 'an inmate of his Majesty's Bench', after having 'eluded the vigilance of the duns and bailiffs for the last six weeks'.

Obviously the admirable intention to present classical drama at the Wells was too ambitious for the powers of the company. Tom Dibdin was no longer there, Grimaldi was a sick man and manager only on paper, while Campbell's over-enthusiasm as an actor was not compatible with the patient self-criticism needed by a producer or, as he was then called, stage manager.

All this was seen in the December of 1830 when Henry Kemble (who never liked acting and joined the army the following year) and his daughter Blanch were introduced by the management 'to such flats as might mistake them for Charley Kemble and Fanny' (his popular father and even more popular sister). They appeared in *Romeo and Juliet, Othello,* and *Venice Preserved,* in which the resident actor Villiers, though greeted with 'Bravo, Villiers!' was not word-perfect and, with Kemble, apologized to the audience. The Jaffier called Belvidera his dear

Desdemona and, when he said to the guard 'Lead me to my dungeon', one wag exclaimed, 'Go by yourself, old chap!' After groans and hisses in the Senate scene, Kemble first appealed, then argued, and lastly joked, so that a fellow in the gallery, remembering the dog-shows, called out, 'Bring the dogs—they will agree better perhaps!'

After this, classical drama was a rarity at the Wells for many years. The original Siamese (Chinese) Twins, Chang and Eng, appeared; *Melmoth the Wanderer* (from Charles Maturin's 1820 novel) provided 'profuse expenditure of cerulean brimstone and the noise of frying-pans and tin pots'; Miss Harvey appeared as *Richard III*; Michael Boai played tunes on his chin, and Campbell reproduced a Jewish wedding.

W. H. Williams, who took the theatre in October, presented Mrs. Fitzwilliam in *The Heart of Midlothian* and *Rochester, or, Charles the Second's Merry Days*. But the standard dropped so low that William P. Mylne of the New River Head wrote recommending Thomas Lloyd Baker (whose father had died) to 'compel these itinerant Theatrical corps to quit the spot for ever': he would then get suitable tenants for decent buildings that could be put up; but 'should you compel the Proprietors to build while their trade goes on, which is now of the lowest description, it will only increase the number of the lodging Houses and Brothels which cover your Tunbridge Wells property and I am sorry to find it is spreading over our Estate altho we make every sacrifice to prevent it'. He suggested that the theatre could be let as a Riding School and Livery Stable or for a Panorama, and that good houses could be built on the rest of the land and ultimately be profitable as well as make the neighbourhood respectable—'as it is, nothing can be worse'.

The new heir to the property did not turn the actors out, and Campbell, still Manager in 1832, tried to fill the house by reducing the prices (even for a dramatization of Sadler's gardener finding the first well).

The non-payment for a site for new back-stage rooms induced Lloyd Baker to refuse any further lease for a time. However, the summer season was taken on by W. H. Williams and Mrs. Fitzwilliam, 'a talented little soul' and as well known to the public as she was respected in private as a mother and wife, though she was once said to have been heard saying, 'I'll give you a *podger* in the *guts*'; still she was the first Wells manager to present a specially written opera (as it was called, though really an operetta).

This was the fourteenth by the thirty-year-old composer, John Barnett, with text by Buckstone. It was called *The Pet of the Petticoats* (originally *The Convent*) and one critic, surprised to hear an opera at the Wells, was even more amazed that, though Barnett had not written down to the audience, the overture had stopped the gods indulging in their usual shouts and catcalls. Even more remarkable, the work had sixty performances in just over two months (how many specially written musical works achieve that number in a repertory theatre today?), though the actors became 'a little slovenly' during the run (not so unusual today).

Mrs. Fitzwilliam not only introduced the vivacious French dancer, eighteen-year-old Madame Celeste, in *The Poetry of Motion*; played the lead in *Charlotte Corday, or, the Revolution*; and presented *Kenilworth* as well as *A View of Scott's Study at Abbotsford* (in which all his principal characters appeared), because of Scott's recent death; she also undoubtedly set out to realize Reeve's frustrated ambition of making the Wells a home for opera in English.

Under her, the usual *Blackeyed Susan*, with Campbell, *Midas*, and Arne's *Judgment of Paris*, were produced, as well as the four-year-old 'Historical Melo-Dramatic Opera' *Masaniello, or, the Dumb Girl of Portici* by Auber (with Freer as Masaniello and Miss Somerville from the English Opera at the Lyceum as Elvira) with the popular Rossini's *Tancredi* overture; Arnold's *Castle of Andalusia*; Mozart's *Figaro* several times, with Miss Somerville as the Countess and Williams as Figaro; and Rossini's *Barber of Seville*.

1832 was a tragic year for old Grimaldi: his son, released the year before from a debtor's prison had, with the help of his father, got an engagement in November at the Queen's Theatre; but after a drunken brawl in a public house off Tottenham Court Road, he died mad on 11th December.

Business at the Wells, 'no longer in that repute it was formerly', had been so negligible for some years that Lloyd Baker was asked to reduce the annual rent by £50, or £100 if the

Wells custom of selling wine, tea and coffee, cakes and sandwiches was stopped, especially as new places of entertainment in the neighbourhood were drawing audiences away from the Wells: a state of affairs that would be worse if, as seemed likely, Parliament passed a Bill proposed by Edward Bulwer of the Reform Party for the licensing of all theatres.

Unfortunately there are no later Wells records in the Lloyd Baker archives; but a mutually satisfactory decision must have been reached as shows went on from Easter 1833 under the actor George Almar, with his fellow-actors Cobham and Robert Honner as Acting and Stage Manager respectively.

Almar was praised for his enterprise, but criticized for his over-advertisement of his artists as flamboyant as the acting of the day—definitely 'penny plain, twopence coloured', as Campbell himself was represented in those popular prints. He dramatized Victor Hugo's novel of that year, *Lucrèce Borgia*, and staged the Cibber-Shakespeare *Richard III*, which, with Cibber's over-theatricalized additional lines, such as 'Off with his head! So much for Buckingham', was highly popular. A description of the average professional actor of the time in that part (as imitated by amateurs who were ready to pay £2 'to exhibit their lamentable ignorance and boobyism on the stage') was given three years later by the twenty-four-year-old Dickens in his *Sketches by Boz*:

> It is very easy to do—'Orf with his ed' (very quick and loud; then slow and sneeringly)—'So much for Bu-u-u-uckingham!' Lay the emphasis on the 'uck', get yourself gradually into a corner, and work with your right hand, while you're saying it, as if you were feeling your way, and it's sure to do. The tent scene is confessedly worth half-a-sovereign, and so you have the fight in, gratis, and everybody knows what an effect may be produced by a good combat. One—two—three—four—over; then, one—two—three—four—under; then thrust; then dodge and slide about; then fall down on one knee; then fight upon it, and then get up again and stagger. You may keep on doing this, as long as it seems to take—say ten minutes—and then fall down (backwards, if you can manage it without hurting yourself), and die game; nothing like it for producing an effect. They always do it at Astley's and Sadler's Wells, and if they don't know how to do this sort of thing, who in the world does?

Such ham acting was, in fact, a mechanical reproduction of Kean's legendary thrilling final fight as Richard, said to have been based on the terrifyingly realistic burnt crawl in the Cherubini-Storace *Lodoiska* at Drury Lane in 1794 by none other than Joey Grimaldi.

In *Eily O'Connor, or, The Banks of Killarney*, from Gerald Griffin's 1828 novel, *The Collegians* (on which the opera *The Lily of Killarney* was later made), Campbell played Danny Mann; *The Man with the Iron Mask* (from the French) was given in November; the great clown, Jefferini, who had appeared at Campbell's benefit the year before, appeared as second clown, Elsgood being the first, with Blanchard as Pantaloon in the December pantomime—which class of entertainment was now restricted to Christmas.

But things at the Wells were not what·they had been, nor were its surroundings. In his autobiography, published in 1834, Tom Dibdin compared the differences: the Wells was now the centre of the 'New Town', though some still thought it so remote from London society that the local *patois* of the inhabitants had to be translated by the watchmen for strangers when lost at night—whereas he remembered that, from the time he first became stage manager of the Wells in 1796 until the 1820s, Myddelton Square (where he wrote his autobiography) had been 'an immense field, where people used to be stopped and robbed on their return in the evening from Sadler's Wells . . . and the ground-floor of the parlour where I sit, was, as nearly as possible, the very spot where my wife and I fell over a recumbent cow on our way home, one murky night, in a thunderstorm: and only regained the solitary path we had strayed from in the dark, by the timely aid of a tremendous flash of lightning'.

By 1834 Almar had regained some of the patronage lost when Joey Grimaldi retired, though when the audience, as they often did (no doubt inspired by the way he waved his arms about like the sails of a windmill when he acted), barked, howled, hooted and hissed at 'some of the most boney, battle-axey and bloody rubbish, that was ever penned', he 'rushed hysterically forward, and darting a glance of rabid fury around the premises, spoke incoherently about the difficulty of obtaining a crust, and hopped off with a frightful air of incipient insanity'. He also knew no restraint when advertising his bloodcurdlers, such as *The Skeleton*

Hand or *The Vampire*, with the picture of a devilish female pouncing on a man and the caption:

> 'Ha! she comes—oh! she seizes me—oh, God!—Lorks, she clutches my throat. Crikey—oh! she chokes me! ah! ah! oh!— I die-ie-ie-ie! oh—ie—oh—ie—oh! oh! oh!

—and an added 'Come Early'.

Yet at the same time Almar appealed to the respectable part of the house by inaugurating conversational advertisement, such as we are so often given in commercial television:

> 'Now, my Dear Thomas, you know you have promised to take me to Sadler's Wells a long time, so take me on Tuesday 16th, there'll be such Beautiful Pieces Performed. You will go with me my Dear, you won't refuse, will you?'

Or, for the cheaper parts of the house:

> 'Oh! Crikey Bill! have you seen what prime pieces there are out at Sadler's Wells Next Tuesday! . . . if you want to get a seat you'd better be in Time for there is enough of my Pals going to fill the Gallery!'

Almar had such a double personality that on one occasion he and his brother Frederick were seen near the boxes punching Mr. Young, the scene-painter, and yet he had the saloon re-decorated like a Chinese Pavilion and presented worthwhile drama such as the first Wells *Hamlet* on 12th May, a dramatic version of Richardson's *Pamela, or, Virtue Rewarded* on the 26th, and in October *The Merchant of Venice*, Sheridan's *Pizarro*, and *The Stranger* by Kotzebue.

Almar's growing failure was reflected in the lowering of both prices and standards in 1835. By May pit and box seats were 1s. 6d. and 2s. 6d. respectively; the titles of the plays (*The Horrors of the Bastille*; or *Dromio, the Drinker, or, the Death Struggle*, with Kemp from the Bowery Theatre, New York, 'a rank amateur'), as well as the way they were performed, were indicative of decay.

Richard III was played by ten-year-old Master H. Smith ('the infant Kean') and a band of juveniles; in *As you Like It* the 'uncommon tall' Rosalind was a foot shorter than Celia: in fact, Almar was advised by the Press to stick to his blue-fire and battle-axes or write over the theatre door Dante's 'Give up hope, all you who enter here'.

In *The Infernal Machine, or, the French Regicides*, about recent attempts to murder Louis-Philippe, the Citizen-King himself appeared in the impenetrable disguise of a Marshal in full uniform complete with feathered hat, attended by torch-bearers, and overheard several conspirators safely hidden in the middle of the street with the gas-light blazing on their faces and interrupting their machinations only to finish a quadrille; and while twenty-five gun-barrels were threatening princes of the blood, 'Numerous Mademoiselles, rejoicing in symmetrical ancles, and a brevity of petticoats truly modest, foot it unconcernedly.' Nor were the dramas better written. In *William the Weaver* (by the Dibdins' nephew, Dibdin Pitt), a husband falsely accused of a murder thirty years before, was regaled by his still-young wife with a tedious recitation about a dulcet lyre. Why not two books of *Paradise Lost*, the Press said.

Nobody would take complete charge of the Wells in the next two years (seats were still cheaper—from 2s. down to 6d., and at half-price time the pit and gallery were free). Almar gave up in 1836 and D. W. Osbaldiston, 'far the best actor that has trod these boards for many years', brought part of his Covent Garden company for two months, playing Sheridan Knowles's *Virginius*, *William Tell*, and *Macbeth*, and gave *Eugene Aram*, based on Edward Bulwer's 1832 novel.

The little comedian William Rogers then took the theatre with T. P. Taylor for three months, producing *The Wife* by Sheridan Knowles, *Jane Shore*, *Rob Roy*, and Bishop's opera *Guy Mannering*. Next Nelson Lee tried it from August 1836 to March 1837 with *Jack Sheppard*, *Richard III*, *Clari*, *Othello*, even *King Lear* with Elton, the brilliant scholar-actor who could never express all he felt, and *Henry IV* 'never acted here' before with Campbell as Falstaff.

To act such plays to a hard-drinking audience with babies squalling must have been discouraging—what can such an audience have thought of the lovely ballad-singing of the famous Mrs. Waylett? But we can admire those managers for making the attempt—especially Rogers and Taylor who came back from Easter 1837 for the rest of the year, first giving shows such as *Boz, or, the Pickwick Club* (the book had been published that year), *The Inchcape Bell*, and Rogers's own *Cyril Woodbine, or, the Old Elm Grove* (on the perils of drunkenness). Then they boldly engaged for one week the St. Pancras-born actor (one-time rival to Kean) who had made his name in America since 1821, the great Junius Brutus Booth, father of the future famous actor Edwin Booth and of the later notorious John Wilkes Booth, murderer of Abraham Lincoln. He played the leads in *Brutus, or the Fall of Tarquin, Hamlet,* and *A New Way to Pay Old Debts,* which were given in addition to *The Children in the Wood, Ivanhoe, or, the Jew's Daughter,* and *Wallace, the Hero of Scotland.*

By now all children over three were charged admission for shows as varied as *Marmion, Jane Shore, Douglas,* even *Heloise and Abelard* and 'an entirely New Native Black Opera, by the Author of "Jim Crow" entitled *Fair Rosamond* ("a Black with songs")'.

In the summer the Wells actors with some from Covent Garden, not Macready, but George Bennett, Pritchard and Mrs. W. West, gave a remarkable programme that included *King John* (a daring choice for an audience not too used to Shakespeare), *Rob Roy, Katherine and Petruchio, The Merchant of Venice, Romeo and Juliet,* and *Julius Caesar.*

Early in July most papers carelessly reported that Mrs. Graham went up in a balloon again at the Wells, whereas in fact her husband went up in her place. This change was no doubt due to the after-effects from a hundred-foot fall the year before while pregnant—a bold aeronaut indeed. Now thirty-three, she was the mother of seven children, but this baby was born dead.

The combined actors in July appeared in *Robert Macaire*; *The Wonder,* by Mrs. Centlivre; *The Castle of Andalusia*; *Timour the Tartar*; *The School for Scandal,* with Benjamin Webster of the Adelphi and Mrs. West as Sir Peter and Lady Teazle ('Victoria our Queen, and England for ever' was sung—a month after her accession); and Shield's opera *Rosina.* In November Mrs. West played *Hamlet.*

Grimaldi had finished his life-story on 18th December 1836, happy to write (though this was found only after his death), 'I cannot recollect one single instance in which I have intentionally wronged man, woman, or child, and this gives me great satisfaction'. On 18th January 1837 he sat at the back of a box during Nelson Lee's pantomime *Fee-Fo-Fum!!!, or, Harlequin Te-To-Tum!!!,* but Jefferini, the clown, pointed him out and the audience so cheered that after some persuasion Grimaldi, in tears, leaning on a friend's shoulder, said:

> You may judge the feelings of one who has travelled through the world of pantomime, and reached the declining years of life without losing one jot of his enthusiasm . . . Years have passed since I had the honour of addressing you and in all probability for the last time. Had I been prepared for this, I should have endeavoured to acquit myself more creditably. I came here but to oblige the manager, and to look once more on scenes which I—

Here he paused, choking with emotion, and hastily throwing out his arms towards the house in a gesture of affection he cried, 'God bless you all! God bless you all!'

He supervised a reproduction of the famous *Mother Goose*, with Jefferini in his own old part, for 15th May; but on 31st May, just over fifty-eight years old, he died at 33 Southampton Street, Pentonville. Five days later he was buried in the churchyard of St. James's Church. Till fairly recently, clowns and variety circus artists from all parts used to go there annually to honour his memory.

As his old friend, the once-famed theatrical engraver Henry Brown (still living in 1881), said, he was no mere clown:

> He was a great comedian born, and in this lay the secret of his superiority over all his rivals in this branch of the profession. And a really kind heart, an even temper, combined with a most child-like simplicity of character, caused him to be as universally beloved in private as he was admired in public.

It must not be forgotten (as it usually is) that originally he was a fine straight actor—his Wild Man alone shows that. 'The Garrick of Pantomime' he was called (and Garrick was one of the few tragedians brilliant in comedy), while a contemporary said, 'We rank the genius of Grimaldi with that of Kean', and *Bell's Weekly Messenger* took leave of him with the following lines:

> The curtain falls—Life's last sad scene is o'er,
> Poor Joe Grimaldi falls to rise no more . . .
> Ye countless thousands, who for forty years
> Bestowed your laughter, now bestow your tears.
> Nor strive your honest feelings to suppress
> For one who laboured for your happiness,
> And in the service, 'stead of golden gain,
> Earned ten long years of unremitted pain.

CHAPTER TEN

AT LOW EBB

1838–1843

THE YEAR 1838 started well when Osbaldiston, having left Covent Garden the year before, moved over again to the Wells. This time he did not bring Covent Garden artists with him, relying on Campbell, little Rogers and others, but especially on his mistress, Miss Vincent, now returning to the stage where she had started as a precocious child fourteen years before: these he advertised in the Dibdin manner with 'New Management! New Music! New Pieces! New scenery! New dressed!' (as well as 'Warm Air Stoves'): again the announcement of new décor, all the more necessary now that Madame Vestris had recently set an example with different and accurate designs for each show.

The new pieces were not remarkable, except for *Esmeralda, the Gypsy Girl of Notre Dame* (from Victor Hugo's 1831 novel), with Miss Vincent as Esmeralda and Campbell as the grotesque Quasimodo, and a version of Edward Bulwer's 1830 novel *Paul Clifford*. Miss Vincent also played Macheath in *The Beggar's Opera*, while Campbell played the Wild Man in the old *Valentine and Orson*, and Osbaldiston himself appeared as *Richard III* and as Pierre in *Venice Preserved* with Mrs. West as Belvidera. He also presented *Pizarro* and *Rob Roy*, and for the now insolvent Almar kindly produced his *Earl of Poverty, or, the Old Wooden House of London Wall*.

But Osbaldiston did not stay, and the Wells started on a more lasting phase at Easter 1838 when Robert William Honner, late acting and stage manager of the Surrey Theatre, who had acted and produced at the Wells five years before, became the lessee. He collected a respectable company—J. Webster of the St. James's, the veteran Williams of the Haymarket, Cathcart from Dublin, Conquest from the Olympic, and C. J. Smith from Covent Garden, with less-known ladies headed by Miss Waylett's rival, Miss E. Honner (his sister?), and his wife, 'a gem that any Manager might be chary of—we mean, as regards her histrionic worth'. His heads of departments too were carefully chosen, while he was in complete charge of the stage.

The theatre, now called the Theatre Royal, Sadler's Wells, was redecorated for the opening on Whit Monday, 4th June; but Honner unfortunately chose shows with good parts for himself and, in particular, for his wife. He was criticized for dictating to the public and relying only on melodramas to fill his coffers at the cheap prices still charged; yet he got the Wells known again.

He forged links with the past by bringing back Jack Bologna for the first time for fifteen years and including Dibdin Pitt among his actors, and kept up to date with contemporary dramas such as Leman Rede's successful *Kohal Cave*; Lacy's *Leila, the Maid of the Alhambra, or, the Siege of Grenada*, from that year's novel by Bulwer (just made a baronet as Sir Edward Lytton Bulwer); Douglas Jerrold's *The Hazard of the Die*; and his own adaptation of another novel, also just published that same year, *Oliver Twist*, in which Dickens wrote that the Artful Dodger, scudding at a rapid pace with Oliver at his heels, reached the turnpike at Islington at nearly eleven o'clock: 'They crossed from the Angel into St. John's Road; struck down the small street which terminates at Sadler's Wells Theatre—' and then went on through Exmouth Street (as it was then) and Coppice Row to Saffron Hill.

Mrs. Honner's Oliver increased her reputation for natural acting, J. Lee (Tyrone Power's rival as an Irishman) was Bill Sykes, and Honner himself played Fagin well: but the critic wondered what had become of the melodiously voiced Miss E. Honner and whether it was true that Honner was giving up at the end of the season, as was rumoured. The first question cannot be answered beyond guessing at family jealousy, but the second was certainly untrue—he represented the Wells at the first general meeting of the new Dramatic Association of all theatres under the chairmanship of Ben Webster, now of the Haymarket, and was praised as a spirited manager under whom the Wells was doing wonders.

He made a great success with Dibdin's arrangement of *The Heart of Midlothian*, with Mrs. Honner as Jeanie Deans; with

Robert Macaire, in which Conquest played Jaques Strop; and with *The Vampire*; while for his benefit the famous T. P. Cooke came to act his original part of William in *Blackeyed Susan*. He introduced the brilliant new scene-designer Telbin, and was so sure of himself that in advertising his Christmas pantomime, *Little Tommy Tucker*, he must have surprised the new young Queen Victoria, who was crowned that year, by putting words into her mouth:

> Attention! vociferated Her Majesty, (from her carriage at Buckingham Palace to her admiring subjects).
> Attention! echoed the loyal thousands to their beloved Queen, (and a dead silence prevailed).
> I would enquire, (said her Majesty, with a countenance beaming with delight,) how many of my subjects have witnessed at our Theatre Royal, Sadler's Wells, in our good village of Islington, the very splendid and clever pantomime at this festive season?
> One hundred and thirty thousand, responded the people.
> There are then three millions of my subjects in London still to be delighted with it: it is therefore my command! (said Her Majesty, assuming her usual dignified and impressive tone,) it is MY command! that the whole body of my people, from night to night, do participate in the enjoyment, by witnessing the best pantomime in London!
> With one universal exclamation the people shouted God bless your Majesty! We will!! And they are nightly in thousands obeying the Royal Command.
>   VIVAT REGINA.

Not that Honner found his task easy. He had to rebuke Conquest and Cathcart 'for what is called larking, whilst the clever Mrs. Honner was playing a serious part', but could not get rid of them: they, with Williams, were said to be 'the chief pillars of the establishment. Mrs. Honner plays a great deal too much either for her own fame or the gratification of the audience.' All the same, Mrs. Honner—like Mrs. Dibdin before her—still commandeered the best leading parts.

But before dismissing the Honners as the Mr. and Mrs. Crummles of a London Minor Theatre, it should be realized how much they did to keep the drama alive in 1839. It is true that at Covent Garden Macready (who had taken over from Osbaldiston two years before) was presenting Shakespeare, good modern plays, melodramas, operas, farces and panto-

mimes, but at the other so-called National Theatre of Drury
Lane Mr. Bunn, having added to that mixture acrobatics and
equestrian dramas with Ducrow's horses, was now displaying
Van Amburgh's famous performing wild animals both on the
stage and at feeding time—Queen Victoria herself went to see
them three times in a fortnight, and the Duke of Wellington and
all society naturally followed where she led.

All the more praiseworthy, then, that in January 1839 the
Wells was said to be becoming daily a more favourite place of
entertainment than before, and that Honner did his best to keep
up dramatic standards, in spite of being attacked by the once
favourable *Town*: this accused him of allowing his 'weak-
minded, illiterate, foolish' little ballad-singer friend, George
'Cocky' Robinson, to 'bounce so much' as if he owned the
Wells (he once, unrebuked, struck one of the audience in Honner's presence).

But even if it were true that Honner was not solely in charge,
things went so well that the Wells was open even on Wednes-
days and Fridays all through Lent, and the shows were of considerable interest, varied as they were—the locally historical
St. John's Priory (the Gate was then threatened with demoli-
tion, but still stands today, looking like a film-set); *The Flying
Dutchman* (revived for Honner to play Vanderdecken); Sheridan's *Pizarro*; the new domestic drama *Grace Huntley*; the historical *Rock of St. Helena!, or, Napoleon in Exile!*; *The Iron
Chest* by George Colman; two new plays by Sheridan Knowles
(*The Hunchback*) and Douglas Jerrold (*The Painter of Ghent*);
the peculiar mixture of Neapolitan Brothers in a Chinese
Grotesque Dance and a Cornish Clog Hornpipe; and at Easter
the pantomime *Sawney Beane, or, Harlequin and the Man-Eater*.

In April both the Wells and Honner were praised by the
Press: the theatre with its row of tall poplars, still countrified
in spite of houses round it, was all cheerfulness and comfort
inside and, though only a few months before no respectable persons would visit it, they now filled the boxes, which were so
well managed by Honner's brother with young, good-looking
educated attendants that they were the *ne plus ultra*, and nobody
left the theatre till the final curtain.

Honner persisted with his worthwhile plays—*Othello, Richard
III, Venice Preserved, Hamlet, Merchant of Venice*—with male

leads by the guest artist Elton, or Cathcart, Marston, or Honner himself, with Mrs. Honner always to the fore.

He was playing in *The Flying Dutchman* in August when Wagner visited London for the first time after a terrifyingly stormy crossing of the North Sea. Unfortunately on this visit Wagner avoided the theatre ('von den Theatern besuchte ich keine', he wrote in *Lehr und Wanderjahr*), and so did not see it. There are several similarities between play and opera versions of the story—the picture, the Dutchman taking a wife (both pointed out by Francis Hueffer in the *Great Musicians* series), maybe the heroine's song at her first appearance, but especially (and most remarkable of all) the striking silence of the Dutchman, so brilliantly exploited by Wagner at the first meetings with both Daland and Senta, with a dramatic outburst at the end of both play and opera.

Yet it was the Wells that planted those touches in Wagner's first typical work, for Heine (who gave the idea to Wagner) had found, as he wrote, the theatre his chief resource when in London in 1827. Having missed the Adelphi production, as can be seen by a comparison of dates, he must have heard much about this talked-of play and seized the opportunity of seeing Tom Dibdin's production at the Wells with young J. S. Grimaldi miming that essentially non-speaking part.

The outstanding new play of the season was Greenwood's version of Harrison Ainsworth's *Jack Sheppard* (published the same year) which was better than the six other versions rushed out (there being no copyright) because the author had attended rehearsals and George Cruikshank had sketched the costumes and made suggestions for the settings: Mrs. Honner was admirable in the first part as the impudent boy of thirteen, her husband excellent in the second part, and the storm was well managed, 'the canvass coming over the stage nearly to the gaslights'.

On Younge's benefit night Miss Mitford's play *Rienzi* was produced; but at the end of the year *Town* had further hits at 'dirty Bob Honner' and not unreasonably: he refused the pantomime audience their usual right to call for extra songs such as 'Hot Codlins' which he considered 'obsolete' and, so that he could superintend Madame Vestris's pantomime at Covent Garden, closed the Wells for eleven nights before Christmas, thereby 'taking bread out of the mouths of nearly a hundred persons, who compose his valuable and faithful company, at a time when their respective salaries would have been of the utmost service to them'. He was supposed to have said, 'I'll take care of *number one.*'

In spite of this temporary closing, Honner did not let the standard down in 1840. He played Dick Turpin in *The Death Omen, or, the Wizard Tree*, Ainsworth's novel *Rookwood* dramatized complete with the ride to York; and presented *Hamlet* with both Elton and Henry Marston from Drury Lane. Marston was such a success he was asked back for a version of the elder Dumas's play of 1832, *The Tower of Nesle, or, the Black Gondola*, and stayed on permanently.

Marston's unnaturally husky voice may have stopped his attaining real distinction (as William Archer afterwards wrote), but he had great successes as Orlando in *As You Like It*, as Triboulet the Jester in *The Curse of St. Vallier, or, the Jester's Daughter* (Hugo's 1832 play *Le Roi S'Amuse*, better known today as *Rigoletto*), and as the chief characters in *The Wife*; *Rob Roy, or, Auld Lang Syne*; *George Barnwell*, and *Katherine and Petruchio*.

He also played one part of great local interest—the murderer in 'an entirely New & Extraordinary Romantic, Local, Legendary Drama, in Three Acts (founded on Facts that occurred in the year 1712, on the very spot on which this Theatre now stands) entitled *The Ruby Ring, or, the Murder at Sadler's Wells'*. This was T. E. Wilks's version of the murder 'near the organloft' with the characters Francis Forcer, the murdered man Lt. Waite, the murderer French, and La Belle Espagnole, while the scenes included the exterior of the theatre in 1712 with the 'celebrated Chalybeate Well', the interior (anachronistically of 1765) with the seats holding bottles and glasses, and the Sir Hugh Myddelton Tavern (the ruby ring that brought ill luck to anyone who wore it, came from a 1673 Hamburg story of the learned Jew, Eleazer of Bruges).

Among other 1840 productions were a ballet, *La Sonnambula*, Boz's *Master Humphrey's Clock*, and a pantomime with a tableau of the young Victoria and Prince Albert, whom she had married on 10th February of this year.

As a contrast Honner also introduced the American Lion King, Mr. Carter, superior to the famous Van Amburgh because:

> He will take the Untamed Lion by the Throat! Do battle with a wild Leopard! And make the Fierce and Ravenous Tiger crouch at his Feet, like a beaten Hound. He will sleep upon a fierce Numidian Lion, His Head pillowed on the Leopard's Glossy Back, While at his feet, the Tiger lies subdued, as though it watched his slumbers.

The continual presentation in unlicensed theatres of spoken dramas instead of dramas accompanied by music did not go unnoticed, and the antagonistic *Town*—ostensibly attacking Honner for not paying the singer Mr. H. Hall on his refusal to act other than according to his contract—accused him of illegally presenting dramas not permitted by the Act of 25 Geo. II— 'a tolerable sample of *Honner*-able management'.

So on 13th February 1841, after productions of Mark Lemon's domestic drama *Gwynneth Vaughan* and *Little Nell, or, the Old Curiosity Shop* (only just published), the management was taken to court. Special reference was made to the 1838 summer season when Osbaldiston presented Covent Garden actors, and on seventy-nine counts penalties of nearly £4,000 were demanded.

Campbell, as Stage Manager at that time, proved that Osbaldiston had ordered such pieces and acted himself, but claimed there was no proof that he had had any reward for his services: the defending counsel, Kelly, did not plead that such efforts had been unremunerative, but maintained there must be proof all through, and the jury brought in a verdict for the defence.

This gave Honner confidence and, though in 1841 he presented Ducrow with his gymnasts and trained horses in his Drury Lane piece, *His Horse of the Pyrenees, or, Moors in Spain*, and the novelty of 'W. Cox's Dissolving Views! Illumined by the Celebrated Oxy-hydrogen Lime Light!', he presented in addition to the usual plays Mark Lemon's successful *Self-Accusation*; Leman Rede's *The Skeleton Witness*; Holcroft's *Road to Ruin*; the 'Petite Opera' *The Swiss Cottage* (Donizetti's *Betly*); and a dramatization of *Barnaby Rudge, or, the Murder of the Warren*. Mrs. Honner played the heroine to her husband's hero in W. T. Moncrieff's entirely New, Grand, Melo-dramatic, Choreographic, Fantastique, Traditionary Tale of Superstition (in Two Acts) founded on the singularly wild and impressive Ballet Pantomime now performing at the Grand Opera in Paris under the title of 'Giselle, ou Les Wilis'.

The Wells dramatic version in August was called *Giselle, or, the Night Dancers* and, with the original music by Adolphe Adam adapted by Collins, ballets by Frampton, and real water in the last scene, it was one of the greatest triumphs at the Wells.

A month later—a week after the death of Tom Dibdin—standards dropped with Almar's *Jack Ketch*, of which one critic wrote:

> This, then, is the state to which the founders of the Newgate school of dramatic literature, and the march of intellect, have brought us. Nothing short of actual hanging—the most revolting and repulsive of all possible subjects to enter, much less to dwell in any mind not actually savage—must now be provided to meet the refined taste of play-goers—the veriest mess of incoherent rubbish that was ever shot upon the plains of common sense.

In the winter the low prices failed to make a burlesque *Othello According to Act of Parliament*, *Othello* itself, and Colman's *Jealous Wife* pay; so three weeks after Easter 1842, by order of 'the Assignees of Richard Hughes, a bankrupt, and with the concurrence of the Mortgagee', an auction was announced of 10/40 shares in the lease of the Wells (twenty-one years from 1833 at the low rent of £338 per annum and sublet to Honner at a yearly £1,000) 'together with its appropriate and well-arranged Stage Machinery, Scenes, etc.'

Honner carried on till the summer but, as he had perhaps been warned not to jeopardize the proposed new Act of Parliament that might license the Minor Theatres for straight drama, he presented only melodramas, mostly with Ducrow's horses— *Harry of England, or, the Battle of Agincourt*; *The Battle of Waterloo*; *Mazeppa*; *Lalla Rookh*; and *St. George and the Dragon, or, the Seven Champions of Christendom* (with the fight that lasted a quarter of an hour). So crammed was the theatre for these performances that only the better ventilation of the Wells than of many other theatres prevented half the audience from being suffocated.

But though Honner grandly called the Wells 'The Theatre Royal, Sadler's Wells and the New Amphitheatre of Arts, under the Patronage of Her Most Gracious Majesty the Queen' (though evidently not with authority, as it had been under William IV, because the advertisements did not include those words for long), he gave up at the end of August, and his Acting Manager and writer, Thomas Greenwood (son of the scenic artist, and the fourth generation of that Wells family) became the Manager, with Henry Marston as Stage Manager and chief actor, performing Minor Theatre melodramas—except on benefit nights when dramas could be given.

Still, things were changing. The theatre gardens had been built over, though the New River still ran by its side (Greenwood had to ask servants of the richer members of the audience to turn their horses *heads* towards the river!) and, while drama was not yet legal, music was increasingly important. There was a tentative concert in March 1843 with the contralto Fanny Wilton (who later married the famous opera-singer Lablache), the composer John Barnett's tenor brother, Joseph; songs from *Fra Diavolo*, lightened by comic duets and Nigger Songs by Abdel Ada, who also did gymnastics with her two infant sons. Later, on a benefit night, a scene from *La Sonnambula* was given with the well-known tenor, Henry Robinson Allen.

Then two things happened in 1843 that materially helped to save the dilapidated Wells from disaster.

Earlier that year the fine, scholarly actor, 'little Elton', so popular as a guest at the Wells, had been one of the victims in the foundering of the *Pegasus* off Holy Isle on the way to America; so to aid his family—a blind father, a wife, and seven children—a benefit night was given with a performance of *Othello*. In this the popular young Wells actress Caroline Rankley played Desdemona, Henry Marston Iago, and from Henry Wallack's Covent Garden company two performers who had previously been at Drury Lane with the recently retired Macready: Mrs. Warner (generally hailed as the modern Mrs. Siddons), who played Emilia, and Samuel Phelps as Othello.

As Phelps himself later recorded about that performance:

> The Wells at that period had sunk to the lowest ebb. The business was so awful that the company were playing down to two or

three pounds a night, and there was the greatest difficulty in
keeping the doors open at all . . .

To the astonishment and delight of everyone the receipts
amounted to fifty-five pounds.

That house and that performance decided my career for the
next eighteen years!

To say that they leaped at us would give but the faintest idea
of the enthusiasm with which we were received.

Tom Greenwood was the manager, and when we settled up,
he said, 'This is going to be a big thing. Come and act here, and
I'll give you twenty pounds a week'.

I had no engagement in view, nor any likelihood of obtaining
one, but I knew that Greenwood had no money, so I took stock
of the situation at once.

'My good fellow', said I, 'don't talk nonsense; I know the
state of the land here, and what you are doing. If the money
don't come in, you can't pay. I'll tell you what I'll do; if you'll
undertake to secure the theatre, we'll go into partnership!'

Greenwood jumped at the idea, and forty-eight hours later
the management by Phelps, Mrs. Warner, and Greenwood was
planned—the first two to have £20 a week each, Mr. Warner
(as a sweetener to her) £5 a week as Treasurer, and Greenwood £5 as Acting Manager and £5 for his Wardrobe—all to
be charged to the current expenses on the weekly pay-sheet, but
variable pro rata according to takings.

The whole project would obviously be more secure when, as
seemed likely, the imminent Bill licensing the Minor Theatres
was passed. So in the meantime Phelps took an engagement up
north, and Greenwood carried on at the Wells from Easter with
popular shows including *The Heart of Midlothian* with the much
liked Mrs. Fitzwilliam, just returned from America.

There was also one extraordinary and full evening when, in
addition to a version of *The Artful Dodger* and Cumberland's
Elf of the Eddystone Lighthouse, one Stafford Smith, a fifty-two-
year-old amateur, formerly trained, he said, by the Opera House
Ballet-Master, gave such a ludicrous performance of *Richard III*
that it was greeted throughout with hoots of laughter and
shouts of advice from his self-indulgent acquaintances, especially
in his final balletic fight: this was loudly encored with cries of
'Put the poor devil out of his misery!' 'Can't you let him die in
peace?' 'His mother ought to be sent for, or, at all events, his
nurse'. When he was called before the curtain at the end, he was

greeted with bouquets and laughter, but he withstood the ironic cheers with great nerve and acknowledged the very equivocal ovation by repeated *salaams* and *congés*, 'which cannot be appreciated for their singularity without having been witnessed'.

Then at last on 22nd August came the other significant event of 1843. The Theatres Act, which Bulwer had so championed, was passed: this licensed all theatres in London and Westminster, Finsbury, Marylebone, Tower Hamlets, Lambeth and Southwark to act regular drama, putting them under the authority of the Lord Chamberlain just like Covent Garden, Drury Lane, and, in the summer, the Haymarket.

So on 16th October 1843 the Wells opened with the announcement for the first time:

> Licensed by the Lord High Chamberlain under the Act 6 & 7 Vic. Cap. 68. Under the Management of Thomas Longden Greenwood, Melbourne Cottage, White Hart Lane, Tottenham.

CHAPTER ELEVEN

PHELPS TO THE RESCUE

1844–1846

VERY wisely Greenwood kept secret the plans he had made with Phelps and the Warners, producing equestrian drama before the Christmas benefits began, and then over the holidays presenting Marston in the melodrama *Alive or Dead* with the pantomime and a farce, all three of which ran well into the New Year.

In February 1844 the dramatization of Dickens's *A Christmas Carol*, published in 1843, was given as *Old Scrooge*, with Marston in the name-part; while *The Wrecker's Daughter* by Sheridan Knowles and, on benefit nights, *The Wonder* and Moore's *Gamester* were also given.

There was also a remarkable concert on 1st March in aid of the 'Hope' Benevolent Institution at which the following artists appeared: Emma Romer (a fine soprano who later presented opera at the Surrey); Charlotte Dolby[1] (for whom Mendelssohn wrote the contralto part in *Elijah* two years later); Emma Lucombe (who later married the great Sims Reeves); the famous John Braham (now seventy, back on the stage where he had sung fifty-six years before) and his twenty-two-year-old son Charles (both just back from an unsuccessful American tour); Frederick Crouch (singer, 'cellist, and composer of 'Kathleen Mavourneen'); Adam Leffler (a Westminster Abbey chorister and opera-singer with a huge range from E below the stave to the G above it); John Parry (well known for his ballad-singing); and thirty ladies and gentlemen of the Sacred Harmonic Society directed by George Stansbury at the piano.

For the ordinary performances business, the Press said, had been 'wretched bad', the theatre open only 'four days last week', and the writer was heartily sorry for Greenwood. One paper,

---

[1] Later known as Sainton-Dolby. At the Royal Academy of Music both a prize and a scholarship are still given in her name.

133

remarking that poor old Sadler's Wells had been for some time in the market, mentioned the rumour that Greenwood might risk taking it again and that the 'sex-decimal-sided building' might be pulled down and rebuilt, which, having been built eighty years ago of old materials, was a consummation devoutly to be wished.

But nobody guessed that the new régime would start, as it did, on Whit Monday, 27th May 1844, after a few alterations outside and inside. Even the new triumvirate felt none too sure. Their opening announcement read:

> Mrs. Warner and Mr. Phelps have embarked in the manage-
> ment and performance of Sadler's Wells Theatre in the hope of
> eventually rendering it what a theatre ought to be—a place for
> justly representing the works of our great dramatic poets. This
> undertaking is commenced at a time when the stages which have
> been exclusively called 'National' are closed, or devoted to very
> different objects from that of presenting the real drama of
> England, and when the law has placed all theatres upon an equal
> footing of security and respectability. . . . These circumstances
> justify the notion that each separate division of our immense
> metropolis, with its two million of inhabitants, may have its own
> well-conducted theatre, within a reasonable distance of the patrons.

Such theatres, they added, should be places 'where all can see and hear at a price fairly within the habitual means of all'. At the same time, while naming *Macbeth* as their opening play, lest it should fail they underlined on the bills their preparation of a new melodrama of the blue-fire species.

After all, not only did a new kind of show have to be estab-lished, but a new kind of audience also. As Dickens wrote in *Household Words* in 1851:

> Seven or eight years ago, this theatre was in the condition of
> being entirely delivered over to as ruffianly an audience as Lon-
> don could shake together. Without, the theatre by night was like
> the worst of the worst kind of fair in the worst kind of town.
> Within, it was a bear-garden, resounding with foul language,
> oaths, catcall shrieks, yells, blasphemy, obscenity—a truly dia-
> bolical clamour. Fights took place anywhere, at any period of
> the performance.

He then refers to the 'improving melodrama' *Jack Ketch* of 1841, and says the management had even contemplated adding 'the physical stimulus of a pint of porter to the moral refreshments offered to every purchaser of a pit ticket, when the management collapsed'. Dickens was wrong in saying the theatre shut up; and he was doubly wrong in saying that Phelps had then 'conceived the desperate idea of changing the character of the dramatic entertainments presented at this den, from the lowest to the highest, and of utterly changing, with it, the character of the audience' and so 'took the theatre and went to work' assisted by Greenwood and Mrs. Warner. As Phelps's own account has shown (perhaps generously), the idea came from Greenwood who was certainly responsible for taking the theatre, and it all happened two years after *Jack Ketch*—but Dickens's version makes more dramatic reading.

Certainly the first night was dramatic enough. The new triumvirate, hoping for a more respectable audience, had looked with qualms at the fair held nightly in the long avenue leading to the theatre from St. John's-Street-road because it was patronized by thieves and courtesans and scared away decent people; so the management took steps with a result described in an article of 1875:

> The showmen, the proprietors of 'shooting-galleries', of 'dollies', of roulette-tables, and other petty gambling arrangements—to say nothing of the exhibitors of pig-faced ladies, Dorsetshire giants, fat babies, and the like—had all been ordered off the premises. Consequently, they vowed vengeance against the new management, and, when the doors opened, crowded into the gallery with the one object of interrupting the performance.

This explanation was left out of Dickens's description of the first night of *Macbeth*, but it does explain the happenings as he described them in the article already quoted:

> It was performed amidst the usual hideous medley of fights, foul language, catcalls, shrieks, yells, oaths, blasphemy, obscenity, apples, oranges, nuts, biscuits, ginger-beer, porter, and pipes—pipes of every description were at work in the gallery, and pipes of all sorts and sizes were in full blast in the pit. Cans of beer, each with a pint measure to drink from (for the convenience of gentlemen who had neglected the precaution of bringing their own pots in their bundles), were carried through the dense crowd at all stages of the tragedy. Sickly children in arms were squeezed out of shape in all parts of the house. Fish was fried at the entrance doors. Barricades of oyster-shells encumbered the pavement. Expectant half-price visitors to the gallery howled defiant impatience up the stairs, and danced a sort of carmagnole round the building.

It being evident either that the attempt to humanize the place must be abandoned, or this uproar quelled—that Mr. Ketch's disciples must have their way, or the manager his—the manager made vigorous efforts for the victory.

There is a story that after the first act Macbeth, having spotted the ringleader from the stage, appeared in the gallery in costume and literally lifted him out of the auditorium, so that there was an instant revulsion: someone called 'Three cheers for Phelps!' which were heartily given, and the rest of the play was heard quietly.

That there was such an atmosphere round the Wells explains why on occasion there had been Press antagonism, especially when lower types of entertainment seemed to encourage it. All the more credit is therefore due to those who had tried to present worthwhile shows certainly from Rosoman and even to Honner, proving that for good works a respectable audience would risk such surroundings.

At the same time, seeing that today a Shakespeare audience has for many years meant a quiet collection of attentive people, the Phelps classical seasons at the Wells suggest to most people 'something like the Old Vic'. How wrong that is! Even when Phelps had trained the Wells audience to be attentive, as he did, he still had to act with the pittites (only one degree less rough than the gallery) crowded on hard benches right up to the stage, some eating apples, oranges, and nuts, some drinking ginger beer or stout bought with bills of the play printed in ink that stained the finger, all sold between the acts by shrill, discordant-voiced women.

Whether or not this is how the theatrical phrase originated, every actor had to 'get over' not only the footlights but also this eager and outspoken cheaper part of the audience in order to get into contact with the presumably better educated folk in the boxes and circle, and so hold the whole house.

It is also only those interested in theatre history who know that, when Phelps went to the Wells, the proscenium was almost a little house, as Clement Scott recalled:

> On either side of the stage proper a little green door with brass knockers and handles, and over each door a window with lace curtains and a balcony with flower pots on it. These proscenium doors were never used, except occasionally in pantomime for the

purposes of the play, but no one dreamed of taking a call or of coming on to make a managerial speech except through these little doors.

Again, it is not generally known that Phelps respected the old custom of always playing tragedy on a green-baize carpet which, Scott said, 'was calculated to give the young playgoer a shudder, no matter if it were *Hamlet* or *The Iron Chest*. We knew then that we were in for it, and that the fatal green baize would sooner or later be strewn with corpses'.

It is also incorrect to speak of Phelps's Shakespeare seasons at the Wells—they never existed as such. He certainly produced thirty-one of Shakespeare's thirty-four canonic plays in fourteen years, but in accordance with the plan to present 'the works of our great dramatic poets' he also produced seventy-one other famous plays both old and recent, as well as eleven new poetic dramas—116 worthwhile plays, an average of over eight new productions a year, a repertory far in extent beyond any we have known in the present century.

Nor was a poetic drama the only entertainment in an evening. Each was followed—even *Hamlet*—by, say, an operetta and a farce, or a pantomime. As a rule the leading actors appeared only in the major plays, but to allow for the lighter shows even the classics had to be judiciously pruned, though a theatre-evening lasted longer than nowadays.

Macbeth, the first production (which was followed by an operetta *The Hunter's Bride* and a farce by Greenwood, *A Row in the Buildings*), was not pure Shakespeare but had Middleton's usual additions (such as Hecate, who with two of the witches sang in the operetta) and included Matthew Locke's vocal and instrumental music of 1672 played proficiently by Isaac Collins and his five talented sons, as one critic said.

The same critic recorded that the dagger scene was greeted with a peal of applause; but more illuminating was the notice in the *Athenæum* for 'this almost forgotten theatre'. It began by saying that in England 'all classes have long ceased to crowd the theatre to witness the legitimate drama', and that every West End theatre was drawing audiences by giving opera, ballet, and other entertainments. At the same time one could always find 'an outlying portion of the population' that still enjoyed amusements voted obsolete by the more refined—'a lord's 'cast off clothes will make a gentleman of the Sunday operative'.

It had been frequently suspected that the neighbourhood of Islington and Pentonville contained many such old-fashioned people, from the fact of the theatre there being always profitably conducted, and sometimes succeeding with the Shakespearean drama, even when under legal interdict. But the locale was despised by high actors, as well as high caste admirers. Destiny has at length found there the only theatre in which the persecuted drama could find refuge; and Mrs. Warner and Mr. Phelps—two among the best tragic performers now in London—have been glad to make it their asylum.

On Monday last they produced 'Macbeth' with new scenery, and got it up certainly in a style which elicited audible exclamations of astonishment from the usual visitors in the boxes. Such, too, was the curiosity excited that it was necessary to pile up elevated forms in the lobbies for the literally overflowing audience, where, we conjecture, they could see little and hear less.

Mrs. Warner enacted the part of Lady Macbeth with great care and force. Mr. Phelps we have never seen before in 'Macbeth', and it was certainly the ablest performance which he has yet exhibited. Since Edmund Kean's we have seen nothing better for vigour and vivid effect. It is essentially distinct from and stands in contrast with Mr. Macready's, which, however fine and classical in its conception, is but too obviously open to the Scotch sneer of presenting 'a very respectable gentleman in considerable difficulties', so studied is it in all parts, and subdued into commonplace by too much artifice; fretfulness, moreover, substituting high passion in the fifth act.

The straightforward and right earnest energy of Mr. Phelps's acting, on the contrary, made all present contemplate the business as one of seriousness and reality; while the occasional pathos of his declamation thrilled the heart within many a rude bosom with unwonted emotion. The spectators were visibly agitated and incapable of resisting the impulse.

The springtide of foreign talent, now at its highest, overflows every place of public amusement whose doors are not closed against the dazzling flood. The annual inundation has swept away the wreck of the tragic drama and the last tidings of the survivors is that Mrs. Warner and Mr. Phelps, having escaped on a plank, had been driven towards the New River and taken refuge at Sadler's Wells. In fact an effort is being made, in the North of London, to carry out the intentions of the legislature in granting the New Theatre's Regulation Act.

After such a reception, the management put away their standby melodrama, having discovered for themselves—as managements are always re-discovering—the fact that 'rude bosoms', the majority of an audience and the mainstay of any theatre, quicker than superiorly educated minds, always appreciate the best when sincerely presented.

But before the Wells could be established as the true home of worthwhile drama the disturbing elements had to be removed. In the words of Dickens:

> The friers of fish, vendors of oysters, and other costermonger scum accumulated round the doors, were first got rid of. The noisy sellers of beer inside the theatre were next to be removed. They resisted, and offered a large weekly consideration 'for leave to sell a call'. The management was obdurate, and rooted them out. Children in arms were next to be expelled. Orders were given to the money-takers to refuse them admission, but these were found extremely difficult to be enforced, as the women smuggled babies in under their shawls and aprons, and even rolled them up to look like cloaks. A little experience of such artifices led to their detection at the doors; and the play soon began to go without the shrill interruptions consequent on the unrolling of dozens of these unfortunate little mummies every night.

To combat the outrageous language, Phelps routed out an old Act of Parliament under which bad language in a public place could lead to a fine, and gave warning on placards and handbills given with gallery tickets that the Act would be enforced,

> and it *was* enforced with such rigour that on several occasions Mr. Phelps stopped the play to have an offender removed; on other occasions he went into the gallery, with a cloak over his theatrical dress, to point out some other offender who had escaped the vigilance of the police.[1]
> Within a month, the Jack Ketch party, thoroughly disheartened and amazed, gave in; and not an interruption was heard from the beginning to the end of a five-act tragedy!

Within that first month after *Macbeth* the Wells saw *Othello* (when Henry Marston played Iago, he always dreaded Phelps's bruising his arm with his intense grip), *The Stranger*, *The Jealous Wife*, Byron's *Werner*, *Merchant of Venice* and *School for Scandal*. Mrs. Warner's Lady Teazle looked to the *Theatrical*

[1] This story was completely denied by Phelps through his nephew W. May Phelps, but certainly for the first few nights extra police were on duty to turn doubtful characters back and refuse admission to even higher-priced parts of the house than the gallery, as John Forbes-Robertson—father of Sir Johnston—remembered seeing.

Journal more like the *Romeo and Juliet* Nurse with her powdered hair: the growing period accuracy was unpopular after the long-established stage custom of wearing modern dress in any play. As the *Journal* said, *School for Scandal* 'is not for a day, or a year, it is for all time'. Strange that the twentieth-century 'novelty' of classics in modern dress was normal till the 1840s!

All plays were of course part of an alternating repertoire, and after June began at 5.45 instead of the long customary 6.30. In July, when the West End had only burlesque, ballet, and opera, additions were *Virginius* ('a masterly piece of acting', but Collins's entr'acte music was inappropriate, and Phelps seemed to be overtaxing his strength acting every night); *The Rivals*; and *Hamlet*, played with *The Blue Devils* and *Dominique the Deserter*. The theatre's dilapidation was shown up when once in *Hamlet* the Ghost under the stage, urgently asked by the prompter why he did not say his usual 'Swear!' shouted, 'How can a man swear-r when he's up to his neck in watther-r?'—and the audience's laugh grew with the next line, 'Rest, rest, perturbed spirit'.

Punch with tongue in cheek urged Mrs. Warner and Phelps, who had made Shakespeare cheap for the people at the Wells, to make him dear for the people (in their own interest), like early peas and strawberries, by taking Her Majesty's and charging opera prices for the aristocracy to talk through Shakespeare as they did through opera. But the Wells went on in August with Colley Cibber's *Provoked Husband*; *The Wife* (with Phelps's Lord Townley 'infinitely superior to Macready's'); and *The Bridal* (Knowles's adaptation for Macready of Beaumont and Fletcher's *Maid's Tragedy*) in which Phelps, though striking, tended to rant and gabble, as he was always liable to do when encouraged by the applause at the Wells.

The *Morning Sun* commented that the Wells, crowded with its most respectable and attentive audience, was rivalling what the Fortune, situated in the same district, was in the days of Elizabeth I. It was remarked that Shakespeare was now filling a theatre even in the hot weather.

The September additions were *The Hunchback*; *A New Way to Pay Old Debts*, with Phelps giving an even greater performance as Sir Giles Overreach, some said, than Edmund Kean's, which was still talked of; a *King John* produced with a degree of splendour that had 'no equal in the history of the stage' (Phelps as John, Mrs. Warner as Lady Constance, and Marston as Faulconbridge were pictured in Park's 1d. plain, 2d. coloured prints); and Massinger's *City Madam*, which was seen by a school (the coarser scenes were always omitted).

The Times compared the tumult at the Wells only a year before with the quiet orderliness since Phelps was acting—and at the same prices. *The Lady of Lyons*, by Sir Edward Bulwer-Lytton (the name which the theatre-liberator had now assumed), and *The Wonder* were given in November when the time of opening changed to 7 p.m. On Boxing Day Phelps and the other leading actors did not appear in the pantomime, *Harlequin Robin Hood and Little John of Merrie England in the Olden Time*, but *The Stranger*, which started the programme, was given to a less orderly house.

Evidently it was an old Wells custom for the acting in the first part of the Boxing Day programme to be transferred from the stage to the audience—the gallery throwing paper pellets, orange peel, and other less cleanly and more dangerous missiles at the pit, which responded with continual explosions of angry noises and discordant sounds, so *The Stranger*

> was performed in 'inexplicable dumb show', and not until the grand desideratum, the pantomime, was commenced, were the gods desirous that all should be quiet, except the performers on the stage.

The beginning of 1845 saw *The Priest's Daughter*, by T. J. Serle (who had written the address given by Mrs. Warner at the opening of the régime) and Sheridan's *Critic*; and Phelps showed great courage and initiative in producing *Richard III* without the Cibber 'improvements'. The restored Shakespeare (though cut) was received enthusiastically and was followed by the well-known farce *Boots at the Swan*. O'Keefe's *Wild Oats*, Cherry's *Soldier's Daughter*, and *The Iron Chest* were also given. The season ended on 10th April with Mrs. Warner's benefit when *Henry VIII* (always finishing with the fall of Wolsey) and *School for Scandal* were both performed.

During the Warner-Phelps-Greenwood first season of 262 nights, 97 plays had been produced (26 major dramas and 71 afterpieces): of these *The Lady of Lyons* had most performances (36), closely followed by *Hamlet* (33) and *The Bridal* (30);

Richard III had 24, *King John* 18, *The City Madam* 16, *Macbeth* 14, and *Othello* 10.

Of course most of the chief plays were in the repertoire of the leading actors of those days, who were expected to be word-perfect in well-known dramas with a mere brush-up run-through (Macready was scornful of anyone needing more than at the most two mornings' rehearsal of a Shakespeare tragedy)—as today leading singers in opera are content with a morning check-up on any of their usual parts before appearing in a strange production with a strange company in a strange theatre. But this does not lessen the achievement of that first season—could present-day leading actors remember most parts they have played well enough to appear without careful rehearsal?

No wonder such exhausting work led to rumours that Mrs. Warner and Phelps were retiring from management. In fact Phelps considered taking the Lyceum, but it was an unlucky theatre and its rent was three times that of the Wells which, after all, though called 'the Little Theatre', held as large an audience (1,100 to 1,200 in the gallery, the same in the pit, and about 600 in the boxes and circle—a little short of 3,000) as any theatre in London apart from Covent Garden and Drury Lane, and the stage could be as deep as Drury Lane and increased in width when required.

So Phelps stayed at the Wells, though he soon began appearing only about four times a week. As a result of acting in a theatre where half the audience sat under boxes, he developed a slower enunciation so that all could hear and insisted that his actors should speak correctly, though his own speech was not faultless (he said 'gargin' instead of 'guardian') and, like all actors, he had his mannerisms, catching fleas on his chest and copying Macready by grunting and growling over a bone.

To ensure a standard, Phelps enforced discipline by twenty-nine rules, the breaking of most of which entailed fines: contracts were terminable at a month's notice on either side; illness—notifiable in writing—after a month led to a cancellation of the engagement which could not be renewed without forty-eight hours' notice; nobody was allowed in the front of the theatre without permission; and forfeits were payable for various faults:

> One month's salary or dismissal for performing elsewhere without written permission.

One week's salary for refusal to appear or causing the cutting or transposing of a scene by missing an entrance.

Half a week's salary for defacing notices, not being ready for a scene, being carelessly or wrongly dressed, or being obviously drunk.[1]

One night's salary for not appearing to sing National Airs or for not being word-perfect.

7s. down to 2s. for being absent from a whole rehearsal or not being word-perfect at the last, according to salary,[2] down to 6d. for being absent from scenes at a rehearsal, for not entering or exiting according to rehearsals, opening scene-doors during performance when not required, standing in the wings nearer the stage than the mark, or not returning the prompt or harpsichord book.

1s. for appearing or exiting when not required to do so.

These forfeits could be taken out of salary due, and if the prompter did not report an offender he himself was liable to pay the fine.

Many think that the impossibility of imposing fines nowadays can lead to a lack of discipline. Fines went on in the theatre till the days of Cochran, and fines today might control slackers who may not be breaking the letter of theatre law: some singers, I am told, leave the theatre after signing in, and I have myself known a chorus-singer wear no make-up for the first act, leave during the second which had no chorus, and return for the third—all without permission or notification: on one opera first night a leading singer who first appeared in the second act arrived only towards the end of the first—surely both inartistic and inconsiderate, as no understudy was ready if the principal were accidentally unavailable. As things are, opera-singers with a large repertoire well know the management dare not replace them by newcomers needing six months to learn all the stock works and might well regard fines for non-professional behaviour as demeaning unless, as in the straight theatre, the majority believe wholeheartedly that their job is more than piece-work.

Phelps was equally strict with audiences in 1845; he allowed no free seats except to the Press, nor was any child under three to be admitted, while all children in the pit had to be paid for.

His second season opened in a re-embellished Wells on Whit Monday, 13th May, with plays of the previous season, to which

[1] This alternatively might lead to dismissal.   [2] £6 down to £1 10s. a week.

he added *King Lear* with a restored text (which he played successfully for pathos); *A Winter's Tale,* played with *Katherine and Petruchio*; Mrs. Inchbald's *Every One has his Fault* and *Animal Magnetism*; Moore's *Gamester*; *Venice Preserved*; Massinger's *Fatal Dowry*; Southern's *Isabella* (in which he did not appear); Shiel's adaptation of Shirley's *Evadne, or, the Statue*; *Pizarro*; *Douglas*; modern plays by Knowles (*William Tell* and *Love*) and Bulwer-Lytton (*Richelieu*), and two new plays, *The Florentines* and Sullivan's *King's Friend.*

Macready saw the Wells *Macbeth* that autumn and thought it 'most creditably put upon the stage and very well indeed *for such a locality.*[1] As a piece of art considered positively, it has been greatly overpraised'. In the Christmas pantomime, *Harlequin and the Steam King*, Mrs. Warner and Phelps were shown arriving from Drury Lane in a first-class steam-railway carriage with a large Shakespeare volume for the Wells.

Before the season ended on 5th May 1846, they added Bulwer-Lytton's *Money*, a new play *Judge Jeffreys*, and *Brutus*, while on the last night Phelps acted in both *Julius Caesar* and *The Rivals*, copying the old Dibdin custom of trying out new pieces at the end of one season for possible inclusion in the next. Usually a famous overture, quadrille or waltz was played during the evening.

But before Phelps's new season started there were many changes. Instead of only about a month's break as had been given between the first and second seasons, each of which had lasted almost unbroken for nearly a year, the Wells was closed for nearly three months so far as plays were concerned before the third season began.

A new portico was erected, a separate entrance for the boxes was made, and a dress circle added. Except for the new circle, prices remained what they had been, and the prices of admission for the 1846–7 season stayed the same to the end of the Phelps régime: private boxes £1 11s. 6d., dress circle, 3s., second circle 2s., pit 1s., gallery 6d.

The biggest change was that Mrs. Warner left. There are no records of any disagreement, though the always prejudiced and jealous Macready said that Phelps thought one great evidence of his own talent was to frustrate or weaken the effects of

[1] His italics.

MRS. FITZWILLIAM AS MISTRESS PAGE

MISS GLYN AS CLEOPATRA

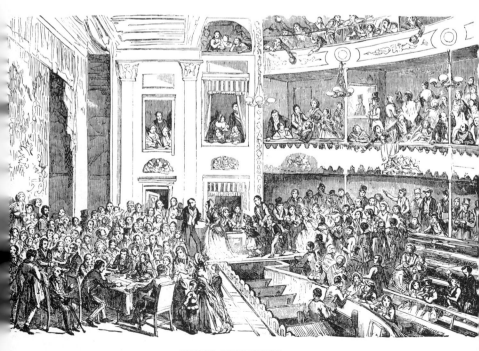

TOTAL ABSTAINERS

1879: OUTSIDE THE THEATRE *and* A SCENE FROM ROB ROY

his superiors (the story that Macready himself engaged Phelps for his company to confine him to secondary parts because his time would come later is well known); at the same time Macready, who had been most correctly grateful to Mrs. Warner for her companionship in her younger days when as Miss Huddart she had 'a strong good sense in her observations, and an acuteness of penetration', later said that she had 'a mind never very elevated'.

Still, perhaps because both Macready and Phelps had automatically overshadowed her, as all leading actors in the classics were bound to cast their leading actresses in the shade (Mrs. Siddons perhaps being an exception), Mrs. Warner left to prove that she too could be a manager—at the Marylebone Theatre; so Phelps was now in sole charge of the production side of the Wells with Greenwood as lessee and admirable business manager.

CHAPTER TWELVE

THE PLAY'S THE THING

1846–1862

MUSIC—AN integral part of the place since before the Wells were discovered—was not ousted by the now firmly established dramas, but Greenwood's composer, William Montgomery (later the editor of Moore's *Irish Melodies*), replaced the older Collins, whose incidental music was below Phelps's standard. Popular pieces were still played before and between the plays and many concerts were given in Lent or the summer with leading artists of the day.

Apart from those already mentioned who often returned, newcomers in 1846 included Sabilla Novello (daughter of the founder of the famous music-publishing firm); the operatic bass Willoughby Weiss, who later that year created *Elijah*; the harpist Frederick Chatterton; the tenor and oboist Grattan Cooke and his brother-in-law, the Islington-born George Kiallmark (whose father had led the Wells orchestra for twenty-five years); the Ethiopian Serenaders; Rossini's pupil, Henry Russell,[1] in a one-man show; the international operatic contralto Mme Albertazzi (born Emma Hewson); J. L. Hatton (best known for his song 'To Anthea'); John Distin (inventor of the keyed bugle and formerly George IV's trumpeter) and his band, consisting of his four sons; the Bohemian opera-singer Pischek; and two Professors of the Royal Academy of Music—the brilliant twenty-year-old pianist Kate Loder, just appointed Professor of Harmony, and George Macfarren, whose eighteen-year-old German wife, Natalie (later, as Lady Macfarren, well known for her opera translations), so mispronounced the start of 'Sally in our Alley' that some of the audience, thinking it intentionally comic, laughed, whereupon she laid down her music and 'in conjunction with her caro sposo' quitted the stage.

[1] Composer of 'Woodman, spare that tree', 'A Life on the Ocean Wave', 'Cheer, Boys, Cheer', and some 700 other songs.

The third drama season, 1846–7, began on 25th July with *Henry IV, Pt.1*, Creswick playing Hotspur and Phelps an amusing but not very fat Falstaff. In comedy, Phelps obliterated his mannerisms so effectively that he effaced his own identity. Though he had a meagre figure, his abstemiousness gave him an elasticity of gait and a singular youthfulness. Some said he was bourgeois, with pale lack-lustre eyes and inexpressive features, but admitted his brow was 'lofty and arched like the dome of a temple', his nose straight, and his mouth and chin powerful and determined. His hands were large-boned, gnarled and even ugly, but eloquently expressive, like his every muscle. His voice (originally weak and piping) was resonant on every word— John Coleman said he was probably the most versatile actor the English stage ever produced.

Unlike most of his contemporaries, he followed the new trend of insisting on good quality performances from each actor, and the high standard of his choice of drama, of his productions and of his own playing continued throughout his régime at the Wells. After *Henry IV*, he presented *Romeo and Juliet* with the original text (his new leading lady Laura Addison a crude but promising Juliet, Creswick a fine Romeo, and himself not light enough as Mercutio but fine in the death-scene), *Measure for Measure* (he played the Duke), and *The Tempest* (Prospero), with George Bennett an excellent Caliban.

Phelps bought from Bulwer-Lytton his *Oedipus* with special music by Mercadante, but it proved too expensive to produce. He gave Ford's *Love's Sacrifice*, Beaumont and Fletcher's *A King and No King* (the first revival for more than a century, and it crammed the house), Morton's *Town and Country*, *The Patrician's Daughter* by Westland Marston, *Ion* by (Sir) Thomas Noon Talfourd (whose Copyright Bill of 1842 was the basis of the present law), Charles Maturin's *Bertram*, Lovell's *Provost of Bruges*, and the first production of the Rev. James White's *Feudal Times* in which Miss Addison created a sensation by her description of a tournament seen from a window. Each play was given with two lighter pieces.

The 1847 concerts introduced Signor Lablache, the great Italian buffo (or, more probably, his son); the mezzo Elizabeth Poole, a Wells favourite for eleven years; the tenor William Harrison; and the original *Bohemian Girl*, Elizabeth Rainforth, who that summer presented the first Wells opera season with an orchestra of forty conducted by J. H. Tully—he often returned to the Wells.

The operas, with Henry Robinson Allen (the most complete English operatic artist, the critic H. F. Chorley said), Signor Borrani, the nineteen-year-old Rebecca Isaacs (popular at the Wells for six years) and Miss Rainforth herself, were *La Sonnambula* (for six nights running), *Maritana*, and *Norma* (each for three nights running), all followed by farces. For Tully's benefit some of his own *Forest Maiden* and Dibdin's *Quaker* were given, and at her own benefit Miss Rainforth sang in both *The Barber of Seville* and *The Beggar's Opera*.

Phelps began his 1847–8 season on 23rd August playing Leonatus in *Cymbeline* to a crowded house; the first performance lasted nearly four hours, with so many of the audience following the text in a 1d. copy of the Wells version 'that the representation might have been taken for that of an opera or a French play'. Though well presented, *Cymbeline* was not popular, but the next production, Shakespeare's own *Macbeth*, given for the first time for two hundred years, packed the house. Instead of Locke's singing witches, the hags appeared mysteriously behind different thicknesses of black gauze; the alarm-bell scene was naturalistic; and Banquo's Ghost, instead of appearing as usual with his back to the audience and then turning to show 'his gashed brow and livid features', rose facing the audience. The scene with Lady Macduff, usually cut, got unqualified praise. Miss Addison was passionately energetic as Lady Macbeth though she did not convey determination, intellectual power or dignity in the Siddons way. Phelps showed extraordinary power. In fact, 'if any sceptic still doubts the influence that Shakespeare possesses over the hearts and minds of English people', wrote one critic, 'let him visit Sadler's Wells Theatre any evening'.

Macbeth was followed by Colman Junior's *Heir at Law* and James White's fairly successful *John Savile of Haysted*, a play about Felton's murder of Charles I's Duke of Buckingham commissioned by Phelps for £400: this might have been 'one of the most stirring dramas of modern times' if the first three acts had not been so thin and the murder stultified by the heroine's unnecessary suicide.

Then came Colman Junior's *Poor Gentleman*, *As You Like It*, Henry Milman's *Fazio*, Colman the Elder's *The Jealous Wife*, Southern's *Isabella*, *Twelfth Night*, Arthur Murphy's *Way to Keep Him*, and *The Merry Wives of Windsor*, with of course, a grand pantomime at Christmas (pantomime now meaning the extravaganza fairy-tale as we understand it today).

In the summer of 1848, after the ventriloquist Mr. Love gave the first of his yearly 'Lucubrations' or 'Lenten Entertainments' with other artists, Miss Rainforth gave another season of operas—*Fra Diavolo*, *Sonnambula* with *The Quaker*, *The Barber of Seville* 'with, for the First Time on any English Stage, The Whole of the Original Music' (Bishop's version had always been used previously), together with Thomas Haynes Bayly's musical burletta *Why Don't She Marry?*, an amazing double bill consisting of *Norma* and a two-act version of *The Barber* (with Rainforth singing only in *Norma*); *The Bohemian Girl*, and Rossini's *Cinderella, or, the Fairy and the Little Glass Slipper* as well as plays such as Bickerstaffe's *Hypocrite* (that is, Molière's *Tartuffe*) and a Dickens burlesque *The Crummleses*.

For the fifth Phelps season, the theatre had been redecorated and opened on 27th September 1848 with *Coriolanus* in which a new leading lady, Isabella Glyn, was good as Volumnia. The great success of the production was the intensity of the mob that banished Coriolanus: after the usual curtain call for the lead, the cry of 'Supers!' went up. 'By Gad!' said Phelps, 'they are calling for the supers; and, damme! they deserve it—I never saw better acting in my life!' The curtain opened and the crowd was loudly cheered. *Coriolanus* was so successful that Phelps, who usually changed the play twice a week, gave it ten performances running.

It was followed by Beaumont and Fletcher's *Rule a Wife and Have a Wife*, *Much Ado about Nothing* (without Phelps), Robert Browning's *A Blot on the 'Scutcheon*, and a full *Henry VIII* instead of ending as was usual with Wolsey's fall. On Boxing Day *Venice Preserved* was followed by *Harlequin and the World turned ՈԺSIԺƎ ԺOMN*, and in 1849 came Fletcher and Massinger's *Honest Man's Fortune*, Morton's *School of Reform*, Murphy's *All in the Wrong*, *Calaynos* by G. H. Boker of Philadelphia, and 'Monk' Lewis's *Castle Spectre* two nights before the end of the season on 30th May.

*

The Wells now gave up its former summer season to non-resident entertainments. Concerts given in the next five years introduced in 1849 the New-York-born Spanish Mlle Nau (the original Page in *The Huguenots*, 1836), the future famous opera-singer Louisa Pyne and her sister Susan (both under seventeen), Braham and his son, and one of Mendelssohn's few pupils—the young conductor, W. S. Rockstro[1]; in 1850 several internation-ally known operatic singers—the tenor Sims Reeves (aged about thirty[2]), who often returned to the Wells; the wonderful but careless Irish soprano of twenty-five, Catherine Hayes, and the bass Karl Formes; the famous Irish-English actress Mrs. Glover; the brilliant twenty-eight-year-old 'cellist Alfredo Piatti (already settled in England), and at the piano Julius Benedict[3]; in 1852 Bottesini, aged thirty, who could play violin-music on his three-stringed bass (*basso da camera*) better than most violinists; and in 1853 Pell, the original 'Bones', with his African Troupe and the seven Shapcott brothers playing Verdi selections on Sax Horns.

The novelties of Phelps's sixth season, opening on 25th August 1849, were Mrs. Cowley's *Belle's Stratagem*; Cibber's *She Would and She Would not*; a remarkable *Antony and Cleopatra* in which Miss Glyn excelled herself (her ornaments, including a lily headdress of magnificent brilliants and coloured stones, an asp bracelet and a large paste bird, were stolen); Mrs. Centlivre's *Busie Body*; *She Stoops to Conquer*; *Garcia* by F. G. Tomlin, Secretary of the Shakespeare Society; and early in 1850 *The Honeymoon* by John Tobin; and a very successful new Cavalier and Roundhead play, *Retribution*, by Phelps's chief supporting actor, George Bennett. For his benefit Phelps played *Macbeth* and his famous Jerry Diddler in *Raising the Wind*.

Colman Junior's *John Bull* was specially given to raise funds for the Great Exhibition of 1851 under the patronage of the Duke of Cambridge, with a committee of Dickens, Leigh Hunt, Charles Kemble, Douglas Jerrold, Thackeray, Maclise R.A., and H. F. Chorley. The same author's *Mountaineers*, with Michael Kelly's music, was also given, the season ending on 24th May. Shortly before February 1850, the twelve-year-old

---

[1] Later well known for his musical biographies and text-books.
[2] Born 1821 according to himself, 1818 according to *Grove*.
[3] The composer, knighted in 1871.

John Brodribb, who, as Henry Irving, was to make his mark in the British theatre, was taken by his father to see his first play, *Hamlet*, with Phelps, whom he often again saw act and once followed at a respectful distance in the street.

The 1850–1 season, with, as new productions, *The Duchess of Malfi*, which ran for almost a month on account of the amazing wolf-madness scene at the end by Phelps as Ferdinand (he would have preferred to play Bosola); Leigh Hunt's *Legend of Florence*, and *The Cavalier* by C. Whitehead led the *Lady's Newspaper* to congratulate Phelps on achieving what the Government should have attempted long ago—the presentation of the highest class of drama.

In February 1851 Macready sent Phelps, as his successor in *Richelieu*, his cross of the Order of the Holy Ghost: in the same month Phelps received a letter after *Hamlet* saying, 'There is nothing new in saying that ghosts never knew how to vanish till they learned to do so at Sadler's Wells. You have taught managers the use of darkness'. On 27th February, the day after Macready's farewell to the stage, Phelps appeared at his benefit both as *King John* and as Jeremiah Bumps in *Turning the Tables*, and received a great ovation as the stage's future leader. This may have led him to bid for Drury Lane that year, but as Greenwood failed to put up the deposit of £500, he lost it to E. T. Smith.

The several summer concerts included Henry Phillips's musical version of *Our Village*, and for the start of the 1851–2 season Mrs. Warner returned to play her famous parts before leaving for America. Miss Glyn refused to play the Queen in *Hamlet* (though she had often played it before), so Phelps replaced her with a Miss Goddard from Hull—his fourth leading actress in eight years.

The outstanding novelty was *Timon of Athens*, with Phelps so much finer than Kean that it had forty performances between the 15th September and Christmas—a 'literary' play, 'long voted unfit for theatrical representation', as John Oxenford wrote in *The Times*, but greeted with 'shouts resounding from that quaint-looking building which is the home of Pentonville legitimacy'.

Phelps also revived Morton's *Secrets Worth Knowing*, Mrs. Lovell's *Ingomar* with *The Critic*, Macklin's *Man of the World* (in which he proved a finer Sir Pertinax Macsycophant— Macklin's original part—than the great George Frederick Cooke), and Planché's *Jewess*; then in James White's new play, *James VI, or, the Gowrie Plot*, he showed his versatility by his Scottish accent and a perfect make-up.

In the summer an opera season was given by Priscilla Horton (who had acted and sung for Macready) and conducted by her husband Thomas German Reed (musical director for Macready, the Charles Keans, and the Cushmans), the singers including Rebecca Isaacs, William Harrison and Louisa Pyne (so foreshadowing the famous Harrison-Pyne Opera Company).

The operas were *Sonnambula*, *The Bohemian Girl*, *Fra Diavolo*, *Lucia di Lammermoor*, *Maritana*, John Barnett's *Mountain Sylph*, *The Daughter of the Regiment*, Auber's *Crown Jewels*, and *Freischütz*, each of which was followed by one or other of *Midas*, *No Song No Supper*, *The Quaker*, *The Waterman*, *The Beggar's Opera*, or *The Swiss Cottage*—eight major and six minor operas for soloists who sang every night for seven weeks. *Sonnambula* was once followed by *The Daughter of the Regiment* on the same evening. For Miss Horton's benefit the programme included two acts of *Lucrezia Borgia* (in which Evelina Garcia also sang) and the play *The Model of a Wife* with the well-known actors Mr. and Mrs. Alfred Wigan. For the benefit of Harrison and Pyne, Balfe's now forgotten 'admired opera of *The Enchantress*' was given with the last act of *Lucia* and a play, *The Chameleon*.

August 1852 to April 1853 saw productions of *All's Well that Ends Well*, and *Henry V*, in which Phelps showed great ingenuity: in the march past before Agincourt, his forty supers defiled behind a breast-high 'set piece', each having two wickerwork dummies in armour lashed to his waist with heads modelled by Madame Tussaud, so that it seemed they were marching three abreast. 'As they tramped past, banners streaming, drums beating, trumpets braying, the stage seemed crowded with soldiers, and the illusion was so perfect that the audience never once discovered the artifice'. At one performance of *Henry V* there was an uproar in the audience: Phelps learned from Douglas Jerrold, in a box with Dickens, that the theatre was over full so, quite unperturbed, he came in front of the curtain and made the novel suggestion that if some would leave they could have their

money back. The overflow rushed to the doors, and the house
settled down. The last night of that season, *Henry IV, Pt. 2*,
Phelps played both the King and Justice Shallow. During the
summer Mrs. Fitzwilliam came back to the Wells for three days
to act with J. B. Buckstone, now manager of the Haymarket;
so did Mrs. Honner for a benefit night when the brilliant little
comedian Frederick Robson appeared, as well as the famous
sixty-six-year-old T. P. Cooke in his original part of William
in *Blackeyed Susan* (which he repeated for another benefit).

The only new major production in the tenth season, 1853–4,
was the lovely *Midsummer Night's Dream* with its green gauze
curtains instead of the then popular glitter, so that Phelps with
his poetical feeling but without extravagance produced a more
absolutely satisfactory spectacle, wrote Henry Morley, 'than
anything I can remember to have seen since Mr. Macready was
a manager'. The Wells audience was now so earnest, Morley
went on, that when Phelps as Bottom volunteered to roar
high or low, a galleryite's query whether he could 'roar like
Brooke' (Drury Lane's popular ranter, Gustavus V. Brooke)
was taken badly by the gods. Douglas Jerrold in *Punch* suggested that the Queen, who had not been to the Wells, might
well command Phelps to take the ass's head to Windsor for her
children. But though strings were pulled, Dickens wrote to
Phelps on 25th February 1854 that the difficulties in the way of
the Queen's coming to Sadler's Wells were insurmountable—
one wonders what they were.

In February 1854 a sixty-year lease of the Wells was granted
by Thomas John Lloyd Baker's daughters, Mary Anne Lloyd
Browne and Catherine, and Catherine's husband, the Rev.
Thomas Murray Browne, to Julia Bennett, Jane Dixon (a rela-
tive of Grimaldi's partner, Dixon of the Horse Repository), and
John Hooper, from whom Greenwood and Phelps rented it.

After the season ended on 2nd March with Fielding's *Miser*
for Phelps's benefit, visiting companies gave varied programmes
—a coloured four-piece band (violin, concertina, banjos and
bones) with a dancing singer and conjurer; a Chinese troupe
of magicians, jugglers and acrobats, who included 'impaling a
human body to a board with huge knives'; Howard Payne's
company with plays including *The Follies of a Day* translated

from *Figaro*; the Adelphi comedian Wright in *Sweethearts and Wives* and other plays; Flexmore, the Princess's Clown, and Mlle Auriol in the ballet *Esmeralda*; E. L. Davenport and Fanny Vining from Drury Lane in stand-by dramas (with the future dramatist T. W. Robertson successful as Captain Crosstrees in *Black-eyed Susan*); and the Lyceum company with a musical piece, *The Welsh Girl*, and three farces including *Box and Cox*.

One Saturday the theatre was let for a meeting of Total Abstainers with the sixty-two-year-old artist George Cruikshank in the chair. Originally he had always liked a drink—once in 1838 he 'seemed set for a booze', Macready recorded with his usual superiority: but in 1842 he produced a series of pictures called 'The Drunkard' and in 1847 'The Bottle' which showed the tragic effects of drink on an entire family, ending in murder (it sold in tens of thousands), while a later series, 'The Drunkard's Children', was played as a drama everywhere. At the Wells meeting, after only one speech had been made, Cruikshank exhorted the audience to take the pledge, and they swarmed across the orchestra to sign.

Soon after the 1854–5 season started, at a benefit for Mrs. Warner, now mentally ill, T. P. Cooke again played in *Black-eyed Susan* and Phelps played *Henry VIII* (instead of his usual part of Wolsey) with the famous American actress, Charlotte Cushman, as Queen Katherine: nine days later on 24th September Mrs. Warner died.

One of Phelps's most remarkable productions was *Pericles, Prince of Tyre* on 14th October 1854, played for the first time for nearly two centuries. Oxenford in *The Times* said that as a spectacle it was a marvel. Morley praised the Wells audience for not applauding rant but for feeling the truth of the Marina recognition scene as acted, while in the panorama voyage to the Temple of Diana the whole theatre seemed transported to the Temple at Ephesus, the 'crowning scenic glory of the play'. Douglas Jerrold in *Lloyd's Weekly News*, though he thought the spectacle was the best part, recommended 'all who love to see their poetical dreams realized' to visit the Wells, and commented that though other managers might spend more money on Shakespeare, none spent it so well as Phelps.

In 1855 the young Brodribb, having learned elocution and pantomime from the Wells actor, William Hoskins, with whom he refused to go to Australia, was advised by Phelps, 'Sir, do not go on the stage: it is an ill-requited profession': but as the seventeen-year-old was determined Phelps said, 'In that case, sir, you'd better come here and I'll give you two pounds a week to begin with'. The offer was refused and Brodribb started acting in the north under the name of Henry Irving.

Notable summer performances in the next few years included in 1855 Benjamin Webster in *Tartuffe* with Madame Celeste (an actress for the twenty-four years since she danced at the Wells); and the sprightly kitten Mrs. Keeley (Weber's original Mermaid in *Oberon* when Miss Goward) as *Jack Sheppard*—for realism actually carving the name on a beam at each performance —and Topsy in *Uncle Tom's Cabin* (her fat puppy of a husband also appeared in 1857). In 1856 Miss Cushman played her famous part of Meg Merrilees (which she despised) in Henry Bishop's dialogue opera *Guy Mannering*; the fine but unreliable Charles Dillon gave his fine *Belphegor* with Adam's opera *The Swiss Cottage* and Dibdin's *Waterman*; and a grand three-week opera season was given by Mrs. Glover's composer-violinist son, Howard, with Sims Reeves, his wife (Emma Lucombe), Miss Poole and Weiss in *The Bohemian Girl*, *Fra Diavolo*, *La Sonnambula* together with *The Waterman* (Reeves sang in both), conducted by Glover, Benedict and the great Balfe himself. In 1858 the Christy Minstrels appeared and Tully gave an opera season (in which Charles Lyall, later of the Carl Rosa Opera Company, sang) including *Il Trovatore* with *No Song No Supper*, the first *Luisa Miller* in England, and *La Traviata, or, The Blighted One* (given with either *The Beggar's Opera* or *The Daughter of the Regiment*—and on Saturday the last act of *La Sonnambula* as well!). In 1859 the Lyceum Corps de Ballet danced, and Tully gave a lighter opera season (with the contralto Fanny Huddart singing), including his own *William and Susan, or, All in the Downs*, T. R. Reynoldson's *An Accidental Son* (based on Rossini's *Bruschino*) and *Midas*, but it ended disastrously during *Martha* when the artists, singing before the curtain in protest for being unpaid for a fortnight, broke the drop-cloth by scrabbling for halfpence showered on them by the audience. In 1861 the famous comedian J. L. Toole appeared in

The Spitalfields Weaver for a benefit, and J. B. Howe played *Richard III*.

The only novelties of the 1855–56 season were *A Comedy of Errors, Hamilton of Bothwellhaugh* and, in *The Tempest*, the restored ship-scene with a realistic storm. But Phelps never let his excellent scenery distract from the plot and while F. G. Tomkins in the *Morning Advertiser*, noting how attentive the audiences were, said 'whoever desires to see the true uses of the stage, and the value of a national drama, be he scholar or unlearned, high or low, should certainly wend his way to Sadler's Wells', Morley, in the *Examiner*, stressed what should always be copied in the theatre:

> The actors are content also to be subordinated to the play, learn doubtless at rehearsals how to subdue excesses of expression, that by giving undue force to one part would destroy the balance of the whole, and blend their work in such a way as to produce everywhere the right emphasis.

Phelps's thirteenth season, starting on 6th September 1856, introduced *The Taming of the Shrew* with Phelps as Sly and *The Two Gentlemen of Verona* without him.

By this time, the Wells was regarded as an example to other London theatres. It was about now that among the audiences were young Squire Bancroft and Henry Irving, now aged eighteen, who later often told how the Wells acting in Phelps's time impressed him. Morley commented that in the pit and gallery could be seen 'our working classes in a happy crowd, as orderly and reverent as if they were at church, and yet as unrestrained in their enjoyment as if listening to stories told them by their own firesides'.

On 6th April 1857 at the Royal General Theatrical Fund dinner, with Phelps in the chair, Dickens, after remarking on the disgraceful condition of the Wells when Phelps took it over, said that

> with one of the most *vagabond* audiences that ever went into a theatre utterly displaced from it, and with one of the most intelligent and attentive audiences ever seen attracted to it and retained in it—I believe I am not very wrong in my rough calculation when I say, that that theatre has been open under Mr. Phelps's management 3,000 nights, and that during 2,000 of those nights

the author represented has been Shakespeare. (Cheers.) Gentlemen, add for the other thousand nights sterling old plays, tragedies and comedies, many new plays of great merit, accepted with a real sense of managerial responsibility, and paid for, as I have reason to know in the case of a friend, with a spirit and liberality that would have done honour to the old days of the two great theatres—add to that, that all these plays have been produced with the same beauty, with the same delicacy and taste, with the same subservience of the scene-painter and the mechanist to the real meaning of the play—(cheers)—and with the same indebtedness to the creator of the whole for his admirable impersonation of a great variety of most opposite and diversified characters, and surely we must all agree, to say the very least, that the public is under a great debt to the profession—is under a great debt of obligation to Mr. Phelps—and that it has a strong legitimate interest in the continued success of his undertaking. (Cheers.)

Phelps extended his fine work in his fourteenth season 1857–8 with *Love's Labour's Lost*, with himself as Don Adriano, *The Clandestine Marriage*, in which he played Lord Ogleby, and Marston's *Patrician's Daughter*, in which his performance inspired a visitor from Devon to shout from the gallery, 'Where be Charles Kean now?' In January 1858 Kean, the Court Master of the Revels, was furious that when he declined to let his Princess's Theatre company play *Macbeth* at Her Majesty's as part of the festival for the wedding of the Princess Royal to Prince Frederick William of Prussia (afterwards Emperor of Germany), Phelps and the Wells company performed it. Phelps, chuckling, went on his way calmly and contentedly; but the mention of the Wells to Kean 'excited him almost to madness. He writhed like a skinned horse'.

As a result, the *Islington Gazette* compared the two theatres: the painter, the tailor, and the upholsterer were Kean's interpreters of Shakespeare, but the Wells 'is as much before the Princess's in point of acting as the Princess's is before Sadler's Wells in point of scenery', but 'scenery is an adjunct of acting, and not, as Mr. Kean's friends suppose, acting an adjunct of scenery'. Shakespeare in sheepskin was better than Kotzebue in gilded morocco, and the Princess's would come to rank with Madame Tussaud's, while a revival of dramatic taste rested with the Wells, where the 'unhallowed union of music with the drama' (as Morley called it) had been dropped.

*

In the 1858–9 season Phelps introduced Richard Cumberland's *Wheel of Fortune*, and in *The Hypocrite* played Dr. Cantwell with Mrs. Charles Young (at the Wells for a second season) who was so good that the *Weekly Dispatch* presumed she would soon be stolen away for the West End, as the Wells was almost the only school of acting in London so that Phelps must be ready 'to see the birds trained in his nest take wing westward as soon as he had taught them self-sustainment'.

After an artistically successful tour of Germany in the summer of 1859, Phelps opened his sixteenth season by presenting (on Macready's strong recommendation) Miss Heath from the Princess's in *Romeo and Juliet*: the production was taken to Windsor Castle and Miss Heath became Queen Victoria's reader, later marrying the actor Wilson Barrett. The principal novelty in 1858–60 was Tom Taylor's *Fool's Revenge* (based at Phelps's request on *Rigoletto*, but more closely linked with Hugo's *Le Roi S'Amuse*). Phelps, playing the Jester Bertuccio excellently, produced it scrupulously, especially as to the pronunciation of names. Tom Taylor later recalled, 'I never saw rehearsals more thorough, more careful or more business-like. Phelps was as able as he was indefatigable in stage management. He did the work of guidance and governance of his actors singly, and of the action as a whole'. Once a member of the audience enjoying *Twelfth Night*, having seen only the previous day's bill for Taylor's play, did not understand until the end why it was called *The Fool's Revenge*!

Greenwood, who had managed the Wells for Phelps for sixteen years, retired at the end of this season, and from April 1860 Phelps was left on his own.

This no doubt kept him too busy to produce any novelties in his seventeenth season, when his son Edmund made a successful debut as Ulric in *Werner*, but in his 1861–2 season, though Edmund got poor notices for his immature Prince Hal in *Henry IV, Pt. 2*, and Roderigo in *Othello*, Phelps amazed the Press as *Louis XI* in Casimir Delavigne's play of that name, by making the King historically real, unlike Charles Kean's hysterically grotesque interpretation. Yet Phelps revived the Cibber-Shakespeare *Richard III* ('Off with his head', and all that) because it did not include the part of Queen Margaret, which his nephew, W. May Phelps, remembering Mrs. Warner's superb performance, was sure the new Miss Atkinson could not play.

In January 1862 the remainder of the Wells lease (an un-expired term of fifty years from the previous midsummer) was put up for auction—Phelps having the use of it for seven years from Lady Day 1860 at £1,000 a year subject to deductions for ground-rent (£277), insurance (£90), etc. The lease was not sold; but on his nephew's advice Phelps, who must have felt the loss of Greenwood and had for some time seen his wife (his constant companion and dresser at the theatre) suffer from cancer, decided now to act only for others.

Under him the 'little temple at Islington maintained a high and unsullied name when all other theatres in the metropolis were falling into a barren reputation, and looked for nothing beyond momentary success. Mr. Phelps unfurled the banner of Shakespeare at a time when Shakepeare was going out of fashion, either through lack of actors or through lack of taste', and he had done this with 'no patronage from "fashion" or assistance of any kind, relying entirely upon the support of what may emphatically be termed the "people" ', as he wrote in a letter two years later. He complained that the Wells 'was and is an old-fashioned wretched place, devoid of all modern im-provements both before and behind the curtain, and to conceal which defects cost much both in money and labour which would have been saved in a better building'. He also said that it was not only locally patronized—'great numbers came long dis-tances', though its situation 'militated much—very much—against pecuniary success'.

This parrot-cry of the inaccessibility of the Wells has been repeated all through its history when a management is not doing well financially, it being forgotten that something worth seeing —especially when novel (like Wroughton's French Revolution dramas, Dibdin's aquatic shows, Phelps's classical revivals)—always draws an audience even to somewhere less convenient than the Wells. In 1931, referring to this letter of Phelps's, Sir Johnston Forbes-Robertson wrote that at the age of seventy-eight he walked to the Wells 'a few days ago from my Blooms-bury home. It took me exactly twenty minutes; which should, I think, dispose of any idea that this historic building is still in an out-of-the-way corner of London'.

It was the originality of Phelps's honest approach to worthwhile drama without any claptrap that filled the Wells and restored its name. He closed his régime, during which he had pretty well run the gamut of the best-known worthwhile classics, on 15th March 1862 with Massinger's *City Madam* and, as the usual afterpiece, *Doing for the Best*, in both of which he appeared. He ended, as he had begun, without any great flourish.

CHAPTER THIRTEEN

'AN EXPLETIVE BARN'

1862–1878

TO FOLLOW Phelps's remarkable eighteen seasons was an insoluble problem for several managers who made a brave attempt. For over a year Miss Catherine Lucette and Captain Morton Price (some Press notices said Rhys) tried varied shows, always with future opera in mind, with Tully as musical director, but the mixture of operettas, melodramas and classics played by poor resident actors and good visitors, such as the Hermann Vezins, Madame Celeste, J. L. Toole and Phelps himself, were notable only for a Bournonville ballet, *Echo Fra Balsalan*, *The Lady of the Camelias*, and the first appearance of the fourteen-year-old Nellie Farren, later famous as the incarnation of the Cockney spirit—'she could play anything, dress in anything, say and do anything', from Shakespeare to burlesque.

Then in 1863 Miss Marriott and her husband Robert Edgar[1] ran the Theatre Royal, Sadler's Wells, as it was still called, for five seasons with 'Legitimate Drama', stressing the good standard by copying Alfred Bunn's innovation at the two Patent Theatres in 1833 of having smart seats, called stalls, price 3s., at the front of the pit, while the first or dress circle, as it was called, was reduced to 2s. 6d. Most of their plays, however, were repetitions of those Phelps had done better, apart from *The Corsican Brothers* and *A Winter's Tale* with the sometimes sober leonine Gustavus V. Brooke and Miss Marriott. They both acted in *The Merchant of Venice* on Shakespeare's birthday in 1864, after which Cruikshank played the *Macbeth* dagger scene, with Buckstone in *Box and Cox*. That same year the British Operatic Association gave two Belfe operas, *The Rose of Castille* and *Satanella*, *Ernani* and other operas.

In 1865 the circle prices were restored to 3s. and the stalls

---

[1] Their son was the father of Edgar Wallace.

reduced to 2s. This is when the Islington-born eleven-year-old Arthur Pinero first tasted the theatre. Sixty years later, Sir Arthur recalled that in those days the Wells was 'a smallish house with a few rows of stalls and an eighteenpenny pit in which one sat on a bare plank with nothing to rest one's back against'. (From his earliest years, his family encouraged his playgoing and gave him the 1s. 6d. when they could.) In the intervals a man in a white apron with a basket cried, 'Ginger-Beer, lemonade, bottled ale or stout, almond cake!' There was a green baize curtain and an act-drop of classical design, the lowering of which signified the end of the play; interior and woodland scenes had green baize on the stage, street scenes or trap-scenes had bare boards. Front scenes were pairs of flats run on by not always invisible stage-carpenters and sometimes the flat failed to come together perfectly—hence the advice to a literary novice, 'Be sure to join your flats'; while sometimes 'half a street went out to meet half a landscape'.

His first heroine was Miss Marriott.

> She played, though already a somewhat mature lady, the leading 'juvenile' characters, and, with no consideration for Mr. Edgar, I, being at the time about ten years of age, fell deeply in love with her.

In 1866 the Edgars reduced the price of stalls to 1s. 6d. and, though the summer manager W. H. C. Nation (step-uncle to the future stars Irene and Violet Vanbrugh) boldly installed 'spring stuffed seats and backs' for stalls at 4s. and, for programmes such as two Dickens adaptations (Dion Boucicault's *Dot* from *Cricket on the Hearth* and *The Golden Dustman* from *Our Mutual Friend*), forbade the wearing of bonnets, 1s. 6d. was the price for the last two Marriott seasons. In 1866–7 Reade's *Masks and Faces* and a 'most faithful version of Washington Irving's *Rip Van Winkle* were outstanding; and in 1868 young Pinero's passion for Mrs. Edgar cooled enough for him to adore the notorious and beautiful Adah Isaacs Menken, who appeared at the Wells for three weeks in May 1868, under the management of Henry Powell of the Pavilion, 'in her World-Renowned Impersonation of Mazeppa, as performed by her at Astley's Royal Amphitheatre, and throughout America, etc. etc. A Powerful Stud of Highly-Trained Horses and Ponies . . . Stupendous Platforms erected expressly at an enormous expense' (with, of course, a comedietta and a farce). In her third week, as well as *Mazeppa*, Powell played the last act of *Richard III* with horses and *Dick Turpin's Ride to York*.

Young Pinero stood at the stage-door to see Menken go in and wrote verses to her when she died three months later. He hoped, he said, that the verses would never be recovered, as they were rubbish, but added he believed 'poor Menken was at heart a good woman—one of those who knew better and, in stress of circumstance, did worse'.

The comments by the *Era* on 17th May 1868 on Menken's performance at the Wells destroy the legend that her nakedness was a scandal:

> Though Mademoiselle causes a sensation by appearing very sparsely clad in the course of her performance, she is splendidly dressed at the commencement of it [in a gorgeous page's costume]. Whatever may be thought of the propriety of a lady making a public exhibition of her figure, with the outlines of it almost as distinct as those of a piece of undraped sculpture, there can be no question that the beauty of form which is displayed by Miss Menken is of a remarkable character. It is a mistake, however, to represent this distinguished lady Mazeppa as appearing on the stage indelicately undressed, the fact being that there is less of the body actually uncovered than is presented to view by many fastidious dames and damsels who profess to be shocked at what is much less indecent than their own approximation to the nude.

For the next ten years things did not improve at the Wells. Once young Pinero took an active part in complaining from the pit against badly printed programmes as one example of the slovenly condition of the theatre, and was rebuked from the stage as 'the boy in the scotch cap'. In 1869 Phelps unwillingly made two return appearances under contract to F. B. Chatterton of Drury Lane, whose father had been box-keeper at the Wells and whose great-uncle had played the harp there in 1843 (he himself, when a child, got 6d. a performance for walking on in the 1842 pantomime), and infuriated Edgar by comparing the decadent condition of the theatre with 'the temple he had reared', calling it 'an expletive barn'.

The 'Sadler's Wells make-up', as it was called, indicates what conditions had come to. It consisted of a little red on a whitened face. If in a hurry, the actor 'rubbed his hands on the whitewashed walls of his dressing-room and smeared them over his face', Pinero recalled in 1910.

Some eleven managers took the theatre for odd weeks in four years with programmes varying from variety with the great Vokes family through *East Lynne* to melodramas in the modern sense (with a boy drawn towards a circular saw or a train dashing towards the unconscious heroine) or a female *Hamlet*. In 1872 R. Delatorre, lessee of the Royal Victoria Theatre (later nicknamed The Old Vic) attempted to save the Wells with good performers, for example, George Belmore, Walter Lacy, Emma Kerridge in strong dramas such as *Atonement* (from *Les Misérables*) or *The Ticket of Leave Man* at prices from 2s. 6d. to 4d. 'to meet the exigencies of the time': he even anticipated future events by trying to alternate shows between the two theatres, but by Easter 1873 he gave up.

Miss Marriott returned for a time and the dignified Jennie Maurice daringly presented the Greek tragedy *Medea*, while Bessie Reid starred in equestrian dramas including *Mazeppa*, *Turpin's Ride to York*, *Joan of Arc*, and *The Bells in the Storm* (a version of Irving's 1871 success, *The Bells*—but the horse drawing the sleigh always stood still!).

Nothing succeeded—not even *Macbeth* with a different Macbeth in each act or *Babes in the Wood* in which the Boy Babe was the future comedian Bert Coote, then aged five—and in June 1874 the Wells was ordered to wind up as being unregistered, and in December it was to be turned into baths and washhouses.

In 1875 cobwebs filled the Wells and 104 pounds of lead were stolen from its roof. In August the unexpired thirty-eight years' lease was put up for auction together with fixtures and fittings. The ground rent was £277 a year and the estimated rental value £1,000 a year, which Phelps had paid, the auctioneer claiming it could still be one of the best paying theatres in London as in Phelps's time (a voice: 'We don't have a Phelps every day!'), but after a first bid of only £800, the Wells was bought in at £1,020.

After further rumours that the building would become a furniture warehouse, the Wells, drastically converted, opened in June 1876 as the New Spa Skating Rink and Winter Garden (complete with Pump Room for those who liked to take the old spring waters) for the latest craze, roller-skating (invented in 1865 by Mr. Plimpton of New York) and the 'oldest Theatre in London has ceased to exist'.

Within a month, however, this enterprise failed, and the building in a ruinous condition was bought by the lessor, W. S. Chenall, who leased it to a company with Walter Stacey as manager. Pending a hoped-for theatrical licence a 'Grand Science Festival' was put on for a run in January 1877, with 'Professor Pepper (late of the Royal Polytechnic), Honorary diploma of Physics and Chemistry of the Lords Committee of Council on Education, Associate of the Institute of Civil Engineers, etc.'

The performances were, in fact, of highly developed conjuring—especially with Cynthia:

Who is Cynthia, what is she? *Shakespeare.*
Answer: She is the brother of Psycho.

This dubiously sexed creation was, in fact, an automaton, like the illusionist Maskelyne's Psycho which wrote a word which was *then* chosen at random from a dictionary by a member of the audience.

A lecture on Vibratory Motion was announced: 'a lady will float in the air'; the famous Pepper's Ghost (invented by Henry Dircks) was shown, and the audience was also promised 'The Ghost of Joey Grimaldi'.

Several boxing and wrestling matches took place (even on Good Friday), while in April prices ranged from 6d. to one guinea for Broekman's Monkey Theatre and Circus from Berlin: but in October after nearly two hours of boxing police appeared and 'the large audience cleared out of the theatre in double quick order'. No arrests were made but warning was given of legal proceedings in the event of such exhibitions in the future.

In 1878 an application for a theatre licence was refused out of hand in March until stone stairs replaced the dangerous old wooden ones, but to try to keep the Wells alive, the mortgagees of the theatre put in one Arthur Harrison in April to give a Masked Ball with 'a number of females present in Ballet costume'. No tickets were sold, on the pretence that it was a private party, but masks had to be bought at 3s. each, and though there was no liquor licence, a policeman with an ulster over his uniform was told, when he ordered 3d. worth of whisky, that there was nothing under 6d. and that as there was no water he would have to drink it neat. Harrison was fined £50 with £5 costs, with the alternative of one month's hard labour.

In July the unexpired lease for about thirty-three years was put up for auction by order of the Court of Chancery but the highest bid was £2,000, and the Wells was not sold.

A month later, however, Mrs. Bateman who, with her late husband, had been running the Lyceum on Phelps-Greenwood lines, left that theatre to Henry Irving, her leading man, and bought Sadler's Wells. Hoping to establish her three daughters, she planned to run the Wells as a country theatre with low prices. She had little capital, but the rent might, she considered, be offset by the saloons. 'The neighbourhood has much improved—is without a place of amusement and the facilities for getting to Sadler's Wells by trams and omnibuses have greatly increased.'

As, however, it was 'impossible to open the house in its existing condition of ruin and decay', she decided to rebuild the interior. Work began in the first week of November 1878, the very week that Samuel Phelps died.

CHAPTER FOURTEEN

EMPTY HOUSES, SHABBY SHOWS

1879–1893

ONLY THE old walls were left for the new theatre, the twenty-third designed by C. J. Phipps. The roof was raised, the pit, hitherto sunk, made level with the street, and the auditorium raked. It was fitted up with Phipps's patent theatre chairs; there was a carriageway in St. John's Terrace, a covered portico in Arlington Street like that at Her Majesty's, and a row of trees in front 'thus reviving one of the olden peculiarities of the place'.

But now, at latest, one 'olden peculiarity' was gone, never to be restored: the doors on each side of the proscenium. While they lasted, Clement Scott said, the actors did not take their calls in a prepared group smiling fixedly, hand in hand, but,

> They all came out of that dear little green proscenium door . . . just the kind of door belonging to such a house as Charles Lamb . . . inhabited in Colebrooke Row[1] . . . I think I am right in saying that the proscenium door, which dates as far back as the earliest Greek plays, disappeared for ever with the old Sadler's Wells Theatre . . . Actors and actresses have no home from which to appear and to take their cheers, and so return to what would otherwise be the broken illusion of the scene.

Now there were to be large electric lamps in front of the theatre and a 'powerful sunburner' in the auditorium, which was to be cream, sky-blue, crimson, and gold. The Theatre Royal, New Sadler's Wells, as it was to be called, which the *Era* said 'may now claim to be one of the largest and most conveniently constructed in London', opened after seven months' delay on 9th October 1879.

When the audience had entered through the new lobby with its Morris pattern of pomegranates and its open fireplace, John O'Connor's act-drop of the Wells in 1799 (replacing Hawes

[1] Still to be seen.

Craven's originally intended design showing the Wells as a spa) rose to disclose blue curtains, and Mrs. Bateman spoke Tom Taylor's address recalling past Wells glories—Kean with 'his childish treble', Braham's 'boy-notes', Grimaldi with his 'monkey baby-face', the real water, T. P. Cooke who 'with Black-eyed Sue A hundred nights "Blessed her dear eyes", and drew'[1], and finally how:

> When e'en Clown's red and white turned blue and yellow,
> And Melodrama grew more stale than mellow,
> Old Sadler's Wells' dry bones that slept, bemired,
> By brave old Phelps with a new life were fired. . . .

The play given that night, to increased prices—Balcony stalls 4s., Family Circle 2s. 6d., Pit stalls 2., Pit 1s., and Gallery 6d., with private boxes at £2 10s.—was Isaac Pocock's old musical drama *Rob Roy*. In the company were many well known players —the three Bateman daughters Miss (Kate) Bateman (Mrs. Crowe, who had acted with Irving at the Lyceum), Isabel, and Virginia Frances; Mrs. Charles Calvert, Hermann Vezin, who had acted with Phelps; Charles Warner and Walter Bentley; F. W. Wyndham (son of the Scottish actor-manager for whom Irving made his first appearance on the stage in Sunderland and who later started the still existing Howard & Wyndham management); Rowland Buckstone, William Farren Junior, and others. Other plays this year—each put on for a run—were *The Hunchback* and *Leah*, while on Sundays the Wells was open both afternoon and evening for religious services with hymns and sermons.

The Times thought the winter's pantomime, *The Forty Thieves, or, Abdullah's 'arrys*, excellent and in February 1880 *Macbeth*, preceded by a farce, filled the house, in which 'opera-shawl, and snowy front, clerical stock (very numerous by-the-bye) and sealskin cap indicated that a real play-going public was there'. The Middleton witches and Locke's music were restored, but 'all that was grotesque in Phelps's time' had disappeared: 'No longer a red-besmeared *Banquo* shot Conquest-like up a trap, but a spirit-like apparition seen through one of the supporting pillars'; and the witches, no longer appearing 'melodramatically' from behind acres of black gauze, had trained voices. The title-rôles of *Macbeth* and *Othello* were played by L. Martin

---

[1] At the Surrey, not the Wells: see p. 111.

Eiffe of the famous highly developed Ducal Theatre, Meiningen. Evening dress was now essential in the dearer seats.

After Tom Taylor's historical *Clancarty* and *Romeo and Juliet*, while the Bateman company went on a long tour, *The Danites* by Joaquin Miller, a play about the revenge of the 'Destroying Angels' for the mob-murder of Joseph Smith, founder of Mormonism, was given for a run by McKee Rankin's American company, so that the 'peculiar dialect, manners and customs should be accurately given' of a 'striking picture of life in the Far West, as described in the sketches of Bret Harte'. It was preceded by *Box and Cox*.

Next came *A Midsummer Night's Dream* with Mendelssohn's music and children as the fairies (Puck being Little Addie Blanche—later well known as the musical artist Ada Blanche). Charles Warner, arriving from Dover an hour late for the first night, played in Charles Reade's *Drink*, adapted from *L'Assommoir*, and had a double call after the famous delirium scene; Jennie Lee played her well-known title-rôle *Jo* (adapted from *Bleak House*).

The Bateman company returned with stock dramas in September (Warner in his celebrated part in *The Road to Ruin* and Miss Bateman in Lytton's *The Lady of Lyons*); it looked as if the great days were back again. As one Islington newspaper said, *The School for Scandal* could not have done better if it had been a pantomime. Then Mrs. Bateman, who had not spared herself, caught a chill while economizing by waiting for a bus to the Wells, and died on 13th January 1881.

Her three daughters were left at odds; only Kate enjoyed acting, but was jealous of Isabel, while Virginia, who like Isabel hated acting, would not appear with Kate. For a time Isabel carried on. Henry Arthur Jones specially wrote his first full-length play, *His Wife*, while J. L. Toole played for a week to help. But from that summer through the next eleven years the Wells had as many managers and was constantly advertised as 'to let'.

Policies varied from Shakespeare and stock drama through melodrama to burlesque and variety, or even a mixture of them, while the performers equally varied from the excellent to the rank amateur. The second half of 1881 was typical—the Olympic company in *Delilah, or, Married for Hate* (from Ouida's *Held in*

Bondage), Hollingshead's Gaiety company in burlesque, Rose Leclercq (the original Lady Bracknell in *The Importance of Being Earnest*) as Queen Elizabeth in *Richard III*, Miss Marriott back again in *Elizabeth, Queen of England* (specially written for the famous Ristori), *Hamlet* eked out by the comic vocalist G. H. Macdermott, F. B. Chatterton's *Ali Baba* pantomime which, in spite of Fred Evans as the Clown and Master (Will) Evans as the cat, was, John Coleman wrote, 'the saddest sight I have ever witnessed. An empty house and a shabby show which would have discredited a respectable barn'. The gas was cut off on 10th January 1882 and the theatre closed. In August the Wells and Whitecross Street houses were sold for £20,030 and eight months later the Wells was bought for £4,750.

Among events worth noting in the next few years were the three-year tenancy of Matthew Robson and his wife Marie Forde with adaptations from Ouida's novels *Moths* and *Folle Farine*, poorly acted dramas and poor melodramas (desperadoes kept at bay with a garden syringe or hospital-ward trapdoors leading to dungeons); in 1885 the famous Gaiety burlesque team of Arthur Williams, Nellie Farren ('the Vital Spark'), Ada Blanche and Edward Royce (one show being *A Mere Blind* from Offenbach's *Les Deux Aveugles*), weekly melodrama by the Olympic company with Isa Bowman as Little Eva in *Uncle Tom's Cabin*, also Goethe's *Faust* colloquially translated (Marguerite called 'a little duck'), the audience admitted free at early doors and those who would not scream out 'Brayvo!' chucked out; James Deacon from his own music hall opposite the present Wells entrance mixing drama such as *Lady Audley's Secret* (from Miss Braddon's novel) with variety artists including the serio-comic Tom Costello ('At Trinity Church I met my doom'), Bessie Bonehill (one of the first male impersonators), and Charles Coborn ('Two Lovely Black Eyes' and 'The Man who Broke the Bank at Monte Carlo') who got £6 a week or during the twice-daily pantomime £14; in 1887–8 visiting melodramas at prices from 4d. to 1s. 6d.—Edmund Tearle from the Standard Theatre, Bishopsgate, Shiel Barry in his famous part of the Miser in *Les Cloches de Corneville*, J. A. Cave in *Robert Macaire* and *The Mystery of the Hansom Cab* (soon after Charles Reade's *It's Never too Late to Mend* he went bankrupt).

' The bravest venture was in July 1889, when thirty-six

artists, forming The Actors' Co-operative Company, took the Wells with £100 from London managers and £5 each from Sarah Thorne (who ran the excellent Margate Theatre, where Irene and Violet Vanbrugh were trained) and Elliot Galer (who had sung in opera at the Wells in 1867). They let the bars for £24 a month and opened with the 1864 Surrey melodrama *The Orange Girl*, which brought them only £46 12s. 3½d., so that each actor only got 12s. in the £: the fine *Silver King*, by permission of Wilson Barrett, did no better, Galer's own Drury Lane drama *A True Story*, did half as well, and *Rob Roy* brought nothing: they went bankrupt and the theatre closed on 3rd September.

In the spring of 1890 *Maria Martin* and *The Man in the Iron Mask* were the best plays given, and in the autumn C. Wilmot and H. A. Freeman established the Wells as a weekly London shop-window for touring companies, but only some three shows now call for notice—*The Dangers of London* with F. A. Scudamore and 'the introduction of the marvellous invention The Phonograph!'; the appearance of Master Percy Hutchinson (later the romantic stage and film actor) in *Wedded to Crime*; and that fine comedian Huntley Wright's performance in Fred Wright's burlesque *Merrie Prince Hal*.

After a tentative week of variety in November 1891 (with two comedians, the black-faced Sam Redfern and his surprisingly tragic drink-saga 'Any Excuse for a Booze' and Charles Chaplin, whose later world-famous son was then two years old), the Wells closed for a month pending the completion of the new Rosebery Avenue over the old New River, though on Boxing Day another variety programme included Daisy Lloyd, a younger sister of the already famous Marie Lloyd.

Dramas were tried again early in 1892 (including *Aurora Floyd* from Miss Braddon's novel), but the Wells was up against it. No manager since Phelps had found a successful policy—the best touring companies now visited the Grand Theatre, Islington, which then stood just across the Angel cross-roads; at the Agricultural Hall a little farther on were the black-faced Mohawk Minstrels; while at Sam Collins's Music Hall by Islington Green the best variety artists were appearing—Deacon's was no longer standing.

Following the trend of the day, Wilmot tried to get a variety licence for the Wells, supported by five thousand Clerkenwell parishioners petitioning the L.C.C. that it would attract other builders to the many vacant sites on the new desolate road and so increase local trade, if a handsome structure were put up 'in the place of the present deformity called Sadler's Wells'. But the licence was refused, so popular plays went on—among them two by Dion Boucicault, *Arrah-Na-Pogue* and *The Streets of London* (localized as *The Streets of Islington*), and even a poor *Henry VIII.*

It was left to a new manager, George Belmont, who took over on 3rd November 1893, to keep the Wells alive for the next ten years.

CHAPTER FIFTEEN

POOR WOUNDED PLAYHOUSE

1893–1925

GEORGE BELMONT, whose real name was Belchett, was a remarkable character. He had been one of 'the greatest "knock-about brothers" that ever adorned any variety stage' and his nickname 'Barnum's Beauty' suggests that he may have appeared with the eighty-year-old Barnum's Circus at Olympia in 1890—though I can find no evidence of this. Since 1885 he had made a success in Hackney of the Sebright Music Hall, then called Belmont's, introducing 'twice-nightly' to London. Because of the way his advertisements were worded, he became known as 'The Autocrat of Alliteration'.

Though a variety licence had been refused, so long as drama was performed at the Wells there was nothing to stop Belmont (on behalf of Wilmot and Freeman) from annoying the authorities by adding solo variety acts. In a way this was a new idea, but it really was a hark-back to the Wells of the eighteenth century when solo performers (for instance, La Belle Espagnole) appeared as well as a long exciting drama (then perforce mimed to music). Belmont paid only £7 a week rent for the Wells, including the bars, and his opening production on Saturday, 18th November 1893, was *The Coiner* in seven scenes—as well as a large number of turns including the great Marie Lloyd, who came to launch him at the Wells in gratitude for his having given her a chance at the Sebright in 1886 when she was sixteen. To suit her other engagements that night, the play was stopped two-thirds of the way through and resumed after her act.

Other performers that evening were the seventeen-year-old Alice Leamar ('Her golden hair was hanging down her back'); Harry Champion ('Boiled Beef and Carrots', with which he started best-selling records, and later 'Henery the Eighth I am' and 'Any Old Iron?'); the Sisters Lloyd (Alice and Gracie,

173

sisters of Marie, who could 'twinkle their tiny toes'); George Vokes (of the famous pantomime family which monopolized Drury Lane for so many years); long eccentric Tom Leamore, The Wrinkle Wrecker; 'and a multitude more, the whole forming the grandest, greatest, and richest show ever seen in this mundane sphere at so small a sum, 2d., 3d., 4d., 6d., & 1s.'

Two performances were given that evening and the *Referee*, after remarking that the Wells had been '—for some inscrutable reason which has very little reason in it, and certainly no justice—denied a music and dancing licence by the London County Council', said that both houses were crowded and enthusiastic.

After this special performance Belmont ran the Wells successfully till May 1902 with a weekly change of both play and variety—his 'Vaudeville bifurcation', he called it—a remarkable achievement. What he called 'sensational dramas' were in themselves of little value though usually performed by leading actors, while the chief variety artists were either of the first rank or soon to become so.

In 1893 *The Lily Flower, or, Fleur de Lys* about the Franco-Prussian war was acted by the leading actor of the Britannia Theatre, Hoxton, Algernon Syms, who returned each of the next two years, while George Vokes, Tom Leamore with his energetic dancing, and Harry Champion ('always a favourite here', 'the Merry Man who Mends his "Unmentionables" with a Yard or Two of Tripe') came back—the last two often returning through the years.

In 1894—when a new entrance was made from Rosebery Avenue—the actors included G. H. Macdermott for several weeks, J. B. Howe, and George Lupino in *Robinson Crusoe* with Nelly Lupino and Arthur Leslie. Marie Lloyd at Whitsun gave up at her first performance because of laryngitis: the audience, though offered their money back, left only after Belmont proceeded to 'do his mite by giving them a few steps'. Marie returned to the warmest reception in June and her sister Daisy came back as Dainty Daisy Wood (the real family name), refusing to cash in on her sister's fame. In September Belmont introduced 'pretty, clever, engaging young' Lily Morris, who scored with her 'Naughty Boys' (and was later famous for her 'Why am I always the Bridesmaid and never the Blushing

Bride?' and 'Don't have any more, Mrs. Moore'): she also came back the next two years.

Sam Redfern returned to the Wells in 1895, Syms acted in the 'dramaëttes' *In the Trenches*, 'a Military Morsel of the Cold Crimea', *Murder Will Out* (a story of Mining Life), and a three-scene version of *Jane Shore*. New to the Wells that year were Wal Pink in his own comic sketches; the famous Kate Carney with coster's barrow and donkey, singing 'Three pots a shilling', 'Strolling along the Walworth Road', and 'Polly Johnson'; and the cockney comedian Gus Ellen. Gracie Lloyd 'with all the archness that is a distinguishing trait of the family' sang about finding a man under the bed and, instead of screaming, locking the door, while Marie herself was re-introduced by Belmont in his typical manner as

> the Star Comedienne of the Stage, the Divine Droll, the Music Hall Manager's Mascot, the Svengalian Songstress,[1] a Star supreme in a Sphere of its own Setting, possessing power of hypnotising the hugest houses into deliriums of delight. Where can one be found so naive, so full of archness, so piquant and delicious in her gurgling laughter and superabundant vitality, whether as the Poetess of Motion, or portraying 'The Barmaid'. She is young, personable, gay, witty, and good; radiant as a rose, sweet as a violet, chaste as a lily, loving everybody and by everybody beloved.

Belmont, whose portrait now adorned the programme, had proved himself able to engage expensive topliners in spite of the cheap prices. He introduced in 1896 the eccentric Wilkie Bard; the bombastic parodist Charles Bignell, 'Sadler's Special Sadness Shifter'; the jaunty, voluble R. G. Knowles (who walked about to stop his stammer) with his 'On the Benches in the Park'; Mark Sheridan singing 'There was I in a little short shirt Running up and down our stairs' and 'I do like to be beside the Seaside'; and two artists who often returned to the Wells— Jolly John Nash with his laughing songs, and nineteen-year-old Lottie Lennox the Lavender Lady. Tom Costello came back, as did the now grown-up Will Evans, an 'Extraordinary Eccentric Entertainer' who played the concertina, cornet, bells and tins that were thrown at him.

But the most remarkable introduction of that year to the Wells was that of moving pictures. Finding that Edison's recently

[1] *Trilby* with her hypnotic Svengali had just been produced by Tree.

invented Kinetoscope was not patented outside the United States, R. W. Paul improved on it and became the British pioneer of cinematography, showing his Theatrograph first at the Finsbury Technical College on 20th February (just after the Lumière brothers had shown their first films in Paris and London), then at the Alhambra, and on 12th December at Sadler's Wells. Belmont said that it

> Debars Analysis and Delights Audiences because of its Wonderful Simulation of Human Beings in Action. Pictures, Life-size, Life-like, and full of Character and Colour, thrown on a Screen. This Theatrograph is a mighty Mirror of Promethean Photography, and an act of Artistic and Mammoth Magnificence.

It showed Passengers Disembarking from the Paris Express; Traffic and Pedestrians on Blackfriars Bridge; Children at Tea, Laughing, Playing and Crying; 'The Soldier and his Sweetheart Spooning on a Seat'; Sunday Morning in Whitechapel; the Czar going to Versailles; David Devant conjuring; probably the waves at Dover which so terrified the front rows when shown that year on Broadway; and certainly the first topical event ever filmed in Britain—the Prince of Wales's Persimmon winning the Derby with 'Thousands of Persons rushing on to the Course'—and all of this, as the advertisement said, in colour (surprising at that date, but explained by the fact that each frame of the film was hand-coloured by a laborious stencil process).

Belmont now nicknamed the Wells 'Sunny Old Sad's', and began 1897 by introducing the comedian George Merritt; James Berry, hangman of 193 murderers, in a lantern lecture showing prison flogging rooms, the hanging beam and the Black Maria; and the Fred Karno Trio; giving the patriotic shows *For the Queen* depicting Her Majesty, the Prince and Princess of Wales, and Dr. Jameson (imprisoned May–December 1896 as leader of the disastrous raid against Kruger), and *Under the Red Cross* in which 'a real Machine Gun, as used in the Matabele Campaign, does some splendid service without the aid of the BRUTAL DUM-DUM BULLETS', and ending the year with 'the new Motion Picture Photograph Device Triumph', the Velograph of the Croydon Syndicate of that name, throwing pictures on a sheet with titles on a screen.

MISS MARRIOTT
AS HAMLET

SIMS REEVES IN
LUCIA DI LAMMER

MARIE LLOYD

ROY REDGRAVE

On 20th January 1898 Pinero put the Wells of the 'sixties on the stage at the Court Theatre, pretending—to avoid possible libel?—that *Trelawny of the 'Wells'* concerned Bagnigge Wells. Two days later Belmont seized the opportunity for publicity by attacking Pinero's 'inaccuracy', offering money prizes 'for the most Humorous and Belmontese Argument . . . showing why the "Court" *Trelawny of the "Wells"* is Trelawny of Sunny Old Sadler's Wells. Bagnigge Wells was demolished in the 'forties, and never boasted a Theatre'.

Twelve years later Sir Arthur Pinero part-identified his 'Wells' characters. By 1910 only 'Avonia Bunn' was still an actress, highly respected; 'Ferdinand Gadd' and 'Rose Trelawny' had really existed, though she did not marry 'Arthur Gower' and had been 'dead some time now'; 'Telfer', the manager ('husky, dignified and uncertain of his h's') with his wife 'Violet Sylvester', tall, massive, and middle-aged, a faded queen of tragedy, may, I suggest, have reflected Edgar and his wife Alice Marriott; 'Colpoys', Pinero said, had the last three letters as part of his real name (so may have been C. Lloyds who played Danny Mann in the Wells *Colleen Bawn* in 1863—or W. Worboys, who played in *Money* the same year); 'Denzil' was John Hare, and 'Mortimer' Sydney Bancroft (as Sir Squire Bancroft first called himself)—both new-type actors 'outwardly greatly superior to the older actors'; while the 'recent manager Phillips' was, of course, Phelps. The Clown Tavern,[1] where the company rehearsed, of course existed, but the only character who had definitely appeared at the Wells was 'Tom Wrench'—the playwright Tom Robertson, who in 1854 when he was twenty-five had played small parts (such as Osric in *Hamlet*) with Phelps. But Pinero's picture of a 'Wells' Theatre of some thirty-five years earlier was a good boost for Belmont, though he called his shows 'Concerts'—presumably to satisfy the law that here was no music-hall.

In 1898 Belmont introduced George Mozart 'in a Comic Musical Gallimaufry' and Joe O'Gorman in a comedy double act with his partner Tennyson. The White-Eyed Musical Kaffir, Chirgwin, black-faced with a white diamond round one

---

[1] Recently a Territorial H.Q., it still stands in St. John's Street but is no longer a public-house.

eye, was a great draw with his 'sempiternal song', 'The Blind Boy', his violin and his dancing clay-pipes.

Outside the theatre in those days, I was told by an old family friend, pig's trotters, split, salted and vinegared, were sold: she said it looked more like a private house than a theatre (its exterior still roughly what it had been in Rosoman's time). Inside a man went round calling 'Almond cakes or Banbury! Bottle of beer a penny! Housebill 'apenny!' Not allowed by her father to go to music-halls (she was about seventeen), she and other girls nevertheless skipped their afternoon piece-work and made up with odd farthings the 2d. a head charged for sitting on the wooden forms close behind the band (early doors, perhaps?). She especially remembered the skin-tightly dressed Chirgwin with his immaculate long straight dressing-gown and his three-foot-tall top hat who, after singing 'Blind Boy' on the constant demand of the audience, made his clay-pipes on the tray twirl and high-kick like dancers—and when he broke them, 'We silly girls screamed and he took the mickey out of us'.

A new artist in 1899 was G. H. Elliott, 'a Jollier from Jollyville' (later known as the Chocolate-Coloured Coon) with his 'Silvery Moon', but the dramas were mere sketches—even *The Corsican Brothers* and Longfellow's 'Village Blacksmith' with a 'Choice Crowd of Charming Clerkenwell Children'. Then the South African War started and patriotism was reflected by shows such as 'an Ntirely New and National Novelty, Ntitled *Under Which Flag?*' and Flo Penley reciting Kipling's 'Absentminded Beggar' (by permission of the *Daily Mail*).

Patriotism and blood-curdlers like *The Worst Man in London* dominated the Wells in 1900 (Belmont ignoring the rumours that it would be demolished to 'make room for model dwellings') and it was besieged for tickets for the popular Minnie Palmer in *Rose Pom-Pom* and Leonard Mortimer's almost resident company in *Blackmail*, supported by the Edisonograph pictures.

Belmont spent £2,000 on redecoration in the winter, having removed a 'hideous hoarding in front of the house', and in 1901 presented many famous names—Gertie Gitana of 'Nellie Dean' fame (then only twelve and billed as 'Little Gitana' with her 'Daddy's Dream' and imitation of Marie Lloyd); Leo Dryden of 'The Miner's Dream of Home' fame, popular at the Wells ever since he first appeared there in 1893, in *The Only Way*; the 'title-rôle ruler of "The Britannia" that rules Hoxton', Regal Roy Redgrave, 'in a thrilling French drama of deep and dark dungeon horrors, and entitled *The Executioner's Son, or, The only Garçon of " Monsieur de Paris" '*; Joe O'Gorman as a solo act; tall, distinguished Marie Kendall ('Just like the Ivy on the Old Garden Wall'); Nathan Jackley with jumps that had 'never been attempted by any other human being'; Daisy James, 'un chic typesse'; George Leyton with his patriotic sketches; the black-faced coon-singer May Henderson; Arthur Reece with his 'Sons of the Sea'; Dainty Daisy Dormer; the Six Brothers Luck; the Eight Lancashire Lads; and Marie Blanche (Ada Blanche's daughter).

Pictures were shown of the Cup Final by the British Biolograph, and the Historiograph showed 'verified views from Venice, Vienna and the Virgin's Valley, Piccadilly'.

Plays included *East Lynne*, *The Sorrows of Satan* (from Marie Corelli's novel), and in a ten-week season from the end of December *Captain Kettle* (Cutcliffe Hyne's popular character), *The Great Detective* (Sherlock Holmes), *I am Innocent* (about Dreyfus, retried only two years before), and other dramas with Redgrave, the 'Cock of the North' (always a great success and foreshadowing his son, Sir Michael) and 'luscious' Louisa Peach or Judith Kyrle upholding 'the Dramatic Dignity of Phelps's Happy Acting Ground'.

The 1902 novelties included an eight-foot bear; several boxing contests (one with Bill Nolan and Bill Corbett, both Champion Belts, together and against all comers); the comedian Arthur Rigby ('I'm the Plumber'); the German-American illusionist Carl Hertz (whose vanishing canary and cage caused high-up enquiries about cruelty to animals); the black-faced 'Miniature May Yohe'; and yet another cinematograph device, the Erascope, with singing pictures.

By now Belmont was paying £45 a week rent—the highest commanded for the Wells: yet he claimed he was the only person since Phelps to make it pay. But on 26th May 1902 the theatre was closed for alterations (many also complained that smoking was not allowed, though not forbidden in nearby music-halls). Belmont went off to the Continent to be 'free from the bustle and turmoil in which London is now engulphed' for the Coronation of Edward VII, and never returned to the Wells.

Summer rumours that the Wells was to be demolished were denied by the owner, H. A. Freeman, but when it reopened in September 1902 under Howard Harvey, it closed three days later. Then in November Frank Macnaghten, manager of the East End music-halls, the Foresters Vaudeville and the Palace in Bow Road, made the Wells part of his Vaudeville Circuit, using it as well for his Bow rehearsals. His weekly programmes were of as high a standard as under Belmont with the return of popular artists; his pantomime *Aladdin*—the first since the 'eighties—lasted till February 1903, in which year he introduced the comedienne Vesta Victoria ('There was I waiting at the Church'); and in November the London County Council granted Freeman a music-hall licence, which however meant that drinking was no longer allowed in the auditorium as it had been under the Lord Chamberlain's dramatic licence—a point to be remembered when considering Phelps's achievements and the attempts of his successors.

Plays naturally became fewer up to the end of 1904, though there was a *Richard III* as well as *Todd! Fleet Street* (a version of *Sweeney Todd, the Barber*), and Macnaghten introduced the bashful Jack Pleasants ('I'm twenty-one today'); Fred Karno and Company (was Chaplin with them then?), Ella Shields ('Burlington Bertie'); Florrie Forde ('Down at the Old Bull and Bush'), Johnny Danvers (uncle to but younger than Dan Leno, to whom he acted as 'feed'); and the Australian Billy Williams, the man with the velvet suit ('John, John, go and put your trousers on').

But in 1905, though the weekly *Entr'acte* still advertised artists' Monday rehearsals, no stage paper gave any names, and after 18th November even the rehearsal advertisements stopped. The Macnaghten records were destroyed in the air attacks of the Second World War and so, apart from a few bills in the Finsbury Library Collection and an occasional journalistic reference, the next twenty years of Wells history remain dark.

At the end of 1910, when Macnaghten gave up the lease for a year, there was a twice-nightly pantomime *Dick Whittington* at this 'Popular Theatre for London Toilers' (prices 2d. to 1s.)

and at the start of 1911 *Babes in the Wood* was supervised by Macnaghten's General Manager, Frederick Baugh who, Wee Georgie Wood tells me, always lifted his hat as a cue to pull an unsuccessful artist into the wings by the long hook.

Sir Walter Besant in his book *London North of the Thames*, published that year, said that then the Wells had 'dirty stucco peeling off the frontage in patches, and the bricks of the body of the house showing a leprosy of damp and old age'.

A Grand Charity Concert was given every Sunday and Frank Harvey's *Ring of Iron* was performed in June when Macnaghten transferred his rights to the new Sadler's Wells Theatre Ltd., Baugh becoming the leaseholder and paying a yearly rent of £1,100 to Charles Richard Wilmot and Louie Emily Wall, wife of Henry Wall of Stamford Hill.

Though no other details of the 1911–13 programmes have come to light (apart from an address by Major Archer-Shee on Tariff Reform and Imperial Preference), I am told by a Finsbury resident that the usual fare was twice-nightly drama, mostly murder-thrillers, the leading lady being Dolly Elsworthy, who married the Moss Empire's popular manager, Ernie Wightman. That fine present-day actor George Merritt (whose uncle, the comedian of the same name, was at the Wells in 1897) tells me the place was then known as a 'blood-tub': he remembers that when he had an audition there (for a job he did not accept) the interior was dilapidated with torn linoleum curling up from the floor.

Then in January 1914 it was announced that Russell's Bioscope Company would open the Wells as a Picture Palace. This started a rumpus, begun by the *Daily Chronicle* theatre critic, S. R. Littlewood, and the well-known actor-manager, Edward Compton (husband of Mrs. Bateman's daughter Virginia, and father of Fay Compton and Sir Compton Mackenzie). Littlewood asked—

> Can it really be true . . . that old Sadler's Wells—the oldest surviving theatre in London . . . where if only in memory of 'brave old Samuel', the very spirit of Shakespeare himself must love to linger . . . has been, in the heartless language of the paragraph, 'acquired for the cinema'? . . .
>
> Poor wounded old playhouse. Here it stands, even now shabby and disconsolate, its once familiar frontage half-hidden with flaring posters. But there is still a certain dignity about it. It is

used for a picture-show on Sundays, but during the week it struggles along in the strictest and most loyal devotion to legitimate drama.

He described how he saw 'from a coign of vantage in the inch or two of standing-room left at the back of the twopenny gallery' a cowboy melodrama 'of an entirely stimulating and honourable sort', in which Reindeer, the faithful Indian, planted 'his gleaming knife in the breast of Mexican Joe, while the snowy-bloused heroine had for the moment retired to pack the hero's portmanteau in the log-cabin':

> Anyone who imagines that the great public has lost its taste for live human drama should have seen or heard that twopenny gallery at Sadler's Wells. It was one seething, roaring mass of human sympathy . . . You should have heard the shouts of rapture when Mexican Joe rolled over and the moccasined hero rushed up in the nick of time and hurled his hat into a stage-box, and clasped the heroine at the lime-lit curtain fall.

As a result of the protests, Frederic Baugh suspended all negotiations and said he was prepared to make over his rights for the next twenty years to a new company, if it was formed 'forthwith with public-spirited enthusiasm and business methods and theatrical experience on the board'. If the new company could start with £4,000, he would accept £1,500 in shares for his rights.

The *Islington Daily Gazette* boosted the idea by printing three excellent articles on the Wells by H. G. T. Cannons, Finsbury librarian, and the proposal was supported by Beerbohm Tree, Sir George Alexander, Sir John Hare, T. P. O'Connor, Arnold Bennett, Edward Compton, William Archer, William Poel, Ramsay MacDonald, Bernard Shaw, Alfred Mond, Sir Arthur Pinero, Gilbert Murray, Seymour Hicks, Weedon Grossmith, Arthur Collins, and many others.

Compton was prepared to bring his own company to give a week of classical drama at the Wells (where the Mayor and Mayoress of the borough attended a Good Friday service); and there was a public meeting there in April attended by Alexander, Henry Arthur Jones, Matheson Lang, Poel, Compton, and Rosina Filippi to urge for a low-priced People's Theatre. But it failed to catch on—the Wells was not even mentioned at a similar meeting at Drury Lane the following Sunday: so that the performance on Saturday, 25th April, of *A Woman from Scotland Yard* was generally expected to be the last play given at the Wells.

On 26th September the Mayor of Finsbury opened the Wells as a cinema, with tip-up chairs instead of the old wooden seats, the proceeds that day patriotically devoted to those in distress through the Great War that had started on 4th August.

But in 1915 it closed, in 1916—marked 'Advertising Station' —it was noted in the Finsbury Valuation list as 'pulled down' though walls and other parts were still standing, and in 1917 the rates were paid by the owners Mrs. Wall and Mr. Wilmot.

On 10th March 1919, however, a report alleged that boys had done £1,000 worth of damage since it had been shut up for twelve months and that ten boys, between ten and fourteen years old, had been caught swinging in the flies and turning on taps. They were tied together with string by the police, marched off, and fined 5s. each.

In 1921 a rumour that Ernest Rolls would turn it into a cabaret theatre came to nothing: and in 1923 the *Evening News* reported that the custodian of the place, Ardeen Foster, once Charles Hawtrey's manager, 'a man with a big heart', gave small money prizes for the best 'house' built in the ruins every evening by 'The little Housewives of Sadler's Wells', children chosen from North London schools which had been contributing to a fund for rebuilding.

But the Wells (its site rejected for a pickle factory) was not finished: two years later the most important chapter in its twentieth-century history began.

CHAPTER SIXTEEN

ENTER 'THE LADY'

1925–1933

WITH THE revival of Sadler's Wells, this book takes
on a different atmosphere—not only because it deals
with the recovery of the theatre's great name which
has lasted till the present day, nor because it is now concerned
with events easily within living memory and people most of
whom are still alive, but because it is impossible for me to write
about it impersonally.

Almost everybody mentioned from now on I have known,
some intimately, and many I have worked with, elsewhere and
at the Wells itself. Not that these next pages will become auto-
biographical, but as I have been closely associated with the
Wells socially and professionally for almost the whole of
its latest period both as actor and director, and in a small way as
composer, it would be ineffectual camouflage to avoid the first
person.

The difficulty—and it is a difficulty that faces all historians—
is that, while the truth (so far as it is known) can be told
freely about the distant past, the nearer one comes to the present,
the more careful (one might say, the less candid) must one be.
This is ironic, since a writer should know more about his own
day than about past generations; but while it is one thing to try
to tell the truth, telling the whole truth where living people are
concerned, either as history or criticism, is a custom which unfortunately died out a century ago.

The occasional comment cannot—and surely should not—be
avoided by the historian; but I shall do my best to set out the
facts without taking sides. Criticism is healthy, and I only hope
that anything read as criticism in the following pages will be
taken—as it is meant—constructively and without offence
especially as comments are from newspapers or other publi-
cations.

*

184

Since 1898 the Old Vic,[1] on the south side of the Thames, had been managed by Lilian Baylis—first for her aunt, Emma Cons, then from 1912 by herself, to further the cause of drama and opera at popular prices.

In the 1920s the idea of expanding similarly into North London, was suggested by the actress Estelle Stead to Lilian Baylis who, with her tireless enthusiasm for what was worth while, interested so many people that on 30th March 1925 the Duke of Devonshire made a public appeal for funds

(1) To purchase Sadler's Wells (freehold), reconstruct the interior, and save it, with its historic traditions, for the Nation.
(2) To establish it as a 'Foundation', not working for profit, under the Charity Commissioners, and, by providing for its use by the 'Old Vic' Shakespeare and Opera Companies, conjointly with their present Theatre in the Waterloo Road, to give an 'Old Vic' to North London.

With him on the Committee were Viscount Hambleden, J. R. Clynes, Sir Thomas Beecham, Sir Sydney Lee, Sir Johnston Forbes-Robertson, Sir Edmund Gosse, Arthur Bourchier, John Drinkwater, S. C. Harper (Mayor of Islington), Edward Marsh, J. C. Squire, J. T. Wallis (Mayor of Finsbury), who formed the Executive Committee, and Stanley Baldwin, Lord Balfour, Lord Oxford and Asquith, the Bishop of London (the Rev. A. F. Winnington-Ingram), Winston Churchill, J. H. Thomas, Lady Cunard, Dame Ethel Smyth, G. K. Chesterton, John Galsworthy, Cyril Maude, George Moore, Maude Royden and Alfred Sutro on the General Committee with Reginald Rowe, an Old Vic Governor since 1920, as Hon. Treasurer—a list that in itself bears tribute to Lilian Baylis's pertinacity.

Subscriptions began to pour in, the three months' option on the property was taken up by the New Sadler's Wells Theatre Trust, and throughout the summer speeches and garden fêtes were given as well as concerts, and a performance of *Trelawny of the 'Wells'* (with Ernest Milton as Tom Wrench and Marie Ney, Andrew Leigh, and Robert Atkins in the cast) was presented at the Old Vic, all to further the fund. The Finsbury

[1] It was Emma Cons who, when she took over the management in 1880, gave the name The Royal Victoria Hall and Coffee Tavern (popularized into The Old Vic) to the theatre opened in 1818 as The Royal Coburg, renamed The Royal Victoria in 1833, The New Victoria Palace in 1871. The Old Vic was in 1963 absorbed into the National Theatre established in that year.

Borough Council gave £2,000 and issued a public appeal; Sir Arthur Pinero wrote his memories of the old Wells for the *Evening News*; the *Islington Gazette* started a fund of £1,000 to secure a Carnegie Trust grant of £10,000; and by October £20,000 had been subscribed towards the £60,000 necessary to buy, repair, and equip the theatre. By December the Wells had been bought for £14,200, leaving between £5,000 and £6,000 in hand towards its reconstruction; some £40,000 more was still needed.

Not that everyone was in favour of the scheme: one magazine —the cutting in the Finsbury Library is not identifiable—attacked it with a mixture of sense and woolly thinking:

> The story is always the same with the Old Vic. When it's money that's wanted, appeal to the educationalists: where there's a blunder to absolve or a debt to meet, put it all down to education . . . let there be no misunderstanding about this. The stage is preserved especially for those of theatrical talent; this old estate of ours is not to be the dumping ground of the incompetent.
>
> Miss Baylis we find incompetent, for she has not done the things expected of a sound manager of a theatre which is 'not run for profit'.
>
> Such a manager must run it for something positive—the negative virtue of not selling enough tickets, so as to cover every expense, is really insufficient . . . The sole healthy idea of a theatre is to run it for Genius *and* a thundering profit too: aiming deliberately for both, sniffing at neither.
>
> Miss Baylis has sniffed at both.

(Many people nowadays wonder why subsidies, without which commercial managements often achieve both artistic and profitable results, do not always guarantee either.)

> But Miss Baylis has shown us what it is she can do. The Old Vic represents the kindly spirit towards the poor of the Surrey side; and now this warm-hearted woman wishes to do the same to the poor of another edge of London . . . by forcing quasi-intellectual food down their throats sugared with the awful phrase, 'It will do you so much good . . . really it will'. . . . What the Carnegie Trust wastes is of no importance . . . But this further £60,000 which is now being slowly extracted from Londoners' pockets is a grievous business, and that it will also be so much waste is a little too bad.

But the 'warm-hearted woman' (always known as 'The Lady') still urged people to collect funds for which a great many special matinées, concerts, recitals and meetings were organized. The leaders of the entertainment world took part: —in 1926 the sixty-seven-year-old Dame Nellie Melba, in *La Bohème* at the Vic, after her farewell performances; in 1927 Sir John Martin-Harvey, Sir Gerald du Maurier, Phyllis Bedells, Sybil Thorndike, Edith Evans, Nigel Playfair and others, in a special matinée at the New Theatre which included a new sketch by Edgar Wallace; Sir Johnston Forbes-Robertson, with eleven of his family and others in *Twelfth Night* at the St. James's; a National Sunday League Concert at the Palladium, with Sterndale Bennett, Marie Dainton, Plunkett Greene, Tex McLeod and John Henry 'of Wireless fame' (still a novelty); and at the New Clown Club Room (formerly the Old Clown) a 'Gathering of Descendants, 1683–1879' of Sadler, Rosoman, Grimaldi, Phelps and Mrs. Bateman.

On 12th October 1928 it was announced that the rebuilding of the Wells would begin in a few weeks, incorporating a little of the old walls where possible, with a stage like that of the Old Vic but larger.

In 1929 Lilian Baylis was made a Companion of Honour (she said that with a handle *before* her name she would be expected to pay out more money). The Islington Borough Council, though the Labour members suggested a hundred guineas, voted 40–21 against contributing to the Wells scheme because children already learned enough Shakespeare at school, a decision greatly deplored by the *Islington Gazette*. (An article in the *Gazette* claimed that Forcer built a theatre on the site in 1570 and early Wells fund appeals said 1573, but I can find no evidence of this.)

Early in 1930 more appeal-entertainments were given by Sybil Thorndike and Gracie Fields among others, but in May an autumn opening was pronounced impossible, unless £6,000 was received by 'tomorrow'. An opening on Boxing Day with *A Comedy of Errors* was planned in August, but in October the Committee announced the Wells would definitely open on Twelfth Night, 6th January 1931, with the appropriate *Twelfth Night*.

The new theatre was designed by F. G. M. Chancellor and built under the architects Frank Matcham and Co. by the firm of F. G. Minter, with steelwork by Smith, Walker Ltd., and fibrous plaster by Veronese. Externally, with a canopy over the principal entrance, and a group of three stone-dressed windows and a decorative panel by Herman Cawlturn above, it relied for architectural effect chiefly on the proportion of the masses and the texture of the wall surface.

The interior had no boxes, no pillars to obscure the view, and no visible supports of circle and gallery. The walls were light buff relieved with gilded arabesques and silver-grey natural oak woodwork. Over the proscenium was an old ivory panel in relief of a scene from *A Midsummer Night's Dream* (by Cawlturn) topped by Finsbury coat-of-arms. There was an apron-stage effect with imitation marble stairs from stage to auditorium for certain Shakespeare plays, and an uncommonly large orchestral pit for the operas. The carpets were mauve and vermilion, the lighting was hidden, and all 1,650 seats were tip-up. Prices ranged from 1s. 3d. amphitheatre, 2s. 4d. pit, 3s. 6d. and 5s. 9d. circle and stalls, and unreserved seats 6d., 10d., 1s. 3d. and 1s. 10d. Smoking was allowed at performances, but silence was requested after the lights were lowered and no striking of matches during the scenes. The 'Plenum' system of heating and ventilation was installed, and refreshment rooms offered tea, coffee, hot mince-pies, and sausage-rolls. One of the two wells, at the back of the pit, can still be seen when the carpet is rolled back and the cover lifted; the other is under the orchestra.

Although £70,000 had been raised (£14,200—the price of the freehold—came from the Carnegie Trust), a debt remained of about £25,000. The builders generously refused to charge interest on the £10,000 due to them until 'such time as we can discharge the debt'.

The curtain rose on the foggy and frosty 6th January 1931 at 7.45, then the National Anthem was sung (first verse by Joan Cross, second by Constance Willis with past and present members of the Vic Opera and Shakespeare companies). The Mayor of Finsbury, Councillor C. R. Simpson, was in the chair, with Dame Madge Kendall, local Mayors, Lilian Baylis with a sprig of rosemary, the Governors of the Old Vic and Sadler's Wells, and representatives of the Carnegie Trust present. Sir Johnston Forbes-Robertson, alluding to 'my beloved master' Samuel Phelps, declared the theatre open; Captain Rowe read messages from the Prince of Wales ('our chief subscriber'), Sir

Arthur Pinero, Sir Philip Ben Greet, Sir Barry Jackson and others—almost an hour of speeches, as John Gielgud recorded (he and Harcourt Williams, the producer, also spoke), and the play began with the following cast:

MALVOLIO	. . . . .	*John Gielgud*
VIOLA	. . . . .	*Dorothy Green*
OLIVIA	. . . . .	*Joan Harben*
MARIA	. . . . .	*Elsa Palmer*
SIR TOBY BELCH	. . .	*Ralph Richardson*
SIR ANDREW AGUECHEEK	. .	*George Howe*
FESTE	. . . . .	*Leslie French*
ORSINO	. . . .	*Godfrey Kenton*
FABIAN	. . . . .	*Richard Riddle*[1]

Music directed by Herbert Menges.

After the performance the audience remained seated till the curtain rose disclosing the stiff-faced line of celebrities with Miss Baylis in the middle, 'imposing and academic, with her robes of Master of Arts and the cross of the Companion of Honour on her breast', as Gielgud wrote in his amusing account, which went on:

Lilian carried a huge basket of fruit in her right hand and when she began her oration her gestures were somewhat hampered by her burden. However, she ploughed bravely on until, enthralled by the force of her own argument, she swept her right arm out impulsively. An enormous apple fell from the basket with a thud! There was a slight titter from the audience. Lilian looked at the basket, and then, edging towards the truant apple, tried to hide it with her robes. She went on with her speech, but soon sincerity overcame technique, and the basket shot out to the right to accentuate another point. This time a pear fell on to the stage— I gave one look at it and burst out laughing. The audience followed suit and the solemnity of the occasion was irrevocably shattered.

He also recorded, 'How we all detested Sadler's Wells when it was opened first. The auditorium looked like a denuded wedding-cake, and the acoustics were dreadful.'

As planned, each fortnightly play was to be followed by a fortnight of opera repertoire, so on 20th January the first opera was given under the new system—*Carmen* produced by Sydney Russell and conducted by Lawrance Collingwood. The cast was:

[1] Henry Ainley's son.

CARMEN	.	.	.	.	.	Enid Cruickshank
MICAELA		.	.	.	.	Winifred Kennard
FRASQUITA		.	.	.	.	Nora Sabini
MERCEDES		.	.	.	.	Celia Turrell
DON JOSÉ		.	.	.	.	Arthur Cox
ESCAMILLO		.	.	.	.	Sumner Austin
MORALES		.	.	.	.	Franklyn Kelsey
ZUNIGA	.	.	.	.	.	Booth Hitchin
REMENDADO		.	.	.	.	Powell Lloyd
DANCAIRO		.	.	.	.	William Hill

The Ballet was designed by Ninette de Valois, who had been establishing an embryo ballet at the Old Vic.

With the opening of the Wells, a permanent opera company was now possible, including—apart from those mentioned—the singers Harry Brindle, Joan Cross, Leslie Jones, Tudor Davies, Edith Coates, and Rose Morris. More rehearsals were also possible now that the Shakespeare company was no longer in the same theatre. But it was not as yet financially possible to engage a permanent orchestra.

Claude Aveling, E. J. Dent, Percy Pitt, and Geoffrey Toye formed the Opera Sub-Committee of the Governors; Walter Wiltshire was the hard-working Chorus Master, Vernon Corri the Leader of the Orchestra, and Muriel Gough the Hon. Adviser. It was thrilling for Charles Corri (at the Vic since 1895) and Collingwood (long associated with it) to realize that, after operas alternating with dramas within each week at the Old Vic, now at last (apart from Mondays, taken up with transferring and preparing) a repertoire of opera and a play could alternate for a fortnight at each theatre, and for the first time there would be permanent opera in London for eight months in the year.

The opera repertoire was directed by Sidney Russell, formerly with the British National Opera Company. Harcourt Williams directed the plays. Owen Smyth designed the effective scenery ingeniously and economically to suit the two stages. And Ninette de Valois, Choreographist and Prima Ballerina, was in charge of the Vic-Sadler's Wells Opera Ballet (providing dancers for the operas as at the Vic since 1926) and the School of Ballet for which a few vacancies were first advertised on 12th January.

The Opera Ballet consisted of six girls—Ursula Moreton,

Freda Bamford, Sheila McCarthy, Joy Newton, Beatrice Apple-yard, and Nadina Newhouse, but it was hoped to give ballets before the shorter operas, with the possibility soon of having full ballet evenings once or twice a week, and maybe eventually a permanent ballet company.

In the first operatic fortnight audiences heard *Carmen, Faust,* Clive Carey's production of *The Magic Flute,* with Joan Cross a lovely Pamina, *Trovatore, Pagliacci* and *Cavalleria Rusticana.*

Gielgud's sensitive *Richard II* and *The Tempest* followed, each for a week, and then to the Wells *Lohengrin* (with Tudor Davies or Henry Wendon in the lead), *Tosca* (May Busby), and *Maritana* were introduced. *Arms and the Man* was followed by *The Lily of Killarney* (appositely on 17th March, St. Patrick's Day), *Butterfly,* and *Aida.* Then, after *Much Ado about Nothing,* came *Figaro, Tannhäuser, Bohème,* and Verdi's *Othello* (with Cox, Cross and Coates excellent, though 'the ensemble counts more with this company').

On 9th May Gielgud ended the first short Wells season of plays with *King Lear,* and on 12th *The Bohemian Girl* was the seventeenth opera from the Vic repertoire introduced to the Wells (a remarkable number in five months, as well as six fortnights of plays).

A special ballet performance on 15th May brought de Valois's *Danse Sacrée et Danse Profane* (music by Debussy, décor by Hedley Briggs), her *Jackdaw and the Pigeons* with Hugh Bradford's music, Vaughan Williams's *Faun* with Leslie French (of the Shakespeare company) and other works. For this programme Anton Dolin (who had appeared in the same programme at the Vic) got special permission from Jack Buchanan to dance his Spanish Dance and, as often before, he returned his fee to encourage the creating of the Wells ballet company—indeed, only his earlier insistence and encouragement had prevented Lilian Baylis from dropping the idea of an embryo ballet at the Old Vic (a point usually forgotten when handing out deserved praise elsewhere). Six days later Lydia Lopokova, at her own request, also danced in *Cephalus and Procris* (previously produced by de Valois for the Camargo Society); she asked for only out-of-pocket expenses which she gave back to be divided among the young dancers, who as promptly passed the money on to the building fund.

The short first season had resulted in a loss of £3,229: £1,060 had to be borrowed from the bank and besides this, the City Parochial Foundation was still owed £4,350, apart from the main debt now standing at £21,000.

As Lilian Baylis's loyal manager, Bruce Worsley, wrote: 'We had neither experience nor professional opinions, nor advice to guide us, as no one else had ever attempted to run two theatres in the way Miss Baylis intended running hers.' One lesson, however, was soon clear: the cheaper seats sold better. Hugh Walpole wrote that when he sat almost alone in the 5s. 9d. seats (he called them 6s.), though the gallery was packed for the not very good *Trovatore*, Lilian Baylis said to him,

'Tisn't very good, dear, is it?' 'No,' I said, 'it isn't. If they had only filled the six-shilling seats it would be better. If the performance were better they would fill the six-shilling seats.' 'Yes, it's a nasty roundabout, dear,' she answered.

So when, after three unsuccessful summer weeks of the farce *A Warm Corner* and *The House of the Arrow* (by A. E. W. Mason) by the Cecil Barth Company from the Vaudeville, the first complete season started in September 1931, more seats were made available at 3s. 6d., fewer at 5s. 9d., with some in the circle at 2s. 4d., while—to make up for the general reduction—the front two rows of the amphitheatre were increased to 1s. 10d.

The new Shakespeare company (which changed essentially every season) included Ralph Richardson, Robert Speaight, Robert Harris, Leslie French, George Zucco, Richard Riddle, and Phyllis Thomas, and it opened in *King John*. During its run the new custom of giving a ballet evening about once a fortnight was inaugurated with Frederick Ashton's charming *Regatta*, music by Gavin Gordon, designs by William Chappell, and Anton Dolin's sensational Satan in de Valois's impressive *Job* (first created for the Camargo Society), called a 'Masque for Dancing by Geoffrey Keynes based on Blake's illustrations' as the composer Vaughan Williams disliked conventional ballet, with décor by Gwendoline Raverat, masks and wigs by Hedley Briggs. By now the Vic-Wells Ballet was getting supporters, chiefly in the gallery, which showed loyal indiscrimination—

'like the enthusiasm of a crowd at a football match—cheering on the local team, win or lose'.

The opera company, much the same as before, gave *Samson and Delilah*, with Astra Desmond as guest artist, conducted by Percy Pitt; *Rigoletto, Carmen* (with either Olive Gilbert or Constance Willis), *Traviata* (produced by John B. Gordon), and *Dido and Aeneas* conducted by Constant Lambert.

A Midsummer Night's Dream, with Richardson as Bottom, Leslie French as a remarkable Puck, and Robert Harris a poetic Oberon, was followed by *Tales of Hoffmann*: this was produced by Clive Carey, conducted by Aylmer Buesst, and performed by Tudor Davies, Nora Sabini (Olympia), Powell Lloyd (Spalanzani), Edith Coates (Giulietta), Joan Cross ('a great favourite with the Wells'—Antonia).

The day before, Phyllis Bedells had danced in Glinka's *Fête Polonaise*. Then came *Henry V*: Richardson was not rightly cast as the King, but Harcourt Williams repeated the brilliantly characterized King of France he had given years before with Sir Frank Benson.

The year 1931 ended with *The Daughter of the Regiment*; a Scottish programme by Jean Sterling Mackinlay, Harcourt Williams's wife; and, for Boxing Day matinée, *Hansel and Gretel* with a ballet programme including de Valois's *The Jew in the Bush* (Gordon Jacob), conducted by Geoffrey Toye. At the start of 1932 Astra Desmond sang in *Carmen*; the first new production at the Wells, *A Masked Ball*, was set in Naples instead of the historical Stockholm or the Verdian Boston. *Mignon* was also produced. The Wells was once more attacking monopoly: the Government would give £17,500 to encourage opera through the B.B.C., but as Covent Garden was havering over a summer season, Lady Cunard urged a fresh start through the Wells, supported by Francis Toye in the *Morning Post* and Fox-Strangways in the *Observer*. So on 30th January the first broadcast from the Wells was given—of *Hoffmann*.

On the same afternoon, Alicia Markova danced in Arthur Bliss's *Rout* and, barefoot, in the first performance of de Valois's *Narcissus and Echo* (also with music by Bliss). She was supported by Stanley Judson, one of the original five men in ballet at the Wells—the others being Travers or Travis Kemp (both spellings were used), Fred Ashton (as he was then advertised),

Walter Gore, and William Chappell (costume designer for *Narcissus and Echo*).

Tentative beginnings are often accidentally or conveniently forgotten in the blaze of later success, and debts of gratitude are seldom repaid. At first even the gallery's exuberance was loyal rather than ballet-minded: but they did enjoy Markova, and that is mainly how a true liking for ballet developed. As Anton Dolin says in his book *Markova*,

> No one can ever estimate how much the company owes to Markova. Had it not been for her, I doubt whether the Sadler's Wells Ballet would exist today. She, and she alone, put that company firmly on its feet. Others helped most generously— Lydia Lopokova, Phyllis Bedells, Stanislas Idzikovsky, and I were frequent guests—but it was Markova, with her loyalty and hard work, to say nothing of her amazing grasp of an enormous repertoire, that made the company, plus the genius and masterly direction of Ninette de Valois.

Six ballet performances in March 1932 included Markova and Dolin in Fokine's *Sylphides* and *Spectre de la Rose*; Rupert Doone's *Enchanted Grove* (Ravel and Debussy) with Duncan Grant décor; de Valois's *Italian Suite* (Cimarosa) and the first performance of her *Nursery Suite* (Elgar)[1] with Dolin as Georgie-Porgie; and her *Création du Monde* (Milhaud).

In March there was also a concert for the Peel Institute with Ben Davies (whose voice failed), Carrie Tubb, Margaret Balfour, Daisy Kennedy, Irene Scharrer, Toplis Green, and Norman Long.

Plays early in 1932 were *The Knight of the Burning Pestle* (with Sybil Thorndike as the Citizen's Wife); *Abraham Lincoln*, produced by the author John Drinkwater (Harcourt Williams played Lincoln); *Othello* (Wilfrid Walter with Edith Evans as Emilia; *Twelfth Night*; *Julius Caesar* (with music by Gordon Jacob); and *Hamlet* played alternately by Robert Speaight and Robert Harris, who on 7th May played it in its entirety.

It was now clear that opera was more popular at the Wells and drama at the Vic. But, according to the Vic-Wells trusts, both had to be given at both theatres, so the next season would

---

[1] Sir Edward Elgar himself appeared at the end before an audience including the Duchess of York, for whose daughters the music had been written.

give two weeks' opera to one week's drama at the Wells and *vice versa* at the Vic.

To encourage bookings, a system of 5s. vouchers for stalls to be purchased in bulk but spread over nights to be chosen according to the bill, was instituted. £30,000 was still needed to cover debts (the Carnegie Trust had already given over £50,000); and Walter Sickert announced that, because of his adoration of Phelps and his gratitude to Isabel Bateman (of whose Sadler's Wells company he had been a utility member), he would sell his picture of Lazarus in aid of the Wells.

In May 1932 the Sadler's Wells Foundation (first President the Duke of Devonshire) published its Declaration of Trust, vesting any lands and hereditaments in 'The Official Trustee of Charity Lands', and appointing fifteen Governors from Governors of the Old Vic, the Carnegie Trust, the Governors of the City of London Parochial Charities Act 1883, the University of London, the Royal Academy of Music and the Royal College of Music jointly, the London County Council and the Finsbury Borough Council. Income was primarily to provide drama, opera, and other specified entertainments at the Wells or elsewhere in the County of London and to repay moneys advanced— the performances to be 'suited for the recreation and instruction of the poorer classes' at such prices 'as will make them available for artisans and labourers', though the Governing Body could from time to time allow the production 'by any person of high-class opera or high-class drama with a higher scale of prices for admission. Provided that such arrangements shall be made with a view to the benefit of and so as not to be a charge on the income of the Charity'.

Lord and Lady Hambleden founded the Sadler's Wells Society (£1 annually or £5 for life) which granted £500 out of £1,000 already raised towards presenting one play, one opera, and one ballet in the coming season, and as the Government withdrew their offer of a subsidy, Sir Thomas Beecham approved a scheme to use his Imperial League of Opera and all opera funds for a unification of Covent Garden, the Old Vic, Sadler's Wells, and possibly the Carl Rosa Opera Company.

For the coming season Harcourt Williams was the Shakespeare producer for the fourth year, but as an innovation guest-producers were to be invited—Edward Carrick (Ellen Terry's grandson, Gordon Craig's son) to assist him with *Macbeth* and Gielgud to direct *The Merchant of Venice*; Clive Carey, Sumner Austin, and John B. Gordon would share the opera productions.

Lilian Baylis also decided to allot one evening a week to ballet, and wrote to Markova hoping she and others 'who helped us in the past' would come as guest-artists, offering her £5 5s. a performance. During the summer Ruby Ginner and Irene Mawer gave a mime and dance performance at the Wells.

For the 1932–3 season, as *The Times* said, Miss Baylis 'has taken the opportunity—does she ever miss one?—offered by the opening of a new season to refurbish the stock operas of the company'. But though Doris Banner made a great success as the Doll in *The Tales of Hoffmann* and the Queen of the Night in *The Magic Flute*, in which Olive Dyer sang Papagena and Arnold Matters Sarastro excellently, the production of the latter, without the original producer, Clive Carey, 'had been allowed to degenerate'.

In November Geoffrey Toye became co-director with Lilian Baylis (two theatres were too much for one director), and the National Opera Council was formed to unite the various opera companies (each still working independently), with Beecham as Artistic Director of the Covent Garden syndicate and Adviser to the Old Vic and the Wells—the Council to receive £25,000 from the B.B.C. and the same from the Imperial League of Opera.

Among this season's operas were Arthur Benjamin's *The Devil Take Her*, décor by Hans Strohbach[1]; conducted either by Sir Thomas Beecham (who had conducted the first performance at the Royal College of Music) or the composer, together with an inaudible and grotesquely danced *Dido* (W. J. Turner and other critics said); Carey's new *Figaro* with Arnold Matters a good Figaro and Joan Cross receiving an ovation; *Hansel and Gretel* with Olive Dyer looking a child but with the power of an adult (the best Gretel since Jeanne Doust in the original London production in the 'nineties); and *Othello* with Arthur Cox and Joan Cross excellent, but with McKnight Kauffer's scenery (previously designed for a production of the Shakespeare play) inartistically displayed before each scene started, and an in-

---

[1] With whom J. B. Gordon had worked in the Cologne Opera house, and from whom I learned so much.

adequate orchestra, gunfire that drowned the chorus, and an alarm-bell more like that of a muffin-man.

Maggie Teyte sang *Butterfly*, returning her fee to the Directors; *Faust* was visited by José Collins and others who were making a film *The Jewel Song* with scenes from the opera which they had never seen; there was a Verdi week—introducing to the Wells *Forza del Destino* with Ruth Naylor; and *The Snowmaiden* was given for the first time in England with décor by Elizabeth Polunin (a pupil of Bakst), who had worked with her husband for Diaghileff, Olive Dyer in the name-part and Edith Coates as Lehl, the shepherd-boy, both excellent.

The drama company included Peggy Ashcroft, Malcolm Keen, Margaret Webster, William Fox, Charles Hickman, Roger Livesey, Geoffrey Wincott, Marius Goring, Morland Graham, with Frank Napier as Stage Manager. The plays were *Caesar and Cleopatra*, *Cymbeline*, *As You Like It*—a moment from which was painted by Sickert for the Wells fund—*Macbeth*, *The Merchant of Venice* (seen by Queen Mary), *She Stoops to Conquer*, *A Winter's Tale*, Drinkwater's *Mary Stuart* with Shaw's *Admirable Bashville* (Alastair Sim and Roger Livesey), *Romeo and Juliet*, *The School for Scandal*, and *The Tempest* (Harcourt Williams, with Leslie French a wonderful Ariel).

Among the ballets were *Lac des Cygnes*, Act II, with Dolin, Markova and Judson (2,000 attending on the opening night); de Valois's new *Douanes* (Geoffrey Toye); Ashton's *Lord of Burleigh* (Mendelssohn-Gordon Jacob to Edwin Evans's scenario with George Sheringham's décor); de Valois's *Origin of Design* (Handel-Beecham—not a success); her *Scorpions of Ysit* (Gavin Gordon); Ashton's *Pomona* (Lambert) with Vanessa Bell's décor; de Valois's new *Birthday of Oberon* (Purcell-Lambert); and *Coppelia*, Acts I and II, produced by Nicolai Sergeyeff of the old Imperial Ballet as done in St. Petersburg, with Lydia Lopokova as the Doll, Hedley Briggs as Dr. Coppelius and the young Australian Robert Helpmann in the corps de ballet. Dolin also created his justly famous solo *Bolero* (Ravel) which de Valois thought music-hall, no doubt because of the spectacular leap on to one knee—but it was nevertheless presented as often as possible so as to draw an audience.

In the summer of 1933 Lilian Baylis, realizing the value of Markova, offered to double her pay per performance to £10 10s.

and promising that de Valois would revive one classic each season for her if she would join the company as prima ballerina instead of guest artist. This she did till May 1935, carrying the repertoire almost alone. The Wells was now recognized in many quarters as the nucleus of an operatic nursery. R. P. P. Rowe as Hon. Treasurer of the Governing Body supported Sir Gerald du Maurier in his fight against the Entertainment Tax (almost the amount lost by the Wells on shows given for public good), and in spite of a loss of £3,460 by the Wells in the previous season, mainly because of the expense of presenting opera (though it took more than the Vic), all was set fair for success at the Wells.

CHAPTER SEVENTEEN

YEARS OF ACHIEVEMENT

1933–1939

THE 1933–4 season was indeed remarkable. Since opera continued to prove more popular than drama at the Wells, it was decided to open there with six weeks of opera and ballet, to be followed by three of drama.

New members of the opera company included Winifred Lawson, Gladys Palmer, George Hancock, Henry Wendon, and Ben Williams. The producers, as before, were Sumner Austin, Clive Carey, and John B. Gordon. Warwick Braithwaite joined Lawrance Collingwood and Charles Corri as conductor, and the orchestra was increased to forty-five players.

La Bohème (with Albert Coates as guest conductor in place of Beecham who was ill) played to standing-room only; Antony Tudor, who had joined the ballet the previous season, designed the ballet for *Faust*; Joan Cross was superb in *Traviata*; Carey based the first performance in England of *Tsar Saltan* on the Moscow production, Coates and Collingwood conducting alternately (the décor by the Polunins painted by Slade School students); and in *Othello*, Arthur Cox was in stupendous voice—'In most respects this was no doubt the best performance ever given in English of the masterpiece'—'not a stellar affair, and yet it thrilled' so the Wells 'has now good reason to consider itself the real home of opera in London'.

Mary Jarred sang as *Orpheus*, Percy Heming sang Scarpia in *Tosca* with Josephine Wray or Florence Easton, the British soprano from New York's Metropolitan Opera. Beecham conducted Ethel Smyth's *Boatswain's Mate* for the composer's seventy-fifth birthday; *Cosi fan Tutte*, admirably done, was not a success; E. J. Dent's new translation of the *Barber of Seville*, conducted by John Barbirolli 'came as a novelty to the audience'; in the first stage performance of Collingwood's *Macbeth*, produced by Sumner Austin, Joseph Farrington sang the name part,

Clive Carey Malcolm, Powell Lloyd the Porter; and Miriam Licette sang Donna Anna in *Don Giovanni*.

The ballet company, now including Robert Helpmann, the fine character dancer Claude Newman, and Antony Tudor as principals, was headed by Markova and, for the first three months, Stanislas Idzikovsky, a Diaghileff premier danseur and one of the greatest dancers of the time.

Ballets, now given every Tuesday, included de Valois's new *Wise and Foolish Virgins* (music by Kurt Atterberg), *Spectre de la Rose* and *The Blue Bird* (in which Idzikovsky wore Nijinsky's costume); a revival of *Job* in which the 'young newcomer' Helpmann made his mark in Dolin's part; Gordon Jacob's *Choral Waltz*, performed with Markova and Idzikovsky in *Carnaval* (but as yet the company was not successful in Fokine ballet); and Frederick Ashton's first important creation, *Les Rendezvous* (Auber), designed to show off the 'particular gifts of speed, precision, and lightness' exhibited by Markova, more and more like Pavlova, and now the darling of the Wells, who danced it with Idzikovsky, décor being by William Chappell.

Most remarkable was the first performance, on 1st January 1934, by a British ballet company of *Giselle*. Markova having understudied Olga Spessiva in 1932, had pored over lithographs of Grisi who created the character in 1851—only to be told angrily by Nicolai Sergeyeff (consulted by de Valois for authentic tradition) *not* to assemble great moments of past performers—'the character is conveyed by the dancer herself and not by the steps devised by the choreographer'; it should not be danced 'like a highly complicated technical exercise' but every move should have a 'why'—a good lesson to any artist who thinks that imitation is creation.

After six weeks' detailed rehearsal Markova was impressive both as the village girl and as the ethereal vision—unlike most Giselles. Spessiva watched from a chair in the wings; and afterwards Lopokova and Lydia Kyasht congratulated Markova, brilliantly partnered by Dolin as Albrecht. The enthusiastic audience was large in spite of a really dense London fog: Dolin got influenza after the first performance and Judson took his place at twenty-four hours' notice.

Later the same month the first full performance outside Russia of *Casse-Noisette* was given, also directed by Sergeyeff, interpreted by Lopokova who acted all the parts at rehearsal. Markova was the Sugar-Plum Fairy, the Lord Mayor's Boy Pipers were the twelve mice, Helpmann danced the Chinese Dance, and the Arab Dance was given by Sergeyeff to the 'dramateek lady' Elsa Lanchester, whom he had seen rehearse as Ariel in *The Tempest*. The last new ballet of the season was de Valois's *Haunted Ballroom* (Geoffrey Toye), a great success chiefly through Helpmann's dramatic performance.

Through outstanding performances of opera and ballet, the Wells was coming to be accepted as the real home of those types of entertainment, 'the large auditorium [prices 6s. to 6d.], with the exception of a few rows of the most expensive seats, has been packed to the ceiling', though many would-be enthusiasts forgot that the theatre was then only a 2d. ride from Piccadilly. The Camargo Society inaugurated public subscriptions of 2s. 6d. annually towards the cost of one first-class ballet each season; and to facilitate the now frequent broadcasts from the Wells six microphones were installed permanently. Beecham planned the allocation of a considerable annual sum from his Imperial League of Opera to the Wells 'with a view to its becoming the centre of English opera, and the company will visit provincial cities'. And in the New Year Honours, Captain Reginald P. P. Rowe, the Hon. Treasurer of Sadler's Wells, received a knighthood.

But this remarkable season was made even more so by an experiment, the success of which created a precedent difficult to follow, thereby ultimately leading to a stoppage of plays at the Wells.

Until now the Vic-Wells drama company had been headed by recognized or promising West End actors—but not yet accepted as stars—with an occasional guest artist. They were supported by sound performers, often from previous seasons, and beginners, who could profit from a season's co-operative work. For the 1933–4 season, the new drama producer, Tyrone Guthrie, tried a fresh plan.

Established Vic-Wells artists such as Marius Goring, Roger Livesey, and Frank Napier were re-engaged, but leading West End artists—Ursula Jeans, Flora Robson, Athene Seyler, Morland Graham, and Ernest Hare—joined the company, as well as two newcomers to the stage who, as undergraduate and don, had gained something of a reputation in Cambridge University performances, James Mason and myself. But for the first time the company was headed by a recognized world-famous star: Charles Laughton. He came straight from the film successes that had followed his brilliant start on the stage, determined to risk his fame by acting in classics, and with him came his wife, Elsa Lanchester.

Not all the plays we did at the Vic were transferred: the first given at the Wells was *The Cherry Orchard* on 31st October— a successful Guthrie production in which the actors were well cast: Laughton as the *nouveau-riche* Lopakhin, Athene Seyler as the unpractical Madam Ranevsky, Flora Robson the repressed Varya, Ursula Jeans the thought-free Anya, Leon Quartermaine (a guest artist) the feckless Gaev, Morland Graham old Firs, James Mason the boorish Yasha, Marius Goring the would-be romantic Epihodov, Elsa Lanchester the over-bright governess, Roger Livesey the old-fashioned landowner Pischik, and myself Trofimov, the eternal student.

On its reputation, the Wells was sold out for *The Cherry Orchard* (the six opera weeks and three of drama were changed to four and four); advertisements for tickets appeared in *The Times*; the Duchess of York came to see it and it was even revived for a fortnight from Boxing Day 'owing to great demand'.

The next Wells play was *Henry VIII*, produced at the Vic just before the film *The Private Life of Henry the Eighth* was shown in London: comparisons between the stage Laughton and the film Laughton were inevitable. It was 'an admirable and memorable production', with the settings made by Charles Ricketts for the famous Sybil Thorndike and Lewis Casson production, and costumes from the Korda film. Herbert Menges wrote the incidental music—as he did for all the plays; Christopher Hassall (later to achieve recognition as a writer) appeared in the small part of Lovell, and Elsa Lanchester sang the 'delicate' Thomas Linley setting of the 'Orpheus' song which I had 'discovered'.

The bad acoustics of the Wells were brought home to Nicholas Hannen, as Buckingham, and myself, as Norfolk, at the opening of this play when our pride was hurt on finding that, even from the front of the stage, our reputedly good diction was unintelligible through the blurring of the sound by the curve of the walls from the proscenium. *Henry VIII* brought me another experience: Robert Farquharson, playing Wolsey, was ill after the first performance, and I had to learn the Cardinal's part in one day. The words were driven into my head by Laughton, Guthrie, and Elsa Lanchester to such effect that in performance that night it was only in the scene with Queen Katherine (Flora Robson's magnificent interpretation) that there had to be prompters behind each hanging curtain.

Then came *The Tempest*—Laughton, knowing critics were unavoidable wherever he appeared, bravely faced London as Prospero, determined to try verse-speaking. This varied from night to night and was the subject of attack; but his speaking of the Epilogue was masterly. Guthrie's storm did not please everyone, and some said Ursula Jeans as Miranda was hampered by a 'cocktail party dress' not in key with Clifford Evans's Ferdinand. Almost generally praised were Livesey's malignant Caliban; Elsa Lanchester's Ariel; Antonio (I am proud to say); Herbert Menges's incidental music; Ariel's songs and the masque music, all written by me to suit the voices available, with Purcellian echo effects, and sung by Ceres (Flora Robson), Iris (Margaret Field-Hyde), and students:

> It can have been no easy task to follow Arne in setting Ariel's final song, but we felt no regret for the familiar version in listening to this new one, in which there is too a note of wistfulness until the moment when Prospero sets the sprite free . . . One wonders whether music for a Shakespeare play has ever before been written by one of the actors in it. It may be that his participation in it contributed towards Mr. Arundell's success.[1]

James Agate, however, while liking Ariel, Caliban, and the masque music, did not like the 'steel-furniture ditties' for Ariel.

Last play in the Wells season was Congreve's *Love for Love*[2]:

> Half artistic London seemed to have climbed the hill to Sadler's Wells to see this decorative revival . . . and it is to be doubted whether *Love for Love* has ever been given a rendering at once so polished and spirited since Congreve wrote the piece as a challenge to the monopoly of Drury Lane Theatre. The management,

[1] *The Times.*   [2] Incidental music by Purcell, songs and dances by myself.

assisted by a generous financial grant from the Sadler's Wells Society, have done things in style on this occasion, and the costumes, designed by Vivian Forbes, are a delight to the eye.[1]

The costumes, incidentally, were brilliantly devised from furnishing materials. As in *The Cherry Orchard*, the casting was considered nearly perfect. Roger Livesey played Ben; his father Sam (as Sir Sampson) and brother Barrie (as Valentine) were guest artists. Laughton was perfect as Tattle (drenching himself in cheap scent, as that character would, on the first night), Athene Seyler a deliciously wicked Mrs. Frail, Flora Robson Mrs. Foresight, Elsa Lanchester a naughty Miss Prue, Ursula Jeans Angelica, Morland Graham Foresight, and myself Scandal.

In spite of the 'atmospheric chilliness' of the theatre, Guthrie had

> recaptured the atmosphere of Congreve's rather saucy play quite brilliantly. Plague on't, but I warrant you have never seen Mistress Athene Seyler and Mistress Flora Robson so roguish and pert, nor Mr. Roger Livesey so lovable and lubberly. Body o' me, but Mr. Sam Livesey is a very naughty philanderer and Mr. Morland Graham as pitiable a cuckold as you could wish to see. And what of Mr. Dennis Arundell? Does he not swagger his way through and play with the best grace of them all? Stap me, but I had almost forgot Mr. Charles Laughton and Mistress Elsa Lanchester! . . . Plague on't, what has happened to my style? I blame Mr. Congreve and Mr. Guthrie entirely.[2]

At one performance the roguish Athene Seyler, the scented Laughton and the swaggering Arundell, all suddenly sitting on a period settee, broke it and collapsed on the floor.

On Mondays, when there was no resident performance, outside entertainments included Les Comédiens de Paris in Molière's *Le Médecin Malgré Lui*, Labiche's *Grandmère*, and later Jules Romains's *Dr. Knock*; and a concert for the Peel Institute in the presence of the Duke of Gloucester with John Drinkwater, Carrie Tubb, Toplis Green, Bransby Williams, Leonard Henry and Gillie Potter (both of radio fame), Norman Long, Gladys Ripley, Daisy Kennedy, and others.

This was the first season to show a profit—£5 11s. 1d. Conchita Supervia, after breaking with Covent Garden, was amazed at the general excellence of *Hansel and Gretel* at the

---

[1] *Yorkshire Post.*   [2] *Saturday Review.*

Wells, 'due probably to the team work of a regular company'; according to the critic Dyneley Hussey, Covent Garden, except when foreign companies visit it, 'cannot attain the artistic standard which has been achieved, in its modest way, by the permanent company at Sadler's Wells as the result of two years' concerted effort'; Francis Toye considered the Wells 'already one of the best popular operas in the world, and it might develop into an ideal nursery for Opera in English if there were sufficient money'. Of the orchestra, Herbert Hughes said, 'You would have to search the whole of Germany, Austria, Italy, France, Czechoslovakia, Hungary, and so on, to find one of its size more efficient'.

In fact, the Wells was definitely on the artistic map—even Covent Garden recognized this by engaging Joan Cross to sing Desdemona opposite Lauritz Melchior and employing twelve Wells dancers for the summer season.

On Shakespeare's birthday 1934 there was a full-length *Hamlet* with Ernest Milton, Gyles Isham (Claudius), William Fox (Horatio), John Garside (Polonius), Charles Hickman (Laertes), Sybil Thorndike (Gertrude), Marie Ney (Ophelia), John Laurie (1st Player), Tom Heslewood (Ghost), and Leslie French (Osric)—producer, Sir Philip Ben Greet, in his seventy-sixth year: at a repeat performance, Donald Wolfit played the King at a few hours' notice.

In May Granville Barker, who had 'no intention of renewing his connexion with the stage as a producer', nevertheless produced with Harcourt Williams his revised version of *The Voysey Inheritance* 'for the sake of a cause with which he sympathizes'— the Vic-Wells fund. O. B. Clarence played George Booth, which part he had created in 1905, and the cast included Beatrix Thompson, Joyce Bland, Joan Harben, Dame May Whitty, Maurice Evans, Felix Aylmer, Marius Goring, George Devine, and Harcourt Williams, while among the audience on the first night were George Arliss, John van Druten, Thelma Cazelet, Evelyn Waugh, and S. N. Behrman.

T. S. Eliot's *The Rock*, with three hundred performers including the Bishop of London (Dr. Winnington-Ingram), was produced by Martin Browne with music by Martin Shaw to raise money to meet the religious needs of new residential districts.

*

For the 1934–5 season, beginning on 25th September, exemption from Entertainment Tax, though not applied for, was granted; a new floor was laid (that installed only four years before had developed dry-rot); decorations were new; and a fully-licensed bar was installed.

Lilian Baylis had invited Markova to appear for one performance a week, plus a month of Saturday matinées, at £17 a week, altered at Markova's suggestion to £15 a week plus £5 for each extra performance; and opera and ballet were to stay at the Wells till 15th December.

The opera company, which Beecham hoped soon to display on tour, was joined by Ronald Stear and Redvers Llewellyn, with John Barbirolli as occasional conductor.

Among its performances—only for a short time at the Vic to satisfy the charter—was Carey's newly produced *Figaro*, 'probably the nearest approach to the Mozart pattern ever seen in England', Herbert Hughes wrote: Rex Whistler designed the scenery and Covent Garden loaned the dresses, but though some of these 'did not fit either the general scheme or their wearers too well, the effect was excellent'. His production of *Fledermaus*—the score approximated to the original from various sources by Warwick Braithwaite—was a 'wildfire success': though Francis Toye, ignoring the Garden production only four years before, queried its suitability for the Wells, delightful as it was (why not Offenbach, Gilbert and Sullivan, or Sousa? he asked ironically, without foreknowledge of the future).

Gordon produced *Eugene Onegin* for the first time in London within living memory with a first-rate ensemble; but Ernest Newman, while commending the Wells for the production, pointed out that it needed a larger orchestra with a silkier tone, more imaginative settings, a younger cast (especially for the first two acts), and a technique of speaking through music rather than a full-blooded operatic style; Heddle Nash appeared in *Faust*; *Fra Diavolo* was cleverly produced by Gordon with designs by Hans Strohbach (bargain-basement materials at 2s. a yard for the costumes); and the first London production of Stanford's *Travelling Companion*, with Henry Wendon's fine performance, was produced by Sumner Austin (who had sung in it at Bristol in 1927).

On the first night of the ballet, 2nd October 1934, young

Treginnis in *The Haunted Ballroom* was danced by fifteen-year-old Margot Fontes—later Fonteyn—and *Fête Polonaise* had new costumes by Edmund Dulac (presented by the Camargo Society), In the audience were Constance Collier, Lady Mountbatten, Adeline Genée, Mrs. Syrie Maugham, Elsa Schiaparelli, Merle Oberon, and Leslie Howard, while Miss G. B. Stern's walking-stick, 'complete with an electric light in the top, aided by her wit, helped to make the conversation sparkle in the intervals'. A week later came the first English presentation of *The Jar*, choreography by de Valois to a Pirandello story with Casella's music, danced by Helpmann, Gore, Appleyard, and Chappell, who also designed the 'delicious' décor.

But the ballet audience was getting out of hand: after praising the brave resurgence of ballet in England, the *Birmingham Post* rightly pointed out that dancers, like all other artists, cannot always be on top of their form, and yet

> the Wells gallery greets with the same hysterical enthusiasm every single entrance, every single exit of its favourites, often regardless of the fact that its ill-timed applause holds up the performance in a manner exasperating to those whose love and appreciation of ballet is not so personal. Moreover, when in-different execution is received with such violent admiration, there is nothing left wherewith to show appreciation of a really good performance. The serious dancer cannot be helped or encouraged by such lack of taste and discrimination.

As with the unbalanced loyalty of the Old Vic gallery for 'their own' Shakespeare actors in the previous season (their sincere leader, Kate Pilgrim, silenced by Guthrie the previous season in no uncertain terms), the sex-frustrated clapping by hearty females at the Wells, while encouraging, developed among the less dedicated dancers a dangerous complacency.

A junior Vic-Wells Ballet Company was formed in November, and Markova printed her praise of de Valois's spade-work in making British names possible for British dancers (her own name of Marks had been changed by Diaghileff). On 20th November there was the first British performance—indeed, the first full performance for twenty years—of the complete *Lac des Cygnes* with Petipa's original choreography, restored by Ser-geyeff, and with décor by Hugh Stevenson. Markova, 'to whose exquisite dancing the Vic-Wells Company owes so much of its reputation and success', was the first British dancer of the double role of Odette-Odile and was wonderful (she wore Pavlova's brilliants as the Snow-Queen and Pavlova's dresser, Mrs. Manya, made her Wells tutus); the other soloists could not compare, though Helpmann's mime was excellent and he was 'rapidly becoming a dancer of outstanding merit', the first major artist to rise from the Vic-Wells corps de ballet. In one performance Markova spun into a loose rope from the flies that tightened round her throat, but she untwisted, and the audience never knew.

Other ballet performances included *Coppelia* with de Valois as Swanilda, John Greenwood—one of the most useful stage-performers the Wells ever had, 'good in ballet and opera', said *The Times*—as Coppelius, and Walter Gore as Franz; Sara Patrick's *Uncle Remus* (Gordon Jacob); Markova and Helpmann in *Giselle*, Act II, with a correct but mechanical corps de ballet (exemplifying the complacency injected by the indiscriminate gallery); Ashton's *Rio Grande* with Margot Fonteyn, 'a newcomer and quite a "discovery" as the Creole girl', décor by Edmund Burra, piano soloist Angus Morrison, alto soloist Valetta Jacopi, and the Vic-Wells opera chorus, conducted by the composer Constant Lambert.

After the season, Markova and Dolin headed the Vic-Wells company presented at the Wells for a fortnight by Markova and Mrs. Laura Henderson for the Vivian van Damm Productions (through Markova's sister, Doris Marks, a soubrette at the Windmill Theatre). This first run by a British ballet company included the first all-British ballet, *The Rake's Progress* (Gavin Gordon) with Markova as the Betrayed Girl, Walter Gore the Rake, Harold Turner most impressive as the Dancing Master, Ursula Moreton the lewd dancer in the orgy—de Valois really proving herself as a choreographer. On 1st June Markova appeared for the last time at the Wells; she had seen the ballet audience grow from 500 to 2,000 a performance, with standing-room only—especially when she performed.

Drama this season, directed by Henry Cass, was allowed only four weeks at the Wells. For Shaw's *St. Joan*, with Mary Newcombe, Felix Aylmer, Alec Clunes, Maurice Evans, Leo Genn, Philip Leaver, Cecil Trouncer, Alan Webb, and Bruce Winston, I wrote incidental music that sounded to Shaw like all

A PARTY DURING THE GUTHRIE–LAUGHTON SEASON

LOVE FOR LOVE

(top left)
THE LORD OF
BURLEIGH

(top right)
JOB

(middle)
THE RAKE'S PROGRE

(bottom)
PINEAPPLE POLL

the Royal College of Music students practising together—a jumble that he admitted with a twinkle might well represent battle-scenes! *The Taming of the Shrew*, with Maurice Evans, Cathleen Nesbitt, and Andrew Leigh (as Sly), was excellent.

There had been an appeal for £25,000 in December 1934 to free the Vic and the Wells from debt; and the following March Gielgud proposed in the *Observer* a National Theatre by interchanging the Vic, Stratford and the Wells performances without a new building. In 1935 Charles Corri retired after forty years' invaluable service to the Vic and the Wells and Geoffrey Toye, manager of the opera company, resigned to join Covent Garden, leaving a committee of conductors and producers under Lilian Baylis. For the first time, both operas and ballets went on a summer tour (financed by Mrs. Laura Henderson and Van Damm), the Wells being occupied for four weeks by the D'Oyly Carte Company in Gilbert and Sullivan.

The profit at the Wells this season was £278.

For the 1935–6 Wells season the Charity Commissioners cancelled the Trust's interchange between the Wells and the Old Vic so that London for the first time had eight months of opera and ballet. The opening night, 27th September, was remarkable in two respects—'the splendid dancing of the young newcomer Miss Margot Fonteyn, who has a compelling personality and exceptional gifts', though only just sixteen; and to replace Markova the new star-attraction of Pearl Argyle (ex-pupil, like many Wells artists, of the indefatigable British ballet innovator, Marie Rambert) deservedly well known for her dancing in the West End and in films. But Antony Tudor, director of fine ballets for Mme Rambert, allowed by de Valois to direct only *Carmen* and *Faust* ballets because of cost, left to become a great choreographer in America.

During the season Walton conducted his *Façade* with a new Pastoral episode for Pearl Argyle and Helpmann, and Turner and Chappell brilliant in the Popular Song; Ashton produced the first important romantic ballet made for a British Company, Stravinsky's *Baiser de la Fée* (décor by Sophie Fedorovitch), with Margot Fonteyn, who later danced Odille in *Lac des Cygnes* with a corps de ballet which, though not yet good, was improving.

Ninette de Valois's version of *The Gods Go A-begging* (Handel-Beecham), differing from Diaghileff's, was one of the best things the Wells had done; and Ashton produced *Apparitions* (Liszt-Lambert, orchestrated by Gordon Jacob), with décor by Cecil Beaton. Pearl Argyle and Helpmann danced the pas de deux from *The Sleeping Princess*; and de Valois modernized, not quite successfully, Balanchine's *Barabau* (the Sadler's Wells Society contributed £120), with décor by Edmund Burra who introduced Blackshirts. Ursula Moreton became Assistant Ballet Mistress.

Operas new to the Wells included the first performance in England of Moussorgsky's original *Boris Godounov*, produced by Carey with an array of talent—Stear, Matters, Cross, Wendon—and later including the revolutionary scene added by the composer, after which the chorus had to take ten curtain calls; a triple bill—Holst's *Savitri* (conducted by Geoffrey Corbett) and Puccini's *Tabarro* and *Gianni Schicchi*; and (said to be the first time in its entirety in English) Verdi's *Falstaff*, one of the most ambitious and successful performances, newly translated by Procter-Gregg, produced by Austin, conducted by Braithwaite, and finely sung by Matters, Llewellyn (Ford), Joan Cross (Nanetta), Edith Coates (Mrs. Page), Marjorie Parr (Mrs. Ford), Gladys Parr (Mistress Quickly), Roderick Lloyd (Pistol), Powell Lloyd (Bardolf), Morgan Jones (Fenton), and that invaluable member of the chorus for many years, William Booth (Dr. Caius).

Some said the *Figaro* with new bargain-basement costumes was excellent, Audrey Mildmay (Mrs. John Christie) better as Susanna in English than in Italian at her new Glyndebourne opera-house.

From 28th April 1936 the last Vic-Wells plays were given for a week each—*Lear* and *Peer Gynt* (shortened except on Tuesday and Saturday)—with William Devlin, Catherine Lacey, Vivienne Bennett, Ion Swinley, Alec Clunes, and Geoffrey Keen.

At the same time Arnold Haskell, supported by Phyllis Bedells, started a five-year plan for the Vic-Wells ballet to raise £25,000 for teachers, scholarships, productions, recordings, grants, benefits and contracts: this scheme operated till CEMA and the Arts Council took over; the benefits section became the Sadler's Wells Benevolent Fund.

For the 1936-7 season the price of seats rose, to improve production standards—the dearest now costing 7s. 6d., though members of the Old Vic Association and the Sadler's Wells Society could get them for 6s.

Ballet performances, with Constant Lambert conducting, were given on Tuesday nights and alternately on Friday nights and Saturday afternoons, with the usual screams from the gallery. On the opening night, June Brae from the Ballet Rambert danced the Evil Fairy in *Baiser de la Fée*; a refreshing new soloist was Mary Honer; Alan Carter and Michael Somes were in the corps de ballet. Among the audience were Claire Luce, Edith Sitwell, 'a stately figure in black and gold brocade', and the Diaghileff ballerina Danilova who left behind a programme with pencilled notes praising June Brae for her hands and graciousness, *Casse-Noisette*, Act II, the end of *Baiser de la Fée* (though the earlier scenes had bad choreography), and the *Sleeping Beauty* pas de deux, commenting on Fonteyn 'si elle ne soit pas "spoilt", elle va être une grande danseuse' if not overworked and the company 'has all the future before it'.

De Valois's rather over-satirical *Prometheus* (Beethoven), with Helpmann and June Brae, was not successful, but the same dancers were better in Ashton's *Nocturne*, suggested by Edward Sackville-West to Delius's music with Sophie Fedorovitch décor. The ballet company now consisted of twenty women, twelve men, two resident choreographers, a resident conductor, and forty students—a great development from six years before. *Façade* was televised that winter.

Casse-Noisette was given in the only original version outside Russia with Phyllis Bedells's daughter Jean, aged twelve, as Clare and, as the Sugar-Plum Fairy, Margot Fonteyn ('correct rather than dazzling') who later danced her first *Giselle* with Helpmann; she also appeared in Ashton's *Les Patineurs* (Meyerbeer) in which Michael Somes's remarkable elevation was rapturously received. Ashton's *A Wedding Bouquet*, with music and décor by Lord Berners and words by Gertrude Stein, was most witty; de Valois was Webster, the maid, and Helpmann danced a comedy part for the first time.

The *Dancing Times* especially praised Margot Fonteyn ('the first great English dancer ever to be weaned on English rôles'), Harold Turner ('his work nearly always shows vitality and finish'), and Mary Honer ('on a level with Margot Fonteyn. Technically she is finer and more reliable than any of her English contemporaries' though she 'yields too easily to the temptation to give her work a facile piquancy'). There was even talk of making the Wells a National Ballet centre. Lilian Baylis said, 'I don't care a dash about the National Theatre. When I think of all the work that has been done by our three companies . . . I know we are the National Theatre'.

New opera productions in 1936–7 included *Aida* (Carey) with John Wright as Radames, Molly de Gunst as Aida, and Edith Coates as Amneris in Powell Lloyd's excellent scenery; Gordon's new *Butterfly* with Joan Cross and Tudor Davies; and, new to the Wells, his *Meistersinger*, an ambitious but sound performance with Matters playing Sachs, Molly de Gunst Eva, Tudor Davies Walther, Sumner Austin Beckmesser, Ronald Stear Pogner, and William Booth a really good David: Bagnall Harris did the scenery again with bargain-basement costumes. In Austin's new *Rigoletto*, translated by Dent, with the final duet restored (Rigoletto played by Llewellyn with Ruth Naylor as Gilda), every number was applauded, disproving—several papers said—the old myth that opera has no following in this country.

Boris Godounov was revived for the centenary of Pushkin's death; Carey produced a new *Magic Flute*; and Gordon did the first Wells production of Vaughan Williams's *Hugh the Drover*.

Though the Wells was still some £18,000 in debt, and appeals were still made for a further £20,000 odd for the completion fund, this season did show a reasonable profit—£605. It was also the occasion of a charity performance with the radio artists Flotsam and Jetsam, Horace Kenny (with his child-voices), Leslie Woodgate conducting the B.B.C. men's chorus, Troise and his Mandoliers; and also Bebe Daniels and Ben Lyon.

The 1937–8 season saw the most important new ballet since *Job*: de Valois's *Checkmate* (Arthur Bliss) with décor by McKnight Kauffer—first produced in June on a visit by the ballet to Paris—was an impressive success, with June Brae as the Black Queen, Harold Turner the Red Knight, Pamela May the Red Queen, and Helpmann the Red King. The Duke and Duchess of Kent and Toscanini were in the audience.

Sumner Austin made a new production of *Bohème*; *Fidelio* was introduced to the Wells in a production (better than the singing) by Gordon who also did a new *Pagliacci*, conducted by Herbert Menges, with Carey's excellent *Il Tabarro* on 17th November.

Eight days later Lilian Baylis died of a heart attack, aged sixty-three; but, as she would have wished, no performance was cancelled. Bruce Worsley became manager and licensee, Sir Reginald Rowe Managing Governor. The Wells opera was under a committee of producers and conductors (Tyrone Guthrie was in charge of the Old Vic drama), and the ballet was under Ninette de Valois, with Miss E. M. Williams still the indefatigable Clerk to the Governors. The day after the death, Ninette de Valois spoke to the audience before *Job*, and after the ballet the curtain did not rise for the artists, but the audience stood. The public were asked not to send wreaths for the funeral, but subscriptions to the Vic-Wells fund instead—these amounted to £724, one 'very poor person' sending 1s. 6d. As a memorial to 'the Lady', the theatre was to be improved.

After one of Ashton's loveliest ballets, *Horoscope* (Constant Lambert), with Sophie Fedorovitch décor and Michael Somes's first major part, was produced early in 1938, Arnold Haskell said, 'Ballet, now truly indigenous in England, reaches a splendid maturity'—a fitting tribute to Lilian Baylis.

Another was paid by Sir Hugh Walpole in a letter to *The Times* concerning *Meistersinger*: 'There was at 6 o'clock a long queue of people waiting down the street, and these people were, you could see, drawn for the most part from neighbouring districts'. (Different indeed from his comment in 1931!) He said he had heard better performances of the opera, 'but I have never anywhere seen a performance in which there was so much enjoyment, radiating from the stage out to the audience and back from the audience to the stage again'. Lilian Baylis 'has broken down barriers between two different forces, the performers and the audience'.

Sumner Austin produced the first Ring opera at the Wells, *Valkyrie* with Matters as Wotan and Cecilia Wessels from South Africa as Brünnhilde; a new *Faust*, and a new *Cavalleria*. Carey gave a new *Don Giovanni* with décor by Charles Reading, conducted by Geoffrey Corbett, and also Nicholas Gatty's revised *Greysteel*, given with Mozart's *Impresario*, produced and conducted by two of my Cambridge University colleagues, Camille Prior, widow of the French Professor, and Boris Ord, organist of King's College.

De Valois's new ballet *Le Roi Nu* (Jean Français), with décor by Hedley Briggs, was not effective because—not unnaturally— the Emperor was *not* 'wearing no clothes at all'. On 10th May Ashton's *Judgment of Paris* (Lennox Berkeley) was first given before Queen Elizabeth (who had often been to the Wells when Duchess of York) at a Ballet Gala for the Extension Fund when seats were from ten guineas down to 1s. The Lord Mayor's Boy Players formed a scarlet guard of honour, and a crowd of 10,000 broke through the cordon of 200 police.

For the extension, several houses in Arlington Way were demolished, including one where Barnett Deitch, a bespoke and surgical shoemaker, had lived for twenty-eight years: he had made shoes for Pavlova, and remembered Chaplin as a boy living a few yards away, playing in the street and dropping in for a cup of tea.

After digging some ten to fifteen feet down, the hidden springs rose, threatening to drown anyone in the hole, and by July it could be announced, 'The last surviving portion of the original walls of the Old Sadler's Wells Theatre, built in 1765, is now being demolished.'

The Wells, now re-established as a theatre of repute, no longer gave exactly the kind of entertainment originally planned either by Rosoman, who had built the long-lasting theatre, or by Baylis, who had created a standard of performance. But strangely enough what was left of the Baylis plan was virtually what Rosoman had given his public in the musical shows of the eighteenth century, namely good music, panto-mimes and dancing (now modernized as opera and ballet).

The reconstructed building had more dressing-rooms (these had been so inadequate that some costumes had had to be put on in the passage), an orchestral library, a wardrobe, offices, a canteen, shower-baths, a committee-room, rehearsal rooms for opera and ballet, and a control room for broadcasting, as well as, for the first time, a way across the back of the stage, a lift from rehearsal rooms to basement, and a scene-dock to hold most of the scenery (previously brought over from the Old Vic). As for the inadequate acoustics (though better for opera than drama), it was announced that, while they might 'come in for attention a little later', the back of the auditorium would be of sprayed asbestos—though the architect on the premises admitted that 'all is not yet known about the science of acoustics' (as might still be said today).

Rebuilding delayed the opening of the 1938-9 season; but it began well with Owen Mase as Director of the Opera, Charles Reading as Production Manager for Opera and Ballet, Henry Robinson (who had joined the Old Vic chorus in 1930) as stage-director, and Sir Adrian Boult as guest conductor. Prices were increased—now ranging between 7s. 6d. and 2s.

Carey reproduced *Tannhaüser* and Ashton his pleasant *Harlequin in the Street* (Couperin) with André Derain décor—originally made for the Arts Theatre, Cambridge; Margot Fonteyn danced Odette-Odile in *Swan Lake* for the first time, and Austin produced *Don Carlos* at a gala première in aid of Queen Charlotte's Maternity Hospital.

The improved building now made it possible to present the long-intended full-evening *Sleeping Princess*, given in aid of the Housing Centre in February 1939, under the gracious patronage of Queen Mary, Princess Helena Victoria, and the Grand Duke Andrew of Russia: the décor was by Nadia Benois. Margot Fonteyn proved she was a prima ballerina, June Brae, Ursula Moreton, Pamela May and others were outstanding; but poor Helpmann as Prince Florimund had to wear a 'blond page-boy affair that flapped as he danced'. Ashton's burlesqued *Cupid and Psyche* (Lord Berners) was loudly booed. But by now the galleryites were not only ballet-drugged, they were so divided into partisan gangs that sometimes they even hung banners over the edge of the amphitheatre inscribed with the name of their respective deities, Helpmann or Turner. The operas, enthusiastically but not hysterically received, included to the end of the season Gordon's new *Trovatore*; a *Rosenkavalier*, with Hamish Wilson's décor, produced by Carey; and Austin's production of Ethel Smyth's *The Wreckers*, designed by Powell Lloyd—fifty-four different operas in nine years.

And then—as a prelude to the 1939-40 season—the Second World War began, on Sunday 3rd September 1939.

CHAPTER EIGHTEEN

OPERA AND BALLET

1939–1951

AT FIRST Sadler's Wells under its new Lessee, Director, and Licensee Tyrone Guthrie seemed prepared to carry on, war or no war: indeed, it was decided to give ballet three times a week. But considering how uncertain the London theatre situation was, the Ballet Company under de Valois left London for Cardiff. The Ballet School stayed at the Wells, where only opera, under Joan Cross, was planned for 1939–40— the Pilgrim Trust giving £25,000 to aid the Arts in wartime.

For several Sundays, the Royal Philharmonic Society gave concerts at the Wells—Sir Henry Wood conducting the Sadler's Wells Symphony Orchestra with Joan Cross and Moseiwitch, Myra Hess and Edith Coates as soloists; the Stratton String Quartet, with John Wright singing tenor songs and Owen Mase as pianist; the Menges Sextet; the Menges String Quartet; and Sir Adrian Boult conducting the Wells Symphony Orchestra with the pianist Cyril Smith. Austin produced a new *Othello*; the Sadler's Wells singers performed in aid of Finsbury's evacuated children; the Ballet Company came home for a trial month, presenting on Boxing Day *Sylphides*, newly dressed by Alexander Benois; and Hedley Briggs produced a new *Fledermaus* (at one performance the sprinkler-release—to be used in the event of fire—was pulled and water cascaded on to singers and orchestra).

On 23rd January 1940 was the première of Ashton's moving *Dante Sonata* (Liszt), danced barefoot by Fonteyn, May, and Somes as Children of Light, and Helpmann and Brae as Children of Darkness. A week later came a Jubilee performance of *Fledermaus*—the fiftieth performance of opera since war began; then a concert, with Sybil Thorndike and Walter Süsskind, for child refugees from Spain, Austria and Germany; and Gordon's new *Traviata*.

In April the Government, realizing that entertainment could

216

sustain the country's morale, proposed to help, among other enterprises, drama at the Vic and opera and ballet at the Wells. *Coppelia* was produced in its entirety; Ashton altered the old Atterberg ballet into the peaceful *Wise Virgins* (Bach-Walton), with lovely designs by Rex Whistler; and there was a symphony concert with Sir Henry Wood, Myra Hess, and Edith Coates.

In July the Ballet Company—having lost everything when their May tour in the Netherlands was cut short by the German invasion—performed de Valois's hilarious *Prospect Before Us* (Boyce-Lambert): based on John Ebers's *Seven Years of the King's Theatre* (1828), with Roger Furse's designs inspired by Rowlandson and Helpmann.

Ballet (including a revised *Façade* with Dolin's *Bolero* burlesqued) stayed at the Wells till 6th September. But when the Opera Company returned from tour the next day, while Mephistopheles dragged Faust to Hell on the stage, on the theatre's roof Guthrie and others watched the real inferno of the first big fire-raid on the City of London.

This was the last Wells performance for nearly five years, the theatre becoming, until it suffered minor damage from enemy action in 1941, a rest-home for some hundred and eighty local people bombed out of their homes. It was then used as London offices for the Ballet, Opera and Drama Companies touring in fit-up style for troops and factory-workers. The main headquarters were in Burnley, later returning to the New Theatre, London; but that story has no place here.

Five weeks after Germany surrendered, the Wells reopened on 7th June 1945.(Sir Reginald Rowe, the managing director, had died at seventy-five on the previous 21st January.) That date saw the first performance of a new British work: Benjamin Britten's first opera *Peter Grimes*. The cast on this doubly celebrated occasion was

ELLEN ORFORD	*Joan Cross*
PETER GRIMES	*Peter Pears*
AUNTIE	*Edith Coates*
THE NIECES	{ *Minnia Bower* { *Blanche Turner*
MRS. SEDLEY	*Valetta Jacopi*
SWALLOW	*Owen Brannigan*

NED KEENE . . . . . *Edmund Donlevy*
CAPTAIN BULSTRODE . . . . . *Roderick Jones*
BOB BOLES . . . . . . *Morgan Jones*

Eric Crozier was the producer, Kenneth Green the designer, and Reginald Goodall the conductor. The theatre was sold out three days in advance, and memory recalls a great ovation both as a welcome home and as a greeting to a new British opera composer, disregarding some booing and hissing from conventional opera-lovers unused to 'new' music who expected the usual heró-villain drama instead of the lonely non-hero (exquisitely sung by Peter Pears) psychiatrically helped by Joan Cross's sensitive schoolmistress.

Sasa Machov produced a new *Butterfly* with décor by Reece Pemberton and conducted by Muir Matheson; and the Ballet returned to the Wells for eight summer weeks, giving Ashton's *Wanderer* (Schubert), with Graham Sutherland décor, first produced on tour in 1941.

The companies came back to a more adequate theatre, hardly tested before the war: this alone made efficiency more possible than in the past. While genuinely admiring the operatic achievement at the Wells since 1931, and at the Old Vic before that, one must admit that intention often counted for more than fulfilment in Lilian Baylis's magnificent fight for the good of the theatre—it could not be otherwise: without adequate resources, she rallied round her theatre and musical friends who came so gladly 'to help' (as her letters so often said) that the remarkable successes outweighed the necessarily unsatisfactory conditions at the Old Vic, which were accepted as normal when inherited by the Wells.

Much of the ambitious approach to the solving of artistic problems inherent in Lilian Baylis's great aims was amateur in the best sense. As Dent said, the amateur usually has 'a will to beauty' that many professionals lack: unfortunately a will to beauty is often regarded as an end in itself and the results are praised as very good, 'considering'.

There had always been fine individual performances and a high general standard, and shortly before the war the material deficiencies that Corri, with his 'mixture of idealism, determination and skill', had had to put up with at the Old Vic since 1900

—an orchestra of fifteen, a scanty chorus doubling round the stage to reappear as other Egyptian soldiers, only the essential scenery, and 'home-made', though cunningly designed, costumes—had become a thing of the past. By 1945 the orchestra was of full size; so was the number of singers; designers were more varied. The producers had always been experienced theatre musicians—and now there was a theatre more fully equipped to deal with its own problems independent of its parent and partner near Waterloo Station.

It was also a relief to come back to such a home after the fit-up war conditions—at first both a chorus and an orchestra of four conducted by Collingwood at the piano, two folding screens, two chairs and a backless settee, later a chorus of fourteen and an orchestra of twenty-three all sleeping in air-raid shelters. Audiences, partly opera-trained when serving abroad, were more understanding, and there was more money to spend, the Arts Council (CEMA's offspring) allowing the Wells £10,000 for the 1945–6 season (Covent Garden got £25,000).

But in establishing the post-war Wells, some eggs were broken. About 1942 there had been talk of reviving Covent Garden with only some of the Wells soloists (maybe in lesser parts than were theirs at the Wells) and chorus; so, apart from any sentimentality towards the Wells, it seemed unfair if some who had worked loyally to build up that theatre at low salaries (the soloists' £12 had recently been raised to about £17) were now to be passed over. This led to a split between performers for or against Guthrie, Cross, and de Valois (a split not discouraged by the management, some said). The result was that when the 1945–6 contracts were drawn up, some artists were left out, and others were offered a lower status than before.

Managements of course should always be free to employ only those they wish, and artists are free to accept or refuse offers; but the Wells—the only resident English-singing opera company—was gaining a monopoly, and a monopoly can easily dictate terms.

Whatever the reasons, Joan Cross left to join Britten's new English Opera Group, and Clive Carey with his long operatic experience became temporary manager. But as 1945 was an abnormal year, the 1945–6 season could not start till Boxing Day, when the opening production was *The Bartered Bride* with the young Belfast tenor James Johnston, Rose Hill, Edmund Donlevy and Morgan Jones, conducted by Walter Süsskind. Then at the start of 1946 the finances of the Wells received a shock. Its reserves were now £75,000: but Lord Keynes (Lopokova's husband), perhaps naturally preferring ballet to opera (though an enthusiastic amateur organizer of all arts), suggested that the Sadler's Wells Ballet should move to Covent Garden—and this it did on 23rd February.

The result was a loss of income to the Wells of £15,000 a year—a sum which had largely paid off the building debts, the cost of the Ballet School, and the launching of the new resident Theatre Ballet. No recompense was paid to the Wells for this transfer (unlike football-team transfers), though the Arts Council did allot £5,000 to the Ballet School.

Audiences at first were confused by Sadler's Wells standing for ballet at the Garden and opera at the Wells where at the same time the Sadler's Wells Theatre Ballet was successfully developing under clever Peggy van Praagh as rehearser and de Valois's Assistant Director.

The junior corps de ballet lacked precision as yet, but Leo Kersley, who had returned with June Brae, danced finely in Andrée Howard's gay *Assembly Ball* and Honor Frost designed striking décor for Celia Franca's *Khadra* (Sibelius).

The operas showed the hand of 'someone who knows music' —Clive Carey, who wisely gave many of the chorus (Marion Lowe and Marjorie Shires among them) their chance in leading parts on tour at an extra £1 per performance, though seldom with more rehearsal than private indications by the enthusiastic but careful resident producer, John Donaldson.

Austin produced Vaughan Williams's *Sir John in Love*, with décor by Bagnall Harris, and a new *Cavalleria*; John Moody produced a new *Tabarro*; and at the end of the season I produced my first Wells opera—the first performance in England of Wolf-Ferrari's *I Quattro Rusteghi* (from Goldoni), translated by Dent and named *School for Fathers*. This, with the composer's approval, we transferred from Venice to eighteenth-century London, with St. Paul's in the décor by Michael Whittaker (who was made Production Manager) and a real cat alone on the garden wall to end the first act, thus stripping the bourgeois comedy of any falsely romantic association. Though 'one of the company's best productions, beautifully dressed and admirably sung', it seemed too slight for Wells habitués.

Before the 1946–7 season James Robertson became Director; he and Michael Mudie were resident conductors with Richard Austin as guest; Sumner Austin became Technical Director and John Moody resident producer with myself as guest. He produced a new *Snow-Maiden* with Barbara Heseltine's décor: though some critics thought the singing not as good as it had been, this was described not only as 'the best production of the opera at Sadler's Wells', but 'the best that has ever been seen in London'. The *Scotsman* said, 'Great efforts have been made to improve the opera standard in the last few years and we are now beginning to reap the fruits of these efforts'; and W. J. Turner wrote in the *Spectator*, 'It looks as if the powers that be, at last, are alive to the importance of making Sadler's Wells into an opera house of the pre-war Continental standard, such as we have never yet had in England.'

The next new production was mine of *Tosca* (also designed by Michael Whittaker) with James Johnston, Victoria Sladen, Roderick Jones (brilliant as Scarpia) and, as Angelotti, Douglas Jones (later well known as the opera-producer Douglas Craig); with good intentions I ill-advisedly introduced the Attavanti hiding the key at the opening to make the story clearer to those who did not know it (and there are many).

Having been refused permission for Tosca to put lighted candles at the head of the dead Scarpia, I was amazed the evening before our opening performance to see on the first night of another *Tosca* (by the Pomeroy company at the Cambridge Theatre) real flaring candles. Enraged, I learned from the Chief of the Fire Service that while lighted candles are forbidden in London theatres (except, I believe, Covent Garden), they are allowed if their flame serves a practical purpose (such as burning the piece of paper in *The Scarlet Pimpernel*): so, forbidden to move two lighted candles from an out-of-the-way table to the head of the body, we were allowed to have a flaming candelabra on the supper-table, round which Cavaradossi had quite a rough fight, so that two *unlit* candles on a side-table could be lit for placing by the body.

Two guest artists came to sing at the Wells, the Carl Rosa star soprano Ruth Packer in *Tabarro* and the sweet-voiced newcomer Joyce Gartside in *Butterfly*; John Moody produced a new *Cavalleria*, and his new *Pagliacci* in modern dress had Redvers Llewellyn as an excellent Tonio and Marjorie Shires establishing herself as Nedda. An opera new to the Wells, Vaughan Williams's *Shepherds of the Delectable Mountains*, was sensitively produced by William Chappell, with Roderick Jones's moving performance as Pilgrim.

The young 'Theatre Ballet encouraged young choreographers with Alan Carter's light *The Catch* (Bartok); Anthony Burke's *The Vagabonds* (John Ireland), in which Leo Kersley was outstanding; Andrée Howard's *Mardi Gras* (Leonard Salzedo), with young Anne Heaton, Donald Britton (who, with Nadia Nerina, made his name that season), and John Cranko (most exciting as the negro pugilist; Celia Franca's *Bailemos* (Massenet); and Cranko's own first ballet *Adieu* (Scarlatti).

Before the end of the 1946-7 season, James Robertson, finding it impossible to run a theatre and conduct, even occasionally, single-handed, was joined by Norman Tucker, a pianist till now without opera-house experience; a great opera enthusiast, who might well superintend the business side of the Wells, since he had been a Treasury secretary under three Chancellors—Sir Kingsley Wood, Sir John Anderson (later Lord Waverley), and Mr. Hugh Dalton (later Lord Dalton).

As he himself said later, his Treasury experience 'came in jolly useful afterwards when I had to argue with the Arts Council about subsidies and things'; it certainly enabled him to persuade the Arts Council to step up its 1947-8 grant to £23,000 (as against the Garden's £98,000).

But Arts Council Grants are not made till January, when a season is well under way, so there was not much to spend on the first new production of the 1947-8 season, *Faust*. The scenery and costumes (mostly out of stock) cost only some £1,400; but the Wells, and I as producer, luckily had Joseph Carl to design impressionistic settings effectively (except the garden) with an unusually long back-cloth which, let down, showed a dark sky and, when raised, clustered houses for the Kermesse, simplifying sudden scene-changes achieved by the enthusiastic stage staff headed by John Greenwood, John Glass, Jack Church and Bill Lavender.

My aim was the 1863 psychological Covent Garden première

planned by Gounod, who despised the simultaneous realistic
Haymarket version. Some 1947 critics thought the 'rum-tum-
tuppety' music demanded an 'exaggerated nineteenth century
"period" style', but Ernest Newman had always hoped some
producer would 'consign to the rubbish heap all the vulgar
trash that has accumulated about "Faust" performances and
restore to the work the dignity that is its due'. He added that
my production

> replaces the crude realism we have been used to by a general
> atmosphere of mystery, sometimes almost of mysticism, makes
> Mephistopheles a dark force of evil instead of a pantomime
> Demon King, sets over against him a Faust and Marguerite
> woven into a joint pattern that is symbolic rather than realistic,
> . . . and altogether shows us how much fine stuff there is in a
> work that has too long been a mere vaulting-horse for every
> mountebank of the theatre.

Dyneley Hussey, though dubious, found a 'remarkable cres-
cendo of tragic feeling' in the Cathedral scene (placed as intended after Valentine's death), Stephen Williams recalled that
soldiers returning war-wounded (as mine did) sing 'vulgar'
tunes, whether the Soldiers' Chorus or 'Tipperary', and Desmond Shawe-Taylor admitted the 'unsuspected depths of evil'
in the 'airy-fairy' ballet music, daringly transformed by Pauline
Grant into an accurate Walpurgisnacht—its obscene perversi-
ties implied by Pauline Wadsworth (Queen of the Sabbath),
Donald Britton (a Renegade Monk), Anne Heaton (an Initiate),
and David Poole (the sensational Goat-King).

Michael Mudie gave 'a spirited and sensitive reading of the
score' and the singing was greatly praised of Marion Lowe in
her first Wells appearance as a principal (Marguerite), of James
Johnston (Faust), Roderick Jones (Valentine) and Howell
Glynne (Mephistopheles)—though some missed spangles on
his eyes! At the first performance, Josephine Proust from the
chorus suddenly deputized for Anna Pollak, later a sympathetic
Siebel, who lost her voice that morning. This production of
Faust stayed in the repertoire longer than that of any other
opera till the present time, the last performance being on 22nd
March 1956.

Hedley Briggs produced and designed a new *Fledermaus*, with
Valetta Jacopi an excellent Prince Orlovsky and Howell Glynne

superb as the silently drunken gaoler hanging up his hat on the bare wall—a meticulous but apparently spontaneous performance in the real tradition of the mute comic as performed at the Wells in the past by Grimaldi and others. Richard Lewis sang in *Cosi fan Tutte*, and there was a new *Trovatore* produced by John Moody, as well as Geoffrey Dunn's production of the first performance of young Anthony Hopkins's *Lady Rohesia*, taken from the *Ingoldsby Legends*, with décor by Tania Moseiwitch, the wit of which, both verbal and musical (there was said to be a quotation from *Peter Grimes* played backwards), did not get over to most of the audience.

New ballets included Ashton's *Valses Nobles et Sentimentales* (Ravel), Anthony Burke's *Parures* (Tchaikovsky), Cranko's *Children's Corner* (Debussy), Angelo Andes's two ballets, *Jota Toledana* (traditional) with the striking Pirmin Trecu and Sheila O'Reilly, and *Farruca del Sacro Monte* (Azagra).

In December 1947 the direction of the Wells was taken over by a triumvirate—the two conductors James Robertson and Michael Mudie, and Norman Tucker. At the same time Joseph Hislop, the Scottish tenor who had made his name at the Stockholm opera, became adviser to singers at both Covent Garden and Sadler's Wells.

For the 1948-9 season the Arts Council raised their grant to £40,000—only £105,000 below that to Covent Garden. The first new opera production was an impressive *Simone Boccanegra*, cleverly adapted and translated by Norman Tucker, produced by John Moody, décor by John Piper, Moody, and Reginald Wooley, finely sung by Arnold Matters, Howell Glynne, and Joyce Gartside; this brilliant young soprano was overstrained by being given varied leading parts too early.

Then came Weinberger's gay *Schwanda the Bagpiper*, translated and produced by myself, with Roderick Jones a real country Schwanda, Howell Glynne a grandly incompetent Devil with a lighter in his tail for his pipe, Hervey Alan a gigantic Magician, and Pirmin Trecu an impertinent page-boy in the Earth-to-Hell lift in Pauline Grant's ballet. Michael Whittaker designed the romantic scenery and Una Simmons the costumes.

When Schwanda swears to his wife that if he has kissed a woman while away from her, the Devil may take him to hell at once, he has to vanish instantly, though there were no trapdoors in the Wells stage. This trick was devised by the production manager, John Glass, who had been at the Old Vic since he was fourteen and was the most brilliant 'behind-the-scenes' man the Wells has had in recent times. With his assistant, Mary Owen,[1] he should never have had to leave the Wells.

A weakness of most opera-singers the world over was well illustrated before *Schwanda* rehearsals started: of all the intelligent cast, each provided only with a translation of their own part, only Hervey Alan asked to read the story. How unlike the famous Mario and Grisi of the mid-nineteenth century, who invariably studied the words first: 'then, and not till then, was the music learnt by heart', for they believed that no singer could do himself justice unless 'he had all he was singing about thoroughly in his head as well as in his throat'.

There was also Guthrie's extraordinary *Carmen* which had a very mixed reception on the first night because of its apparent perversity: during the vigorous opening music of the inn-scene, everyone was lying flat and motionless on the ground in a garden far too open for smuggler's plotting; and the last scene outside the arena was ingeniously but surprisingly changed to a room overlooking the entrance. But it remained popular for many years, chiefly because of Anna Pollak's bold personality and dominating performance, though she was as impeccably dressed 'as any Kensington lady'.[2]

The ballets, with Guy Warrack as conductor, included Andrée Howard's *Selina* (Rossini-Warrack), with Stanley Holden as the Witch, Hans Zullig and Elaine Fifield; Nancy McNaught's *Étude* (Anthony Hopkins); and young John Cranko's dramatic *Sea Change* (Sibelius).

To keep the Theatre Ballet and the Ballet School going cost the Wells £6,500 more than the Arts Council grant allowed. The position of the Wells Ballet Companies in 1949–50 was highlighted in a letter from Sir George Dyson to *The Times* in February stressing the serious loss to the parent theatre since the transfer of the senior company to Covent Garden four years before, without any compensation:

> Sadler's Wells have lost a principal source of income. They still nourish the ballet at Covent Garden, train and provide new talent

---

[1] Her actor-husband, Alun, is now the well-known dramatist.
[2] *News Chronicle.*

for it. But they get no adequate revenues from it. Nor do they get enough to compensate them from the subsidies which the Arts Council make to ballet. The lion's share of these also goes to Covent Garden. The mother is being starved to feed the child. This is a macabre absurdity which must not be allowed to persist. Sadler's Wells have used up all their hard-earned reserves of money. They are now in serious financial straits . . . The money available to ballet . . . must be re-allotted with greater regard to equity and to facts.

By now Peggy van Praagh was Ballet Mistress to the Theatre Ballet, and especially notable among the works performed were the new ballet by the already remarkable choreographer John Cranko, *Beauty and the Beast* (Ravel), in which David Poole gave a moving performance; another by Angelo Andes with Pirmin Trecu—*El Destino* (Manuel Lazareno), with décor by Hugh Stevenson; and the first ballet invented by Michael Somes—the simple but good *Summer Interlude*, for which, however, Respighi's music was not a satisfactory choice.

The two youngsters, Patricia Miller and David Blair, began to make their mark. In April 1950 young Svetlana Beriosova from the Metropolitan Ballet, New York, joined the company. On 15th May the Sadler's Wells Ballet celebrated its twenty-first anniversary at the Wells with a gala performance attended by Princess Margaret: the programme, with the original artists as far as possible, included *Façade*; Gore, Sheila Macarthy and Ursula Moreton in the *Rake's Progress* orgy scene; Margot Fonteyn as young Treginnis in *The Haunted Ballroom* (the part she had danced years before) and as Julia in *A Wedding Bouquet* with Mary Honer as the bride (partnered by Helpmann), Constant Lambert reciting Gertrude Stein's words, and Ninette de Valois—dancing for the first time since 1937—in her original part of Webster, the maid, with a giggle.

There was no new opera this season, but there were new productions of *Don Giovanni* (a scholarly version by Geoffrey Dunn), *Falstaff* (brilliantly, if some said over-exuberantly, produced by Guthrie), *Traviata* (sensitively produced by Joan Cross, who had inspired Marjorie Shires with her own subtle understanding of the character), and Powell Lloyd's very British *Hugh the Drover*.

For the 1950–1 season the auditorium was redecorated in

grey and red, and the orchestral pit was enlarged to hold a normal-sized opera orchestra. In September *Falstaff* was given both at Covent Garden by the Milan Scala company and at the Wells; but, apart from the orchestral playing, critics praised the latter more, especially Rowland Jones as Fenton and Arnold Matters in the title-rôle.

In October *School for Fathers* (often unsuccessfully revived) now drew good audiences—this time perfectly cast in every difficult subtle part. Those who saw it then cannot forget the angry fathers, Howell Glynne and Stanley Clarkson, becoming dirty old men, with presumably, 'French' drawings—some done by David Low but never displayed—only to be embarrassed by the sudden arrival of Lady Pinchbeck (Marion Lowe) who later silenced them with her quick-firing nagging aria. Marion Lowe established herself as a first-rate comedienne, but it was 'teamwork in excelsis', with acting and singing so knit together it would be hard to equal such an operatic blending again, and the audibility of the words proved that English is singable—as I said in 'one of the briefest curtain speeches on record', 'There is such a thing as opera in English'. One West End management would have transferred it for a run but for the orchestral expenses. (After one performance, at which Mary Garden and Beecham were my guests, Sir Thomas, trousers above his knees, entranced my supper-party by wickedly burlesquing an old operatic friend of ours persuading him she could play Salome.)

There was a new *Barber of Seville*, which had 'several kicks administered in the seat of the pants'. 'If only Mr. Guthrie would leave well alone' instead of dulling the work by fussily spinning chairs during the sextet (a surprising lapse by a producer of genius), and by replacing Rosina's shut-up room with an interior-exterior with a flag-pole in the centre. Norman Tucker at the time said, 'There are some fine producers on the "straight" stage, but few of them are adequately qualified to produce opera' and at the Wells the producer should allow the conductor the last word, whereupon one critic asked about the *Barber* conductor—'Was he struck dumb, perhaps?' (No conductor should have the last word if he is only a musician: he cannot settle the tempo of, say, a march unless he is ready to march himself, as Beecham was when he and I were settling *tempi* for the Festival of Britain *Bohemian Girl*: nor should a producer direct opera singers without understanding music, technically if possible.

A blow came in December 1950 when the Chairman of the Governors, the Hon. James Smith, confirming the financial loss to the Wells when the Ballet progressed to Covent Garden (of which he was also a Director), announced that the Wells Opera might have to close in the following July.

For the time being, however, new opera productions continued. Norman Tucker translated and admirably shortened *Don Carlos*, restoring Schiller's ending and cutting the auto-da-fé scene: in this Joan Hammond as the Queen and Amy Shuard as the Countess of Eboli were outstanding. The effective scenery was by Roger Furse, and the production by the drama producer George Devine was praised for its directness, though several critics disliked his making performers fall to the floor in moments of high emotion. (One straight producer at the Wells, being asked by a singer how she was to sing her top-note lying full-length on some steps, told her that that was her affair; while another said to me that he thoroughly enjoyed producing his first opera but didn't know what to do with the twiddley bits between the lines.)

Amy Shuard gave one of her finest performances in the title-rôle of Janacek's strangely-moving *Katya Kabanova*, 'a glorious failure'. This was translated by Norman Tucker, conducted by Charles Mackerras and produced by myself—the first performance in England of a Janacek opera, I believe—with realistic sets so cunningly devised by John Glass that a complete change took only some fifteen seconds.

There was also a new non-classical *Dido and Aeneas* which, though effective, had too many tricks for Purcell; but opinions about it differed. The chorus was permanently in the orchestra with action mimed on the stage by dancers produced by Alfred Rodrigues in collaboration with Geoffrey Dunn.

The Sadler's Wells Theatre Ballet had a remarkable season. Before Christmas, George Balanchine introduced his new *Trumpet Concerto* (Haydn) and John Cranko his *Pastorale* (Mozart), both with Beriosova and Blair. (Ninette de Valois became Dame Ninette de Valois in the New Year Honours, 1951.) During the Festival of Britain in the summer of 1951, the Theatre Ballet was rightly praised for giving more new ballets than the senior company. Most noticeable was twenty-three-year-old Cranko's amazing versatility as a choreographer. First, in March had come his enlivening *Pineapple Poll*; this, though just too long, was all brilliantly amusing, with Charles Mackerras's cunning *mélange* of Sullivan tunes (the first practical indication that the Sullivan copyright had expired), Osbert Lancaster's designs, and all the dancers, especially the girls disguised as old sea salts, David Blair as gallant Captain Belaye, and David Poole unforgettable for his solo dance as the pathetic Pot-Boy.

Then in May came his oddly poetic *Harlequin in April* (Richard Arnell) based on a couplet from T. S. Eliot:

> April is the cruellest month, breeding
> Lilacs out of the dead land.

In this David Blair showed his versatility by his remarkable dancing as Harlequin.

So good was the Theatre Ballet becoming under Peggy van Praagh that the Press of the day remarked that it lived—unlike the senior company at the Garden—more on its future than its past, and that it was to be hoped 'all the big guns from Covent Garden will come down to the Wells to watch the sister company at work. They could catch from them a sense of their old excitement again.'

Though the threat of having to close did not materialize, the triumvirate of management was disbanded by the next season (1951–2), Norman Tucker becoming the sole Director and Director of Music for the Theatre Ballet while his adjutant, Stephen Arlen, took over the post of General Manager of the Wells from Lilian Baylis's loyal lieutenant, George Chamberlain, Clerk to the Governors, Licensee and till now General Manager of both the Vic and the Wells.

CHAPTER NINETEEN

SUCCESS AGAIN

1951–1957

THE NEXT three seasons were remarkable for a number of reasons. The Theatre Ballet could at least hold its own in competition with the parent-sister company, which some thought was resting on its oars. In September 1951, the juniors, after Loudon Sainthill had given a new décor to *Coppelia* and Cecil Beaton one to *Casse-Noisette* arranged by Ashton (in which Elaine Fifield and David Blair really arrived), were taken by Sol Hurok to follow their seniors and tour more than sixty cities in Canada and the United States of America.

They also danced at the Edinburgh Festival in August 1952, and on their return presented Cranko's new *Reflection* (John Gardner) in which he perhaps over-reached his capacity—it was depressing and incoherently subtle—and Rodrigues produced his *Île des Sirènes* (Debussy).

In January 1953 Margaret Dale (like Rodrigues, of the senior company) produced her first ballet *The Great Detective* (Richard Arnell), in which Kenneth Macmillan danced both Sherlock Holmes and his rival Professor Moriarty—an idea which Miss Dale's humour as a dancer promised would be 'screamingly funny', but resulted only in a Victorian jumble that did not foreshadow her skill as a television choreographer.

In February Kenneth Macmillan for the first performance of the embryo Sadler's Wells Choreographic Group produced his *Somnambulism* to the progressive jazz of Stan Kenton; and in April the Theatre Ballet toured the Netherlands, Belgium, and Germany; after which came Rodrigues's gripping and fast-moving *Blood Wedding*, a version of the Lorça play. In July the company appeared at the Rhodes Centenary Exhibition at Bulawayo, and in August again at the Edinburgh Festival.

In 1953–4 the Wells saw *Puerta de Tierra* (Albéniz) by Roberto Ximenes; Cranko's moving and, in the best sense,

theatrical *The Lady and the Fool* (Verdi-Mackerras); and
Rodrigues's *Café des Sports* (Anthony Hopkins); and in April
1954 the company had a twelve-week tour in Africa.

The first new opera production in the 1951–2 season was
Figaro. In this I reflected the Beaumarchais play, convinced that
no opera-composer changes characters of near-contemporary
plays: so Marion Lowe as the Countess was not the familiar
middle-aging Marschallin from *Rosenkavalier*; 'Non piu andrai'
was not sung militaristically, but to hoodwink the Count with
satirical ultra-heroics to hide Cherubino's staying; and, as roses
would not suit Figaro, Susanna sang the most un-Susanna-like
'Deh vieni' as part of her impersonation of the Countess,
roguishly peering between her ultra-romantic lines to be sure
she is overheard—what else do the semiquavers mean?

Most critics approved, but some said the great hall looked like
a London furniture shop display, when in fact it was Johnnie
Glass's detailed copy of an eighteenth-century building in the
actual locality where Almaviva 'lived' (truth is not always real
on the stage); some thought the servants' revolt was over-
stressed and considered the repertory casting of the aristocracy
too suburban: but all agreed that the final scene, filled with pine
trees as the play-plan shows (but usually as empty as an un-
planted garden), provided all the necessary hiding-places. Elsie
Morison was a delightful Susanna and Anna Pollak the perfect
Cherubino, while the Goya-like costumes by Anthony Boyes,
the ingenious Wardrobe Master at the Wells, were for the
most part highly praised.

After *Figaro*, *The Times* made an apposite comment that
should in fairness be considered by all who believe that static
performers bring out the musical beauty of the arias—they have
obviously never read Mozart's letters in which he distinctly says
marvellous singing in opera needs acting to enhance it, nor do
they remember that when rehearsing *Don Giovanni* he pinched
Zerlina's bottom in the wings to make her scream for help
instead of vocalizing an interesting modulation. As *The Times*
said: 'However wrong our distinguished producers, the Eberts,
the Guthries, the Arundells, may go in particular cases, their art
is essential: the dramatic element in opera must be properly
served'.

This does not mean that acting is more important than singing, nor that producers of drama are necessarily suitable producers of opera, nor does it justify over-fussiness; but the three opera-producers mentioned—not necessarily at one on detail— would all agree that clarity of atmosphere and story is essential, and that comedy should not be damped by a 'shushing' of laughs by the knowledgable. It should also be remembered that true comedians (funny without effort) are rare in opera companies, and that performers, when less than first-rate, need 'something to do' to be effective.

Arnold Matters, who had played Figaro well, and Marion Lowe were perhaps more suitable for the Bailie and Charlotte in Massenet's *Werther* which I produced in February 1952. In this intricately subtle work there could be no fussiness as the whole atmosphere is one of restraint. The opera had been well translated by Norman Tucker, and I was lucky to have as designer Ernest Stern who had worked so much with Reinhardt. Stern's designs were so lovely, the cast fitted the characters (Rowland Jones as Werther, Frederick Sharp as Albert, Marion Studholme as Sophie), and the opera was conducted so sensitively by James Robertson that it is hardly surprising one critic praised the performance as a 'model of tact, imagination and good taste'.

George Devine's straightforward production of *Eugene Onegin* would have 'won credit for an opera house of far more than Sadler's Wells pretensions': the décor by Motley—apart from what one paper called the 'suspended' bedroom for Tatiana— was sumptuous without ostentation. The ballroom with Cranko's choreography was generally admired, Rowland Jones was beautifully lyrical, Frederick Sharp also again happily cast, and the first night was another triumph for Amy Shuard.

Another straightforward production was that of the first Wells presentation by Clive Carey of Mozart's *Seraglio* with Jennifer Vyvyan's fine Constanze in an amusing new translation by Dent who, to 'help out', had translated so much for the Vic-Wells for nothing. But at last I persuaded my old friend that Shaw had been right when he told me he always insisted on full payment for performing rights, since if he allowed performances by deserving companies for nothing (as he could have well afforded), his example would be quoted against authors who entirely depended on their royalties. To hand back a fee in a good cause is one thing: to be expected to work for less than one's deserts for art is another and can lead to charitable blackmail.

There was a new production of *Samson and Delilah* by the drama director Basil Coleman, with Ralph Koltai's colourful décor, clever crowd manipulation, and a fine last scene in which Cranko's choreography, though somewhat out of style, certainly gingered up Saint-Saëns: the name-parts were sung by Jean Watson and a Covent Garden giant from Iceland, Thorstein Hanneson.

Three more operas new to the Wells were produced in the 1952–3 season—the tuneful documentary opera-drama *Romeo and Juliet* by Sutermeister which had swept Germany before the war, but did not sweep London; *The Immortal Hour*, with too much ballet and none of the dream-like quality that so caught the audiences in the famous London long run of 1926 with its less good voices but more convincing Celtic Twilight; and Carey's tense production of Vaughan Williams's setting of the Synge play *Riders to the Sea*, conducted by Muir Matheson with a moving performance by Olwen Price, another ex-member of the chorus who did valuable work as a principal.

In 1953 the Duchess of Kent attended the first performance of Verdi's *Luisa Miller*, translated by Norman Tucker and Tom Hammond, the most thorough and musical *répétiteur* at the Wells. The new tenor was the handsome young Maltese, Oreste Kirkop, who glamorized the gallery; with him sang the new soprano Victoria Elliot, whose adaptability proved invaluable to the Wells. Then came *Don Pasquale*, amusingly translated by Dent and well sung by Majorie Shires (later by Marion Studholme), Owen Brannigan, and Denis Dowling—though some said more in the Gilbert and Sullivan style than Donizetti's (a criticism encouraged by Osbert Lancaster's delightful doll's-house scenery). Critique-headlines included: '*Don Pasquale* was never like this', 'In line with the rest—a success', and, perhaps more correct, 'Oh, it was so different'. Both those operas, new to the Wells, were produced by Basil Coleman and conducted by James Robertson. For Christmas Vilem Tausky conducted Powell Lloyd's charming new *Hansel and Gretel*, beautifully played by Marion Studholme, Anna Pollak, and Sheila Rex, a comfortably wicked old aunt of a witch.

In January 1954 James Robertson left to conduct the New Zealand Broadcasting National Orchestra. In the same month *Carmen* was enlivened when Robert Thomas (5 ft. 9 in.), whose breeches had split when he picked up Carmen's rose, reappeared in those of David Ward (6 ft. 3½ in.), to sing 'What a look! What brazen assurance!' Jennifer Vyvyan and Owen Brannigan were successful as Donna Anna and Leporello in the Prague version of *Don Giovanni*, though Thomas Round sang the Vienna 'Dalla sua pace' beautifully instead of the original 'Il mio tesoro'.

Kirkop, having conventionally outshone team-work for some four months in *Cavalleria*, *Rigoletto*, *Butterfly*, *Tosca*, and *Bohème* (where even Richard Austin's sensitive conducting could not temper his bravura), left in February to make *The Vagabond King* film in Hollywood, giving a few performances at Covent Garden on the way.

The Pearl Fishers had its first performance in England in Geoffrey Dunn's translation, produced by Basil Coleman with David Ward an impressive High Priest—yet another ex-chorus singer who had been making his mark in small parts such as Monterone in *Rigoletto*. For the centenary of Janacek's birth, Rafael Kubelik's conducting of *Katya Kabanova* made the revival memorable with subtlety and silences, so that Desmond Shawe-Taylor wrote, 'The whole performance underlines something which, in my indignation with the slighting attitude now generally adopted towards the singer, I have sometimes been tempted to underestimate: the paramount importance of the operatic conductor' (which I take to mean the operatically-minded conductor, not the conductor of an opera). We even added maroons to the storm-scene.

In July I produced for Edgar K. Bruce the old melodrama *East Lynne*, interpolated with Victorian songs which I had searched out: Rosalind Fuller played the lead, Bruce the villain, and Derek Oldham of D'Oyly Carte fame proved that a sincere artist can reap storms of genuine applause even in a near-burlesque and when raising his hat at his exit after a sentimental song. Joan Young was magnificently exuberant, especially in a cockney scene and when marching as a full-blown principal-boyish Britannia in clever routines by Tony Stuart, danced by him, Kim Grant, and the Munks Twins: old-fashioned limelight was used from the gallery, and the only disappointment was that we could not sell water from Sadler's original well. Tests proved it undrinkable.

Then came trouble for the Wells.

The thirty dancers in the Theatre Ballet, after a successful African tour, when the principals had their names in lights (not a Wells custom) with all salaries at commercial rates (as before in America), were supported by British Actors' Equity in asking for a 30s. increase on their basic weekly pay for the 1954–5 contracts already issued.

Till now the corps de ballet had had only £7 a week (less than the opera chorus), while leading dancers got less than a third of what non-subsidized companies paid—the Festival Ballet salaries were from £8 to between £15 and £30, it being reported that Tamara Toumanova received £500, while Fonteyn with the senior Wells company got about £100.

The Wells directors refused a flat-rate increase on principle, as they were 'the best judges as to whom is the most deserving' (as their statement put it). Pointing out that all dancers got £3 extra on tour, a year's contract including holiday pay, sick benefit, and encouragement towards an established career, they proposed £7 for first-year dancers rising to £9 in the third year and between £16 and £18 a week for those of higher status, but stressed that the delay in signing contracts prevented the ballet from opening on 6th September.

The *Daily Herald* deplored the use of 'sweated labour—in the name of art', and Equity said it would 'regret it very much' if singers were to be embarrassed by operas replacing ballet at the start of the season.

No meetings had taken place during the three weeks' argument, and the management next stated that failing an agreement 'before Monday' the provincial ballet tour would be cancelled: but the following day they were prepared to accept arbitration if the dancers would carry on as before for three months.

The *Manchester Guardian* thought the Wells Trust ill-advised in its attitude and £7 a week 'shockingly low pay' for skilled dancers (even if juniors) from an institution 'which gets £60,000 or so a year of public money'.

If ballet directors refuse to give way,
A lockout their action compels,
Swans, fairies, and sylphides must all dance away,
With skaters, senoras, and belles . . .
But London can hardly believe, when they say
No dancing at Sadler's Wells.

The *Sunday Times* disliked 'the pro-consular tone' of the Wells assertion that, as an institution, it could not be compared with independent companies—'it was not by craving the status of an institution that Diaghilev created, year after year, the ballets on which other companies are now happy to thrive'.

The dancers, though still ready to consider new proposals, unanimously turned down the *status quo* proposition, but the Wells stressed that some twenty-one dancers would get £2 or 30s. more on the management's terms, the non-acceptance of which within forty-eight hours would mean the company would be disbanded.

Dame Ninette, when asked by the Press, 'Are you prepared to lose the Sadler's Wells Theatre Ballet for a question of principle?' was reported to have replied, 'Well, it sounds a little pompous, but that is it', and to have commented, 'We are like a miniature Civil service'.

The Wells then made a new compromise offer—a minimum rise of £1 with an average of 30s. (newcomers starting at £7 and rising to £9 in the third year—as in the management's original offer), plus increased holiday pay and a guarantee to review the whole structure, including the possibility of a year's contract, that is fifty-two weeks at full pay.

This was accepted—with the odd result that some of the Theatre Ballet would now get more than some of the senior company: so the Hon. James Smith undertook to arrange a discussion with Equity on the Garden salaries.

It was the first time any ballet company had made a stand, and it had taken twenty-six days.

Many have thought that to work at the Wells implied a dedication 'comparable to that of a financial expert who chooses to remain in academic life rather than to accept a highly remunerative post with an industrial organization': but the *Yorkshire Post* not inappositely commented that the Wells was following the Baylis policy of stressing the cachet of appearing at the Wells—inevitable because she couldn't pay more—but, the article went on:

> With the present management it is different. They stepped into a ready-made reputation, and they now appear to be trading on it, although they have no cause to cry poverty. They are subsidized, they have a great following, and they can spend money on experimental enterprises, which to some people do not seem to have been worth while.
>
> The least that can be expected of them is that they will pay salaries equal to those paid in the commercial theatre, where all the risks have to be taken by the management.

For the 1954–5 season several changes were made. Prices were increased—Circle seats now cost from 6s. 6d. to 12s. 6d., Stalls 7s. 6d. to 10s. 6d., Pit Stalls 5s., Amphitheatre (the front of the gallery) 4s., unreserved Pit 2s. 6d. and Gallery 2s. Stephen Arlen, handing over his place as Manager to the experienced Douglas Bailey, now became the Licensee instead of George Chamberlain, who with Annette Prevost, the Treasurer, both invaluable to the Wells, from now on, instead of serving the two theatres, had their services confined to the Old Vic.

The season began with Lennox Berkeley's new *Nelson*, an eminently singable setting of a good libretto by Alan Pryce-Jones, in which Anna Pollak gave a touchingly restrained performance as Lady Nelson; Victoria Elliot sang Lady Hamilton, Robert Thomas Nelson, and David Ward Hardy—the last two and the composer having been in the wartime Navy. The producer was George Devine, and Felix Kelly's scenery was effective till entrances stultified his false perspective. Lady Churchill and the Austrian and United States Ambassadors were at the first night, when the whole performance was broadcast.

The English Opera Group with Peter Pears, Joan Cross, Alexander Young, Rose Hill, and others then gave *The Beggar's Opera* in Britten's version; *The Rape of Lucretia*; *Love in a Village*; *The Dinner Engagement*; and the first performance of *The Turn of the Screw* with Britten's remarkable orchestration and the gripping piano and churchyard scenes.

I then produced Menotti's *Consul*, cleverly designed by Quentin Lawrence of television-production fame: in this Rowland Jones was the conjurer (complete with dove), Anna Pollak was brilliant as the Secretary (conveying the character's underlying sympathy—as approved by Menotti—avoiding the obvious hard interpretation), and Amy Shuard superb as Magda. It was vitally conducted by Alexander Gibson, a former Wells *répétiteur* brought back as conductor in 1951. In the final dream-sequence, with dry-ice clouds for, I believe, the first time in a theatre, the singers were understandingly trained by Tony Stuart to move like dancers, and I used Irving's trick from the *Corsican Brothers* ballroom scene of having children at the back of the stage, to increase the effect of distance, but more as it was done in Purcell's dramatic operas—each succeeding entry (in the *Consul* the dream-images of John and the Mother) farther upstage successively by shorter figures—Menotti, who himself dislikes his last scene, paid us the compliment of telling me we had made it effective.

George Devine produced a new *Magic Flute*, designed by Motley and conducted by Rudolf Schwarz. *The Merry Widow* was announced but had to be cancelled through royalty difficulties. *Faust* was still in the repertoire, conducted by Marcus Dods; *Katya Kabanova*—now more popular through Amy Shuard's greatly increased stature as an artist—was revived, but she then left to join Covent Garden, her place in the usual repertoire being taken in 1955–6 by the Australian Betty Fretwell.

Powell Lloyd, always reliable, produced a straightforward *Rigoletto* conducted by Leo Quayle; and Douglas Seale, another 'straight theatre' director, produced a new *Figaro* conducted by Rudolf Schwarz: the lovely great hall scene by the clever designer Malcolm Pride was spontaneously and rightly applauded, but its brilliant perspective, with dwindling-sized chairs by farther windows, was spoilt (as Felix Kelly's setting for *Nelson* had been) when normal-sized people, entering at the back, nearly touched the lintel of an apparently 'nine-foot' door.

A Gala Performance on 6th January 1956 for the twenty-fifth anniversary of the reopening of the Wells had been given in the presence of Princess Margaret, President of the Sadler's Wells Foundation (of which Queen Elizabeth the Queen Mother was Patron). After a prologue by Christopher Hassall, spoken by Joan Cross, the programme included the Prelude and duet from *The Pearl Fishers*, sung by Robert Thomas and Alfred Orda who joined the company this season; Rowland Jones, Stanley Clarkson, and Joan Stuart in the Prison Scene from *Faust*; Victoria Elliot, Howell Glynne, John Hargreaves (who did so much good work at the Wells), James Johnston, and Frederick Sharp in a scene from *Boccanegra*; Kenneth Macmillan's *Danses Concertantes* (Stravinsky); the Letter Scene from *Figaro*, sung by Patricia Howard and Marion Studholme; the second act of *Hansel and Gretel* with Anna Pollak, June Bronhill (a young newcomer from Australia) and Ava June (from the chorus); Fonteyn and Michael Somes in the pas de deux from *Lac des Cygnes*; and the Circus Scene from *The Bartered Bride* with seventeen others of the company and the chorus.

On 31st May Norman Tucker's C.B.E. was announced.

At the end of the season the Theatre Ballet gave a farewell[1] three-week season in which there was de Valois's new production of *Coppelia* for the first time in London, and Kenneth Macmillan's new *Solitaire* (Malcolm Arnold).

Instead of the theatre's being left empty for the summer months, as had recently been usual, there was a reversion to Phelps's general practice, and the Wells was once more let to outside companies. The Carl Rosa Opera Company played there for a fortnight, giving *Manon Lescaut*, *Tales of Hoffmann* and nine stock operas with singers including Gwen Catley, Estelle Valery, Ruth Packer, Charles Craig, conducted by Arthur Hammond and Edward Renton.

Then came a week of the Welsh National Opera Company in a more unusual programme: *I Lombardi*, *Nabucco*, *Trovatore*, and *Sicilian Vespers* were sung by Ruth Packer, Rosina Raisbeck, Tano Ferendinos, Alfred Hallett, Brychan Powell, Bryan Drake, Roderick Jones, and Hervey Alan, and conducted by Warwick Braithwaite and Charles Groves.

For the 1956–7 season admission prices were stepped up yet again—for the second time in two years—Circle now 7s. 6d. to 15s., Stalls 7s. 6d. to 12s. 6d., Pit Stalls 5s., Upper Circle 6s., Pit and Gallery, if booked on the day of performance, respectively 3s. 6d. and 3s., and if paid for at the doors 3s. and 2s. 6d.

---

[1] Following this season, the junior company joined the senior company at Covent Garden as part of the Royal Ballet, granted a Royal Charter by Queen Elizabeth II on 16th January 1957 and incorporating the Sadler's Wells Ballet, the Sadler's Wells Theatre Ballet, and the Sadler's Wells School of Ballet.

At the same time, a form of season ticket for six performances was introduced—one 15s. seat costing £3 10s. and so on down to one 9s. seat for £2 2s. 6d. (but four performances had to come from a list marked 'A' and two marked 'B').

In Powell Lloyd's production of *Martha*, conducted by Leo Quayle, June Bronhill was charming; and in a new *Fidelio* with Malcolm Pride's clever scenery, produced by Douglas Seale, and conducted by Rudolf Schwarz, the Australians were outstanding—Elizabeth Fretwell a grand if somewhat cold Leonora, and Ronald Dowd a vital Florestan.

For some years Michael Mudie, one of the original triumvirate of 1947 and a sensitive musician with a real feeling for opera, had been suffering from multiple sclerosis; an Operatic Concert was given in December 1956 to raise a Testimonial Fund for him.

In January 1957 the interesting programme included Puccini's *Trittico*; *Il Tabarro*, conducted by Leo Quayle and sung by Victoria Elliot and Ronald Dowd; *Suor Angelica* (the first performance at the Wells), conducted by Marcus Dods and sung by Elizabeth Fretwell; and *Gianni Schicchi*, conducted by Alexander Gibson and sung by Patricia Howard, William McAlpine, and Denis Dowling.

Charles Craig from the Carl Rosa sang at the Wells as a guest-artist in February: at Joseph Hislop's suggestion, Sir Thomas Beecham and I had 'discovered' him in 1951 in the Covent Garden chorus, but when I first had introduced him to the Wells his singing with a dreadful cold had not made a mark. He sang again at the Wells in April when the Carl Rosa added an interesting revival of *Benvenuto Cellini* to their repertoire, with Gita Denise, William Aitken and Walter Midgley in the company.

In May the Wells gave the première of John Gardner's setting of Patrick Terry's libretto from Somerset Maugham's *Moon and Sixpence* (the seventy-fifth opera in the twenty-two production years at the new Wells). This was conducted by Alexander Gibson and most effectively produced by Peter Hall, new to opera; the cast included Elizabeth Fretwell, June Bronhill, Anna Pollak, Chin Yu, Thomas Round, Edith Coates, Owen Brannigan, and, in the lead, John Hargreaves, the last three being especially good. On the first night (to which I took Oiva Soini, the head of the Helsinki Opera, where I had often worked)

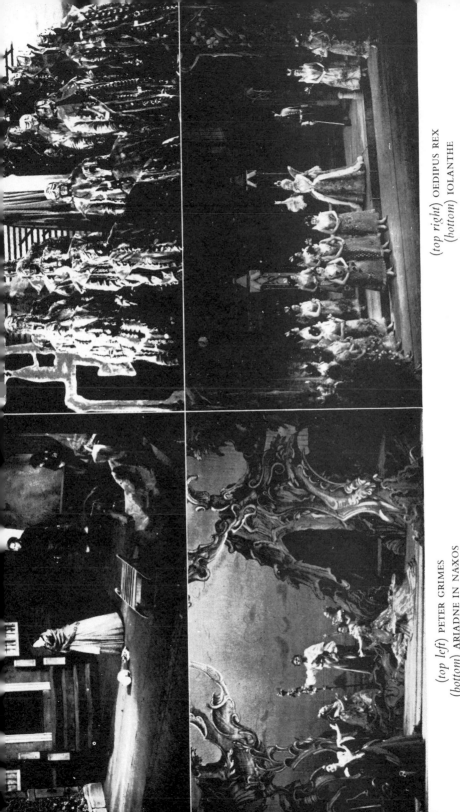

(top left) PETER GRIMES
(bottom) ARIADNE IN NAXOS

(top right) OEDIPUS REX
(bottom) IOLANTHE

THE FLYING DUTCHMAN

THE RISE AND FALL OF THE CITY OF MAHAGONNY

there was overwhelming applause for cast, conductor, producer, and designer (Leslie Hurry); and then, to the great surprise of my guest and many others, an enormous booing cruelly hit the composer when he appeared: the reason, I suspect, was not that the audience disliked the effective modern music, but that the many interesting interludes between the numerous scenes were so extended that there seemed more music with the curtain down than up.

In June, at raised prices, the Kurfürstendamm Theatre Company acted Georg Buchner's *Wozzeck* with his comedy *Leonce und Lena*, G. E. Lessing's *Philotas* with Heinrich von Kleist's comedy *Der Zerbrochene Krug*, and *Ein Traumspiel* by Strindberg. Then the Welsh National Opera returned and introduced Boito's *Mefistofele*.

The former Theatre Ballet returned in July from the Garden with the first London revival of Ashton's *Apparitions* and a new *Giselle* with Anne Heaton, Michael Boulton, Donald Macleary, and Donald Britton. Then came the New Opera Company, with Vaughan Williams as its president, an amateur-professional group started at Cambridge University by Peter Hemmings and Leon Lovett, its conductor. They gave the first London stage performance of Stravinsky's *Rake's Progress*, already given in Cambridge, produced by Brian Trowell with Doreen Murray and Kenneth Bowen in the leads; and the world première on the stage of Arthur Benjamin's *Tale of Two Cities*, libretto by Cedric Cliffe, produced by Anthony Besch, and well sung by Ruth Packer, Heather Harper, Leyland White, and John Cameron, with an exceptionally beautiful performance by Heddle Nash as Dr. Manette; the Goldsborough Orchestra, leader Emanuel Hurwitz, played for these two operas (both of which I had previously produced for the B.B.C.).

There was a fortnight by the Ballet Rambert including Andrée Howard's new *Conte Fantastique* (Caplet), a new *Coppelia*, and Ronald Yerrell's *Mirror* (Lars Erikk Larsen); a week of the Ximenes and Vargas Spanish Ballet for the first time in England; and a fortnight of the José Limon American Dance Company.

For the third time in three years prices were raised for the 1957–8 season—front Circle seats now cost 17s. 6d., and though Stalls remained unchanged, the Gallery was now bookable one day ahead for 3s. 6d., while subscribers of 3s. 6d. a year could book ahead of the general public—signs of growing financial difficulties. The site, size and suitability of the Wells were all blamed and Norman Tucker's suggestion in 1954 for rehousing the company on the South Bank near Waterloo Station was welcomed by the Treasury, the L.C.C., the Arts Council, and the Wells Trust—obviously the Director's previous association with Chancellors of the Exchequer was no hindrance—but the scheme collapsed owing to the 1957 credit squeeze.

Alexander Gibson was now Musical Director, and a revival of *Samson and Delilah* started the season, with Patricia Johnson and the fine-voiced Charles Craig, now a member of the company.

But then came more trouble.

CHAPTER TWENTY

STEPS TO FAREWELL?

1957–1961

THE START of the 1957–8 season had suddenly to be re-planned because the chorus, as the Theatre Ballet had done three years before, made a stand for increased pay. In 1947 they had earned £6 10s. a week, in 1948 £7, in 1950 salaries rising to £8 10s. in the third year; in 1952 the top figure was £9, in 1953 £9 10s., while in 1955 the scale was:

For the 1st 3 months	. . .	£7 per week.
„ „ next 9 „	. . .	£8 10s.
„ „ 2nd year	. . .	£9 10s.
„ „ 3rd year and on	. . .	£10 10s.

—the rates at which they were now working.

In October 1956 they asked, through British Actors Equity, for a scale rising to £14 14s.—in line with the general increase of similar salaries (B.B.C. chorus, etc.)—but no answer came till March 1957 when the Wells and Covent Garden (where a similar claim was made) announced that they wished the claims to be considered together. In May the managements' offer of £1 a week increase was rejected; so was their June offer of 30s., and in August the managements suggested arbitration, to which the chorus agreed, providing they received an immediate rise of 30s. This the managements refused; and the chorus stood on their reduced claim for an increase of £2. No reply was made.

Instead, the Wells management changed the already adver-tised programmes for the September start of the 1957–8 season so that only operas without chorus would be given, announcing that money for bookings already made, especially for *Tosca* and *Martha*, would be returned.

Some performances were cancelled; *The Consul* and *School for Fathers*, being non-chorus operas, were revived; one programme consisted of one act each from *Martha*, *Samson*, and *Bohème*; and the first Wells performances of Menotti's *Telephone* and Bartok's

243

Duke Bluebeard's Castle were given with *Gianni Schicchi*—David Ward and Victoria Elliot doing their best in the rather atmosphereless Bartok production.

During the dispute Norman Tucker claimed on television that the chorus appeared in only half the Wells repertoire; but Equity pointed out that in the 1956–7 season the chorus had been in all the nineteen operas (some 241 performances) and commented that the choristers had to know some forty operas. Out of 46 singers, 11 had been at the Wells since before the war, 13 for 10 years or more, 6 for 5 years or more, and 8 for 3 years or more, so that only 8 did not qualify for full chorus salary. They therefore proposed starting rehearsals at the 30s. increase and then a new scale from £9 10s. up to £13 in the third year. The management refused, and the appointed arbitrator, my old friend and fellow Cambridge don, C. W. Guillebaud, decided for the management's increase of 30s. only.

After the chorus came back, Adele Leigh sang as a guest in *The Magic Flute* in November, and the normal repertoire got going again. Then on 20th January 1958 came the long-intended *Merry Widow*, translated by Christopher Hassall, produced by Charles Hickman, with décor by Thea Neu and choreography by Pauline Grant.

Though normal fare for a People's Opera-house abroad, the *Widow* was a new line for the Wells: its style was also new for the singers, but thanks to Charles Hickman's experienced coaching, not only was the whole cast good, but the four leads were outstanding—the piquant June Bronhill, Marion Lowe in her 'French' number, Thomas Round (now 'by permission of D'Oyly Carte') with his polished insouciance and elegant tenor singing, and Howell Glynne becoming a broad operetta-comedian as to the manner born. The *Widow* was so often sold out that in March extra performances were given instead of already announced operas.

But that same month brought another and more serious crisis. In the autumn of 1957 the Arts Council had realized their allotted funds could not cover adequate grants to all the opera companies—the Garden, the Wells, the Carl Rosa and the Welsh National—so it was 'convinced that some degree of integration' was desirable. The Wells Trust (which runs the operas) therefore suggested some amalgamation with Covent

Garden; but the Wells Governors (who own the theatre) could not agree on what lines.

The Trust then (entirely on its own initiative, the Arts Council reported) approached the Carl Rosa and on 21st November 1957 the two companies jointly announced their mutual and unanimous agreement that their amalgamation would 'bring advantages both artistic and practical to both organizations'. The Arts Council then proposed to give the new combination £215,000, to ensure some eighteen weeks at the Wells and some thirty weeks in the provinces—breaking the continuity at the Wells, but preferable to a complete close-down.

Mrs. Phillips, the Carl Rosa Director, though remaining on the Board, retired in favour of Professor Humphrey Procter-Gregg, and the Wells Trust accepted the new plan. But, at the beginning of March, before the terms could be agreed by the Carl Rosa, and some three months after the original agreement in principle between the two companies, Norman Tucker, the Director of Sadler's Wells, Stephen Arlen, the General Manager, and Alexander Gibson, the Musical Director, resigned.

The Trust and the Governors at once abandoned the amalgamation idea, as it would have meant 'the end of Sadler's Wells as we know it', and an appeal was started by the Hon. James Smith and David MacKenna, Chairman and Vice-Chairman of the Trust, announcing a lack of funds that could be rectified, Mr. Tucker said, by an additional £25,000.

The National Press enthusiastically supported a public letter signed by the Mayor of Finsbury and written by the Borough Librarian, Reginald Rouse (a champion of the district and a Wells Governor for the Council in 1956–7), pleading that 'London pride can surely afford a trifling subsidy to keep its opera going' seeing that a mere one-tenth of a penny rate for all London would provide £38,000 to save the Wells.

Viscount Esher became Chairman of an Appeal Fund, an anonymous donor gave £15,000 and, after approval by the Finsbury Council through their Leader, Alderman M. Cliffe, the Metropolitan Boroughs Standing Joint Committee asked the London County Council to make a grant, there being no other convenient machinery for a composite grant from London boroughs.

In April the Governors and Trustees of the Wells announced

their determination to preserve and develop the Wells opera as a separate company (rather different from their previous attitude), being equally determined to find the necessary money. So the management withdrew its resignations. In June A.B.C. Television promised an annual £3,000 for seven years; in July the L.C.C. granted £25,000; and the Wells was saved.

For the whole of the 1958 summer the Wells was occupied by visiting companies. First came the Carl Rosa—into the lions' den, as it turned out—giving more or less the same programme as in 1957 with William Aitken, Kevin Miller, John Heddle Nash, John Holmes, Stanislav Pieczora, Victoria Elliot, Joan Stuart, Charles Craig, John Hargreaves, and James Johnston— all of whom would soon sing (if they had not already sung) as members of the Sadler's Wells company.

Then Peter Daubeny presented the famous Moscow Arts Theatre in *The Three Sisters, Uncle Vanya, The Cherry Orchard,* and Rakmanov's *Troubled Past*; the three-week season was an enormous success and the demand for seats could not be satisfied, though prices were, not unreasonably, raised—the highest being 35s.

This was followed by the first appearance in England of the Ballets 1958 des Étoiles de Paris (Director and chief dancer Milorad Miskovitch) at ordinary prices: they danced *L'Échelle, La Dryade, L'Écuyère, Le Rideau, Rouge, Prométhée, Cache-Cache,* and *Quatuor*. Then came, for the first time in London, the Piccolo Teatro di Milano playing Goldoni's *Servant of Two Masters* in delightful *commedia dell' arte* style.

Next the Opera de Camara de Buenos Aires presented an interesting variety of short operas, mostly unknown to present-day London—Handel's *Apollo e Dafne*, Pergolesi's *Serva Padrona*, Telemann's *Pimpinone*, Hindemith's *Hin und Zurück*, Galuppi-Goldoni's *Filosofo de Campagna*, and Cimarosa's *Maestro di Capella*; their regular conductor was Enrique Sivieri, but Charles Mackerras conducted as a guest.

The New Opera Company then gave *A Tale of Two Cities* again; two English premières—Werner Egk's *Government Inspector* (based on Gogol, translated by Norman Platt) produced by Anthony Besch, and Menotti's *The Unicorn, the Gorgon and the Manticore*, produced by Colin Graham with choreography by Peter Darrell (who had been with the Wells Ballet some time before); Stravinsky's *Soldier's Tale*; and Brian Trowell's production of *Sir John in Love*. The company was joined by the Western Ballet Company.

During the New Opera Company's visit, the Wells boldly tried a new venture—successfully opening at the London Coliseum on 31st July with *The Merry Widow*: but this is the story of the Wells itself, not of the Wells opera company.

Then followed at the Wells seven weeks of ballet—four of Feliks Parnell's Ballet from Poland in small works, but including *L'Après-midi d'un Faune*; two of the Ballet Rambert (with Miskovitch as guest-artist) including two new ballets, Dervk Mendel's *Epithalame* (Jean Guillaume) and Norman Morrice's remarkable *Two Brothers* (Dohnanyi)—the first short ballet entirely telerecorded—as well as an American Night with Anthony Tudor's ballets *Lilac Garden*, *Judgment of Paris*, *Dark Elegies*, and *Gala Performance*; and lastly a week of the famous Spanish dancers Susanna and José, in England for the first time, with guitar, piano and flamenco singer.

For a week the Düsseldorfer Schauspielhaus gave Schiller's *Maria Stuart*, Hauptmann's *Michael Kramer*, and Lessing's *Nathan der Weise*. Then came the Edinburgh International Ballet (Dance Director Peggy van Praagh, Musical Director Charles Mackerras, assisted by Maurits Sillem): the dancers included David Poole and, as guest-artists, Beryl Kaye, Gillian Lynne, Wendy Toye, Milorad Miskovitch, George Skibine, and Paddy Stone.

After the summer the Arts Council, unable to reconcile the dissentient members of the Carl Rosa Board, invited Professor Procter-Gregg to take those of the Carl Rosa ready to serve with him on an autumn tour as the temporary Touring Opera 1958, at the same time withdrawing all support from and association with the Carl Rosa Company.

So, after eighty-three years of success, that famous company, weakened by lack of competition 'on the road', closed down, and Sadler's Wells, able after its Coliseum success to tour operetta with a second company and orchestra, gained what was virtually a monopoly of long-term opera in English with two interchangeable companies—one resident in London, the other on tour.

Norman Tucker, with Stephen Arlen now designated Administrative Director, opened the 1958-9 season at the Wells on 29th October with my production of *The Flying Dutchman*. I was intrigued when Norman suggested it might be done in the Wieland Wagner modern Bayreuth manner on an empty stage with projected 'magic-lantern' scenery. But then I realized that a projected ghost-ship needed as a contrast a solid ship and solid rocks: so inexorably we logically adopted the 'old-fashioned' naturalistic style of the composer himself (not a bad approach, by the way, to any composer).

This was a challenge because such a production calls for a large stage equipped with all mechanical devices (it was said the Covent Garden stage-hands were laughing in anticipation), but the result was one of the best examples of co-ordination and co-operation in an opera-house.

The co-operation began with the prime problem of making the distant ghost-ship approach through the storm apparently with ghost-sailors aboard. Three months before rehearsals I discussed this with Charles Bristow, the lighting expert in charge at the Wells. As a result the opening storm-clouds were constantly changing (unlike the usual rhythmic succession of the same shapes), and the arrival of the dark ship from the far distance was amazing, considering the shallow stage (only 43 ft. from the proscenium to the back wall instead of Dibdin's 90 ft.), especially when the gaunt figure of the Dutchman came ashore on to the high rocks where every foothold had needed constant rehearsal. The intricately simple lighting scheme—involving no less than twenty-two effects lamps—meant that we had to insist that the young A.B.C. Television designer, Timothy O'Brien, added a rock he thought artistically unnecessary into his attractive scenery because it was the only place to hide one of the lamps.

In the title-rôle David Ward made his name and soon became an international star—proving the value of a system that allows a chorus artist to improve technically by playing ever-larger parts with an experienced team in preference to being trained for leading parts, as happens in opera-schools the world over.

Elizabeth Fretwell was the Senta, Harold Blackburn (another

former member of the chorus who had been making his mark for some time) a rugged Daland, William McAlpine a lyrically tortured Eric; and Alberto Remedios (whom the management was grooming) was the Steersman. The very effective costumes were by Anthony Boyes and, owing to the illness of Alexander Gibson (who later conducted the opera with real Wagnerian stage-sense), the first performance was successfully conducted by a junior Wells conductor, William Reid.

In November the brilliant orchestral musician Colin Davis came to conduct *Il Seraglio,* and in the new year *Russalka* was first produced at the Wells by Wendy Toye with fairy-book décor by James Bailey: it was conducted by Vilem Tausky, and the two chief parts were sung by Charles Craig, bravely fighting laryngitis to avoid a cancellation of the first night, and, in the title-rôle, Joan Hammond sang beautifully, for the first time on the stage, the well-known aria 'O Silver Moon' of which she had already made a famous recording. She also sang *Butterfly* this season.

A Committee of Inquiry on Sadler's Wells—Sir Frederick Hooper, Sir Adrian Boult, Lady Fermoy, Lord Latham, and Mr. Philip Hope-Wallace—set up to advise the London County Council, reported early in March 1959 that the Wells was essential to London both as opera-house and as training ground for young singers; that the lowest prices there could not be raised 'without departing from the spirit of the charter' catering for the 'student public', nor could the highest—low compared with West End prices; that the organization was efficient and on the whole not extravagant; that the Wells and the Garden were complementary—the Garden containing a permanent national opera, the Wells serving the broad London public; that the L.C.C. should help the Arts Council to aid the artistic development of the Wells while the Coliseum profits should reduce the accumulated deficit; that 'the technical deficiencies of the theatre (cramped offices and storage space, defects of seating, acoustics, proscenium, apron and orchestral pit) now impose an artistic barrier which will have to be removed if further progress is to be possible'; that the Wells should entertain audiences of every kind; and that improvements should be put in hand at once over the next few years at an estimated cost of £50,000.

The Committee therefore thought the L.C.C. should grant £35,000 a year for three years, subject to reconsideration, and an extra initial £15,000 for immediate maintenance, provided the gift of the same amount already held was also used, as well as £10,000 of the second and third year annual grant; that grants for the succeeding triennium should be considered not later than the end of the second year, and that after that the Wells should be able to rely on £25,000 a year at least.

By public demand, the *Dutchman* was given three more performances at the end of the season, when Alexander Gibson ceased to be Musical Director, and Peter Hemmings, a founder of the New Opera Company, became Personal Assistant to Stephen Arlen.

The summer was filled with visiting companies, though the Wells Trust was associated with the first presentation—that of Tamara Toumanova with Wladimir Oukhtomsky in programmes including *The Dying Swan* and excerpts from *The Nutcracker Suite* and *Romeo and Juliet*. They were followed by the return of Susanna and José, and they by the Ballet Rambert. In June 1959 (when the L.C.C. granted the Wells £120,000 over the next two years) the Handel Opera Society performed *Rodelinda*, produced by Anthony Besch, with Joan Sutherland, Janet Baker, Margreta Elkins, Patricia Kern, Alfred Hallett, and Raimund Herincx, and *Semele*, produced by Ande Anderson, with Heather Harper, Monica Sinclair, Helen Watts, Owen Brannigan, John Mitchinson, and John Noble; Robin Pidcock was the designer, Charles Farncombe the conductor, and Thurston Dart was at the harpsichord.

Then came La Famille Hernandez for the first time in London; Le Ballet-Théâtre de Maurice Béjart in his choreographic drama *Orphée*: and the New Opera Company gave the English premières of Dallapiccola's *Prisoner*, impressionably produced by Anthony Besch with designs by Ralph Koltai, and Carl Orff's *Tale of the Wise Maiden* (*Die Klüge*).

In the autumn structural alterations, especially of the proscenium and orchestral pit, were made by the Festival Hall expert Hope Bagenal to improve the acoustics, at a cost of £15,000, and the new season of 1959–60 opened with two new productions—*Andrea Chenier*, produced by Anthony Besch with Leslie Hurry designs, sung by Victoria Elliot, Charles Craig, and young Peter Glossop, a fine baritone; and Douglas Craig's effective *Cinderella* (*Cenerentola*), conducted by Bryan Balkwill and well performed by Nancy Creighton, Patricia Kern in the name-part, Anna Pollak, Alexander Young, Denis Dowling, Howell Glynne, and Stanley Clarkson.

The acoustic improvements soon had to be drastically altered (perhaps acoustically unsatisfactory buildings can as yet never be adequately improved): during a full rehearsal of a revival of *Katya* (with Marie Collier, Monica Sinclair, William Macalpine and Stanislav Pieczora) I heard an expert, when told that the conductor, Charles Mackerras, could not hear the singers adequately, first advise less loud orchestral playing and then, learning that Kubelik in the same theatre had added maroons to that same essentially noisy key-scene (Ostrovsky's original play was called *The Storm*) comment, 'Mozart never scored like that'.

A rather bare *Tannhaüser* was produced by Anthony Besch, with designs by Motley somewhat after the modern Bayreuth manner and conducted by Colin Davis, in December 1959— the year in which Sir Robert and Lady Mayer extended their excellent Youth and Music organization (founded 1954) to include operas from the Wells repertoire for young people, a practice they have kept up ever since; and in January 1960 Michel Saint-Denis's admirably stylized production of Stravinsky's *Oedipus Rex*, with costumes and masks by Abdul Kader Farrah, was given: in that Monica Sinclair and Ronald Dowd were especially good and the admirable chorus had to be motionless for so long that rests were made for them to lean against.

Colin Davis, who had conducted *Oedipus*, at the end of the season conducted equally brilliantly my completely new production of *Tosca* including passages restored from Puccini's first version. For this Paul Mayo's excellent sets included a secret torture-chamber off Scarpia's room and iron gates in the Sant' Angelo fortress that Tosca manipulated to stop the soldiers reaching her before her suicide (usually an unconvincing moment); only the lack of stage-depth somewhat stultified the Cardinal's procession and the singing of the Te Deum in the main body of the church (an effect I willingly tried at Norman Tucker's suggestion).

Beatrice Dawson, the designer for many first-rate films, proved how effective a mixture of cheap and expensive materials can be and surprised some by giving Tosca no petticoats under a transparent skirt (such as Grimaldi sang about)—this Marie Collier would have correctly worn damp to cling to the legs, had I let her risk catching the prevalent cold of the period. Her Tosca was the convent-bred singer of Sardou's original play (a reading supported by Puccini's accompanying her first entry with an anticipation of her sincere appeal to God in 'Vissi d'arte'); Charles Craig sang beautifully as Cavaradossi; Peter Glossop achieved a restrained and sinister Gestapo-like Scarpia; Harold Blackburn's Sacristan was humorous but not a comic; and two invaluable chorus singers, Rees Williams and Charles Draper, made Spoletta the nervy underling of a dictator state and the Gaoler an official with a heart.

It was about now that I introduced for rehearsals, instead of the usual method of marking out the floor, portable single screens to make scene-shapes—an ingenious aid to the artists that I had learned at the National Theatre in Helsinki (in four of whose theatres I did some eleven productions and where I had spent most of the previous year).

Visiting companies then included the Ballet of the Théâtre Royal de la Monnaie, Brussels, with which the Wells was now linked through Stephen Arlen, with performances of *Le Sacre du Printemps*, an *Orphée*, Charrat's *Fantaisie Concertante* (Prokofiev), his *Concerto de Grieg*, and *Les Algues*, Peter Darrell's *Prisoners* (Bartok) and Béjart's *Symphonie pour un homme seul* to *musique concrète*; and the New Opera Company in Schönberg's *Erwartung*, Stravinsky's *Nightingale*, and Humphrey Searle's *Diary of a Madman*. For four weeks in May the Wells presented Geoffrey Dunn's version of Offenbach's *Orpheus in the Underworld*, directed by Wendy Toye: in this lively, though inevitably British, reading of the French original, Kevin Miller as Orpheus, Eric Shilling as Jupiter (with a cloak marked 'Invisible' as in Wordsworth's day), and June Bronhill as Eurydice were outstanding.

Then came a stage history of the neighbourhood, *The Finsbury Story*, to which the Borough Council, local celebrities such as

Eric Newton, the art critic (whose wife produced it), Frederick Crooke, who designed it, local firms, schools, and sewing-parties, as well as Pikemen and Musketeers of the Hon. Artillery Company, contributed. John Betjeman wrote the foreword, David Lytton the script, and John Gardner the music, which was conducted by Leonard Hancock: unfortunately mixed interests and standards of experience hardly made for smoothness.

Next the Handel Opera Company performed *Hercules* and *Radamisto*; the Rose Bruford Training College of Speech and Drama gave Noel Coward's *Cavalcade*; and the Ballet Rambert gave the first London performance of Norman Morrice's interesting *Wise Monkeys* (Shostakovich) and the first British production of Bournonville's *Sylphide* (Loverskjold) of 1832.

After a tour, my production of *Merrie England* as reshaped and with new dialogue by me, with the consent of Edward German's family, was the first August production by the Wells, with choreography by Andrée Howard. It had earlier been planned for the Coliseum, but the Wells company gave its last performance there the previous year—some said the West End disliked the operatic practice of varying the cast.

Peter Rice cleverly adapted his Coliseum designs for the smaller revolve-less stage, while Joan Stuart, John Carolan, John Hargreaves, and either Denis Dowling or John Holmes had the right romantic spirit for Bessie Throckmorton, Raleigh, Essex, and the actor Wilkins; Leon Greene was fine as Long Tom and Anna Pollak as Queen Elizabeth.

Incidentally, at the first chorus music-rehearsal, when they sang during the welcome to the Queen

> Held high thy sceptre is
> Over thine enemies,

they were advised to improve their tone by broadening the final short vowel, so that they lustily sang

> Over thine enemas

—and nobody smiled but myself.

The £15,000 acoustic alterations of 1959 had been further readjusted by Mr. T. Somerville of the B.B.C. for £1,200, and the 1960–1 season began with Colin Davis as principal conductor, assisted by John Barker, Michael Moores and

William Reid and six guest-conductors, while the thirty-three resident principal singers needed the addition of no less than eighteen guest-artists, including Marion Studholme, who had been an invaluably versatile member of the company for some years.

A new *Traviata* was produced by another well-known drama producer, Frank Hauser, and a new *Barber* by Douglas Craig, followed by Wendy Toye's gay *Fledermaus*, as seen at the Coliseum. New to the Wells were *Ariadne in Naxos*, a notable production by Anthony Besch, baroquely designed by Peter Rice and well sung by Elizabeth Fretwell; and, in Colin Graham's production, Janacek's *Cunning Little Vixen*, picturesque but not wholly convincing to a British audience.

In the summer of 1961 operas new to the Wells were presented by the New Opera Company—F. Burt's *Volpone*; by the Welsh National—*The Battle* by Verdi (translated by John and Nell Moody from *La Battaglia di Legnano*), and Rimsky-Korsakov's *May Night*, produced by George Foa (well known for his television productions); and by the Handel Opera Society—*Rinaldo*.

It was encouraging to read in the annual report that, while in 1959–60 the deficit was £55,375 (after receipts of £532,746 from Wells and Coliseum takings, a share of the tours, the Arts Council grant, and sundry extras), in 1960–1 the total receipt of £556,437 (from the Wells, tours, grants from Arts Council, L.C.C., and A.B.C. Television and other sources) resulted in a deficit of only £17,186.

But when Geoffrey Dunn's version of Offenbach's *La Vie Parisienne*, directed by Wendy Toye with gay designs by Malcolm Pride, was given, the Directors announced with very great regret an appreciable increase in admission prices—entirely due to 'the very heavy increases in operating costs which the Theatre is having to meet'; while 'in view of the great demand for seats' on Saturdays and first nights, they claimed the innovation of increasing prices further for those nights was justified. Prices were now to be:

Dress Circle   normally £1 to 12s. 6d.: Saturdays £1 5s. to 15s.: first nights £1 10s. to 15s.
Stalls   normally 15s. 6d. to 8s. 6d.: Saturdays and first nights £1 2s. 6d. to 15s.

Upper Circle   normally 8s. 6d.: Saturdays and first nights
               10s. 6d.
Gallery   normally 5s. in advance, 4s. on the day: Saturdays
               and first nights 5s. only.

In July Rose Bruford's college gave the first London produc-
tion of the American Don Marquis's play on the Crucifixion,
The Dark Hours; the Ballet Rambert gave the first British per-
formance of George Balanchine's new *Night Shadow* (Bellini-
Riety), the première of Norman Morrice's finest achievement to
date—*A Place in the Desert* (Carlos Surinach), and the first
London performance of Walter Gore's *Night and Silence* (Bach-
Mackerras); and the Wells revived the popular *Orpheus in the
Underworld*.

The decision by Selwyn Lloyd, Chancellor of the Exchequer,
on 12th July, that he would release the £1,000,000 earmarked
in 1949 towards the building of a National Theatre on the
South Bank of the Thames, plus an annual grant of about
£400,000, at first sight did not seem to affect the Wells. But
now it was announced 'in small print' that the Government and
the L.C.C. would consider creating a National Theatre (first
mooted about a hundred years earlier) not only out of the Old
Vic and the Stratford-upon-Avon Shakespeare company (as had
been rumoured in 1946) but also including the Sadler's Wells
Opera Companies.
    In the *Daily Mail* Robert Muller commented that, if this
meant the closing of theatres, 'this "embrace" may well be a
kiss of death . . . And if this is so, then it's clearly time that the
kissing stopped . . . Theatres cannot be established on take-
over lines . . . We want *more* theatres in Britain; not fewer'.
    The enthusiastic originators of the National Theatre scheme
(whether of the 1840s, the 1920s, or the 1940s), mostly experienced theatremen, would have been the first to stress the im-
practicability of housing both opera and drama in the same
theatre except as a make-do method, as at the Old Vic in its
younger days and at smaller municipal theatres abroad.
    The new plan—to build not one but two theatres, one large,
one intimate, for interchange of large and small productions,
whether operatic or dramatic—would not make the fusion
easier. This National Theatre planning, however, would have

nothing to do with a history of the Wells itself, had it merely concerned the move, much criticized in the Press, of the established régime from that theatre.

On the face of it (though other views will be given later), the Governors and Trustees of the Wells were empowered to agree to the moving of the company. But, to provide extra funds for the National Theatre, they claimed they were entitled to sell the Wells itself.

CHAPTER TWENTY-ONE

'SO MUCH ACHIEVED ...'

1961–1964

THE DECISION to remove the opera organization from the Wells rallied people to the defence of the theatre and what it stood for. One of the first shots was fired by Leo Kersley, a principal dancer with the Wells Ballet in 1950, asking in a letter to the press what experts, theatrical or musical, had been consulted as to the advisability of the move: the Wells Press Officer merely replied—the Governors and Trustees. No other names of more experienced persons were given, and not even the mixed experts on the Arts Council's Music Panel (of which I was then a member) were asked their opinions. Kersley also enquired, like Robert Muller (who thought the Chancellor's announcement 'a form of gentle blackmail'), 'Is it a matter of money, pure and simple? "You may move to the South Bank, *or else*" . . .?', and queried whether the Wells Opera could function more efficiently, or indeed at all, 'when thrown in piecemeal with several other organizations, all, doubtless, pulling different ways'.

A former Director of the Sadler's Wells Trust, Evert Barger, wrote to the *Daily Telegraph*,

> No architect has yet built a theatre which has solved the acoustic problems of an opera house and met at the same time the more intimate requirements of Shakespeare and Shaw—

a view supported in an *Opera* editorial. Barger further said that some £30,000 had been spent two years before on improving the Wells acoustics and amenities, and that the stage could be enlarged for about £125,000, 'a very small slice of the £2,300,000 now to be spent on the building of a National Theatre', while

> it would . . . be a grievous mistake if the Sadler's Wells organisation were absorbed, lost its home, and its separate identity, and performances ceased in Islington.

257

Some time later (for clarity the arguments quoted are not given in strict chronological order) Norman Tucker wrote enthusiastically in favour of the two auditoriums,

> one predominantly for opera and the other for drama, with all the possibilities of cross-communication and mutual help that can arise in the circumstances,

and the critic Desmond Shawe-Taylor thought that to put two auditoriums under one roof would 'test, but hardly defeat, the ingenuity of a good architect', while it was good to get drama and opera together—after all, some of the best opera-producers came from the straight theatre.

The chief reason given at first for the move was the time-old cry that the Wells was inaccessible, that it had no passing trade, and that the South Bank was more central.

Eric Newton, Chairman of the Finsbury Art Group, and A. H. Ley, Chairman of the Finsbury Theatre Society, pointed out that the Wells was no more isolated than the Old Vic, the Royal Court, or the Lyric, Hammersmith, and that the Government and Trade Unions encouraged local enterprise in the arts.

Opera draws only lovers of opera, not seekers for casual entertainment: Glyndebourne and Salzburg hardly rely on passing trade.

Near the Festival Hall there are few easily accessible amenities, such as pubs, for the man in the street (the modern 'artisan and labourer'), and, while on the map the South Bank is nearer to Piccadilly Circus, the Wells is more accessible for similar customers—the Waterloo stations (main line and Underground) are five minutes from the Festival Hall with twelve bus-routes (five of which do not run on Saturday evenings) three to seven minutes away: less than three minutes from the Wells are thirteen bus-routes and the Angel Underground station with King's Cross one and Euston two stations away. By bus and foot, as this book was going to press, test journeys took seventeen minutes from the Festival Hall to Piccadilly Circus street level and from that spot to the Wells twelve and a half minutes.

The Wells Directors said the transfer would help touring, though how was not apparent; while the proceeds from the sale of the theatre site, to be at the disposal of the Joint Council of the National Theatre, would not clash with the provisions of the Foundation or the use of income derived from the theatre in the Charity Commission scheme of 1931. As for the constant quoting of the 'artisans and labourers' clause from the original Baylis intention, 'a reasonable proportion of relatively cheap seats' would be kept on the South Bank 'as at present', said Norman Tucker, while 'whatever happens, the name of Sadler's Wells will be kept by its companies, whether they perform on the South Bank, in the provinces, or abroad'.[1]

Opponents doubted whether, under the Charity Commission, the Wells could be sold—it allowed the Governors to present entertainments anywhere in the County of London, but expressly added 'subject thereto in improving or enlarging the theatre'. Some thought the Governors and Trustees in charge of the Wells were breaking their trust by approving the transfer and sale and by being represented on the National Theatre Committee, and that therefore they should resign.

British Actors Equity sent a memorandum to Selwyn Lloyd disapproving of the inclusion of the Wells opera in the National Theatre scheme (which otherwise they approved), especially if it meant the closing of Sadler's Wells theatre. As Leo Kersley wrote, 'Were Lilian Baylis alive she would be behind the barricades at this very moment. But she is gone, and who is left to care?'

In the theatre itself performances were more easily supervised, as heads of departments could now listen-in from any part of the building through ear-plugs connected with a one-way transistor-radio system.

On 12th September a new opera company, Rostrum Ltd., with Wells personnel on the committee, backed by business firms, presented the Brecht-Weill *Seven Deadly Sins* with Rodney Bennett's first opera *The Ledge*, 'a promising failure', and Stravinsky's ballet *Renard*. Then the 1961–2 season opened with John Barton's production of *Carmen*—strangely unexciting in spite of Ralph Koltai's sets and costumes by Annena Stubbs, but later most successful when Joyce Blackham sang the lead.

[1] This is either like calling the Prime Minister's residence 'No. 10', whether in Downing Street or not, or refuted by the natural eagerness of the Sadler's Wells Ballet at Covent Garden to become The Royal Ballet.

Colin Davis, after his great successes with the orchestra, was appointed Musical Director and Principal Conductor in November, but he did not conduct the first two new productions. Of these, *Iolanthe* was the first Gilbert and Sullivan opera to be presented at and by the Wells since the Gilbert copyright expired, produced by Frank Hauser, well designed by Desmond Healey; in it Patricia Kern was exceptionally good in the face of rather self-consciously 'different' touches in presentation. Then came a new *Bohème*, produced by the Australian Robin Lovejoy, unrealistically designed by Voytek, the two chief parts sung by William McAlpine and a new young singer Wendy Baldwin.

Colin Davis then conducted Glen Byam Shaw's production of *The Rake's Progress* beautifully performed by Elsie Morison, Edith Coates, and Alexander Young, with designs by Motley. There were two more new productions that season—*The Bartered Bride* with Ava June and later Wendy Baldwin, produced by Pauline Grant and modernistically designed by Timothy O'Brien, and Delius's *A Village Romeo and Juliet*, produced by Basil Coleman as sensitively as Leslie Hurry designed his atmospheric décor, with lovely performances by Elsie Morison and John Wakefield as the lovers.

At the end of the season Glen Byam Shaw, known for his skill at the Old Vic, Stratford-upon-Avon, and in the West End, was made Director of Productions—a new position created with the idea that a channelling of drama with Colin Davis's musical understanding should merge into opera.

The attack in the press on the South Bank scheme went on. One letter pointed out that the Arts Council seemed to be concentrating on opera for London to the neglect of the provinces. Mrs. Phillips, the Carl Rosa Director for so many years, while agreeing that touring opera now needed some subsidy, commented that the Wells, which had already approached provincial cities for support, could no longer tour without support from the ratepayers as well as the taxpayers, and remarked that 'central administrative costs' at the Wells 'are said to reach £3,000 or £4,000 a week in addition to the £5,000 quoted as normal weekly expenditure'. Certainly the Wells administrative staff—according to the 1959–60 report numbering from

96, plus 76 concerned with production (not counting 132 singers, 24 ballet, 108 orchestra)—seemed more numerous than that employed by the largest commercial managers (though opera is complicated, and there were two companies).

A blow hit the National Theatre planners with an implied criticism which they refused to notice: the Stratford-upon-Avon Governors of the Royal Shakespeare Company, despite their belief in the need for a National Theatre, withdrew because the proposed terms of amalgamation either raised constitutional difficulties in relation to their Royal Charter or envisaged a framework too cumbersome, in their view, to operate smoothly. They agreed with Equity that different bodies had different needs: 'Such a wholesale fusion might also reduce the variety of theatre available to the community without creating a National Theatre with an authentic personality'.

Four days later Sir Isaac Hayward, Leader of the L.C.C., forecast a postponement of the completion of the National Theatre from 1964 to 1965 because of Government restrictions on spending; and after a month it was agreed to build two separate buildings (opera and drama would not, therefore, be playing Box and Cox after all), while the withdrawal of Stratford would mean a reduction of the annual grant from £400,000 to £300,000 (a sign of the 'gentle blackmail').

So the Wells directors could now look forward to having a theatre holding 1,850 instead of the actual 1,550, not—as Norman Tucker said—with the aim of becoming 'the National Opera' and a rival to Covent Garden, but so that 'we will be able to display ourselves to rather better advantage' than could be done on the existing Wells site, as was emphasized by David McKenna (by now Chairman of Sadler's Wells), who was criticized for not disclosing earlier that the decision was made in 1957. Asked now if the Wells would retain its name on the South Bank, Mr. Tucker now said, 'That is something we just don't know.'

At the Wells itself the Welsh National Opera returned with works they had done there before; and then on 30th May the Wells presented *The Mikado*, produced by Keith Beattie, an experienced theatre man now on the staff. Peter Rice did the charming designs; but the separately designed collapsible bamboo fan-curtain had to be scrapped before the first performance as, though built at considerable expense, it masked the lights and was not satisfactory: this, some thought, was the type of wasted expenditure the Arts Council should examine when considering grants in general.

Then the New Opera Company presented Henze's *Boulevard Solitude* (with April Cantelo as the modern Manon) which was given with the English Opera Group's *Albert Herring*; and the first London performance of Pizzetti's *Murder in the Cathedral*.

The following day, 3rd July, the Government gave the go-ahead to the National Theatre scheme, subscribing with the L.C.C. £400,000 a year for the two buildings, and the B.B.C. signed up with the Wells to televise between four and six operas or operettas from the studios in three years, starting with *The Mikado*, for £40,000.

The Handel Opera Company introduced a staged version of Handel's last oratorio, *Jephtha*, produced by Anthony Besch with Peter Rice's designs; and Marie Rambert, at long last a Dame of the British Empire, presented the first British performance of *Don Quixote* (Petipa's story from Cervantes) with choreography by Alexander Gorsky and Zakharoff, music by Ludwig Minkus, arranged by Geoffrey Corbett, and designs by Voytek; the first performance of Norman Morrice's *Conflicts* (Bloch) with Ralph Koltai's costumes; and a revival of Antony Tudor's *Soirée Musicale*.

Thanks to a grant of £20,000 from the Calouste Gulbenkian Foundation (half of it repayable), the Wells was able to buy ten road vehicles, including a travelling information bureau, to take productions on tour.

At the end of August the National Youth Theatre acted *Henry V* and *Julius Caesar* in modern dress, directed by Michael Croft. Then in September the famous Hamburg State Opera made its first London appearance (reasonably at very high prices—from 10s. 6d. Gallery to Front Stalls or Dress Circle at £3) with *Lohengrin*, produced by Wieland Wagner and conducted by Horst Stein with Arturo Sergi, Elisabeth Grümmer, Astrid Varnay, Herbert Fliether, and Ernst Wiemann; Henze's *Prinz von Homburg*, produced by Helmut Kaütner, conducted by the composer and sung by Vladimir Rusdak, Liselotte Fölser, Helmut Melchert, Heinz Hoppe, and Mimi Aarden; and the two Berg operas, *Lulu* and *Wozzeck*, produced by Günther Rennert and conducted by Leopold Ludwig with singers including Helge Pilarczki, Toni Blankenheim, Gisele Litz, Ratko Delarko, Kurt Ruesche, Kurt Marschner, Sigmund Roth, and Jürgen Förster. Wieland Wagner's 'boldness in unfurnishing the stage and de-hamming the action' in *Lohengrin* was praised by some; others blamed him for using 'ramps and rostrums better suited to a trade fair', but the singing as a whole was wonderful, especially Astrid Varnay's 'bloodcurdling Ortrud', who 'with a voice like a beautiful serpent' succeeded in stopping the show. Through lack of storage-room the scenery had to be put into the grounds of the MetropolitanWater Board next door, a fact later stressed by Norman Tucker.

The 1962–3 season began with Glen Byam Shaw's new *Idomeneo* designed by Motley and conducted by Colin Davis, who in a revival of the *Dutchman* gave such Wagnerian breadth to the start of the third act that it was difficult for the sailors to dance or be drunk—in my opinion a theatrical lapse in his otherwise brilliant conducting which he most understandingly corrected in a later revival.

The Wells now commissioned three full-length operas from Rodney Bennett 'because he could write reasonably quickly, and his music was not so complicated that it needed "six months'" orchestral rehearsal'.

Puccini's melodramatic *Girl of the Golden West*, produced by John Blatchley, conducted by Warwick Braithwaite, and sung by Elizabeth Fretwell, Donald Smith, and Raymond Herincx (surprisingly in black as the villainous Sheriff), seemed somewhat over-hammed, perhaps intentionally; the effective sets were by Timothy O'Brien though with a large free-standing electric log-fire and, in the last act, a mining-sluice more prominent than the Californian forest of the score.

In the second week of November 1962 Sadler's Wells Theatre was put up for sale, 'and I'm hoping', said Norman Tucker, 'that it will fetch at least a million from Mr. Cotton or Mr. Clore'. It would be three or four years before the South Bank opera house would be ready; but he dreamed great dreams about the opening night in their new home—'prominent among these fantasies is a vision of the Queen arriving by Royal Barge'.

There were no bidders up to mid-December, when a delegation of the Finsbury Art Group and the Finsbury Theatre Society handed the Town Clerk a petition, signed by nearly 3,000 people, against the sale; the Federation of Theatre Unions had already approved of the campaign against closing the Wells.

For the first time in three years the Wells was able to announce in January 1963 that it had made a surplus in the previous season—reducing the company's deficit from £93,436 to £62,083 (their grants from the Arts Council and the L.C.C. alone had amounted to £405,000).

The next Wells production was the Brecht-Weill *Rise and Fall of the City of Mahagonny*, revelationary to the younger audience but old-fashioned to their elders. One critic hailed it as 'a fierce triumph' and an achievement 'which would be even more impressive if they could articulate the words more clearly', and though others regretted the too many irrelevant un-Brechtian tricks of the producer, Michael Geliot, it was certainly something not to be missed. Miscasting (the underplaying April Cantelo as a mulatto tart, Ronald Dowd as a 'riotous young animal' and the softly lyrical Patricia Bartlett in the 'Edith Coates' part of Mrs. Begbick) was no reason for withholding praise from Alberto Remedios for his eating-himself-to-death scene and the performances of Inia Te Wiata and John Chorley (another valuable soloist from the chorus); but the real triumph was Colin Davis's conducting 'with an unfailingly keen sense of the music's expressive range, its tempi, rhythms and textures'.

Then came Rossini's delightfully ribald *Count Ory* with Alexander Young's witty performance, the whole neatly pointed by Bryan Balkwill's conducting, Anthony Besch's production, and Peter Rice's scenery. A new *Cosi fan Tutte* was distinguished for the singing of John Wakefield and Donald McIntyre as the two officers and Thomas Hemsley as Don Alfonso; Glen Byam Shaw's production was both 'laudably free of arch or extraneous byplay' and adorned 'with distracting detail', while Motley's sets were both 'simple and effective' and 'often much too pretentious'! Prokofiev's *Love of Three Oranges* (in association with the New Opera Company) was produced by Peter Coe with designs by Tony Walton and slapstick instead of satire—bogus clergymen jumping up in the audience, for instance; and one critic commented, 'If anything goes, if everything is distorted, no norm of meaning or feeling is left . . . Everything is self-destructive . . . every gesture immediately satirized, and because it is also heartless, it quickly becomes a disintegrating bore.'

The last new presentation that season was Basil Coleman's successful production of *La Belle Hélène* which 'went like a frothy sugar-candied delightful waltz dream', though it was 'a somewhat prolonged romp, especially in a performance on Friday that with difficulty shook off the feel of a dress rehearsal' —no wonder when many of the cast had to be sewn into their ultra-elaborate clothes for first-time wearing on the opening night, and expensive properties had been tried out and scrapped. Still, 'Anthony Powell's Victorian Greek décor is uproarious, Geoffrey Dunn's translation racy, and Joyce Blackham queens it nicely in the title-rôle', while Kevin Miller's sincerity as Paris and John Frear from the chorus as Menelaus were nearest to Offenbach.

In the summer the Handel Opera Society's new presentations were *Xerxes*, conducted by Anthony Lewis—perhaps over-amusing with Brian Trowell's production and Geoffrey Dunn's translation, but John Holmes was an admirably irrepressible Elviro and Alexander Young sang beautifully as Xerxes; and *Giulio Cesare* (producer Norman Ayrton, designer Michael Warre, conductor Charles Farncombe)—'one of Handel's richest operas, but no very clear impression of its riches came across': Margreta Elkin's superb performance did not make a female Caesar convincing and in Cleopatra Joan Sutherland found a part which 'musically suits her voice, but not her temperament'.

On 26th June Princess Margaret, arriving for a gala performance of *Giulio Cesare* in aid of the Sunshine Homes and Schools for Blind Children, composedly walked into the theatre though a middle-aged man came out of the crowd in the street and made as if to grab and kiss her.

The Rostrum opera company (in association with the Arts Council, the L.C.C., and Hoover Ltd.) then gave the first performance of Malcolm Williamson's setting of a libretto by Sidney Gilliat based on Graham Greene's *Our Man in Havana*, expertly produced by John Blatchley in a double-stage setting by Carl Toms and conducted by James Loughran. The music combined the conventional with jazz and 'pop' idiom, and 'Raymond Nilsson's butterfly-tummied James Bond of a Bramble was one of the most original things he has done', but 'most of the thunder was stolen by Owen Brannigan's humorous and touching Hasselbacher'.

The Ballet Rambert came with a varied programme of ballets, especially notable being *The Travellers*, a new ballet by the 28-year-old Norman Morrice. This up-to-date story of a ballet-company held up at an airport, a loudspeaker voice of authority, brain-washing and sudden death—'a protest against the barriers to freedom'—with 'steel-sheeting' walls and 'Army blanket' costumes designed by Ralph Koltai to accentuate the grimness, was hailed both as a weak ballet and as a new ballet-winner.

On 26th July an *Opera Gala At Midnight* was a tribute to Joan Cross and Anne Wood for their work over the last fifteen years at their National School of Opera before continuing at the London Opera Centre which was to open in September under Professor Humphrey Procter-Gregg:[1] the Gala was organized by a large number of distinguished musicians and leaders of society and performed by former students of the School and others who had studied there.

Financial difficulties, like the performances, went on as before. The Management regretted that, though in the last two years the deficit had been reduced to £50,000, it looked as if, though the Arts Council grant had been increased, the current season might result in a loss of some £30,000, largely owing to salary increases negotiated through the unions.

The controversy over the departure of the opera company (now disapproved of by the St. Pancras Borough Council) was concentrating rather on argument against losing the theatre itself. A new opera house elsewhere might be necessary, but 'All we ask is that it should not be founded on the corpse of Sadler's Wells'; the loss of the Wells was 'too high a price to pay for the establishment of a new Covent Garden on the South Bank'.

[1] In less than a year internal differences led to changes at the London Opera Centre.

The suggestion that the Wells might be used for homeless opera and ballet companies, such as had performed there on many occasions, was unofficially supported by Norman Tucker, though he would be willing to welcome them at the South Bank when the resident companies did not need the new opera house. More were now led to think the Governors had been tempted to forget the terms on which the Wells had been saved and entrusted to their care: the power to sell was not included in the Charity Commission scheme of 1931 and the 'Power to Lend or Let' was allowed in paragraph 32 only for certain purposes which would 'not unduly interfere with the use of the building for the specified purposes'.

The 1963–4 season began with Glen Byam Shaw's production of Weber's *Freischütz* with designs by Motley and conducted by Colin Davis, but the essential magic seemed lacking, which could not be said of the more than solid eagle. Then came the Frankfurt City Opera with *Salome, Entführung aus dem Serail, Zar und Zimmermann,* and *Fidelio.* The Wells then gave a new production by Basil Coleman of *Peter Grimes,* conducted by Meredith Davies and designed by Alan Tagg on the lines of Sir Tyrone Guthrie's Covent Garden production with the cross-section of Grimes's hut in the open rather than shut in as at the effective first performance of 1945. The first Wells production of Verdi's *Attila* by Basil Coleman by being more or less static in a modern Bayreuth saucer—the designs by Ralph Koltai—concentrated on the music conducted by John Matheson and sung well, especially by Harry Mossfield and Donald McIntyre; this was followed by the experimental New Opera Workshop's single performance of the world première of Daniel Jones's first opera *The Knife,* conducted by David Lloyd-Jones, produced by John Cox, designed by Colin Winslow, having been commissioned by the Welsh Committee of the Arts Council; then for Christmas came Glen Byam Shaw's new production of *Hansel and Gretel.*

In February Charles Mackerras as conductor and Marie Collier in the principal part made notable successes with Janacek's *Makropoulos Case,* translated by Norman Tucker, produced by John Blatchley with Motley's designs; Colin Davis then conducted Basil Coleman's new production of *The Seraglio;*

and the last new work of the season was Johann Strauss's *Gipsy Baron* conducted by Vilem Tausky and produced by John Blatchley with sombre designs by Abd'elkader Farrah which seemed to damp even June Bronhill, Nigel Douglas and Derek Hammond Stroud.

In July 1964 the Handel Opera Company's new production was *Richard I*, and in the Ballet Rambert's two weeks Morrice's new *Cul de Sac* was given with music by Christopher Whelan and designs by Ralph Koltai, as well as the first London performance of Walter Gore's *Sweet Dancer*, music by Frank Martin, designs by Harry Cordwell who had danced with the Wells opera ballet.

At the end of the same month the American Merce Cunningham Dance Company delighted in surprising, mystifying and amusing audiences: Carolyn Brown was hailed as a superb classical ballerina who added modern contractions and kicks—her feet as controlled and elegant as most ballerinas' hands, uniquely able to turn a middle toe up while the rest were normally pointed or turn them all up with an arched instep: by contrast Merce Cunningham himself was rather wooden. His invention was best when handling *pas de deux* rather than a number of dancers in a monotonous idiom: but he avoided anything resembling a story and often even a theme, preferring well-rehearsed movements spontaneously improvised to numbers displayed in the wings—often with accidentally chosen haphazard props such as a length of hosepipe found behind the scenes—with the dancers usually in tights and leotards against a blue skycloth with skimpy lighting, all planned by his designer Robert Rauschenberg, an American *avant-garde* painter.

The movements were carefully 'out of synch' with music that was cerebral and 'aleatory' (i.e. random), usually by John Cage, with long pauses for dancing and two-piano sounds made 'to correspond to imperfections in the paper upon which the music was written' or an orchestra whose players were given different music or instruments each night—in other places instrumental parts were changed *during* a piece of music, while at the Wells the clarinet one night was asked to play without the reed and the next was given a bunch of keys, a roll of wire, a comb, pieces of wood, a box of matches, a bottle and a box of pills to be rubbed, banged or scraped on a sheet of thin plywood (reminiscent of Grimaldi's famous act in 1800 of accompanying a mock-Italian air by Dubois with a salt-box).

After this the start of the 1964–5 season reads conventionally, especially as it began with the bane of modern critics, the popular *Faust* in a new translation by Leonard Hancock, which had shared a prize offered by the Arts Council for improving on the old version: Colin Davis conducted and Glen Byam Shaw's production with Motley's designs was most successful with the Study and the Kermesse scenes but lost magic with the difficult Garden scene and the 'Oxford Street store's Christmas display' of the last scene. Donald McIntyre was an authoritative Mephistopheles and there was good but 'English oratorio' singing from Wendy Baldwin as a not too simple Marguerite; Alberto Remedios was a pleasant Faust, who surprisingly stabbed Valentine in the back, while Marguerite's stabbing of the baby with Mephistopheles's dagger stressed the melo-dramatic side of the story.

To aid performances, especially the conducting of off-stage singing, closed television was at last introduced behind the scenes.

In October the City Ballet Society presented the Sadler's Wells Opera Ballet in a Workshop Evening of Ballet (it is intriguing that the Wells did not present their own dancers) but though the inventions by their ballet-master Philippe Perottet (*Sarabande* with modern characters interrrupting a seventeenth-century ballroom, and *Patterns* with black-clad gentlemen dancing round white-clad ladies chained to the stage), and by Susan Salomon (*The Necklace*, based on a Maupassant tale), were valuable for the dancers as 'a useful stretching of wings', the dancing showed that performance in opera-ballets 'is about the worst conditioning' for straight ballets.

In November a deliberately untraditional *Madam Butterfly* 'in keeping with present-day theatrical ideas . . . without too many vigorous tugs on our heart-strings' was credited with a coldness 'which accords uncertainly, to say the least, with Puccini's score', though Ava June, beginning rather too robustly, grew in pathos till she made her death-scene tragic rather than sentimental, and William McAlpine, singing finely in character as Pinkerton, 'made a perfect fit'. The critics' comments on the presentation were puzzling: Colin Graham's production, 'safely conventional without being stale', and Alix Stone's authentic-looking costumes hardly join up with her 'travel brochure setting', especially of Act I—'an avant-garde nest of coffee-tables' or the 'Bamboo Room in a Swedish hotel': this would suggest that the Wells might be following a modern stage tendency of segregating the departments that should co-ordinate into a presentation, were it not that Norman Tucker has always sincerely worked for opera as a whole.

For the two Mondays 30th November and 7th December the New Opera Company with the support of the Arts Council, the L.C.C. and the Vic-Wells Association gave the world-première of the late Arthur Benjamin's *Tartuffe*, the libretto by Cedric Cliffe after Molière—the fifty-fourth opera presented by a non-resident company since 1945 and the 156th different opera given at the Wells since the new theatre was built in 1931 (not counting the nine operettas).

In view of such a record it was depressing to read in August that a Property Company hoped to redevelop the site as part of the New River Company's plans for twenty acres that it owns in the neighbourhood, but as yet no approach has been made nor proposals for buildings when the Opera Companies move to the South Bank—whenever that may happen.

The record certainly justified the Governors' now saying that the sale of the premises would not necessarily mean that the theatre would be demolished: 'if means can be found to preserve the theatre as a centre of culture and entertainment, this should be done'. The *Stage* had written on 18th April 1963,

> Opera-goers rightly maintain that the Wells is one of the most accessible theatres in London, but for some unaccountable reason theatregoers imagine it is a bit off the map. If the theatre can be saved, it would be better, therefore, to continue to devote it to opera.
>
> Students may provide the answer. Why not make Sadler's Wells available to the opera singers of the future, to the young people who are at present studying at the principal music schools of London? Many of these establishments have their own minia-ture theatres, but if they had the use of Sadler's Wells students would have the advantage of being able to sing in a real London theatre under the same conditions they will encounter later on when they start their professional career . . .

Public performances could be given at prices far below normal opera-house charges, and this might lead to a new opera public being created from younger people who cannot possibly afford to patronize either Covent Garden or the Wells at the present time. Who is to buy the Wells and maintain it as a Student Opera House? The Ministry of Education might be approached, as it would be a decided asset to those studying music, and the borough of Finsbury[1] might spend some of that much-discussed sixpenny rate on saving their famous local theatre from the bulldozers.

That is one suggestion. Another is that with London's de-centralization places of entertainment will be needed away from the West End centre—and indeed are already being considered: not only is there the Peggy Ashcroft Theatre at Croydon and the Mermaid by Blackfriars, the Royal Shakespeare Company may now be given a theatre in the Barbican. Old suburban theatres have made way for offices, shops or bingo halls, and new theatres will be needed to train performers for theatre, film and television.

Many schemes for the Wells are in the air—idealistic, prac-tical, cheese-paring, expensive. It was going to be destroyed many times in the past 280 years, but each time another enter-prise was rewarded by the success this theatre can give. So what now? Let some enterprising young men like Rosoman, Wrough-ton or Phelps, experienced theatre-men or far-seeing commit-tees get together and their enthusiasm will find enough backing to start yet other regular entertainments at 'The Wells',

> Founded to England's honour, yet a shrine
> To Music that admits no boundary line . . .
> So much achieved, and still a mounting sum,
> So much achieved, and greater things to come!
> Christopher Hassall, *Twelfth Night*, 1956

[1] Since then joined with Islington.

I

BREAKING BOUNDS

1965–1968

IN THE twelve years since this book was first published there have been drastic changes at the Wells. There were hints of this when Stephen Arlen, the Administrative Director, stated in the Annual Report of May 1965

> If we are to continue we need more support... it is difficult to say at what point it will no longer be possible to play ducks and drakes with cash balances,

adding that the increases of the Arts Council and Greater London Council grants (to £380,000 and £45,000 in 1962–3 and to £400,000 and £45,000 a year later) were more than absorbed 'by block salary awards'.

He warned the Press that the accumulated deficiency by April 1965 was £157,000 and that the higher Saturday night prices might have to apply through the week, the highest rising from 20s. to 25s. and the lowest from 4s. to 5s., though for 1965–6 the G.L.C.'s grant would be £75,000 and the Arts Council's £520,000.

In January a lavish *Ballo in Maschera* had been booed at the end, a 'rare occurrence at Sadler's Wells', because apart from Elizabeth Fretwell the recently high standard of singing 'had slumped badly'[1]. But a month later Catherine Wilson, Gregory Dempsey and John Fryatt had excelled in the world première of the Wells' first new British work since the 1953 *Nelson*, Richard Rodney Bennett's first full-length opera, the strong and uncanny *Mines of Sulphur* commissioned by the Wells.

At the same time a new-style illustrated and informative programme was introduced. The Wells saw its first *L'Enfant et les Sortilèges* in March and in April Charles Mackerras, now doing more conducting at the Wells, restored the long-missing Mozart-style ornamentations to *Figaro*. The Theatre Ballet under Philippe Perottet who had made dancing in the operas

[1] *The Times*

272

DER JUNGE LORD:
COLOGNE OPERA

BLACK THEATRE OF
PRAGUE

KATHAKALI DANCE TROUPE

KABUKI THEATRE

homogeneous was replaced by the Western Ballet under Peter Darrell, while the Gulbenkian Foundation gave £4,500 for the commissioning of young creators of opera.

In May *The Rake's Progress* had Otakar Kraus as Nick Shadow, the part he had created, and was one of the operas taken on a Continental tour by the Wells (Zagreb, Paris, Amsterdam, Geneva, Vienna, Bratislava, Prague and Hamburg). Meanwhile at home the Welsh National Opera presented Michael Langdon as London's first Rossini *Moses* since 1850 and Gwyneth Jones as Lady Macbeth and Beethoven's Leonore.

For the Handel Opera Society Geraint Evans gave 'a vivid portrayal of Saul's decline' in their staged version of Handel's oratorio in June, and in July Marie Collier was 'all compelling' as Renata in the New Opera Company's first British staging of Prokofiev's *Fire Angel*.

Translated by John Arden as a story of ordinary people, the 1965–6 season saw *Fidelio* staged with a Commonwealth cast on the opening of the Commonwealth Arts Festival. Despite Colin Davis's conducting it 'failed to come alight' in Leslie Hurry's one-unit set. Monteverdi's *Orfeo*, realized and conducted by Raymond Leppard for its first London showing, was the only Wells opera apart from *Oedipus Rex*, not sung in English. It was sung in Italian 'and not very good Italian at that'.

But the first London *House of the Dead*, conducted by the Janacek expert Mackerras, and produced by Colin Graham with my own translation (originally for the B.B.C.) was 'altogether a fine achievement'. *The Thieving Magpie*, using tattered old Covent Garden orchestral parts, with Peter Rice's sets and sung by Catherine Wilson, Patricia Kern, John Fryatt, and Denis Dowling with Harold Blackburn in the difficult coloratura bass role, 'did Rossini proud', while a *Faust* revival was 'lacklustre'.

Then on 8th March 1966 during three months' 'leave of absence' for 'health reasons', however they were started, Norman Tucker, Director of the Wells since 1948, had his association with it 'abruptly terminated'[1] before the end of the season.

The official press announcement stated that, 'in order that the Trust should feel completely free to design an appropriate

[1] *Evening Standard.*

organisation . . . best suited to their work' which had become 'increasingly complex and extensive', he had offered his resignation which had been accepted.

Opera Magazine mentioned various rumours 'neither confirmed nor denied of grave differences between Norman Tucker and the Trust', and the *Daily Telegraph* reported that Colin Davis, the Musical Director, had recently resigned as he felt that he had not enough control of music policy. The *Birmingham Post*, reporting that the administrator of the proposed new Midlands Opera Company (which unfortunately never materialized) might be Norman Tucker, correctly stated 'There is no one in the country that knows quite as much as Mr. Tucker does about the running of opera companies'.

Stephen Arlen immediately became managing director of the Wells' resident and touring companies with the former music critic Edmund Tracey responsible for repertory planning, Brian Balkwill and the young Canadian Mario Bernardi as joint music directors, Glen Byam Shaw in charge of the dramatic field, Edward Renton as co-ordinator of production and stage, Leonard Hancock as assistant to the musical directors and John Hargreaves as opera general manager.

In a later *Opera* editorial[1] Harold Rosenthal said that, like many of us, he was convinced that

> the two company plan with the two musical directors and the present dilution of vocal talent has resulted in a lowering of standards since the departure of Norman Tucker.

In May the Hamburg State Opera, returning after four years, included the first London staging of *Frau ohne Schatten*. Then, extending the season, the Wells gave an Offenbach cycle of which *Bluebeard*, Gillian Lynne's first opera production with John Fryatt's King Peppin in Kenneth Rowell's delightful settings, was uproariously received. The *Daily Express*, however, thought it an 'over-squeezed, rather shrilled musical lemon'.

Before the 1966–7 season started visiting companies were the Western Theatre Ballet, the Handel Opera Society, with Janet Baker 'splendid in the name-part' of *Orlando*, produced by Birmingham's Barber Institute, and the Sierra Leone National Dance Troup.

[1] November 1967.

The new season opened with Alexander Gibson conducting *The Queen of Spades* with Anna Pollak's not surprisingly 'gripping' and 'superb' Countess, her last new Wells part. But many asked why the Wells did a large-stage opera while Covent Garden did intimate works.

Sylvia Fisher's Queen Elizabeth was 'the performance of her career' in Colin Graham's October production of *Gloriana*. In November Malcolm Williamson's *Violins of St. Jacques*, commissioned by the Gulbenkian Trust, was 'admirably produced' by the librettist William Chappell with Peter Rice's delightful decor, and was enthusiastically received. Its tunefulness however, made some people think it was more suitable for Drury Lane, 'splitting critical opinion more sharply than any modern work in the last few years'.[1]

Colin Graham joined the Wells staff in December, and while the first London *Dr. Faustus* by Busoni never materialized, *Ernani* appeared in February 1967. Finely sung by Pauline Tinsley and Ronald Dowd, it was surprisingly produced as 'a play within a play' with an applauding stage audience and inscribed banners explaining the scenes. Later in the year, this was called 'a perversion' (*Musical Times*) and 'an enormity' (*Opera*). In March—despite the excellence of Derek Hammond Stroud's High Priest and John Fryatt's Menelaus—the *Evening Standard* headed its notice of the revived *Belle Helene*: 'Saucy French? No, boring English'.

In the growing need for expansion Camperdown House in the Aldgate district, formerly a youth club settlement, was leased in March for conversion into rehearsal rooms, library, warehouses and also a small experimental theatre that never materialized. The South Bank scheme which was now abandoned, even though models had been prepared, in favour of a provincial Opera House[2] that also came to nothing.

Then, at a Press Conference in May 1967, Arlen, boosting the next year's touring pattern with a month in both Manchester and Glasgow and the running-in of new productions on tour before London and grumbling about the Wells' inadequate facilities, 'worked himself up into such a frenzy over the fact

---

[1] *Opera.*
[2] Referred to in the Arts Council Report on Opera & Ballet in the United Kingdom 1966–9.

that the South Bank plan for a new opera-house had been abandoned, that he snapped a wine-glass in two.'[1]

In May the outstanding Netherlands Dance Theatre first came to the Wells and in the summer Flemming Flindt of the Danish Ballet appeared with the Western Theatre Ballet.

In July the English Opera Group included Colin Graham's productions of *The Beggar's Opera* and the first London performances of Lennox Berkeley's *Castaway*.

In 1967 DALTA (Dramatic and Lyric Theatres Association) was formed to co-ordinate through the Arts Council Britain's subsidized companies: The Royal Opera, the Royal Ballet, Sadler's Wells Opera, the Royal Shakespeare Company, and the National Theatre at the Old Vic.

The 1967–8 season, opening for the first time in August instead of September, began with a generally considered 'wrong-headed' newly-translated *Magic Flute* with 'gimmicks a-plenty'; a *Figaro* which was called by Alan Blyth 'the most stylish and best integrated in Europe today'; and Alexander Young singing Orpheus in the Paris version of Gluck's *Orpheus*.

In October Richard Rodney Bennett's *Penny for a Song*, commissioned with the Gulbenkian Trust and based on John Whiting's play which *The Observer* thought it too closely resembled, was praised as a 'blend of light-hearted comedy and elegiac sentiment'. Produced by the librettist Colin Graham it contained notable performances by Joan Davies, John Fryatt and Harold Blackburn who 'will doubtless remember this as the opera in which he spent the entire evening sitting on the branch of a tree'.

Thea Musgrave's first full-length opera *The Disaster*, showing a mining calamity and its aftermath partly in flashbacks, and introduced by the New Opera Company, was recommended by Alan Blyth for adoption by the Wells for its vocal writing although, as with other serial writers, 'the pacing is apt to become monotonous . . . and personal emotions are not always clearly enough defined'.

Andrew Porter's singable, but not always audible, new translation retaining the Italian vowels was the success of Michael Geliot's *Rigoletto* production because only the smaller parts, such as Stafford Dean's Sparafucile, were well sung and Annena Stubbs' natural sets had too shiny a floor.

[1] *Opera.*

But outstanding was *The Mastersingers*, produced by Glen Byam Shaw and John Blatchley, in January 1968 with the combined resident and touring companies and conducted by Reginald Goodall who 'unfolded the score in a magical manner'. It included Norman Bailey's finely sung Sachs, Gregory Dempsey's David and Derek Hammond Stroud's excellent Beckmesser with his every word of Fredrick Jameson's translation (revised by Norman Feasey and Gordon Kember) crystal clear 'unlike some singers'.

Among revivals that followed, *Cosi fan Tutte* had as Despina Margaret Neville, 'the best heard at Sadler's Wells since Rose Hill'. But the formerly effective *Flying Dutchman*, now rehearsed by a staff producer from the stage-manager's notes of my 1958 production (regrettably the last opera I was asked to do for the company) with the 'real Wagnerian but too serene' Norman Bailey, was 'a sorry revival'[1] with 'an elderly circus ghost-train and higgledy-piggledy stage movement'. However on the season's last night Gregory Dempsey was an exciting *Peter Grimes* in the last Sadler's Wells opera to be performed at Sadler's Wells because of the biggest change there since Lilian Baylis reopened it in 1931.

On 24th April 1969, because of the pressure of accommodation and criticism of the acoustics at the Wells, whose 'activities had outgrown the building'[2] Stephen Arlen, after many rumours, had announced at a Press Conference that at the end of the season Sadler's Wells Opera would move to the London Coliseum on a ten-year lease.

The alterations to the Coliseum[3] would cost about £130,000 of which £110,000 had already been given or promised, while the Arts Council grant to the companies in their new home would be increased by £75,000 to £787,000, the G.L.C. grant staying at £100,000.

Some 2,000 of the Coliseum's 2,400 seats would remain at the present prices of the Wells' 1,450 seats, while some at higher prices would still be less than their Covent Garden equivalents.

The ten performances a fortnight at the Wells would at the

---

[1] *The Times.*

[2] *Arts Council Report on Opera & Ballet 1966–9.*

[3] Most extensive before and behind the curtain, to be done in nine weeks, leaving the company 2½ weeks' rehearsal before opening. *Opera* September 1968.

Coliseum be increased to eleven and, though to start with there would only be twelve touring weeks as opposed to the usual twenty, the target for later seasons would be thirty.

After the last Wells' Opera performance Charles Farncombe, the conductor of the Handel Opera Society's July revival there of *Saul* was still inclined to 'substitute speed for inner animation'[1]. In *Deidamia*, however, although the singing in Italian 'for artistic reasons' (the programme said) made the long recitatives with their 'faint touches of ironic humour' unintelligible to most, Harold Rosenthal said David Thompson's production with Hans van Langeveld's decor made it visually the best Handel opera production he had seen in England.

Then, after the Wells companies started at the Coliseum in August, Rosenthal's October *Opera* editorial was headed 'Outlook stormy and unsettled'.

He admitted he had been fascinated like everyone else by Arlen's *volte-face* with his 'sudden enthusiasm for the London Coliseum' after the loss of the South Bank Opera House: but a misgiving, voiced to me at the time by Dame Eva Turner, was shared by him for young singers in a theatre 'with an auditorium larger than that of Covent Garden and with a proscenium wider than that of La Scala, Milan . . . where *are* young singers now to serve their apprenticeships?' As for the danger of young voices singing too big roles too soon, that 'is just what Sadler's Wells seems to be asking them to do'. An authoritative excuse at the time was 'What does that matter? There are plenty more where they come from.'

The editorial ended:

> One has the uneasy feeling that the move . . . has been hastily planned and ill prepared. . . . It is, to put it bluntly, very, very depressing—and one really wonders whether the Arts Council knows what it is about.

Through the move to the Coliseum, Sadler's Wells itself immediately lost not only all its financial grants and prospects but also certain stage equipment, press notices, letters and archives hurriedly but carefully packed by the Wells' archivists, Mander and Mitchenson, as instructed, and from rehearsal and dressing rooms chairs, tables, and even bits of carpet.

---

[1] Alan Blyth: *Opera.*

II

THE DARK DAYS

1968–1974

FOR SADLER'S WELLS itself the Governors of the Foundation had decided the policy should be

(1) a suitable shop-window for important foreign companies.
(2) a platform for worthy home-based companies in need of a properly equipped and sited metropolitan show case.

(These two clauses, though primarily for opera and ballet, were not to exclude drama.)

(3) a vital stepping-stone in the post-graduate training of opera singers.
(4) an important London link in a DALTA-type circuit of high quality touring presentations.

Accordingly the deserted Wells reopened in March 1969 for visiting companies all through the year.

But this 'theatre for the public', a description strongly endorsed by the Arts Council,

> was not given too good a start in playing its new role because the publicity given to the move to the Coliseum contrived to suggest that not only was Sadler's Wells Theatre no longer good for the Opera Company . . . but that it was no good for anything.

—an impression strongly conveyed to the Greater London Council's representatives who inspected the premises[1].

However the Sadler's Wells Trust[2], naturally also in charge, with Arlen, of the opera companies now at the Coliseum, did invite companies to the Wells at a presumed economic rate.

The first visiting company, which has also returned almost every year up to the present 1977, was the London Opera Centre. In December 1968 its students presented *Albert*

[1] Recorded in the *Report to the Governors of the Sadler's Wells Foundation* from the Administrator Douglas Craig in June 1973.
[2] Created to present provincial tours as the Foundation was limited by the Charity Commissioners to London performances only: see page 195.

279

Herring, Ibert's *Angélique* and, with the future international soprano Kiri te Kanawa, *Dido & Aeneas* all in a dangerously freezing theatre for which they had to hire lighting equipment and borrow back from the Wells Company at the Coliseum the closed circuit television for back-stage conducting.

The General Manager of D'Oyly Carte's Gilbert and Sullivan company, Frederic Lloyd, has told me that when, greatly shocked at the lack of stage equipment and even dressing-room tables and chairs on this the first of their now annual visits to the theatre they were hiring, he told Stephen Arlen, the reply was 'Look, we're very busy! As far as I am concerned, I couldn't care less!'

From now on, as there were now more visiting companies each year—a full list is given in the Appendix—than there had been noteworthy operas when the season was from autumn to early summer, these records will be classified according to the Wells' financial year which ends on the last Saturday in March.

First in the 1969–70 period the London Opera Centre included the seldom-seen *Opera Rehearsal* by Lortzing; in July the Handel Opera Society had 'one of their most successful seasons', with *Xerxes* and *Susanna*; in August the top notes of one soprano in the London Opera Group's *Turn of the Screw* apparently made the auditorium's emergency gas-jets flare up; in September the English Opera Group gave Colin Graham's new production of *Rape of Lucretia* (a triumph for Janet Baker) and the first London performances of Crosse's *Purgatory* and *The Grace of Todd* and of Birtwhistle's *Punch & Judy* (enjoyable in spite of the libretto').

The Cologne Opera in December brought Jean-Pierre Ponelle's unfussy production of *Clemenza di Tito* with the women, including Lucia Popp and Yvonne Minton, better than the men and the British première of Henze's savage comedy *Der Junge Lord*.

Then, in March 1970, the New Opera Company gave the British première of Hindemith's original version of *Cardillac* with John Cameron in the title-role and Elizabeth Robson outstanding as the Lady, and the London Opera Centre gave the first London *Coronation of Poppea* by Monteverdi as realized by Raymond Leppard.

That first period's dance companies showed perhaps more

clearly than ever before the great differences between classical, folkloristic, experimental and national dancing.

The April visit of the Netherlands Dance Theatre, which later often returned, was followed by Les Grands Ballets Canadiens under their artistic adviser Anton Dolin, opening with a Royal Gala Performance before Princess Margaret and Lord Snowdon: that company included Orff's *Carmina Burana*. And in June, attracted by ballet differing from that 'emanating from the 19th century' and working 'in close alliance with other arts' (as was first greeted enthusiastically in 1964 when Merce Cunningham visited the Wells), a young public thronged to the Alwin Nikolais Dance Theatre.

In the winter the Scottish Theatre Ballet, impressive with their liveliness and also their 'immaculacy'[1], included London premières of Peter Darrell's *Beauty & the Beast* with Thea Musgrave's specially commissioned score and *The Frontier* by the American choreographer John Neumeier. Finally the Dutch National Ballet's first London season presented Nureyev as a guest artist in *Apollon Musagète* and Rudi van Dantzig's *Monument for a Dead Boy*.

For the first of their yearly visits till 1973 the Black Theatre of Prague had come in May 1969 with its magical movements of both objects and humans in ultra-violet light with 'all the charm and humour we associate with the best of cinema cartoons'[2].

In November the B.B.C. started a concert series called *Sunday Night at Sadler's Wells* and in March 1970 Cleo Laine, John Dankworth and John Williams took part in a concert in aid of the Africa Bureau.

However in December 1969 the Arts Council, though now neither financially nor officially concerned with the Wells, had declared that the Theatre's new programming was

> not intended to be a permanent policy, and it is hoped that the Theatre will, in time, become the home of a permanent company —be it drama, opera or ballet—or it may be that its most effective use will be as London's third opera house.

That last possibility, though badly needed for the more intimate operas as is generally recognized, has not materialized.

Financially things at the Wells were far from good. The

[1] *The Sunday Times.*   [2] *The Financial Times.*

rentals charged were pitched too low and at a specially reduced rate for companies that were 'old friends'. So the first year's deficit was £31,168, which was met by Sadler's Wells Trust Coliseum Ltd. and caused a complaint from the Arts Council 'having, they said, been given assurance' (by whom, one would like to know)

> that the theatre would run without need for further subsidy, but neither they nor the G.L.C. were disposed to offer financial help, for various reasons—they had already committed large sums to 'Sadler's Wells', there was no more money for London, etc.[1]

On the separation between the Wells and the Coliseum the Governors of the Foundation were rumoured to be having differences with the Trust,

> legal advice was sought in negotiations which at times became acrimonious and which are in fact still [1973] not wholly concluded and could at any moment be re-opened by anyone who had a mind to do so[2]:

and on 20th March 1970 David McKenna, Chairman of the Governors, stated that the running of both theatres by one authority was 'becoming increasingly unrealistic' and 'a separate management for each will be more efficient'.

So, while the Trust would run the Coliseum, the Foundation would control the Wells although, as the latter received no subsidy 'from any quarter whatsoever', between £25,000 and £45,000 per annum had to be found in order for the Wells to survive.[3]

Opera at the Coliseum, wrote *Opera*, would probably run 'ultimately under another name'[4] to avoid such confusions as when the Wells Ballet was at Covent Garden and the Wells Opera at the Wells.

Meanwhile the position of 'Administrator, Sadler's Wells Theatre' was advertised at a salary of 'not less than £3,000 per annum'. After being in charge of the Welsh National Opera, Douglas Craig was appointed in July about twenty-five years after he had sung in my first *Tosca* production there.

From 1970 till now there have been more dance companies than opera presentations, which in the 1970–1 period were

---

[1] Quoted in *Report to the Governors of Sadler's Wells Foundation by the Administrator*, Douglas Craig: June 1973.
[2] *Ibidem*.   [3] *Opera*: May 1970.
[4] Later it was rightly renamed the English National Opera.

only given by the constant visitors—the London Opera Centre, the Handel Opera Society with an impressive *Scipio* and a disappointing *Samson*, and the regular D'Oyly Carte winter season.

Of the 1970–1 dance companies the 'unusual and spectacular' Polish Mime Ballet in April had to be extended a week, the 'eminent and splendid' Vyjayanthimala gave two performances of her Indian classical dances, and there was a week of the exciting Kathakali Dance Theatre from India with 'richly ornate costumes . . . highly traditional but often funny and sometimes wildly gruesome':[1] that last company however, when asked to make a return visit, not surprisingly was persuaded to join Peter Daubeny's celebrated World Theatre season, as was also the Greek National Theatre after gladly agreeing in principle to perform at the Wells.

In July, after the Paul Taylor Dance Company's 'original' performances, the Scottish Theatre Ballet included the world première of Peter Darrell's 'intriguing' *Herodias*, and in the autumn the pastoral dancers and singers of the Yugoslavian Opanak were welcomed by a reception committee that for publicity purposes included sheep 'kindly lent' from Hadley Wood!

But in November, before the Alvin Ailey American Dance Theatre had such a success that on their last night they were giving encores for over an hour after the final curtain, the Netherlands Dance Theatre returned with their 50 minute *Mutations* by Glen Tetley and Hans von Manen.

This had been banned at the Edinburgh Festival by the City Fathers because in its last few minutes a British audience would see for the first time some dancers in the nude. Douglas Craig has told me that before the company came to the Wells 'I probably received more letters and postcards consigning me to hell-fire and brimstone than David Webster did when the Garden did *Moses and Aaron*' (in which an orgy had few holds barred). He did not allow photographs showing nudes to be displayed outside the theatre, but

> we had more House Full notices (and sold more front stalls) than the theatre had seen for years. Nor do I remember a single moralizing criticism, for the simple reason that the beauty and seriousness of the performance was all-compelling.

[1] *The Times.*

There were protests on the first night when the opening scenes, on a ramp extending into the stalls, couldn't be seen by other parts of the house, and on the last night some itching substance sprinkled on the ramp made the scratching dancers in their tights leave the stage to be treated by Dr. Norman Newman, a local doctor friend of their British manager, William Beresford, and myself, before they could carry on.

At a Press Conference in February 1971 it had been stressed that, in spite of the now apparently encouraging situation at the Wells with an increased number of playing weeks, some £50,000 a year from some source were essential if the planned objectives were to be achieved, and the only operas in the first half of the 1971–2 period were given by the London Opera Centre which in July included *William Tell* in a collaboration with Northern Opera, using three North of England choruses in Tom Hawkes' production.

Of the dancing of this period the Burmese National Dancers on their first Western Europe appearance in April made 'an immediate appeal'[1] with their colourful costumes and fascinating musical instruments, followed by the 'gentle charm' of the Dora Stratou Company's first British visit with Greek folk-dancing and singing.

Then on their first return to the Wells since leaving in 1957 the Royal Ballet with their Touring Group included the first two ballets choreographed by Joe Layton, the successful Broadway director,—*Overture*, a curtain-raiser using the music of Bernstein's *Candide*, and the witty *Grand Tour* to well-known Noël Coward tunes whose contemporaries, such as Mary Pickford and Bernard Shaw, were shown on a ship's cruise,— that 'had great impact'.[2]

In the autumn the famous and exciting Chitrasena Dance Company of Ceylon first appeared in London and the charming Little Angels of Korea, twenty-nine little girls and three little boys, were 'fresh and exhilarating'.

A double chance in May 1971 had led to the presentation of the first modern English play at the Wells since the 1959 production of *Cavalcade*. The New Theatre, Bromley, burned down when Graham Greene's *The Potting Shed* was about to

---

[1] *Financial Times.*
[2] John Percival: *Theatre 72.*

be produced and the visit of the Kalakshetra Dance Company to the Wells was cancelled. The play was therefore staged at the Wells with the popular young singing star Cliff Richard wearing his own beard for his first straight character part.

Then in September 1971, because without financial support from the public the Wells now would have to close, a Sadler's Wells Theatre Appeal Fund was proposed.

A draft leaflet stressed what was obvious to theatre professionals, that while the Coliseum and Covent Garden were too large for intimate operas the Wells was ideal for housing companies of all kinds and encouraging the development of embryo opera stars. But, although British companies abroad received financial support from the countries they visited, distinguished European companies had had to be turned away, as the Wells could not pay their keep in London because since 1969 it had received 'not a penny from the Government. It has lived on its capital and is now struggling to survive'.

Apart from individual donations a Friends of Sadler's Wells Society was proposed with Company membership subscriptions of at least £100 per annum (or £85 if covenated) or a single donation of £1,000, while individual membership should be £6 per annum (or £5 if covenanted) or a single donation of £50.

In the autumn the English Opera Group introduced Colin Graham's brilliant production of his version of *King Arthur*. Cleverly reduced for a small cast the work was misleadingly distorted, partly through Philip Ledger's 'realization' which cut Purcell's score and gave other Purcell arias to characters originally played by actors. And partly by raising guffaws at the 'Restoration näivety' of modernly added lines as when Merlin told Ariel to drown the wicked magician's book 'Where none but fish will have the wit to look', though no book was ever drowned or even mentioned by Dryden in his *King Arthur* opera-text.

The first revival since Handel's days of *Ottone* by the Handel Opera Society with Andrew Porter's new translation and Patricia Kern's splendid Matilda was noteworthy, as was the vitality of Paco Peña's Flamenco Puro dancing, and the London Theatre Company's *Under Milk Wood* with Marian Grimaldi, descendant of the great Joey of the Wells, in the cast.

There was a concert for India's Prime Minister's Relief

Fund for East Bengal refugees, but the Oxford Playhouse's presentation of Aristophanes's *A Diet of Woman* was cancelled after the Musicians' Union's objection to the use of taped music.

A statement to the Press by McKenna and Craig in November 1971, pointing out that the Governors' policy (like that of the Théatre des Nations in Paris) of an all-the-year-round theatrical festival of all kinds had resulted in twenty-one companies from thirteen different nations performing at the Wells that year with all but four weeks of the following year pencilled in and, apart from return visits by British companies, twelve sporadic weeks already booked for 1974, stressed that the Wells would not abandon its standards: at the same time

> The sort of financial help we are looking for in order to develop our policy is modest compared with the money spent elsewhere and is estimated at 15 new pence per seat sold or £30,000.
> But the fact remains, that unless this is found, Sadler's Wells Theatre will shut within a year.

So with the Wells losing £20,000 per annum, the Appeal was launched with a target set at £300,000 over five years and the Society of Friends formed with several distinguished patrons.

Meanwhile the theatre had been improved for entertainments with musicians in close contact with performers by covering the orchestra pit with a removable apron-stage, making the whole stage 62 feet deep.

The Royal Philharmonic Orchestra gave a Gala Concert on 21st November for the Musicians' Union's fiftieth anniversary; in the first of two Master Classes for the London Opera Centre's students Sir Geraint Evans and John Copley performed the Marcellina-Susanna duet from *Figaro* hilariously though in the second Sir Geraint gave the young singers valuable advice; and the usual D'Oyly Carte winter season included a new *Sorcerer* production designed by Osbert Lancaster.

In March 1972 Elisabeth Lutyens' 'charade in four scenes with three interruptions' *Time off? Not a Ghost of a Chance* admirably produced by Anthony Besch for the New Opera Company had contradictory notices—'a brilliant presentation of a dazzling piece'[1] and 'made a rather painfully pretentious impression'.[2]

[1] *The Financial Times.*   [2] *The Daily Telegraph.*

The Royal Academy of Music's students celebrated its 150th anniversary with Donizetti's *Belisario* well sung and played, and in the Leppard realization of Cavalli's *L'Ormindo*, imaginatively ´produced by Colin Graham for the London Opera Centre, students Elisabeth Connell and Stuart Harling were outstanding.

In February 1972 the Royal Ballet's New Group (so-called because of its smaller size and its concentration on new ballets) had included the world première of Joe Layton's *O.W.* to some of Walton's music, with Michael Somes 'magnificent' as Oscar Wilde. It was during their fortnight that Douglas Craig had, as he told me, one of the most heart-warming experiences he had ever had. In his own words:

> When we launched the Appeal, one of the things we did was to give little 90-second speeches in front of the curtain just before the start of the show. I did most of them, but Colin Benham did quite a few and so did David McKenna.
>
> The boys and girls of the Ballet heard these and were so upset that we were in such appalling financial circumstances that they themselves suggested they should give a midnight charity performance.
>
> It was conceived at eleven o'clock on a Friday evening and the curtain went up on it at exactly the same time the following Wednesday. Everybody concerned, including Princess Margaret, Fonteyn, Nureyev and Lord Goodman had been mobilized in the meantime. All the performers donated their services. I was temporarily nicknamed 'Mr. Instant Gala'.

The result of this sudden Midnight Gala was £7,849 for the Appeal fund.

The first year of the Appeal was answered by 700 people (excluding those who put money into collecting boxes) of whom over 500 were registered as Friends of Sadler's Wells, 58 companies or charitable trusts, 25 local authorities including 16 London Boroughs and the G.L.C. which gave £5,000 a year for three years, and the Arts Council which 'made a once and for all' donation of £10,000.

From the resultant £55,082 the Wells received £15,000 for 1971–2, which meant that, as the box office receipts had also increased from £188,874 in the 1969–70 period to £228,000 through more playing weeks in the year, this year's deficiency had amazingly decreased from £31,162 to £1,700.

1972–3 began with the first drama season at the Wells since

that of the Moscow Arts Theatre in 1958 (unless the two National Youth Theatre's Shakespeare plays in 1962 can be called a season) given by the London Theatre Company on its second visit. It comprised Oscar Wilde's *Lord Arthur Saville's Crime* with the popular stars Elsie Randolph and Jack Hulbert, Rose Hill (fondly remembered from her Wells Opera days) and Bill Kerr, Arthur Miller's *All My Sons* with Malcolm Hayes, a revival of their *Under Milk Wood* and Sheridan's *The Rivals* with Maxine Audley.

That year's outstanding operas were Delius's *Koanga* produced by Douglas Craig for the Delius Trust and the Camden Festival, with Charles Groves conducting the London Symphony Orchestra and the coloured principals Eugene Holmes and Claudia Lindsey, who were in the recent U.S.A. production in Washington; the English Opera Group's London première of John Gardner's *The Visitors*; and the Handel Opera Society's new production of *Jephtha*, and a revival of *Scipio*, with Philip Langridge taking over the name-part after David Hughes' sudden death during rehearsal time.

Dancing that year included the Royal Ballet New Group's revival of the original *Façade* with Peter Pears narrating; the 'skill and zest' of the Chhau Dancers of Bengal; the 'racy and sharp' Jamaican National Dance Theatre; and the return of both Merce Cunningham and the Little Angels of Korea.

Just before the 'gracefully attractive'[1] Ballet-Theatre Joseph Rusillo's visit, (the last ballet-company of 1972–3) the North Korean Mansudai Dance Company came for ten days with acrobatics, jugglings and 'inexorably smiling young ladies' with pink paper azaleas showing folk art of 'the most simpering and inscrutable quaintness'[2] but at the same time breaking the Wells' coach party records, since one huge party came all the way from Glasgow. On the other hand, as Douglas Craig says,

> There are members of the Wells staff past and present in whom the mere mention of this company is likely to induce something approaching a nervous breakdown.

Incredibly protracted discussions in halting English and equally halting French resulted in decisions to their advantage rather than to that of the Wells' and in spite of constant vigilance

[1] *Dancing Times.*
[2] Clement Crisp: *Theatre 74.*

they were exceptionally 'adept at breaking all the G.L.C.'s rules': however Craig adds:

> On the other hand, their technical accomplishment was staggering Their orchestra was amazingly competent and their technical equipment outclassed anything I had experienced up to then, especially their remarkable back projections. It was only a pity that this was all employed in the service of such tinsel.

On their first appearance in England in June 1972 the famous classical Japanese theatre, the Kabuki, with their impressive 'slow, stylized movements' had drawn a larger audience than had any company from 1971 to 1973.[1] There was a Royal Philharmonic Orchestra concert on Sunday the 25th and, on the same day, a sponsored walk in aid of the Appeal, which also benefited from the opening Gala performance of Julian Slade's 'gently charming' musical *Trelawney*, based on Pinero's *Trelawney of the Wells*, presented by Bristol Old Vic with Max Adrian in his last part before his death.

A Gala Opera Concert in support of the Appeal which was presented as a part of the July Islington Festival was followed by Marcel Marceau's brilliant miming and the Black Theatre of Prague again while, in November, Judi Dench and Michael Williams contributed to *The Man Trap* (a Sunday poetry reading) before the D'Oyly Carte season.

The New Opera Company in April 1973 gave the first British stage performance of Shostakovich's *The Nose* produced by Anthony Besch with Alan Opie as the 'vigorous hero' and with a revival of Elisabeth Lutyens' *Time Off?* and the première of her 'absorbing and moving' two-character opera *Infidelio* composed twenty years before.

As an earnest of their faith in the Wells the Governors had recently approved a capital expenditure of £103,000 over five years for improvement and modernization: in 1972–3 new boilers had been installed and steelwork repaired, and this August both stage and roof were repaired, the stalls re-seated, and the theatre rewired for a new sound-relay system for off-stage conducting and the installation of the Rank-Strand's computerized lighting consoles.

Especially impressive was the visit to the Wells in the autumn of the Scottish Opera with *Pelléas & Melisande* which I

[1] *Report to the Governors 1973*

had staged for their 1962 opening season in Scotland, now beautifully produced by Colin Graham with John Fraser's lovely settings 'perfectly lit' by Charles Bristow and John Shirley-Quirk outstanding as Golaud. As Rosenthal wrote in *Opera*:

> it was wonderful to hear this opera in a theatre the size of the Opéra Comique, where it was originally produced, and made one regret yet again the lack of a suitable medium-sized *modern* auditorium for works of this kind in London.

They also gave *Tristan* with fine playing from the Scottish National orchestra under Alexander Gibson with Helga Dernesch the ideal Isolde in voice and figure.

New productions of Tchaikowsky's *Iolanta* and Gilbert and Sullivans's *Trial by Jury* were brought by the English Opera Group, and of *Atalanta* by the Handel Opera Society, 'not one of their best efforts',[1] but with an 'enjoyable' revival of *Ottone*.

Then in December 1973 the adventurous Royal Northern College of Music gave five varied opera nights (*A Midsummer Night's Dream, The Rake's Progress* and *Purgatory* with *The Bear*) which were rightly applauded for several fine student performances, though some of their overlarge Manchester scenery had to be cut down for the Wells.

The first of the 1973–4 dance-companies was the Royal Ballet with eight out of sixteen one-act ballets new to London, including David Drew's *Sacred Circles* with 'excellent dancing'. Then came the return of the Netherlands Dance Theatre and Alvin Ailey's Dance Theatre with a 'tremendous' guest performance by Lynn Seymour in *Flowers*.

The New York Paul Taylor Dance Company only had full houses when Nureyev appeared as a guest, but in September the Ballet Rambert, returning after eight years in their new 1966 form, had a fortnight's artistic and box-office success including the world premières of Louis Falco's *tutti-frutti*, Norman Morrice's *Isolde* and Christopher Bruce's *Duets*.

The Royal Ballet New Group in October gave a tribute to John Cranko who had died recently, and then to large audiences the London Contemporary Dance Theatre brought Robert Cohan's spectacular evening-long *Stages*, a multi-media show with jazz, electronic music and flying effects, with the dancers

---

[1] *The Guardian.*

trained in gymnastics by Pauline Prestidge of the National Olympic team.

The 'exceptionally gifted dancers' of the Louis Falco Dance Company from New York with 'mixed offerings' were followed by the Ballet Contemporain from Amiens's second visit with world premières of *Cycle* and *Whisky-Coca* to Stockhausen's music, the London première of *Hymnen*, and four ballets to Stravinsky's music including *Rossignol* with Anne-Marie Rodde singing as the Nightingale in a feast of bright colours.

Hans von Manen's light-hearted *Septet Extra* to Saint-Saëns' music was introduced by the Royal Ballet in February 1974 and, after Galina Samsova's 'outstanding dancing' with the New London Ballet's first visit in March, von Manen's *Adagio Hammerklavier* was 'the best new ballet this season'[1] in the triumphant return of the Dutch National Ballet. On their first night however tape-recordings of their music had to be used as some of their larger orchestral instruments were held up in transit.

Pete Sinfield had given a pop concert in June 1973. The Black Theatre of Prague returned in September and the Salzburg Marionettes came back in February 1974 to be the first foreign group to give a benefit performance for the Appeal.

There were great developments in 1973–4.

An after-theatre bus service was instituted to take patrons without their own transport to specified West End destinations for only 10p during popular seasons such as the Royal Ballet or D'Oyly Carte. The Sadler's Wells Entertainment Excursion Plan (S.W.E.E.P.) ran in conjunction with British Rail Eastern region. There was a student concession scheme for standby tickets half an hour before performances at 30p for a stalls' ticket, subject to availability, and on 19th February 1974 the Wells started special coaches with theatre ticket services for patrons such as Women's Institutes and Sports Clubs from outlying districts, St. Albans being the first town so served.

But of the greatest importance in 1973 was Douglas Craig's brave and justified twelve-page report to the Governors in June about the 'scandal of the year . . . that the Wells was in the grip of a financial crisis'.[2]

---

[1] *Daily Telegraph.*
[2] Clement Crisp: *Theatre 74.*

After sketching the Wells history since 1968 and blaming the loss of impetus for the Appeal on an over-optimistic Press report in January 1973, he declared his belief in the continuation of the existing policy with adaptations, and London's need for the Wells with its rehearsal rooms, orchestral pit and stage available for opera, ballet—and even the right sort of drama— especially since with the entry of Britain into the European Economic Community it had become London's link with the European Theatre Circuit.

So he proposed the Governors should follow Sir Thomas Armstrong's plea, supported in many professional circles, for a new resident company to perform operas needing a smaller stage than at the Coliseum or Covent Garden, both for established repertoire works and new works which would be financially risky for the larger opera houses. This would enable young singers 'to mature *as an ensemble*' safely, the opportunities for this being 'actually less now than they were a few years ago'.

As such money as was available was now more committed to the regions than to new London ventures, he stressed that such a Young Wells Opera, if formed, would chiefly tour the regions with only some eight weeks a year at the Wells: but for such a scheme unfortunately 'so far the Arts Council[1] (without whose help the proposition is null and void) have been able to offer no encouragement at all'.

Concerning the Wells itself he reported that 'unless a radical improvement is made in our subsidy from public funds we shall not survive beyond the next three years' chiefly because, though the Wells was now 'the Mecca for many of the best companies in the world, it would seem that we are the only theatre in the world which is unable to offer a guarantee'. Many of those companies found 'it is simplicity itself' to get guarantees from provincial cities but, after haggling 'down to the last penny', could not be afforded by the Wells for London.

He quoted a long letter from the Director of the most friendly Netherlands Dance Theatre, so popular at the Wells, pointing out that it was 'the only theatre in the world where we have performed since 1968 that is unable to offer us a guarantee' and therefore regretfully, because of

[1] Which had originally mooted such a scheme: *see page 279.*

enormous increases in hotel, orchestral and living costs, the
introduction of V.A.T., the devaluation of the £ (which is not
offset by the minimum increase in theatre prices) we cannot
begin to contemplate another season at Sadler's Wells unless you
are able to vastly improve your financial conditions.

He also suggested the Arts Council should make it possible
for the Scottish Opera, the Welsh National Opera, the Glyndebourne Touring Opera and other regionally based companies
to be seen at this London theatre. But as for companies from
abroad—seeing that even the Royal Swedish Opera, which the
Wells had been unable to afford in 1971, went with international
stars to a Brighton Festival—it followed that unless the subsidy
of £1,000 a week as suggested in 1971 could be obtained, the
Wells—and therefore London—would have to secede from the
European Theatre Circuit, and then

if Londoners want to see the kind of international fare we are
now offering them, they will have to be prepared to go to
Brighton or Norwich or Sunderland.
  Our counterpart in Paris—the Thèatre de la Ville—has an
annual subsidy of £225,000.

Still, as he said, the Arts Council had in fact, after a second
approach, given in 1973 a grant-in-aid of £7,500.

III

A NEW BEGINNING?

1974–1977

AFTER DOUGLAS CRAIG'S Report to the Governors Sir Hugh Willatt, Secretary-General to the Arts Council, wrote on 22nd November 1973 to his Chairman, Patrick Gibson (now Lord Gibson), that though the Wells Opera had gone,

> there remains a theatre building which, putting it at its lowest, serves a very useful purpose. Its facilities make it unique in London for short term visits by opera, ballet and large scale companies: an orchestra pit to house a full opera house orchestra, extensive back-stage accommodation and quite large seating capacity. Secondly, it is the only large theatre, apart from the Royal Opera House and the Coliseum, even if they were available more than occasionally, to have comparable facilities.

He added that, although the visiting companies' performances had not all been of top quality, nevertheless 'the artistic life of London and the country had benefited from quite a number of these foreign visits.'

The increase in box-office receipts from 1969–70 to 1972–3 with a growing number of playing weeks (from about 35 to 51 in the year) meant that, with the £15,000 grant from the Appeal Fund, instead of a deficiency in the latter year there had been a paper profit of £247; despite the not too happy progress of the Appeal Fund, this augured well for the future. But the 1973–4 year, in spite of a further increase of box-office receipts by £12,625, had a working deficiency of as much as £16,950 (not counting £10,000 spent on re-seating, etc.) largely due to the introduction of Value Added Tax.

On 1st April 1974 Douglas Craig, the Administrator, became the Director of Sadler's Wells and the highspot of the next twelve months was the celebration in May of the Centenary of the birth of Lilian Baylis, without whom the English National Opera at the Coliseum, the Royal Ballet at Covent Garden and the National Theatre on the South Bank would never have been established.[1]

As an introduction to the celebration the B.B.C. broadcast a hilarious version of the *My Music* programme, recorded at the Wells before an invited audience on 27th April, in which, with Steve Race as Chairman, Frank Muir and John Amis competed with Denis Nordern and Ian Wallace in a light-hearted quiz on this book's story of the Wells.

The Centenary Celebration, organized by the Governors of both the Old Vic and the Wells, opened after a meeting of the Association of Ballet Clubs on Sunday 12th May with performances on Tuesday and Wednesday by the Royal Ballet's New Group and Ballet for All based on the early years of the Vic-Wells but also including *Harlequinade* by de Valois and Ashton which was new to London.

On the Friday Hugh Jenkins, Minister for the Arts, planted a tree in memory of 'the Lady' and the London Opera Centre gave a largely double-cast *Figaro*. This was produced by Joan Cross, who had joined the Old Vic in 1923; conducted by Lawrance Collingwood, who had last been in the Wells orchestra pit in 1946 and over fifty years before had played the piano for the Old Vic's operas for 5/– a week; and designed by William Chappell with guest artist Douglas Craig as Antonio the gardener.

Before Princess Margaret on 19th May, in an Opera Gala Concert, Charles Mackerras conducted the Royal Ballet Orchestra and distinguished singers from the Coliseum and Covent Garden in a 'rag bag programme of bits and pieces'[2] largely by Verdi.

The receipts from the Celebration, which amounted to £1,604, went to the Wells.

On Monday 20th May the English Opera Group gave a concert performance of *The Rape of Lucretia* conducted by Steuart Bedford, on Wednesday there was an Evening of

---

[1] Although at present she is still not included among those commemorated at the National Theatre, Sadler's Wells now plans to rename their 'Wells Room' buffet the 'Baylis Room'.   [2] *Opera.*

Operetta conducted by Terence Kern, London Opera Centre Director James Robertson, Royston Nash of the D'Oyly Carte Company and Bryn Jones of the Gwalia Male Voice Choir. Finally on Thursday with supper, wine, dancing and 'an Entertainment' there was a Party on the Stage ('Period Dress Optional: 1974–1937').

The first opera of 1974–5 was Opera Rara's witty adaptation of Offenbach's *Robinson Crusoe* with William Chappell's brilliant production for the 1973 Camden Festival now performed by London Opera Centre students. Then also in April, Alexander Goehr's first opera *Arden Must Die* had a lukewarm response, perhaps partly because Jonathan Miller's 'debilitating production'[1] updated the Elizabethan period to the Victorian.

In the summer, Keynote Opera Society, founded by the Workers' Music Association with donations from over two hundred distinguished musicians and companies, gave the first British stage performance of Alan Bush's dedicated *Wat Tyler*, which had been so successful in Leipzig in 1953. This was unhappily a 'shoestring production' with student and professional singers of whom one 'in the important role of the King . . . made me feel Richard (II) deserved to die in Pontefract'.[2]

There was a 'sparling production' of *La Vie Parisienne*, with Joyce Blackham, in July by the Phoenix Opera with whom it had been suggested the Wells might make a liaison when the Arts Council made it quite clear that they gave support to companies and not to bricks and mortar. But such a liaison (which might have vitalized both institutions), suffered the same fate as the Arts Council's 1969 hope that the Wells might be the home of a permanent company. It never materialized.

The English Opera Group in October included the London première of *The Voice of Ariadne* by Thea Musgrave, which 'musically gave great pleasure' with the singing of Jill Gomez and Thomas Allen, but was 'handicapped by a libretto which did not hold up for three acts',[3] and a pretentious production of Puccini's operetta *La Rondine* with the former Wells'

[1] *Opera.*
[2] Frank Granville Barker: *Music & Musicians.*
[3] *Opera.*

star June Bronhill handicapped by a music-hall landlady costume.

Two box-office records were broken in the winter—those of the Handel Opera Society with Richard Lewis in a revival of *Jephtha* and, with ninety-five per cent audiences, those of the D'Oyly Carte in their Centenary season.

In 1974–5 the Royal Ballet New Group in the spring had included the London première of Ronald Hynd's *Charlotte Brontë*, while in June the ritual ceremonies of the Mevlevi Whirling Dervishes had a 'hypnotic fascination'.

The only black classical ballet company in the world, The Dance Theatre of Harlem, on their first London visit was 'irresistible'.[1] Precarious finances had prevented all attempts to engage them since 1970: Craig now suggested to the Governors that this was the time when 'to live cautiously was to die, and to live dangerously was to survive' and the Governors magnificently supported him. So the Wells introduced this unique though expensive company to Britain and they not only broke all records for a foreign dance company but also (after the Bat Dor Dance Company from Israel, who had to have security guards in the theatre) they returned with acclaim a fortnight later to dance for another week—in all to a ninety-four per cent capacity audience. They were then the second company to appear at a Royal Command Performance on the Wells' recommendation, the first being the Little Angels of Korea.

The London Contemporary Dance Theatre in November 'had never looked better' and the Ballet Rambert's ballets in three weeks varied from Anthony Tudor's *Dark Elegies* to the première of John Chesworth's 'pretentious' *Project 6354/9116 Mk. 2*.[2]

Sunday lettings of the theatre for such as a Youth Gala in August 1974 and a Macnaghten Concert of Italian Music in March 1975 helped the Wells financially, as did the letting of the rehearsal rooms.

For the first time since 1968 the G.L.C. gave the Wells a direct grant of £15,000 plus a guaranteed £10,000, the Arts Council gave £7,500 again and a supplementary £2,000, and from the Appeal Fund came £5,000 including £3,000 from the

[1] *The Guardian.*   [2] *Sunday Telegraph.*

London Borough of Islington. But in spite of further increased box office receipts the year's deficiency was £10,187 due to the payment of £32,357 in V.A.T. The dress circle was now re-seated and recarpeted.

Through the generosity of the Greater London Arts Association the Sadler's Wells Bus Service was extended—although unable to run throughout the year. The Coach Service had in 14 months transported from 12 outlying districts nearly 3,000 people of whom 90 per cent were 'new' audience. The Wells with the Coliseum, Covent Garden and the Royal Shakespeare at the Aldwych were part of the two Hotel/Theatre weekend projects; and almost 30,000 patrons came in Party Bookings with tickets at £1 (50p for children or senior citizens) and reduced for certain shows.

But in December 1974, because the Coliseum's benefit performance of *The Magic Flute* was suddenly cancelled as a result of an industrial dispute, the Appeal Fund lost a possibly substantial profit and months of work were wasted.

It was during 1974–5 that Colin Benham O.B.E. relinquished the chairmanship of the Appeal which he had pioneered from its inception, saving the Wells in the dark days of 1971–2: he was succeeded by Grenfell Huddy.

A Gala for the Society for Autistic Children was the first operatic evening in 1975–6. In May after the Royal Academy of Music students' performance of Massenet's *Cendrillon* the New Opera Company had their greatest success to date with the British première of Szymanowski's *King Roger* with Charles Mackerras conducting the Royal Philharmonic Orchestra and Anthony Besch producing with a spectacular first act and Peter Knapp in the name-part. The production was later adopted by the Coliseum.

In October for their 21st anniversary the Handel Opera Society's *Alcina* was 'revealed . . . as one of the masterpieces of the 18th century' and 'banished memories of less stylish productions' with Eiddwen Harrhy, Hannah Francis, Della Jones, James Bowman, David Cusick and Bryan Drake together with the Society's amateur chorus sensitively produced by David Thompson in Bruno Santini's decor under their conductor Charles Farncombe.[1]

[1] Alan Blyth: *Opera.*

1975–6 Ballet companies included the 'uncommonly exhilarating' Tokyo Ballet, the splendid Netherlands again, the
Ballet Rambert with the world première of Christopher Bruce's
'imaginative and brilliant' *Ancient Voices of Children*, and the
New London Ballet with Fonteyn as guest artist.

In May there had been an 'East End and Theatreland' Party
for the Appeal Fund and a B.B.C. Gala Performance for
television with the British debut of the dancers Valery and
Galina Panov. In August Marcel Marceau gave, he said, his last
London solo appearance, and in November there was a 'Twenties
Ball' for the Appeal (for which Covent Garden had given a
Gala performance of their new *Peter Grimes* in July), together
with a Festival of Greek music, poetry and a benefit Gala for
the Phoenix Opera.

The Annual Report for 1975–6 shows that the year's deficiency had dropped to £8,523, which means there would have
been a credit without V.A.T.

Grants for the year were £25,000, again from the G.L.C.,
£4,500 direct from Islington, £7,000 from the City Parochial
Foundation to reduce the cost of repairs and redecorations to the
Upper Circle, and £12,000 from the Arts Council. The Appeal
Fund contributed only £1,899 because of the new policy of
the Directors of the Appeal to give the Foundation only the
interest on the accumulated Fund, thus reserving a contingency
fund.

The Appeal Fund's capital was greatly helped by the Arts
Council's second donation of another £12,000, but this gift was
qualified by a letter from the Secretary-General to David
McKenna on 5th January 1976 stating that this donation

> will enable the Foundation to draw upon this as and when re-
> quired in the light of the likelihood that no Arts Council Funds
> will be available to Sadler's Wells Foundation in 1976–7.

The student standby stalls ticket-price was raised from 30p
to £1.00, and Party Booking tickets from £1.00 to £1.50
(children and senior citizens from 50p to 75p); but the Theatre
Bus Service now ran all the year round thanks to a travel
subsidy from the Greater London Arts Association and about

4,000 people used the Coach Service from as far as 100 miles outside London.

The first 1976–7 opera was Wolf-Ferrari's *School for Fathers* by the London Opera Centre conducted by its Director James Robertson, as it had been in what was my first Wells production thirty years before; but now set, not in London as approved by the composer, but in Venice where he originally set it.

In September the English Opera Group's offspring, the English Music Theatre Company (a name that Rosenthal thought 'one of the most off-putting imaginable' but with Colin Graham and Steuart Bedford as directors to be admired for 'welding . . . an assortment of young artists' in less than a year) opened with the London première of Britten's early operetta *Paul Bunyan* with Auden's 'waggish' libretto rather indifferently sung. So was their Mozart *Finta Giardinera* (re-christened *Sandrina's Secret*, with Edmund Tracey's excellent translation) but to have the scenery visible to the audience on arrival 'savoured of just another gimmick'. But their London première of the specially commissioned *Tom Jones* 'said to be the 18th(!) opera by 26-year-old Stephen Oliver'[1] was thoroughly enjoyable; the singing and acting of Catherine Wilson as the Governess and of Neil Jenkins as Quint were the 'high points' of their *Turn of the Screw* and in the *Threepenny Opera* (the only well-attended work of their season), well directed from the piano by Simon Rattle, Della Jones as Jenny showed herself 'mistress both of this style and of the coloratura flights of Rossini's Cinderella' (which they also gave)—a feat of real distinction 'and Michael Follis as Don Magnifico was one of the company's strongest personalities'.[2] In a new, but inadequately grand *Belshazzar* by the Handel Opera Society Pauline Tinsley and Anne Wilkens were outstanding. Then during the usual D'Oyly Carte season Her Majesty the Queen visited the Wells for the first time and saw *The Gondoliers*.

In March 1977 Lully's *Alceste* by the London Opera Centre's students with the Europa Singers, the Rambert School of Ballet and a Trinity College of Music orchestra proved too much for young performers, though William Chappell's production was a delight. Similarly, the Royal Northern College of

---

[1] (*sic*) Arthur Jacobs: *Opera*.   [2] Arthur Jacobs: *Opera*.

Music's expensive and fussy production, with overlarge stair-cased sets on an unnecessary imported Manchester revolve, showed that the *Bohème* score 'is heavy on student voices and too subtle for an inexperienced conductor of opera'.

The Royal Danish Academy of Music however, reciprocating the R.N.C.M.'s earlier visit to Scandinavia with the help of the Arts Council, had Frans Rasmussen confidently conducting Ib Norhoff's specially commissioned hour-long *The Garden Wall*, with young singers excellently enunciating the English text in Daniel Bohr's controlled production, followed by the early 'pre-reformed' Gluck's 'piece of Metastasio artificiality' *Le Cinesi*.

The R.N.C.M. then introduced to London Brian Hughes' *Stars and Shadows* with a 'show business' libretto by Ursula Vaughan Williams, cleverly designed to display as many singers as possible but so that it 'would not vocally tax the most im-mature student'. Andrew Penny conducted 'with the same control evinced by the singers' with the chief part sung by Marie Jagus 'who scored a notable double by going on to sing Maurya in *Riders to the Sea*'[1] which followed, with Euan Smith's production intensifying the score's emotional impact.

At the end of March 1976 the vigorous Scottish Ballet's opening Royal Gala Performance, raising £8,145 for the Appeal, included London premières of Darrell's *Tales of Hoffman*, *Mary Queen of Scots* and, with Margot Fonteyn and Anthony Dowell, *Scarlet Pastorale*.

In May the 'slick and flamboyant' Brazil Tropical ended their spectacular extravaganza performances with the audience dancing with them on the stage and in the stalls. Then the Royal Ballet which, because of heavy advance booking, had to stay an extra week, included in their programme the world première of Jack Carter's *Lulu* 'bright and breezy as a music hall show'[2] as well as de Valois's 1937 *Checkmate* with Maina Gielgud, Sir John's niece, scoring a triumph.

In June, Princess Margaret attended the Ballet Rambert's 50th Birthday season which was followed by the 'authentic and energetic ethnic dancing' of Dance Senegal.

[1] *Opera.*
[2] *The Times*

Then there came on 29th July the encouraging announcement that the Royal Ballet Touring Company was at last to be based at the Wells, as had been suggested some six years before.

In their approval, the Arts Council, strongly influenced by the findings of their recent enquiry under Wynne Godley's chairmanship into the future of lyric theatre in London, made only two stipulations—first, that the company would have a secure base from which to launch regional tours without adding to their Wells performances, and second that the Wells should still play host to distinguished British and foreign companies.

The Ballet Company would be allotted offices, music library, wardrobe, rehearsal and changing rooms (about 5,000 square feet in all) with a new rehearsal room designed by Fred Rowntree and Sons, the Wells' consultant architects, to be built on top of the theatre for the use of the ballet and visiting companies.

After a return of the Dance Theatre of Harlem in August, the Royal Ballet Touring Company, renamed the Sadler's Wells Royal Ballet by approval of Queen Elizabeth, opened at their old family home on 29th September 1976 with a Gala Performance before their President, Princess Margaret.

After a fanfare by Constant Lambert (1905–1951) and a tribute to him spoken by Dame Ninette de Valois recalling all he had done for British ballet in its early days, this exceptional performance began with Ashton's *Les Patineurs* (music Lambert-Meyerbeer: designed by William Chappell) first given at the Wells in 1937 with Harold Turner, Margot Fonteyn and Robert Helpmann, Mary Honer, Elizabeth Miller, and Michael Somes. Then came *Divertissements* danced by soloists of the Wells and the Covent Garden Royal Ballet companies: and finally Cranko's *Pineapple Poll* (music Mackerras-Sullivan: designed by Osbert Lancaster) first given at the Wells in 1951 and on this occasion with Brenda Last in the title-role and Wayne Sleep as Captain Belaye, the part originally created by David Blair.

In May 1976 David McKenna had retired after fourteen

devoted years as Chairman of the Sadler's Wells Foundation and was succeeded by Sir Roger Falk.

The 1976–7 accounts have not yet been published[1], but the G.L.C. has granted £25,000, Islington £4,500 and the Appeal Fund £4,559.

The first 1977–8 opera was Lars Johan Werle's *Tintomara* produced by its librettist Leif Söderstrom and presented by the Gothenburg Opera in May. The performers' music-drama style obviously derived from their constantly playing together without guest-artists, as had the Sadler's Wells Opera in the past. Now, with no international bravura conventions, they enacted a story of a non-historical androgynous character with incidents connected with Gustavus III's murder, based on an extraordinary 'novel-play' by the early 19th century Almqvist, whose words linked the scenes through a narrator. Singers in and from the auditorium and simultaneous scenes were not disturbing, nor were the merged styles and quotations in the music, and Anna Gisle's scenery and costumes were delightfully simple. But to appreciate the high value Sweden places on this opera an understanding of the Swedish words was essential, in spite of the sensitive performance of the 'boy-girl' by Marie Louise Hasselgren.

In June the English Music Theatre gave *The Fairy Queen* inevitably reduced but with 'Purcell's wonderful music beautifully played by the English Music Theatre orchestra conducted by Steuart Bedford' and with this company of young artists (insufficiently supported, some think, by the Arts Council which values it but cannot subsidize it for a full year's work) 'admirably schooled in speech by Colin Graham' though 'the general standard of singing was not very distinguished' and the 'treatment of the fairy court . . . suggested that they were a very lascivious lot indeed!'[2]

Then they gave an admirable *Albert Herring*, with the cast strengthened by more experienced artists including Janice Chapman, Meryl Drower, Ian Caley and Michael Follis, in the three-year-old English Opera Group production by David William, 'a producer who is prepared to put himself at the

[1] 27th May 1977.
[2] Harold Rosenthal: *Opera.*

service of the work in hand, not one trying to impose some
extraneous ideas on it'.[1]

Next, 'no doubt . . . pressed by the Arts Council to include at
least one box-office attraction' they gave 'a somewhat cosy and
ungrandiose production' of *The Magic Flute* with a strengthened
cast: in *Opera* Rosenthal wrote:

> Unlike many of my colleagues, I found this quite refreshing,
> although at the same time I was more than once acutely conscious
> of vocal and orchestral weaknesses. The one singer who could
> have stood out in any *Magic Flute* cast was Anthony Rolfe
> Johnson.

In July D'Oyly Carte's three-week season included what had
been announced as an untraditional *Iolanthe* produced by
Michael Heyland: but, presumably coming up 'against heavy
opposition' as Rosenthal sympathetically said, he said in a
programme slip he only had to 'regroup where necessary and
sharpen the dialogue'. With overacting the result was not a
success, especially when compared with the English National
Opera's hilarious production, though Royston Nash had raised
the orchestral standard higher than previous seasons[2]. The
company, always hitherto self-supporting, now seems to need
financial assistance, though the Arts Council apparently does not
agree: if its historical brilliance and importance should be
forgotten because it has become unprofitable, unsupported or
unattractive to newer audiences with repetitious traditions
that the enthusiasts expect, it would be a great loss to the art of
the theatre.

Then, as Stanley Sadie wrote in *The Times*, *Figaro*—the last
production by the London Opera Centre before its transformation into the National Opera Studio 'seemed like a hangover
from the D'Oyly Carte season' as 'there seemed to be little
attempt to treat the work as musical drama' but rather as 'just a
funny opera': the conducting was 'bland and sluggish', though
the Guildhall School of Music orchestra 'did well enough'
and Claire Powell as Cherubino was the best of some promising
singers, and, unlike its achievements in the past, this presentation
seemed 'to come incongruously from an institution that tries to

---

[1] Alan Blyth: *Opera*.
[2] *Opera*.

QUEEN ELIZABETH MEETS THE D'OYLY CARTE COMPANY

PRINCESS MARGARET AT BALLET RAMBERT'S 50TH BIRTHDAY CELEBRATIONS

THE RED KING IN
CHECKMATE

THE BLACK QUEEN IN
CHECKMATE

THE ACHARNIANS, GRE
ART THEATRE

teach opera as a living art. . . . One can only wish the new National Opera Studio good fortune'.

In November the renamed Handel Opera gave two works first staged in 1732—the concert-masque *Acis & Galatea* (preceded by Rameau's Prologue to his Fêtes d'Hébé of seven years later) and then the opera *Ezio* in its first revival in Britain. Stanley Sadie found the Rameau delightful as choreographed in period style by Belinda Quirey, conducted by Charles Farncombe and sung by Dinah Harris, Joy Roberts and Anthony Rolfe Johnson, and praised the last two singers as Galatea and Acis with Peter Jeffes as Damon but thought the Polyphemus over-comic and under-thundering, the conductor insufficiently 'giving his singers quite the scope they needed' and the chorus inadequate especially in acting though 'it is not easy to stage' (in fact the 1732 staging of this 1719 concert-work was sung 'in still life').

The presentation of *Ezio*, 'one of Handel's failures', he praised, as did Desmond Shawe-Taylor, for Farncombe's vigorous conducting, the singing of Anne Collins, Anne Wilkens Hannah Francis, Kenneth Bowen, Ian Comboy and John York Skinner, Tom Hawkes' production, Tom Hammond's 'generally admirable' translation and especially the resplendently elaborate *opera seria* baroque designs by Steven Gregory.

The London Contemporary Dance Theatre in April 1977 on their second visit in four months included London premières of Cohan's 'Graham-inspired' *Night Watch* specially choreographed to Bob Downes' taped and live music for the Queen's Silver Jubilee celebrations, Robert North's *Meeting and Parting* to Howard Blake's 'updated Chopin' and Cohan's *Forest* with taped 'bird-calls, thunderstorms and chilly-sounding wind'.[1]

On 26th April, at the Royal Gala in aid of the Building Fund which opened the Sadler's Wells Royal Ballet Season, Lynn Seymour's *Court of Love* was thought unsatisfactory after her stylish *Rashomon*, partly because of Howard Blake's 'sub-*Spartacus*' Khachaturian-type music. The evening ended with Maina Gielgud's Black Queen powerful and menacing in front of Sir Robert Helpmann, welcomed back to the Wells as the splendid doddering old Red King in *Checkmate*.

---

[1] *Daily Express.*

In later performances David Morse's *Birdscape* was little more than dancers dressed as birds, but Glen Tetley's *Gemini*, first created for the Australian Ballet, proved 'a cunning new masterwork'. It was superbly danced by Maina Gielgud and Desmond Kelly, June Highwood and the Australian guest artist Dale Baker—in place of the injured David Ashmole—and brilliantly designed by Nadine Baylis with Barry Wordsworth conducting Henze's theatrical Third Symphony. [1]

John Percival in *The Times* of 10th May, writing of Peter Wright's amended *Summertime* and *The Two Pigeons*, especially praised the dancers (one of whom was on loan from the Covent Garden main company for one performance) but queried the strain on the fewer Wells soloists in their welcomely varied programmes compared with that of the senior company's artists. He also questioned why the transfer of soloists between the two sections of the Royal Ballet worked in only one direction, it having been 'promised last year that they would be on a fair exchange basis'.

The brilliantly performed *Coppélia* had Sir Robert Helpmann not only reminding the audience of his discovery, years before, of how droll Dr. Coppelius could be, but also introducing new tricks such as 'hanging his overcoat on a nail that is not there', which he must surely have remembered (and why not?) from Howell Glynne's drunken Frosch in *Fledermaus* thirty-one years before. [2]

Galina Samsova and André Prokovsky as guest artists in *Raymonda* Act III (in which Marion Tate's Hungarian Dance enlivened the evening before her serenity in *La Fille Mal Gardée*) were object lessons to dancers. [3]

But the last-named ballet on the Company's last night—14th May—mingled 'tears and cheers' as being the sparkling farewell of Brenda Last; initially rejected by the Royal Ballet (though the Adeline Genée Gold Medal winner at the Royal Ballet School) because she was too short, she danced to success through nightclubs and the Western Theatre Ballet, to become the 'backbone' of the Sadler's Wells Royal Ballet and now Director of the Norwegian Ballet. [4]

[1] *Daily Express.*   [2] Page 224.
[3] *The Sunday Times.*   [4] *The Times.*

In July 1977 the London Youth Dance Theatre gave an 'exciting and adventurous' matinee and in August, after Les Danses Sacrées de Bali with 'only a limited vocabulary of movement' though the costumes were colourful, the Korean National Dance Company made their first return to London since their great success at the Round House in 1972: they had a 'marvellously costumed programme of court ritual and folk-dances given by a phalanx of delicious girls'.[1]

Then the Sadler's Wells Royal Ballet included in a three-week season the London première of Balanchine's *Concerto Barocco* staged by Patricia Neary and the world première of the pas de deux by Galina Samsova and André Prokovsky *Soft Blue Shadows*.

During that season H.R.H. Princess Margaret officially opened the new John Cranko rehearsal-room on 22nd September for the use of the Company.

Large rehearsal-rooms are rare in London and finance to build such rooms is not usually available from public bodies, so the cost of some £80,000 for the building of the Sadler's Wells Royal Ballet's rehearsal-room with its essentially sprung floor (completed in fifteen weeks) has had to rely on private donations. The equally go-ahead Festival Ballet under their Director Beryl Grey was therefore very lucky to have the £325,000 needed to convert Queen Alexandra House near the Albert Hall into their first real home largely financed in June 1975 (before there were financial restraints on public bodies) by £75,000 from the Greater London Council and from the Arts Council Housing the Arts Fund £125,000.[2]

In October, presented by Pierre Cardin, twelve men and five women who kept fit by daily marathon runs, the Ondeko-Za (a name meaning 'demon drums') with their traditional dances made their pulsating beating of drums, of which one, carved from a single tree and mounted some 10 feet off the stage floor, weighed 700 lbs, so rhythmically exhilarating that towards the end of their fortnight there were queues round the side of the theatre hoping to gain admission.

In May 1977 the Greek Art Theatre, well known from often

[1] *The Sunday Times.*
[2] *The Stage*: 22nd September 1977.

appearing in the World Theatre seasons, gave Aeschylus' *Seven against Thebes* and showed 'what ensemble can be' in their uninhibitedly phallic but artistic performances of Aristophanes' 2,400-year-old *Acharnians*[1] updated in an honest music-hall manner, but with a traditionally all-male cast acting, singing and dancing brilliantly as mock-serious, burlesque, or female chara·ers, apparently spontaneously but in fact as a result of being constantly together in training and practice.

The totally different but equally brilliant all-male Kabuki (i.e. 'trend') theatre of Japan was presented in August by the Shochiku Company with some thirty-three singers, instrumentalists and actors, mostly trained in the traditional technique since early childhood, and twenty-one stage staff. They gave *The Mansion of Kawazura Hogen* (one act of a ten-hour-long 1747 play) with incredibly expressive hand-movements and long-held motionless positions full of meaning which heightened the apparently instantaneous reappearances through trick scenery with changes of costume and personality from warrior to fox by Ennosuke Ichikawa, whose family has performed Kabuki for generations. The same artist then was equally remarkable in a 1939 Kabuki version of the Noh drama *Kurozuka* as a quiet old woman who is disclosed as a man-eating demon. As *The Times* said, it is 'hard to overpraise the achievement of the Kabuki', but its expense forced the Wells to raise the price of the most expensive seats to £6.50, the highest ever charged there.

On Sunday 7th August Opera Rara had given a Silver Jubilee Donizetti concert entitled *Kings & Queens of England* ranging from 'Alfredo il Grande' to Elizabeth I: Elizabeth Forbes in *Opera* found this so dramatically and musically exciting that credit should be given to the soloists Milla Andrew, Eiddwen Harrhy, Yvonne Kenny, Della Jones, Janet Price, Maurice Arthur, John Brecknock, Graham Clark, Christian du Plessis and John Tomlinson, the Geoffrey Mitchell Choir and the Philomusica of London conducted by Alun Francis.

Since March 1976 the Governors have been trying gradually

[1] *The Sunday Times.*

to write off the accumulated deficiency, and in the first year of this policy about £11,000 have been written off, leaving an accumulated deficiency of about £52,000.

Grants for 1976–7 had come from the G.L.C. (£25,000), the London Borough of Islington (£4,500) and the Appeal Fund (£4,559).

The greatest encouragement in 1977 has come from the return of the Sadler's Wells Royal Ballet, still run of course by the Royal Opera House so their Wells accommodation is at present only rented on a five-year lease and, as old friends or rather relations, not at a commercial rate; hopefully their return is to be permanent.

Actual grants already promised for 1977–8 are £27,000 from the G.L.C. and £4,500 from Islington again. But, although the Arts Council's Annual Report for 1975–6 had said 'Sadler's Wells has achieved much success in becoming an important centre, especially for visiting overseas companies' and had announced plans to set up a new unit (not yet formed, though some progress has been made) to be financed by the Gulbenkian Foundation, the Arts Council, the British Council and the Foreign and Commonwealth Offices to encourage visits by overseas companies and artists to England, Scotland and Wales, the Wells had received no grant from the Arts Council in 1976–7 and seems unlikely to receive one in the foreseeable future.

In the last year of the late Sir Peter Daubeny's important World Theatre seasons, 1973, there had been no criticism from any quarter of his potential losses of £45,000 from his fourteen-week Festival.[1] Amazingly however Craig's Report at the time that the Wells needed only £1,000 a week to carry on with their similar festival that lasted a year still holds good today, despite rising prices and inflation.

Originally the World Theatre seasons had been mainly sponsored by *The Daily Telegraph*, and the 1977 Brighton Festival for example, which presented the Frankfurt Ballet, was sponsored by the Arts Council as well as by local and commercial bodies.

Perhaps in the future the remarkable programmes of the Wells, which gives almost a permanent Festival, might well be

[1] *Report to the Governors 1973.*

supported also by commercial firms, just as are Glyndebourne Opera and, in addition to its Arts Council grant, Covent Garden.

In fact in the Foundation's Annual Report for 1975–6 published 30th September 1976 Sir Roger Falk said he was glad to report

> that Industry and Commerce have also provided help by way of gifts in kind and occasional donations, and we hope to introduce an Industrial Sponsorship Guarantee Scheme for the year 1977–8.

For the Gothenburg Opera's visit, the Wells Foundation was sponsored by Lex Brooklands (London) Ltd, distributors of Volvo Cars, and that of the Greek Art Theatre by Paterson, Zochonis/Cussons, while some ten other companies—including Mars, Guiness Peat and Bulmer's—have sponsored other presentations.

At the same time economies have had to be practised at the Wells for some time as at the Old Vic in the old days, but it is hoped that present rumours of yet more drastic economies will not result in inferior entertainment. After all economy can be as disastrous as extravagance: Lilian Baylis certainly cheese-pared but still kept up good standards, and at the same time the expensive Dance Theatre of Harlem packed Sadler's Wells.

When the Old Vic was on its uppers in the 1920s 'the Lady' appealed everywhere for financial approval of her aims: now the Wells is making yet another Appeal—this time for the Building Fund to complete the financing of the new rehearsal room. This Fund has already benefited from the 1976 and 1977 Ballet Galas and from the donation by the Trustees of the John Cranko Memorial Fund of its accumulated funds as was announced in the 1976 Gala Performance programme.

There are now also plans to open a new day-time box-office and bookshop on the corner of Rosebery Avenue and St. John Street very near the house where Charles Dibdin lived nearly two hundred years ago.

Planning still continues and the Wells goes on.

A FINAL WORD

IT IS GOOD to have this new edition of *The Story of Sadler's Wells*. Surely it should be subtitled 'Story Without End'.

For Sadler's Wells Theatre was meant to live. It was meant to serve not only the North London public, but people from the South, the East and the West of this great city. The Wells did not rear its head on a North London hill to no purpose. Time is proving the necessity of its existence.

Today, due to Mr. Craig's unflagging energy and enterprise, and backed by his board of directors and Islington local authorities, the Theatre welcomes ballet companies of a certain size from England and Scotland and foreign countries, and also sees that the D'Oyly Carte Opera has an annual three months' season in the capital.

Its policy links up with the big West End Opera Houses in an effort to satisfy a great theatre-loving public, and the many companies that travel to the Wells do so with the same zest that the great Grimaldi showed when he ran from Drury Lane to the Wells across the Islington marshlands.

The spirit of Islington's 30s is much alive. People seem to enter the theatre in a relaxed state of mind. To return to Sadler's Wells for any performance holds all the excitement of the old days.

There remains one little story to tell that will show the inevitable passage of time . . . .

I was stepping over the ropes in the Theatre's foyer one morning recently when 'Hi!' yelled a stranger's voice from the box-office, 'Where are going?' 'Backstage', was the brief reply. 'Well, wait until I can get someone to show you the way. . . .'

But the backstage of Sadler's Wells is the one way that no-one will ever have to show me.

Ninette de Valois

APPENDIX

Companies Appearing at Sadler's Wells since March 1969
Number of visits in brackets.

(a) Opera

Season

1969–70   Cologne Opera (Germany) (1)
         D'Oyly Carte (1)
         English Opera Group (1)
         Handel Opera Society (1)
         London Opera Centre (5)
         New Opera Company (1)

1970–71   D'Oyly Carte (1)
         Handel Opera Society (1)
         London Opera Centre (1)

1971–72   D'Oyly Carte (1)
         English Opera Group (1)
         Handel Opera Society (1)
         London Opera Centre (4)
         New Opera Company (1)
         Polytechnic of Central London (1)
         Royal Academy of Music (1)

1972–73   Delius Trust/Camden Festival (1)
         D'Oyly Carte (1)
         English Opera Group (1)
         Handel Opera Society (1)

1973–74   D'Oyly Carte (1)
         English Opera Group (1)
         Handel Opera Society (1)
         London Opera Centre (2)
         New Opera Company (1)
         Royal Northern College of Music (1)
         Salzburg Marionettes (Austria) (1)
         Scottish Opera (1)

1974–75   D'Oyly Carte (1)
           English Opera Group (1)
           Handel Opera Society (1)
           Keynote Opera (1)
           London Opera Centre (2)
           New Opera Company (1)
           Phoenix Opera (1)

1975–76   D'Oyly Carte (1)
           Handel Opera Society (1)
           London Opera Centre (1)
           New Opera Company (1)
           Royal Academy of Music (1)

1976–77   D'Oyly Carte (1)
           English Music Theatre (1)
           Handel Opera Society (1)
           London Opera Centre (2)
           Royal Danish Academy (Copenhagen) (1)
           Royal Northern College of Music (1)
           Salzburg Marionettes (Austria) (1)

1977   D'Oyly Carte (1)
           English Music Theatre (1)
           Gothenburg Opera (Sweden) (1)
           Handel Opera (1)
           London Opera Centre (1)

(b) Dance and Ballet

Season

1969–70   Alwin Nikolais Dance Theatre (U.S.A.) (1)
           Ballet et Choers Basques Etorki (France) (1)
           Ballet Prague (Czechoslovakia) (1)
           Dutch National Ballet (1)
           Fiesta Gitana (Spain) (1)
           Les Grands Ballets Canadiens (1)
           Scottish Theatre Ballet (1)

1970–71   Alvin Ailey Dance Theatre (U.S.A.) (1)
           Antonio Gades and his Ballet (Spain) (1)
           Netherlands Dance Theatre (1)

Opanak (Yugoslavia) (1)
Paul Taylor Dance Company (U.S.A.) (1)
Scottish Theatre Ballet (1)
Vyjayanthimala (India) (1)
Turkish Song and Dance Festival (1)

1971-72   Alwin Nikolais Dance Theatre (U.S.A.) (1)
Ballet Théatre Contemporain (France) (1)
Burmese National Dancers and Musicians (1)
Chitrasena (Ceylon) (1)
Cullberg Ballet (Sweden) (1)
Dora Stratou Dance Company (Greece) (1)
El Sali and his Madrid Flamenco (Spain) (1)
Lado—Croation Folk Ensemble (1)
Litle Angels of Korea (1)
Pace Peña Flamenco Puro (Spain) (1)

1972-73   Ballet Théatre Joseph Russillo (France) (1)
Chhau Dancers of Bengal (India) (1)
Little Angels of Korea (1)
Mahali Dancers of Iran (1)
Mansudai Dance Company of Korea (1)
Merce Cunningham Dance Company (U.S.A.) (1)
National Dance Theatre of Jamaica (1)

1973-74   Alvin Ailey Dance Theatre (U.S.A.) (1)
Ballet Gulbenkian (Portugal) (1)
Ballet Rambert (1)
Ballet Théatre Contemporain (France) (1)
Bayanihan—National Ballet of the Philippines (1)
Dutch National Ballet (Holland) (1)
London Contemporary Dance Theatre (1)
Louis Falco Dance Company (U.S.A.) (1)
Netherlands Dance Theatre (Holland) (1)
New London Ballet (1)
Nigerian National Ballet (1)
Paul Taylor Dance Company (U.S.A.) (1)
Royal Ballet (3)

1974-75   Ballet Gallego (Spain) (1)
Ballet Rambert (1)
Bat Dor (Israel) (1)

Dance Theatre of Harlem (U.S.A.) (2)
London Contemporary Dance Theatre (1)
Mevlevi Whirling Dervishes (Turkey) (1)
New London Ballet (1)
Royal Ballet (3)
Toronto Dance Theatre (Canada) (1)

1975–76 Ballet Rambert (1)
Gothenburg Ballet (Sweden) (1)
London Contemporary Dance Theatre (1)
Netherlands Dance Theatre (1)
New London Ballet (1)
Royal Ballet (1)
The Scottish Ballet (1)
Tokyo Ballet (Japan) (1)

1976–77 Ballet Rambert (1)
Brazil Tropical (1)
Dance Senegal (1)
Dance Theatre of Harlem (U.S.A.) (1)
Libyan National Folklore Troupe (1)
London Contemporary Dance Theatre (1)
Royal Ballet
Sadler's Wells Royal Ballet

1977 Danses Sacrées de Bali (1)
Korean National Dance Company (1)
London Contemporary Dance Theatre (1)
Ondeko-Za (Japan) (1)
Sadler's Wells Royal Ballet (2)

(c) Drama and Mime

1969–70 Black Theatre of Prague (Czechoslovakia) (1)

1970–71 Alfred Jarry Pantomima Company (Czechoslovakia) (1)
Black Theatre of Prague (Czechoslovakia) (1)
Kathakali (India) (1)
Polish Mime Ballet Theatre (1)

1971–72 Black Theatre of Prague (Czechoslovakia) (1)
Bromley New Theatre Company (1)

Ladislav Fialka Mime Company (Czechoslovakia) (1)
London Theatre Company (1)

1972–73   Black Theatre of Prague (Czechoslovakia) (1)
Bristol Old Vic Company (1)
Kabuki (Japan) (1)
London Theatre Company (1)
Marcel Marceau (1)

1973–74   Black Theatre of Prague (Czechoslovakia) (1)

1974–75   —

1975–76   Marcel Marceau

1977   Greek Art Theatre
Shochiku Kabuki Company (Japan) (1)

INDEX

I. GENERAL INDEX

317

II. INDEX OF ENTERTAINMENTS AT SADLER'S WELLS

(a) Ballets and Dances

(b) Operas, Operettas, Burlettas, etc.

(d) Spectaculars, Pantomimes, etc.

(e) Various

SUPPLEMENTARY INDEX
(to 1977 Postscript)
I. General Index

II. Index of Companies & Entertainments at Sadler's Wells

1. (a) Ballet & Dance Companies

(b) Ballets

2. (a) Drama Companies

(b) Plays

3. (a) Opera Companies & Institutions

(b) Operas

4. Other Entertainments